GENDER AND ACADEME
Feminist Pedagogy and Politics

GENDER AND ACADEME
Feminist Pedagogy and Politics

Edited by
Sara Munson Deats
and
Lagretta Tallent Lenker

Rowman & Littlefield Publishers, Inc.

ROWMAN & LITTLEFIELD PUBLISHERS, INC.

Published in the United States of America
by Rowman & Littlefield Publishers, Inc.
4720 Boston Way, Lanham, Maryland 20706

3 Henrietta Street, London WC2E 8LU, England

British Cataloging in Publication Information Available

Library of Congress Cataloging-in-Publication Data

Gender and academe : feminist pedagogy and politics / edited by
Sara Munson Deats and Lagretta Tallent Lenker.
p.   cm.
Includes bibliographical references and index.
1. Feminism and education.   2. Women—Education
(Higher)—Political aspects.   I. Deats, Sara Munson.   II. Lenker,
Lagretta Tallent.
LC197.G43   1994   370.19'345—dc20   94-19946 CIP

ISBN 0-8476-7969-1 (cloth : alk. paper)
ISBN 0-8476-7970-5 (pbk. : alk. paper)

Printed in the United States of America

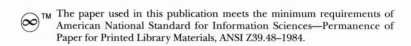 ™ The paper used in this publication meets the minimum requirements of
American National Standard for Information Sciences—Permanence of
Paper for Printed Library Materials, ANSI Z39.48–1984.

To the memory of

Juanita Williams
1922–1991

Professor of Women's Studies
University of South Florida

Teacher, Mentor, Friend

Contents

Part II: How does a feminist perspective influence *how* we teach in the classroom?

Part III: How does a feminist perspective influence *what* and *how* we teach outside the classroom?

Preface

These essays represent work presented at the University of South Florida's first two "Gender in Academe" conferences held in 1989 and 1991, respectively. These national conferences were convened by the Division of Lifelong Learning and were organized by a committee of university faculty and administrators from different disciplines, all of whom considered gender issues to be significant to their professional lives. The conferences received financial support from the University of South Florida Office of the Provost, the Division of Sponsored Research, the College of Arts and Sciences, and the School of Continuing Education. The title of the 1989 conference was "Gender in Academe: The Future of our Past" and featured keynote speakers Gerda Lerner, Sue Rosser, and Bonnie Thorton Dill. The 1991 conference, entitled "Gender in Academe: Who Cares?," presented Toril Moi, Leslie King-Hammond, and Linda Brodky. Both conferences also featured academics chronicling gender theories and experiences in a wide range of disciplines, including fields as diverse as art history and biology.

Both conferences were attended by educators from across the United States and Canada whose written evaluations of the programs indicated a very favorable response to both gatherings. On a local level, subsequent presentations by participants in both conferences to classes and seminars have been equally well-received. These conferences have also led to the formation of the University of South Florida's Women's

Caucus, a group that meets for continued study and discussion of gender issues. The opportunity to meet university colleagues in other areas of campus proved an unexpected benefit for many of the female faculty and administrators involved in the conferences. In a large, diverse institution such as USF, faculty members often meet only when engaged in a common project. These conferences offered a catalyst for collegiality that had been missing for many women.

Numerous inquiries about the conferences and the papers presented led to the inception of this volume.

Acknowledgments

The editors gratefully acknowledge the support of the following University of South Florida colleges, schools, and departments: Sponsored Research, English, Lifelong Learning, Continuing Education, and Arts and Sciences. We also thank the steering committee for the conference that produced the papers for this volume, especially Lee Leavengood, Ellen Kimmel, and Diane Elmeer. This book would not be possible without the contributions of Beth Williams, whose technical skill and unfailing good humor compensate for the editors' many shortcomings in time and technical ability. Megan Lenker's proofreading abilities are valued and admired. We also appreciate the encouragement of Julie Kirsch of Rowman and Littlefield, who recognized what we trust is a good thing.

Finally, we thank our families, Gordon Deats and Mark, Megan, and Mark Lenker, for their love and patience during the completion of this and many other time-consuming projects.

Introduction

Sara Munson Deats

Rationale

In recent decades, a revolution in human thought has occurred, comparable in its cataclysmic effects to the Copernican revolution of the late sixteenth century that jarred the edifices of Western philosophy and science to their foundations. In his literally earth—shaking book, *On the Revolution of the Celestial Spheres*, Copernicus, the prophet of the first revolution, decentered the earth from its privileged position in the universe, calling into question many of the venerated assumptions on which Western civilization was constructed. Approximately four centuries later, Beauvoir, in her equally monumental work, *The Second Sex*, rattled the structure of the social if not the heavenly spheres. With her brief statement, "One is not born, but rather becomes, a woman" (1952, 301), Beauvoir, the prophet of the second revolution, decentered man from his privileged position in society, demystifying gender as natural, essential, and universal, and interrogating many of the revered assumptions on which the nuclear patriarchal family was built. Feminism, at least in its contemporary manifestations, derives from Beauvoir's simple, yet even today controversial, assertion that "woman is not an essence but a social construct in the domain of patriarchal culture" (1952, 305), with its crucial implication that what is merely adventitious rather than essential can be changed.

The revolutionary attitudes toward sex and gender emerging during the past two decades have affected every aspect of contemporary life—the family, the church, the government, the public schools, and, of course, the academy. Indeed, academe, an institution devoted to education—which includes the "educing," or bringing forth of one's fullest potential, as well as the discovery of knowledge and the liberation of the intellect—has, not surprisingly, become a central site of conflict among competing ideas concerning the human subject, sex, and gender. The essays in this collection explore the reverberations of this ideological conflict as they affect every area of academe—including our classroom curricula, our pedagogical techniques, our research interests, our relationships with students and colleagues, and, on a more private level, the books we read, the languages we speak, the sentences we write, and the way we think about ourselves and our world. Some of these essays trace the historical development of feminist thought and its impact on our profession; others confront the challenges that these new ideas and attitudes present to academics today; still others speculate on the future trajectory of feminist influence in the academy. These essays thus consider where we have been, where we are, and where we are going in relation to attitudes toward gender in academe.

Definitions

Misunderstandings frequently arise from unclear definition of terms, and never more so than in the area of feminism. I will thus follow Socrates' dictum and begin by defining my terms.

When discussing issues concerning sex and gender, it is important to differentiate between the frequently related terms "female," "feminine" and "feminist." I will first define two of the most important words in the feminist lexicon: "female" and "feminine." "Female" and "male" denote biological categories, identifying one's physical sex. "Feminine" and "masculine" describe cultural categories, referring to the socially conditioned qualities associated with one's sexual identity (McConnell-Ginet 1980, 16). Feminists argue that the patriarchal ideology makes the mistake of equating "feminine/masculine" (cultural qualities) with "female/male" (biological categories), thus confusing culture with biology (Kramarae and Treichler 1985, 173–74). Feminists also insist that it is important to make these distinctions between sex and gender in order to free both women and men from sexist stereotyping by discrediting essentialist theories of human behavior that designate certain psychological characteristics as female-specific or male-specific. Thus, according to this feminist view, being female does not require one to display stereotypic "feminine" traits, nor does being male compel one to manifest traditional "masculine" attributes. Both women and men are thereby liberated from confining gender stereotyping.

The final term, "feminist," is somewhat more difficult to define. "Feminism" refers not to physiological traits or socially conditioned qualities but to a political position that has no intrinsic relationship to one's sex or gender. Simply being female does not guarantee that one is a feminist, nor does being a man prohibit one from participating in the feminist movement, as the example of leading feminist advocate John Stuart Mill, and those of many other dedicated male feminists, clearly illustrate. The often unintentional confusion of these three key terms—"female," "feminine," and "feminist"—has hindered the progress of the feminist movement, frequently obscuring its agendas and distorting its goals.[1] But simply to define feminism as a political position does not sufficiently clarify its meaning because this political position may be interpreted differently by different women and men, depending on the time in which they live, their race, and their class. I must, therefore, further clarify how the term "feminism" is being used in this study.

In her excellent survey, *Contemporary Feminist Thought*, Hester Eisenstein divides the feminist movement into two phases or waves.[2] The first wave, comprising the last three decades of the nineteenth century as well as the first three decades of the twentieth, concentrated on political and social reform, and although the movement rectified many legal, economic, and educational injustices, it failed to attack successfully the patriarchal assumptions underlying and causing these injustices, assumptions with which both women and men are unconsciously indoctrinated. As a result of this failure, the feminist movement became vulnerable to assaults from the counter-revolutionary forces of the 1920s and 1930s, which ultimately routed the feminist insurgents, precipitating the retreat to the suburbs, the elevation of separate and complementary gender spheres, and the valorization of the "feminine mystique" of passivity, domesticity, and motherhood.

The second wave of feminism, initiated by Simone de Beauvoir and featuring such leaders as Kate Millet, Shulamith Firestone, Betty Friedan, and Germaine Greer, established the framework for the renewed discussion of feminism in the 1970s. This first current of the second wave focused on the socially constructed differences between the sexes as the chief source of female oppression, rejecting the valorization of "femininity" and "domesticity" while seeking to replace gender polarization with some form of androgyny. In the late 1970s the emphasis shifted dramatically. The first feminists of the second wave had sought the elimination of socially constructed differences between women and men as a prerequisite for women's liberation. This view that women's differences were the source of female oppression led to a focus upon these differences and their origins and to the establishment of women's studies as an interdisciplinary area of study in numerous colleges and universities. Paradoxically, this examination of feminine difference gradually led to a change in the terms of the debate. Many feminists began to feel that in ostensibly advocating androgyny, the feminists of the first current were actually elevating the ideal of the masculine woman while derogating the feminine woman. Therefore, rather than considering women's difference from men as a form of inadequacy and a source of inferiority, woman-centered feminists of this second current—such as historian Gerda Lerner, poet Adrienne Rich, and psychologists Jean Baker Miller and Nancy Chodorow—not only accepted these feminine differences as something worth preserving but also lauded them as something to be celebrated. As Eisenstein describes this reaction:

> Instead of seeking to minimize the polarization between masculine and feminine, it sought to isolate and define those aspects of female experience that were potential sources of strength and power for women, and, more broadly, of a new blueprint for social change. (1983, xii)

Most feminists applaud many aspects of this most recent movement, particularly its critique of patriarchal systems and masculinist's values (the privileging of reason over feeling, competition over cooperation, objectivity over subjectivity, the public over the private, autonomy over relatedness, etc.) and its recognition of the worth of feminine experiences and "women's ways of knowing" and feeling. However, many feminists also fear that this movement, with its "Vive la différence" celebration of the feminine, could degenerate into a reverse form of sexism and essentialism in which woman is enshrined as inherently morally superior to man. Like Julia Kristeva, many feminists reject first-current feminism, with its affirmation of androgyny and its failure to critique patriarchal institutions and masculinist's values, as too bourgeois, while worrying that second-current, woman-centered feminism can become an inverted form of sexism. They thus yearn, as does Kristeva, for a feminism that totally deconstructs these socially constructed polarities, exploding these dichotomies and moving into a new area of freedom (1981, 197–98; 214–17). In her essay in this collection, Lisa Starks similarly deplores the dichotomizing of the feminist into either the pro-masculine or the pro-feminine ideal, instead defining the feminist as one who "strives to open up the range of possibility in terms of gender and sexuality and to encourage others to respect differences in particular personal choices about one's 'style' of gender and sexual preference." Jacques Derrida envisions a similar freedom to express a "multiplicity of sexually marked voices," a world in which

> the relationship to the other would not be a-sexual, far from it, but would be sexual otherwise: beyond the opposition feminine/masculine, beyond bi-sexuality as well, beyond homosexuality and heterosexuality which come to the same thing. As I dream of saving the chance that this question offers I would like to believe in the multiplicity of sexually marked voices. (Derrida and McDonald 1982, 76)

I will conclude my definition of feminism with a quotation from bell hooks [sic] that eloquently expresses my own interpretation of the cause to which I am dedicated. For bell hooks, feminism

> is a commitment to eradicating the ideology of domination that permeates Western culture on various levels—sex, race, and class, to name a few— and a commitment to reorganizing U.S. society, so that the self-development of people can take precedence over imperialism, economic expansion, and material desires. (Kramarae and Treichler 1985, 159)

As I hope the above examination illustrates, feminism is far from a monolithic system; indeed its diversity and variability, its "playful pluralism," to adopt the phrase of Annette Kolodny (see Chapter 14), is one of its greatest strengths. In summary, feminism, as defined in this collection, transcends the historical movements outlined by Eisenstein, seeking to achieve the freedom and diversity championed by Kristeva, Derrida, and Starks and the equality and fulfillment envisioned by bell hooks.

Another highly connotative term needing careful definition is the word "patriarchy." The contributors to this volume use this term to describe the particular social system that has prevailed throughout Western civilization since the beginning of history, a "social organization marked by the supremacy of the father in the clan or family, the legal dependence of wives and children, and the reckoning of descent and inheritance in the male line" (Webster's Ninth New Collegiate Dictionary 1990). In employing this term, we are fully aware that this hierarchical social system victimizes men as well as women and children. We believe that the gender polarization and the hierarchical structure of the traditional patriarchal family and state limit the freedom of men, women, and children, and that the creation of a more egalitarian and peaceful society—which is the goal of feminism in all its forms—is a way of liberating both sexes.

The designation "patriarchy," referring to a clearly defined social system, should be carefully discriminated from the term "sexist," which defines an attitude or state of mind. In clarifying this term, I will adopt the definition offered by two contributors to this volume, Evelyn Ashton-Jones and Gary Olson: "Sexism refers to the doctrine that perceived inherent differences between men and women make one sex (almost always men) superior to the other and thereby justify discrimination toward and abuse of the 'inferior' sex" (1991, ix).

Sexism pervades all the institutions of our society, including academe. Yet, because sexism assumes many forms, it is often difficult to recognize. Sandra Harding, a leading feminist scientist, identifies three distinct processes that combine to gender our society and thus to encourage sexism. The first process, which Harding calls "gender symbolism," assigns dualistic gender metaphors to perceived dichotomies that rarely have anything to do with sex differences (1986, 17). By "gender symbolism," Harding appears to be referring to the "metaphysical couples" (to adopt Hélène Cixous' picturesque phrase [1986, 101–2], by which society has gendered its value systems since the time of Pythagoras. For example, society codes hierarchy, authority, order, reason, and objectivity as masculine, designating equality, freedom, flexibility, feeling, and subjectivity as feminine. Almost invariably, a patriarchal society privileges the masculine principle over the feminine one. In academe, this privileging results in the often authoritarian, hierarchical structure of our classes and the high value awarded to reason, order, and objectivity. A feminist approach would oppose gendering or necessarily affirming one value principle over another, instead advocating choice and diversity in value principles and systems. The second process, which Harding terms "gender structure," relies on "gender dualisms to organize social activity," dividing necessary social functions between different groups of humans (1986, 17–18). This division of labor operates in academe as well as throughout society, manifesting itself in the propensity for hiring women in certain disciplines and men in others (thereby encouraging female and male students to choose certain majors); in the proclivity for assigning certain types of classes or academic duties to women and others to men; and in the tendency to award positions of power or authority more often to men than to women. Feminism, of course, opposes the gendering of the labor market, either within or outside of academe. The third process, which Harding designates "individual gender," constructs individuals and identity along gender lines, "only imperfectly correlated with either the 'reality' or the perception of sex differences" (1986, 18), a priori labeling women as emotional, compassionate, nurturing, and subjective and men as rational, logical, detached, and objective. This type of invidious stereotyping often results in the devaluing of women's accomplishments, both artistic and academic, as well as in blatant discrimination against both female students and faculty, a devaluation and discrimination that feminism vigorously opposes. This volume, like feminism in all its multiple forms, is dedicated to resisting all of these sexist processes wherever they are manifested, either within or outside of academe.

Content

To move from precept to practice—a leap of faith that feminism must make if it is ever to become a dynamic force in our society—we must address the tripartite question, "How does a feminist perspective influence *what* we teach in the classroom, *how* we teach in the classroom, and what and how we teach *outside* of the classroom?"

The first section of this volume, comprised of seven essays representing seven different disciplines (art history, communication, English, history, psychology, and interdisciplinary women's studies), examines the impact of feminist ideology on the curricula of the classroom and approaches to those curricula.

The opening essay in Part I, entitled "On the Social Construction of a Women's Gender Studies Major" and jointly authored by five professors from five different disciplines—Blanche Radford Curry, Judith M. Green, Suzan Harrison, Carolyn Johnston, and Linda E. Lucas—delineates the feminist strategies employed by this indefatigable quintet in their successful campaign to establish a women's and gender studies major at Eckerd College. Their carefully crafted, cooperative essay, describing their carefully crafted, cooperative campaign, should provide a useful paradigm for others attempting a similar venture.

The second essay in this section, "Gender and Visual Literacy: Toward a Multidisciplinary Perspective," is also jointly authored, in this case by a female art professor, Colleen McNally, and a male communications professor, Arnold S. Wolfe. This article demonstrates how feminist techniques, an interdisciplinary approach, and poststructuralist critical methodology can be combined to instill in students a "visual literacy," defined in this context as a heightened awareness of the way which the images of women, presented in both canonical art and contemporary media construct society's attitudes toward gender.

A similar heightened awareness and a verbal rather than visual literacy are the concerns of the two following essays written by English professors. The essay by Brenda Gross, "Old Maids and Helpful Husbands: Alerting Students to Gender Bias in Biography, Criticism, and Autobiography," focuses not on blatant sexism but on the "ripple of subtle gender bias that runs throughout much biography, criticism, and autobiography." At the end of her essay, Gross urges teachers to integrate into their curricula techniques of analysis that will alert students to these subtle biases and thus help to shape a new generation of scholars more fully aware of the prejudices that inform their work. Charlotte Templin's essay, "The Male-Dominated Curriculum in English: How Did We Get Here and Where Are We Going?," explores a more blatant form of academic bias, the exclusion of women from English and American literature courses. In her study, Templin traces the process by which women have been systematically excluded from canonicity in the past and continue to be excluded even today, calling upon English professors throughout the nation to strive to open up the canon and make the rich legacy of female authors available to our students, both female and male.

Moving from the humanities to the social sciences, the next two essays probe biases in the discipline of psychology and offer possible solutions to these biases. Sharyl Bender Peterson's essay, "The Nature and Effects of a Gender-Biased Psychology Curriculum and Some Suggestions for Implementing Change," investigates the egregious slanting in college and university textbooks for psychology courses, concluding that despite twenty years of research in this area, little advance has occurred. In the last section of her essay, she outlines suggested remedies for these prejudicial presentations, urging feminist psychologists not only to compensate for these biases in their teaching but also to write new texts that avoid deleterious misrepresentations, omissions, and stereotyping. Shifting the focus from textbooks to curricula, Eleanor Roffman's essay, "The Personal is Professional is Political: Feminist Praxis in a Graduate School Counselor Training Program," illustrates yet another way that a feminist point of view can affect the teaching of psychology. The essay describes Roffman's efforts in a two-semester psychology course to create a classroom situation in which students can "articulate their understanding of self, other, subjective reality, empathy, and the surrounding environment through examination of critical texts on feminist psychology." By incorporating feminist theories into actual classroom activities, this course seeks to bridge the gap between precept and praxis.

The final essay in this section, "Woman as Witch: The Renaissance and Reformations Revisited," by historian Judith Ochshorn, concentrates on a significant historical topic, the European witchcraft craze in the sixteenth and seventeenth centuries. Ochshorn's focus on this horrendous episode in Western history illustrates how feminist historians today are foregrounding episodes crucially important to women that have traditionally been marginalized and effaced within the male-dominated discipline of history. Through these endeavors, feminist historians are helping the female majority at last to discover its past.

Because not only our curricula and textbooks but also our pedagogical methods should reflect feminist theories and emphases, Part II of our collection includes five essays that treat the question: "How does a feminist perspective influence *how* we teach in the classroom?"

Our first two essays in this section detail some of the challenges endemic to the teaching of feminist theory. After rehearsing some of these problems, English professor Lisa S. Starks, in her essay, "Hyper-feminisms: Poststructuralist Theories, Popular Culture, and Pedagogy," recounts some of the methods she employed in an interdisciplinary course in feminist theory in order to deconstruct the pro-masculine/pro-feminine fallacy that plagues contemporary feminism, while also using fashion and video to relate feminist theories to her students' quotidian experience. My own essay in the collection confronts another vexing question: given the authoritarian, hierarchical structure of most classroom situations, how can a teacher incorporate into the pedagogy of a course on feminist criticism the liberatory, egalitarian values advocated by feminist theory? My essay, "Navigating in a Brave New World: Teaching Feminist Literary Criticism," outlines some of my own experiments in steering between the rigid rocks of authority and the whirlpool of anarchy in my effort to transform the study of feminist theory into a genuinely liberating experience for teacher and students alike.

Linda Woodbridge, in her essay entitled, "The Centrifugal Classroom," expands the enterprise described by Starks and Deats and seeks to apply feminist and postmodern pedagogies to the teaching of courses not primarily focused on women and gender issues, in this case, the teaching of Shakespeare. This is a significant effort because we, as feminist teachers, do not wish to limit the use of feminist pedagogy to courses in women's studies but to encourage the use of feminist methodologies throughout academe. In her essay, Woodbridge describes the innovative pedagogical strategies—such as debates and performances of scenes from Shakespeare—that she employs in her efforts to decenter the teacher, empower the students, and create the centrifugal classroom envisioned by feminist pedagogy.

The two following articles examine the adaptation of feminist theory to composition studies. Carol Mattingly's essay, "Valuing the Personal: Feminist Concerns for the Writing Classroom," problematizes one of the sacred cows of feminist theory, the valorization of personal experience writing, pointing out that difficulties sometimes occur when teachers bring practices that have proven successful in earlier, more homogeneous settings into the more diverse writing classroom. At the conclusion of her revisionist essay, Mattingly calls for a rigorous reevaluation of pedagogical strategies in the teaching of rhetoric and composition and a restoration of the balance between theory and practice. The second essay, "Evidence and Ideology When College Students Write About Gender" by Virginia Nees-Hatlen, performs the kind of rigorous evaluation that Mattingly recommends. This essay reports on a research project conducted by Nees-Hatlen which demonstrates that there is very little "carry-over" from academic courses into the students' experience within their social communities. These results led Nees-Hatlen to alter her goals and many of her writing assignments in women's studies and English classes in order to give students practice in writing in the modes of logic and persuasion and to show them ways to articulate their academic learning to nonacademic audiences. Through these exercises, Nees-Hatlen seeks to make academic learning relevant to her students' roles as citizens.

The final essay in this section, "Woman to Women: Understanding the Needs of Our Female Students," jointly authored by a trio of professors of counseling psychology—Mary Ann Gawelek, Maggie Mulqueen, and Jill Mattuck Tarule—considers the question of how individual teaching and pedagogy in general are influenced by gender differences. Concentrating on three theoretical perspectives on gender differences—epistemological development, female sex-role identity and competence development, and intimacy and autonomy drives—this essay describes how these three perspectives have influenced the teaching of these three feminist professors. Like the other essays in this section, this study offers a valuable template for those seeking to integrate feminist praxis with feminist precept in academic pedagogy.

As all of us are fully aware, much significant teaching takes place outside of the classroom. In a number of professional forums—books, journals, conferences, and committees—we often teach our peers, either by sharing our scholarship or by demonstrating our precepts through practice. In other less structured affiliations, such as the all-important mentoring relationships between teachers and students, much valuable, and often reciprocal, education occurs. Moreover, the very language we speak and write, both within and outside of the academy, often becomes an involuntary pedagogical tool, testifying to our perspectives toward ourselves and others. The final seven essays in our collection thus analyze the influence of a feminist ideology on the way we teach, either consciously or unconsciously, in these out-of-classroom pedagogical environments.

The first three essays in Part III treat relatively formal forums of out-of-classroom teaching. The essay by Lagretta Tallent Lenker, director of Lifelong Learning at the University of South Florida, entitled, "A Study in Feminisms: Organizing a Gender Conference," delineates some of the problems and rewards—the agonies and the ecstasies—involved in planning a gender-related conference. In considering issues surrounding the planning of such a conference, Lenker concludes that a pluralistic approach best serves the various constituencies at this essentially multidisciplinary meeting and that the program at such a meeting should reflect the various feminisms that comprise the current fabric of gender studies. Lenker further describes "pressure points," organizational and programatic, that must be dealt with in order to produce a successful gender program. The second essay by psychologist Judith Worell, "Feminist Journals: Academic Empowerment or Professional Liability?" moves from the podium to the press and evaluates the pros and cons—the benefits and the risks—of publishing in a feminist journal. Worell's article considers two important issues: the influence of feminist journals on the direction of research in relevant fields of inquiry and the impact of feminist journals on the professional lives of the academicians who are both the creators and the consumers of the new revisionist scholarship.

The last essay in this group, "Building an Effective Model for Institutional Change: Academic Women as Catalyst," co-authored by Gloria DeSole, director of affirmative action, and Meredith Butler, dean of university libraries at the State University of New York at Albany, narrates a success story. This article describes the network of women's committees, consciously created and integrated within the institutional context of the State University of New York at Albany, that serve as an effective vehicle for social change and a forum for education—for the women on the committees, for the university, and for the community. All three essays, while acknowledging the time, effort, struggle, and even jeopardy involved, affirm the significance of these out-of-classroom forums for teaching feminist ideals.

Progressing from the teaching of peers to informal interaction with students, the next two essays—"The Politics of Gendered Sponsorship: Mentoring in the Academy," co-authored by rhetoric and composition professors Gary A. Olson and Evelyn Ashton-Jones, and "Gender Patterns in Faculty-Student Mentoring Relationships," written by psychology professor Kathleen Day Hulbert—analyze the ways in which faculty-student relationships beyond the classroom shape students' self-perceptions, achievement motivation, and academic and career goals. In their dialogue, Olson and Ashton-Jones examine the multivalence of the term "mentor" as defined in the literature on the subject and summarize critical attitudes toward the mentoring relationship, as well as offering anecdotal material from their own personal experience as mentor and protégé. Their dialogue focuses particularly on the impact of gender on the mentoring affiliation, exploring the scarcity of mentors for women, even though women have a greater need for mentoring in order to succeed, as well as the advantages and disadvantages involved in cross-gender mentoring. Whereas Olson and Ashton-Jones concentrate on cross-gender mentoring, Hulbert examines four possible modes of gender interaction in the mentoring relationship—male faculty to male student; male faculty to female student; female faculty to female student; and female faculty to male student. She concludes that although statistically valid data are unavailable, general consensus agrees that same-gender mentoring seems to be more comfortable and therefore more often occurs. Although their orientation is very different, all three commentators concur that sexism often influences mentoring in many ways and that expanded dialogue is needed to foster an awareness within academe of the gender trouble frequently impeding the success of this invaluable pedagogical experience.

The final two essays in this section move from the particular to the general and consider the language we use and the images we hold of ourselves as unconscious pedagogical tools in our out-of-classroom teaching. The essay by Fran Schattenberg, doctoral student in English, entitled, "If R2D2 is a Male Robot, Then 10^6 is a Female Nothing," critiques the sexist language that even after almost twenty years of feminist protest still pervades academe, and offers a valuable template for achieving "gender neutral" language in all our speech and writing, both inside and outside of academe. The final essay in this volume presents a dialogue between English professors Janet Mason Ellerby and John Clifford, entitled, "The Hidden 'A-Gender' in Intellectual Discourse: A Dialogical Examination." In their dialogue, Ellerby and Clifford explore the dialectic of gender: What it means to be a female feminist intellectual, what is means to be a male feminist intellectual, and how gender affects the way we regard ourselves, our mission, and what we profess both within and outside of the academy. This often illuminating dialogue provides an appropriate closure for our own dialogical examination of "Gender in Academe."

The contributors to this volume do not expect their essays to impact Western thought as violently as did Simone de Beauvoir's *The Second Sex*. They do, however, hope to dispel some of the confusion befogging the debates about feminism within academe and to alert our audience to the host of distorted assertions generated by gender-marked dogmas. Ideally, after completing these next 300 or so pages, our readers will decide that they can simultaneously advocate both hierarchy and equality, authority and freedom, order and flexibility, objectivity and subjectivity, and reason and feeling without being guilty of gender treason.

Notes

1. See the discussion by Toril Moi, "Feminist, Female, Feminine" (204–21) on which I draw freely in my own distinctions between these three terms.
2. I refer the interested reader to the excellent analysis of contemporary feminism by Hester Eisenstein, to which my own discussion is deeply indebted.

Works Cited

Ashton-Jones, Evelyn, and Gary Olson, eds. *The Gender Reader*. London: Alleyn and Bacon, 1991.
Beauvoir, Simone de. *The Second Sex*. Trans. H. M. Parshley. New York: Vintage Books, 1952.
Belsey, Catherine, and Jane Moore. *The Feminist Reader*. New York: Blackwell Press, 1989.

Cixous, Hélène. "Sortis." In *The Feminist Reader*, ed. Catherine Belsey and Jane Moore, 101–16. New York: Blackwell Press, 1989. Originally published in Hélène Cixous, *The Newly Born Woman*, trans. Betty Wing (Minneapolis: University of Minnesota Press, 1986).

Derrida, Jacques, and Christie V. McDonald. "Choreographies." *Diacritic* 12:2 (1982): 66–76.

Eisenstein, Hester. *Contemporary Feminist Thought*. Boston: G. K. Hall and Co., 1983.

Harding, Sandra. *The Science Question in Feminism*. Ithaca: Cornell University Press, 1986.

Kramarae, Cheris, and Paula A. Treichler. *A Feminist Dictionary*. Boston: Pandora, 1985.

Kristeva, Julia. "Women's Time." Trans. Alice Jardin and Harry Blake. *Signs* 7 (1981): 13-35. Reprinted in *The Feminist Reader*, 2, 14–17, 197–98.

McConnell-Ginet, Sally. "Linguistics and Feminist Challenge." In *Women and Language in Literature and Society*, ed. Sally McConnell-Ginet, et al. New York: Praeger, 1980.

Moi, Toril. "Feminist, Female, Feminism." In *The Feminist Reader*, ed. Catherine Belsey and Jane Moore, 115–24. New York: Blackwell Press, 1989. Originally published in *Modern Literary Theory*, ed. Ann Jefferson and Donald Robey (London: 1986).

Webster's Ninth New Collegiate Dictionary. Springfield, Mass.: Merriam-Webster, Inc., 1990.

Part I

How does a feminist perspective influence
what we teach in the classroom?

Chapter 1

On the Social Construction of a Women's and Gender Studies Major

Blanche Radford Curry, Judith M. Green, Suzan Harrison,
Carolyn Johnston, and Linda E. Lucas

On March 20, 1991, the general faculty of Eckerd College in St. Petersburg, Florida, approved without dissent a proposal for a new women's and gender studies major. This event represented the achievement of a long-held dream of the core members of the organizing committee. It was also the result of a substantial investment of time and energy during that academic year by nearly a quarter of the faculty and a group of highly committed students. This core planning committee was diverse in its composition—diverse in gender, race, generation, affectional preference, and academic status. It was also cross-disciplinary, including faculty from all five of the college's disciplinary groupings (collegia) as well as representatives of both the residential or "day" college and the evening division (the Program for Experienced Learners). Our grassroots organizational approach was successful in large part because it coincided with a call from the college administration for faculty groups to propose new liberal arts majors.

It was successful because the entire faculty of Eckerd College participates in teaching interdisciplinary general education courses, giving us a greater familiarity with synthetic interdisciplinary work and with faculty members of other disciplines than is common at most colleges and universities. Our efforts were also successful because a critical mass of our faculty had already developed courses in their own disciplines in which women's experience and gender issues were significant foci of attention; this allowed us to emphasize reorganizational goals in our proposal rather than to justify new hires or additional extensive diversions of faculty course offerings away from disciplinary needs.

Although our singular situation at Eckerd College contributed to the successful outcome, we believe that our method of developing and promoting a successful women's and gender studies major should be of interest and value to others considering similar endeavors. The following sections describe our political, theoretical, pedagogical, and resource strategies.

The Political Construction of a Receptive Climate

In their book, *The Struggle for Equality in the Nineteenth and Twentieth Centuries*, Nancy E. McGlen and Karen O'Connor describe the following conditions as necessary for the emergence of a mass women's movement:

1. The presence of an organizational base or outside resources to facilitate its development;
2. Existence of lines of communication among potential leaders;
3. A sense of collective oppression and a recognition of the need for a common solution within a sizeable group of women; and
4. A critical mobilizing event (or events). (1983, 15)

In order to launch a successful new major in women's and gender studies, these conditions are also applicable. An organizational base must be in place, with communication among potential leaders who perceive a need to teach the new feminist scholarship. After a critical mass of participants has been achieved, timing and appropriate tactics are essential for the program's passage and implementation.

In 1978, Julie Empric (literature) taught a course entitled "Woman as Metaphor," and Carolyn Johnston (history/american studies) began to teach "Women in Modern America: The Hand that Cradles the Rock" and "Becoming Visible: Sex and Gender in America." These courses marked the beginning of the development of an organizational base. Shortly thereafter, Sarah Dean (human development) offered "Male-Female Socialization," and Nancy Corson Carter (literature) developed courses on women in the arts. Thus, we had the beginnings of a women's studies program that was supported by the revival in 1978 of the Women's Resources Committee as a women's advocacy group on campus. We first formalized our academic program as a concentration in women's studies. This concentration was a student and faculty designed major with tracks in history, literature, and human development, based on our course offerings and independent study courses. In this first stage of our efforts, the primary objectives were to sustain as many course offerings as possible and to focus our energies on hiring more women and minorities into tenure-track positions. This meant placing ourselves on numerous search committees (Carolyn Johnston alone has been on twenty-six). In 1978–79, there were about seventy-five faculty members and seven full-time women on the faculty. Now, in 1992, we have twenty-five women out of eighty-six. In 1978 we had no African-American faculty members, and we now have four.

In the second stage of our efforts, our focus shifted as we sought to increase course offerings, thus building the major instead of proposing a major that required new staffing or courses. At the same time, we sought to integrate new scholarship on women and African-Americans into mainstream general education courses. We continued to develop a coalition of male and female faculty members and enthusiastic students. Seven years ago, Judith Green was hired in the philosophy discipline. With expertise in feminist theory, she has contributed immensely to our range of offerings. Along with hiring new faculty, we also recognized that a crucial precondition for the stability of our program was the continued tenuring and promotion of leaders in the program.

By 1990, we believed that we had the key factors in place for the acceptance of the program. Twenty-three faculty members were participating in the program and offering courses from the majority of the disciplines. We had created a receptive political climate, and we had designed a well-articulated program that resulted from weekly meetings throughout the fall of 1990. Thus, when Eckerd faculty were invited by the dean of the faculty and curriculum committee to propose new majors, we were ready with a proposal that included a realistic staffing model, a coordinator, and demonstrated student demand for our courses.

We have found that in order to insure success in proposing a women's and gender studies major, a balance is required between passion and reason, patience and impatience. Our approach was characterized by assumed legitimacy and avoidance of any defensive posture. Before the proposal was presented to the faculty, we were assured of acceptance, and thus the proposal met with genuine enthusiasm. As experience has taught us, resistance to new ideas can be fierce, expressed subtly or blatantly depending on the nature of the opposition. Thus, sometimes political change requires long-term vision and leadership that is not vulnerable to dismissal or budget cuts. Success also depends on stamina, vision, persistence, and the demonstration of excellence as well as efficiency. Because Eckerd is a liberal arts college, we had more freedom to develop new courses easily, and we avoided the bureaucratic impediments present in a university. We decided to call the program Women's and Gender Studies because we felt that this name accurately described the current directions in feminist scholarship, while acknowledging the history of the discipline as grounded in women's studies. This was the only politically delicate issue since some of our male allies in the social sciences objected to the inclusion of the title gender studies, arguing that the male gender was essentially excluded in our courses. We were able to mollify these objections through discussion and detailed course descriptions and encountered no other difficulties in the passage of the new major.

Implementation will be our fourth stage. We have a broad coalition of enthusiastic professors and students with five majors thus far.[1] We are excited about implementing the program, developing internships, and sending our students off to graduate programs.

Theoretical Considerations

In addition to organization and timing, several theoretical aspects of our proposal and our process were important and may offer some useful insights for feminist theory and feminist praxis within the academy. These comments are organized as memories of our extemporaneous answers to two questions about our proposal that were asked at the final general faculty discussion before our proposal was put to a vote. Though the larger political, historical, and practical content of this faculty discussion probably accounted for its favorable outcome, perhaps the extemporaneous answers we were able to give to these two questions accounted in part for the absence of voiced dissent. Roughly paraphrased, these two questions were "Why are you proposing such an awkward sounding title for such a major, instead of either 'Women's Studies' or 'Gender Studies'?" and "Does it make sense to create a new major to remedy a current social problem when the rest of the majors are focused on fundamental subjects of perennial interest?" The answers we gave to these questions, derived from continuing conversations within feminist theory and praxis, sketched a methodology, an epistemology, a philosophy of history, and a set of operative ideals for our new major.

In response to the first question about the awkward-sounding title of our proposed new major, we explained that our shared methodological approach is historically embedded, growing out of developments over the past twenty years in the political field of various women's and men's movements and the theoretical field of cross-disciplinary feminist theory. We continue to work for a more woman-inclusive academic canon and more woman-empowering academic customs, as well as social transformation away from patterns of gender expression in our larger society. Believing that gender systems limit men as well as women, we emphasized that the goal of feminist praxis is the liberation of both women and men from gender restrictions. Yet, we have come to realize that it is necessary to expose the root causes of these problems in order to achieve these goals, and we have come to understand the importance in its own right of gender as a fundamental social and intellectual construct that merits serious academic study. We have come to believe that we cannot adequately understand the situation of women without understanding the broader and deeper issues of gender, and—contra Marx's critique of Feuerbach—we cannot adequately transform what we cannot adequately understand.

This is not to suggest that the feminist political struggle should grind to a halt until the academy has finished its work, but rather that results in each domain are likely to be roughly comparable in adequacy to those in the companion domain. Theory will be no more insightful than praxis and praxis no more effective than theory allows. In short, we have sketched a pragmatic epistemology of theory-in-praxis shorn of a false, impartial objectivity, yet stabilized by cross-cultural, historical, and meta-theoretical reflection. We suggested that we cannot achieve the original compensatory and transformational goals of women's studies as a curricular field without broadening and deepening our understanding of existing gender systems and their feasible alternatives. At the same time, the role and meaning of gender in existing human societies cannot be understood without compensatory attention to the experience of women given the current masculine-focused state of the contemporary academic curriculum.

Our answer to the second question, concerning whether it is appropriate to create a new major focused on women and gender within a curriculum of majors focusing on subjects of fundamental and perennial concern, was related to our answer to the first question. Referring to some of the "Great Books" that have become increasingly important parts of Eckerd College's curriculum as well as favored texts among antipluralist, "traditionalist" curricular reformers, we pointed out that women and gender issues are of perennial concern; indeed, these issues were discussed with careful attention by Plato, Aristotle, Shakespeare, and Freud, and these discussions held great interest for their contemporaneous audiences. Moreover, we reminded the faculty that the struggle to transform the broader gender structure of our society as well as to revalue women's place within it dates to our country's earliest days, making it older than many unquestionably important contemporary academic disciplines such as psychology, sociology, and anthropology.

We argued further that it was modernism's emphasis on the universal sameness of persons in all the significant fundamental ways that allowed feminist women and their supporters to argue for the need to improve women's condition relative to this universal standard yet, ironically, made it difficult to theorize about women's experience per se, even to show systematic injustice, as well as to value differences among women and between women and men. The contemporary critique of the modernist vision to which feminism has contributed has shown the need not only to acknowledge and include aspects of experience and discourse that were excluded and ignored, but also to rethink the fundamental categories of Western thought and experience upon which our academic curriculum rests.

These points sketched half of a temporally grounded defense of the fundamental and persisting importance of women's and gender studies. As for the future, we suggested that the faculty try to estimate by what year gender-based inequality would no longer be a focus of basic interest, anxiety, and concern. Because that future date, whenever it will be, is clearly well beyond the horizon of our own lifetimes, the importance of studying gender and women's experience is as practically perennial as anything else that now matters in academe. We concluded by reminding our colleagues that human liberation has always been the goal of the liberal arts and that widespread literacy and access to books were advocated by democratic theorists in ancient times precisely because deeper understanding and transformative ideas were thought to have the power to free and fulfill human beings. Thus, in calling for the study of women and gender, both in a new major and across the curriculum, we were governing our curricular proposals by one of the oldest and most lasting academic ideals.

Erasing Invisibility: A Multicultural Framework for Empowerment

A critical component of the theoretical construction of an interdisciplinary approach to the study of a multicultural, multiracial, and intergenerational field is its application. Women's and gender studies programs are a natural medium by which we can further recognize and understand significant differences among women. However, since the initial formal development of women's studies programs in the 1960s, the echoes of exclusion ring on. It remains a fact that the leadership of women's studies programs continues to be mostly white women (Zinn 1986, 290–303). The curriculum, in general, still reflects the standpoint of white, middle-class, heterosexual, Christian women. The result is a very distorted theoretical construct of universal womanness that is applied in practice. Accordingly, women of color are relegated to invisibility or at best marginalized in both theory and practice.

The extent and significant costs of exclusionary practices in women's studies programs are well documented by many feminists of color such as bell hooks [sic] (1981), Paula Giddings (1984), Maria C. Lugones (1991), Patricia Hill Collins (1989), and Angela Davis (1989). Such is also the case for some white feminists like Margaret Simons (1979), Alison Jaggar (1983), and Elizabeth V. Spelman (1988). From the research of these feminists, both women of color and white women, it is clear that the exclusion of women of color from feminist theory renders it incomplete and incorrect and perpetuates unacceptable applications of theory. Two examples include the fact that

1. failure to explore fully the interplay of race, class and gender has cost the field the ability to provide a broad and truly complex analysis of women's lives and of social organization; and
2. emphasis on the shared experiences of women has negated the important differences among women. (Zinn 1986)

Maria C. Lugones (1991) points out that the value of including excluded voices is that society needs new models to transform itself to accommodate rapidly changing circumstances. We are in urgent need of a new process of feminist theory construction that respects women speaking in their own culturally different voices, separately if they prefer to do so, or in equal cross-cultural collaboration if they presume to comment on each other's lives and call each other to a common cause. A framework is possible for considering each other's standpoints

without giving up our own or denying another's. As Elsa Barkley
Brown explains:

> all people can learn to center in another experience, validate it, and
> judge it by its own standards without need of comparison or need to
> adopt that framework as their own. Thus, one has no need to "decenter"
> anyone in order to center someone else; one has only to constantly
> appropriately, "pivot the center." (1989, 923)

Research on the invisibility of women of color in women's studies
programs represents the initial step of bridging the gap between
knowing and acting upon our knowledge, through acknowledging other
voices, making a conscious commitment to choose change, and going
beyond knowing what is right to *doing* what is right. This is what
Patricia Hill Collins (1989) calls an ethics of personal accountability.
We at Eckerd College have made the conscious commitment to change,
to do what is right, to be accountable.

After this initial step, the question becomes how to design a
women's and gender studies program for maximum inclusion of other
voices? This question provides the turning point for change. As
Margaret Simons points out, "[our] efforts on a theoretical level are not
sufficient. We must extend our efforts to a personal and practical level
. . . as feminists, we must . . . [act] on both a personal and theoretical
level" (1979, 379, 399). What have we done at Eckerd College to
structure our Women's and Gender Studies Program to make it reflect
an interdisciplinary approach to the study of a field that is multicultural,
multiracial, and intergenerational? To bridge the gap between theory and
application, the knowing and acting upon our knowledge, we began with
two general observations that Maxine Baca Zinn (1986) discusses: 1)
that structural changes in our academic practices and policies are
necessary; and 2) that we should not expect leadership from
administrators. With this understanding, we realized that it rested upon
us to bring about the change in the political construction.

Among the specific efforts we have taken to diversify our Women's
and Gender Studies Program at Eckerd are:

> 1) taking advantage of opportunities for temporary and/or
> permanent faculty positions to include a representation of
> women of color;
> 2) including research by women of color in each of the course
> offerings;

3) engaging in ongoing dialogue with as many women of color as possible to bridge the gap between what is read and what is understood in terms of cross-cultural collaboration;
4) having women of color as guest lecturers or panel participants in each of the course offerings;
5) including discussions of gender and various disciplines by guest lecturers of each gender who specialize in these disciplines;
6) continuing our ongoing evaluation and dialogue with other women's and gender studies programs about what works in enhancing and maintaining diversity.

Our future plans of enhancing and maintaining diversity in Eckerd's Women's and Gender Studies Program include a general focus of broadening the representation of diversity on all levels.

Methodology and Competency in the Major

In addition to our concerns about political climate, theoretical construction, and diversity, we realized that our answers to pedagogical and methodological questions would be essential to the success of our new major. The question of methodology is one that plagues any interdisciplinary field of study. What unity we find in "traditional" disciplines comes not just from the subject matter, not just from the types of texts (in the broad sense) studied, but in great part from the methodology. Thus, studies of *Beowulf*, Virginia Woolf, and Tom Wolfe can be encompassed by the methodologies of literary study. Studies of voting patterns, parking patterns, and language patterns can be encompassed by the methodologies of sociology. The question of how to traverse these wide differences in methodologies becomes important for any interdisciplinary study, especially when differences in methodology are at the heart of so many of the long-standing disciplinary rivalries in academia. Where, then, do we find coherence and agreement in a multidisciplinary field?

The methodological questions that vex interdisciplinary studies are problematic for women's and gender studies in additional ways. First, if we take into account the theoretical issues raised earlier, the issue becomes more complicated: Where do we find coherence in a field that is not only multidisciplinary, but also multiracial, multicultural, and intergenerational? Second, questions raised by writers like Robin Lakoff and Deborah Tannen,[2] who illuminate gender differences in language use; by writers like Carol Gilligan,[3] who suggest gender differences in moral reasoning; or by writers like Nancy Chodorow,[4] who suggest gender differences in psychological and social development, add another layer of complexity. If, as these theorists lead us to believe, our traditional methodologies are predominately masculine, what does it mean to read, write, think, talk, observe, and teach through the lens of gender?

Finally, the questions raised about methodology in a women's and gender studies major often mask a subtext of resistance to the notion of "gender in academe." Questions such as—"But will this be a rigorous major or simply group therapy?" "But will students know how to do X?," and "Will students take my course in X?"—while sometimes expressing legitimate concerns, can also express deep-seated resistance to women's increasingly powerful presence in academic politics.

We formulated our developmental, competency-based women's and gender studies curriculum in response to these concerns. Rather than taking for granted our students' development of a methodology (or methodologies), we sought first to identify skills or competencies common to most academic disciplines, and to include instruction in these areas in all of the courses in the major. We came up with seven areas: bibliographic instruction, writing excellence, close reading of texts, creative problem solving, small group communication, oral communication, and expressive awareness. To reinforce and expand our students' mastery of these skills, we incorporate into both our required introductory and senior level courses explicit discussions of the methodologies of various disciplines.

Under the heading of bibliographic instruction, we ask introductory students to 1) learn to select and read appropriate periodicals; 2) develop familiarity with significant primary sources; 3) locate underlying premises, assumptions, and conclusions in scholarly literature; 4) understand how the disciplines that contribute to the field relate to each other; and 5) complete a collaborative project concerning a human problem or issue in the field, producing an annotated bibliography and summary oral report. In the senior research seminar, we ask students to use these methods to produce an extended bibliography, a review of the significant literature in their subfield, and a thesis that synthesizes these views and advocates a position.

Writing excellence in the introductory course includes 1) reading assigned and/or optional readings accurately, retelling the main ideas, and reacting in the student's own voice; and 2) formulating questions that lead to collaborative writing projects that include shared research, writing, presentation, and critiques. In the senior research course, students are asked to build upon these skills in order to 1) work in a collaborative research group in which members read and critique each other's work, and combine efforts in order to reflect interdisciplinary views on an important human problem; and 2) write a research paper (or senior thesis) on a topic of current research in the field.

Close reading of texts on the introductory level includes 1) analyzing texts to differentiate between fact and opinion, and to identify logic or arguments and point of view, qualifications of author, word choice, and tone; and 2) identifying the modes of thinking and learning within the disciplines by analyzing articles about women and gender in various journals and periodicals. On the senior level we ask students to fine-tune their reading skills, to ascertain accuracy, clarity, and authority as well as validity and reliability of research design and development of arguments, hypotheses, and conjectures.

Creative problem-solving develops students' ability to 1) identify a problem by using a case study and brainstorm multiple solutions as a collaborative small group activity; 2) cultivate open-mindedness by engaging in a debate, defending first one side of an issue and then the other; and 3) express feelings about a gender issue through some artistic medium.

Small group communication on both the introductory and senior levels requires students to evaluate their own and others' contributions to the large group and the small task groups, asking questions such as 1) How well did you listen? How sensitive were you to others' views?; 2) How carefully did you pay attention to the attitudes of others that were hidden below their verbal cues?; 3) What role did you play in the group most of the time?; and 4) What do your answers say about you as a learner?

Oral communication demands of introductory students that they 1) observe models through the use of videotapes, classroom lectures, movies, and guest lectures, and analyze the qualities that make effective speakers; and 2) design and deliver an effective in-class presentation, including a videotape and critique. On the senior level, we ask students to demonstrate these skills through an oral presentation based on their written work. Finally, the expressive awareness competency requires that students become familiar with various plays, paintings, poetry, music, and fiction that give expression to issues relating to women and gender. To this list, in the senior level research course, we added a leadership component requiring that each student become active in an organization in the college or broader community that addresses human problems that are a direct result of issues relating to women and gender.

In our descriptions of the various methods or competencies, we begin to map out a methodology and epistemology for women's and gender studies, and here we employ Sandra Harding's distinctions between method as "a technique for . . . gathering evidence," methodology as "a theory and analysis of how research does or should proceed," and epistemology as "a theory of knowledge" (1987, 2–3). We are working toward a methodology and epistemology informed by feminist theories, one that values women's experiences as well as men's, process as well as product, collaborative learning as well as individual endeavors, listening as well as speaking, and open-mindedness as well as the ability to defend a position. To underscore our emphasis on methodological awareness and to develop our students' ability to identify and articulate their own assumptions as researchers, readers, and writers, we are incorporating into our introductory and senior level required courses presentations on methodology by faculty from the different disciplines.

In considering these questions of coherence and methodology, it is useful to draw upon a metaphor that turns up again and again in feminist studies: the metaphor of quilting, an art of creating coherence from fragmentation, meaning from chaos. Like most women's and gender studies majors, quilting is an art that cuts across the boundaries of race, region, and class. It is also, in Elaine Showalter's words, "an art of scarcity, ingenuity, conservation and order" (1986, 228). In "Piecing and Writing," Showalter describes the process of quilting:

> 'piecing' means the sewing together of small fragments of fabric cut into geometric shapes, so that they form a pattern. The design unit is called the block or patch; 'patchwork' is the joining of these design units into an overall design. The assembled patches are then attached to heavy backing with either simple or elaborate stitches in the process called quilting. (1986, 224)

If the individual courses in our women's and gender studies major form the pieces of the quilt, and gender provides the backing, then our competency-based curriculum serves as the patchwork, the stitches that join the pieces together in an overall design that is multidisciplinary, multicultural, multiracial, multigendered, intergenerational, and rigorous.

Gathering Resources

With our theoretical, political, and pedagogical issues resolved, we faced the question of resources. The resource problem before us was to maximize our course offerings while minimizing additional workload on participating faculty. There was no budget allotted for the new major, and faculty were already pressed to capacity. Through weekly meetings we recognized that creating the major would involve reallocation of some resources and sharing of others.

The first task was to identify all of the appropriate courses that were already being offered. We considered every discipline in the college and approached faculty to discover whether any of their courses not clearly identified as gender oriented might address gender issues or fulfill a competency requirement, such as research or statistical skills. We found twenty-three courses that made up the core and elective selections for the major. Courses existed in American studies, anthropology, art, economics, history, human development, literature, sociology, philosophy, psychology, and religious studies. The diversity of course offerings clearly reflected faculty recruitment efforts over time. Among the courses were "Human Sexuality" (anthropology), "Women in Modern America" (history), "Socialization and Gender Issues" (human development), "Women in Literature," "The Family" (sociology), and "Varieties of Biblical Interpretation" (religious studies). We also identified several courses that were being planned but not yet offered. These included "Gender and Economics," "Gender and Writing," "Spanish Women Writers," and "Women in Cross-Cultural Perspectives." A third category included those offered by independent or directed study: "American Women's History," "The Goddess in Art and Literature," and "Women in the Arts."

We then approached faculty not otherwise included and solicited their agreement to develop a course within the next five years or to begin giving attention to women's and gender related topics in their current courses. Many of these faculty replied that they would be willing but needed guidance in material selection. In the end, we found that we needed only two new courses: an introductory course and a senior capstone course required of all majors in the college.

The final listing of courses well exceeded the minimum to demonstrate that the major would have stability and adequate offerings on a regular basis. Women faculty were underrepresented in the behavioral (social) sciences, natural sciences, and mathematics, and this was reflected in the courses offered. In spite of this, we received commitments from male faculty members in some of these areas to consider developing courses such as "Women and Math." We were able, after this process, to set the course schedule years ahead to accommodate leaves and other demands on faculty.

This process cost us time and energy. We had thirteen two-hour meetings over the fall semester with regular attendance by twenty people. Three people spent additional time drafting and editing the proposal that went before the faculty for approval. All twenty faculty engaged in formal and informal lobbying activity. However, we created a community of interest around a common goal that made the process fun and reduced the stress on particular individuals.

Currently, operational decisions are made by a five-person rotating steering committee drawn from across the disciplines. The current committee includes faculty from American studies, economics, literature, philosophy, and rhetoric. Since the major is interdisciplinary, funding comes from the budgets of various disciplines. The Women's Resources Committee, a faculty standing committee, overlaps in membership with the steering committee of the women's and gender studies major. The Women's Resources Committee has office space and a small budget that has been used for supplemental materials, work scholar hours, and speaker fees. We have used the college's library small grant program to build library holdings. Thus far, no additional faculty lines or funds have been necessary. As student response grows, however, we may need to press for administrative support or course releases. However, we will by then have demonstrated enough student interest and enrollment to support such requests.

Essentially, therefore, we created the new major from existing resources and minimal effort and anguish. This process has deepened our understanding of our shared interdisciplinary field, in addition to enriching the quality of our ongoing collaborative and consultative efforts. However, the fact that our efforts sufficed to achieve approval of the major has not lulled us into ignoring the substantial practical, political, and theoretical obstacles we still face in making the proposal of our dreams a long-term reality. We have been enlightened and uplifted by our success thus far in beginning to realize a broadly inclusive women's and gender studies major. If our initial experience of collaborative energy and cohesion without coercion is any indicator, this new major may have real transformative power within our academy.

Notes

1. Total enrollment at Eckerd College is approximately 1,350, with thirty-four disciplines from which students select majors as well as self-created majors.

2. See Robin Lakoff, *Language and Woman's Place* (New York: Harper & Row, 1975); and Deborah Tannen, *You Just Don't Understand: Women and Men in Conversation* (New York: Morrow, 1990).

3. See Carol Gilligan, *In a Different Voice: Psychological Theory and Women's Development* (Cambridge: Harvard University Press, 1982) and *Mapping the Moral Domain: A Contribution of Women's Thinking to Psychological Theory and Education* (Cambridge: Harvard University Press, 1988).

4. See Nancy Chodorow, *The Reproduction of Mothering: Psychoanalysis and the Sociology of Gender* (Berkeley: University of California, 1978).

Works Cited

Brown, Elsa Barkley. "African-American Women's Quilting: A Framework for Conceptualizing and Teaching African-American Women's History." *Signs* 14 (1989): 921–29.

Chodorow, Nancy. *The Reproduction of Mothering: Psychoanalysis and the Sociology of Gender.* Berkeley: University of California Press, 1978.

Collins, Patricia Hill. "The Social Construction of Black Feminist Thought." *Signs* 14 (1989): 745–73.

Davis, Angela. *Women, Culture, and Politics.* New York: Random House, 1989.

Giddings, Paula. *When and Where I Enter: The Impact of Black Women on Race and Sex in America.* New York: Bantam, 1984.

Gilligan, Carol. *In a Different Voice: Psychological Theory and Women's* Development. Cambridge: Harvard University Press, 1982.

—, ed. *Mapping the Moral Domain: A Contribution of Women's Thinking to Psychological Theory and Education.* Cambridge: Harvard University Press, 1988.

Harding, Sandra. "Introduction: Is There a Feminist Method?" In *Feminism and Methodology*, ed. Sandra Harding. Bloomington: Indiana University Press, 1987.

hooks, bell. *Ain't I a Woman: Black Women and Feminism*. Boston: South End Press, 1981.

Jaggar, Alison. *Feminist Politics and Human Nature*. Lanham, Md.: Rowman and Littlefield Publishers, 1983.

Lugones, Maria C. "On the Logic of Pluralist Feminism." In *Feminist Ethics*, ed. Claudia Card. Lawrence, Kans.: University of Kansas Press, 1991.

Lugones, Maria C., and Elizabeth Spelman. "Have We Got a Theory For You! Feminist Theory, Cultural Imperialism and the Demand for 'The Woman's Voice.'" *Woman's Studies International Forum* 6 (1983): 573–581.

McGlen, Nancy E., and Karen O'Connor. *The Struggle for Equality in the Nineteenth and Twentieth Centuries*. New York: Praeger, 1983.

Showalter, Elaine. "Piecing and Writing." In *The Poetics of Gender*, ed. Nancy K. Miller. New York: Columbia University Press, 1986.

Simons, Margaret. "Racism and Feminism: A Schism of Sisterhood." *Feminist Studies* 5 (1979): 38–401.

Spelman, Elizabeth V. *Inessential Woman: Problems of Exclusion in Feminist Thought*. Boston: Beacon Press, 1988.

Zinn, Maxine Baca, Lynn Webber Cannon, Elizabeth Higginbotham, and Bonnie Thorton Dill. "The Costs of Exclusionary Practices in Women's Studies." *Signs* 11 (1986): 290–303.

Chapter 2

Gender and Visual Literacy: Towards a Multidisciplinary Perspective

Arnold S. Wolfe and Colleen McNally

Mapping the Terrain: Defining Terms, Taking Sides

Feminist perspectives have informed both research and teaching in art history and communication but genuine multidisciplinarity across these fields hardly exists. Images of women made by men for the purposes of men dominate both Western art and such communication forms as advertising and motion pictures. Clearly, a gap exists in both research and teaching about image-making and its relation to gender. For example, H. Leslie Steeves' otherwise exemplary survey of the leading schools of feminism and their relation to mass communication research omits any reference to feminist art history or criticism. Whitney Chadwick's similarly thorough overview of the history of art as seen through several feminist lenses cites only one feminist analysis of cinema among the numerous mass communication studies that could have been used to enrich her otherwise praiseworthy work.

This paper seeks to bridge the gap between art history and communication curricula by describing how feminist perspectives in each field can foster greater understanding of the images of women that have been regarded as canonical by art historians and continue to structure image-making today. The background of the first of the co-authors is in mass communication—television, film, and journalism.

The background of the second is in the fine arts. In our teaching of image interpretation, we use similar approaches. We both teach students about such formal elements of images as color, value, and line and about such compositional principles as size, placement, and space. We both teach students about the relations of such elements to the whole of the images we analyze and the relations of such elements to one another (cf. Olin 1989, 286). But beyond these formal matters, we have also integrated into our teaching such fundamentally feminist questions as: "How are these formal elements and compositional principles as they appear in images used to communicate ideology?"

Ideology may be defined as a usually unconscious culturally-shared belief system that claims to represent reality accurately. Literature professor and critical theorist Alice Jardine elaborates: "Ideology makes culture seem natural" (1986, 85). For Colleen McNally and Arnold S. Wolfe, "Ideology . . . refers to those ideas or forces in a culture that work to create or maintain the notion that what is or was made by humans—and is therefore cultural and changeable—is natural and consequently inevitable" (1991, 291).

According to media analyst Arthur Asa Berger, ideological statements represent and communicate the interests of a dominant class, race, or gender and support the status of the dominant group. Ideology works to "naturalize" what is man- and woman-made; as a result, most people not in the dominant group find "it difficult to recognize that they are being exploited and victimized" (1982, 50-51).[1]

Deconstruction is both a pivotal term and important practice in feminist art historical and communication research. In the context of visual images, deconstructions may be defined as analyses that aim to reveal the ideological meanings of visual communications (Jameson 1981, 291; Scholes 1982, 12–14). We contend that such analyses are a necessary aspect of visual literacy. The visually literate may be defined as those who have been educated to grasp the full cultural and political meaning of visual messages. The visually literate can do this in part because they can perceive the clashes between and among classes, races, and genders in visual communications. Visually literate persons can also grasp key cultural and political meanings of images because they can, according to art historian Griselda Pollock,

1) describe what the particular visual communication is doing to and for each side in a political struggle;
2) specify the means by which images make meanings; and
3) identify whose interests such meanings best serve. (*Vision* 1988, 7)

These proficiencies accord with a definition of visual literacy supplied by an affiliation of visual scholars and practitioners, the International Visual Literacy Association (IVLA). An IVLA brochure defines visual literacy as "the learned ability to interpret the communication of visual symbols (images) . . . " (International Visual Literacy Association 1990). The goal that drives the visual literacy curriculum thus far outlined is empowerment. To develop students' interpretive competence and skills in describing how images make meanings is to empower students. To extend their abilities to *communicate* those interpretations and descriptions and to specify the political and ideological interests served by a given image is to empower students even further. Students are empowered to resist patriarchy not only when they are given tools by which they can deconstruct patriarchal images but also when they learn to create non- or antipatriarchal images.

We maintain that this empowering pedagogy must be driven by a multidisciplinary, feminist theory and practice that must work together in a continuing effort to identify and deconstruct patriarchal conventions that structure image-making in every expressive form. John Berger's *Ways of Seeing* anticipated this pedagogy in its examination of how women have been presented in painting. Berger suggests that the conventions by which women have been portrayed in that medium are reproduced in such mass media as advertising and television (Berger 1972, 7, 135). Advertising, he notes, "relies . . . on the language of [European] painting. It speaks in the same voice about the same things" (Berger 1972, 135). According to art historian Rosemary Betterton (1988, 251), canonical European painting spoke with an ideologically patriarchal voice; European paintings of women were designed by men for their pleasure (Berger 1972, 47-57, 63-64; cf. Armstrong 1986, 230, passim).

Patriarchal image-making practices as they originated and evolved in European painting are echoed in advertising (Williamson 1978). But few studies have attempted to explicate the links between these two cultural forms. One of the most important of these links is the pictorial convention. A convention may be defined as an unwritten agreement between message-makers and -receivers that governs meaning (Katz 1983, 52). One early cultural studies inquiry into mass communication argues that "the conventions . . . should [be] the problematic of cultural studies . . ." (Kreiling 1978, 253). In order to explicate the links between patriarchal practices in art and mass media image-making, we shall make the conventional ways of depicting women the "problematic" of the present cultural study.

The next section will consider an image produced by a canonical European male artist. The succeeding section will show that the conventional and patriarchal way of depicting women that this image embodies persists in a mass media form such as contemporary advertising. The multidisciplinarity of this approach cannot be over-emphasized. Signifying practices, such as image-making, that discriminate against women transcend the boundaries that academe has raised to acquire funds to found departments and majors. It is ironic that students, teachers, and scholars are more confined by these boundaries than patriarchal image-makers are: Conventional art history departments, for instance, do not examine image-making on television commercials. Some mass communication students resist the idea that any painting could have anything to do with the images they seek to broadcast or print. Feminist perspectives are firmly established in neither discipline. Simply stated, the received curriculum has been unable to account for the manifold nature of patriarchal signifying practices. In part, this inability may be traced to the fragmentation of human experience into academic disciplines.[2] Be that as it may, the multidisciplinarity of this study ought not to be considered a trendy or trivial compromise of more established epistemologies. Rather, such multidisciplinarity is best understood as an indispensable tool by which the culture-wide practice of patriarchal visual communication may be grasped and opposed.[3]

The Nude and Visual Literacy

Impressionist Edgar Degas painted female nudes in the late nineteenth century. The study of painted female nudes may offend feminists and nonfeminists alike. Such study is justified, however, not only because it augments understanding of the ideological meaning of images and illustrates compositional principles, but also because the study of nudes promotes visual literacy; as Betterton notes, "The nude in art has been enshrined as an icon of culture since the Renaissance" (1988, 251). The study of images of nudes, therefore, accords with the description of visual literacy this paper promotes; visual literacy must entail historical competencies as well as compositionally and ideologically analytical ones. Apart from these considerations, analyses that enhance understanding of the nude enhance understanding of the visual culture we share.

Edgar Degas. *Reclining Nude*. Musee de Louvre, Paris; Cabinet des Dessins. Giraudon/Art Resource, New York.

Degas' *Reclining Nude* depicts a subject that the canonical white, European, male artist turned to more than once (Betterton 1988, 264). Aside from the significance this subject had for one canonical artist, *Reclining Nude* is a fitting image for deconstruction because it presents a nude free of references to any historical event or any religious or mythological theme (Betterton 1988, 263). Rather, as Armstrong insists, the image is preoccupied with representing the nude female body frontally and horizontally as a landscape. Its limbs are merely elongations of the line created by the supine, stretched-out torso (1986, 237).

Degas' way of painting his model does not individualize her. Consider the figure's face vis-à-vis her torso: It is almost totally concealed by her arm and minimally detailed. In contrast, her naked torso is more finely delineated. As Berger (1972, ch. 3) has explained, this way of depicting women is a convention of the Eurocentric art of the nude. According to Berger, the nude is not a representation of the nakedness of an individual person; rather, the nude represents a body objectified for the pleasure of the male viewer (Berger 1972, 54, 62). We argue that any representation that highlights the body and de-emphasizes the face objectifies and dehumanizes. When the person depicted is female, such representation is manifestly patriarchal and voyeuristic.

The image displays another conventionally patriarchal way of depicting women, viz., as "asleep, or [as] unconcerned with mortal things" (Parker and Pollock 1981, 116). Consider how Degas renders his figure's one visible eye as "a slight linear smear" (McNally and Wolfe 1991, 293), thereby inviting the viewer to conclude that the figure is asleep. Betterton remarks that "the viewer is [thus] given . . . access to a private moment . . . seeing a woman alone and caught *unawares* . . . " (1988, 264; italics added). This is voyeurism. Degas himself conceded that he painted his women models "as if you [were] looking at them] through a keyhole" (Lemoisne, cited in Armstrong 1986, 239). Art historians Rozsika Parker and Griselda Pollock show that such patently voyeuristic ways of seeing women developed into a convention during the nineteenth century. At that time female figures were "frequently [shown as] asleep," or as otherwise withdrawn from material reality (1981, 116). The "device" of presenting the female figure as unconscious, they add, "allow[s] undisturbed . . . voyeuris[m]" (1981, 116). These same conventions continue in advertising. One study of the representation of gender in ads describes how "women more than men . . . are pictured [as] removed psychologically from [any] social situation" that might be presented otherwise (Goffman 1979, 57).

An example would be the ad for a nationally known brand of gin that shows a supine, bikini-clad woman whose left arm frames her head.[4] The model is not nude, but as Berger reminds us, "there are nude . . . poses [and] gestures," (1972, 53) independent of the degree to which a figure is clothed. The resemblance between the Degas and this ad is remarkable in several respects. First, there is the similarity between the gesture of the figure's left arm in the Degas and in the gin ad, and between the shut eyes on both and the shaded faces. For these reasons alone, it can be said that neither Degas nor the advertiser fashion an image of an individualized woman; both images deemphasize the face and highlight the torso. Unlike the Degas, the gin ad does present a face, but the advertiser leaves little doubt that consumers should consider this woman a thing: he paints and dresses her body to resemble the container of his advertised spirit (pun intended).[5] The colors on her bikini echo the colors of the gin bottle; the red emblem affixed to the bikini's top mirrors both the color and positioning of the seal on the bottle's upper half; and the lettering painted on the woman's torso copies that printed on the bottle's label.

We do not believe this is an innocent case of "life" imitating "art." Such a comment fails to account adequately for the social, cultural, and political meanings we have thus far specified for the images we have analyzed. A comment more pertinent to these meanings and one with which we shall preface further discussion modifies literary critic Fredric Jameson's (1981) maxim: "History is what hurts." Jameson suggests that the pain history can inflict may best be treated by historicizing any account of the genesis of that pain. We hope to demonstrate in the following analysis that any pain the ad may inflict or perpetuate may be traced to its art historical antecedents. The ad transmits the signs of art historical convention. Men making art and art history devised both objectified images. With respect to the ad, *art* history is what hurts. Both *Reclining Nude* and the ad exemplify other conventions of the historically significant genre of the nude. Both figures are slender and young and are rendered so as to emphasize their curvaceousness. The curvaceous torso in the Degas is lighter in value than both the darkened portion of the lower body and the arms. The darker values of these body parts are coordinated with the eclipsing arm and dearth of detailing not so much to conceal as to deform the figure's head. Similarly, in the ad no part of the figure's body is darker than her upper head. The value differences in both images work to privilege the torso and further objectify the figure. To the extent that the face is nullified, so is the individual identity of the model (see Millum 1987, 57). The torso of any young and slender woman could be easily substituted. No wrinkles or bulges lessen the degree to which these images privilege the curvaceous torso (cf. Betterton 1988, 266). In the Degas, the towel on which the nude rests echoes the value differences registered across her body; the towel's brightest expanse lies in the foreground *between* the viewer and the illuminated torso immediately rearward. Even the towel is a device used to intensify the objectification and sexualization of the figure.

Degas did not invent the conventional way of seeing women that has been canonized by art historians. But inasmuch as his nude is portrayed as reclining, "passive[, and] submissive" (Berger 1972, 52), and inasmuch as she is presented as embodying an attitude of "languorous, curvaceous . . . self-abandonment," she conforms to the patriarchal conventions of the genre (Armstrong 1986, 230, 233, 237; order inverted for the sake of quotation.) What is more, each and every one of these attributes applies to the figure in the ad. As Berger reminds us, the conventional, canonical nude does not express the "actual feelings" of the person on whom the figure was modeled (1972, 52). Rather, the figure is a specular object for male pleasure. "To be naked," Berger explains, "is simply to be without clothes [and] be oneself. To be nude is to be seen as an object" for the use of males (1972, 53–54).

An alternative way of depicting women is offered by Dorothea Tanning's *The Birthday*. Tanning's figure hardly conforms to the stereotypical female of male sexual fantasy. Though partially naked, the figure is not nude as in the European tradition. On the contrary, this image deconstructs that patriarchal tradition in several moves that may not be evident at first glance. The following section will attempt to describe precisely what patriarchal conventions of the nude *The Birthday* arguably deconstructs.

To accomplish our aims in this section, our discussion must move beyond one obvious difference: that the represented bodies of Degas' figure and the model in the ad are more exposed than the body that Tanning depicts. This analysis will consider such formal issues as the posing of the primary female figures and the nature of their dress. If the Degas is accepted as exemplifying the Eurocentric nude and the ad is accepted as a contemporary extension of this tradition, then Tanning's image, we shall argue, questions and deconstructs several of the tradition's patriarchal conventions. This section will be followed by some remarks on the curricular and the political implications of our analyses.

Degas, The Gin Ad, and *The Birthday*: Comparison and Contrast

The conventions embodied in the Degas and the ad "may be most productively grasped as *meaning with an economy of scale*" (McNally and Wolfe 1991, 297). These conventions may have fallen into disuse in contemporary painting, but they persist in mass media today. This persistence reveals the continuing cultural significance of these conventions and their salience as guides for the production and consumption of what many still regard as socially acceptable visual communications. Whether one likes them or not, these conventions constitute part of our shared cultural inheritance.

The Tanning figure deconstructs many of the conventions of nudity in part because she is standing, rather than reclining, her left hand actively gripping a doorknob. Her unsubmissive, unlanguorous, unself-abandoned, *alert*, open-eyed uprightness unmasks the patriarchal basis

Dorothea Tanning. *The Birthday*. Copyright 1993 ARS, New York/SPADEM, Paris.

of the specified conventions, as does the branch-like matrix descending from her waist. Art historian Uwe Schneede contends that the matrix represents the figure's "closeness to nature" (1973, 132), but a closer inspection reveals that various parts of female bodies hang in the brambles, some in crucifixion-like postures. We can see a disembodied female breast, a disembodied female leg, and headless female torsos, one amputated above the elbow, two others cut off from below the breast. We contend that the matrix cannot be accurately interpreted as a reiteration of the long-standing patriarchal stereotype that assigns the cultural to men and the natural to women (see Schneede 1973, 72, 132);[6] rather, we interpret the matrix as a visual, metaphorical comment on patriarchal culture and its dehumanization of women.

At least one other element of the image encourages this reading: the figure's skirt.   Significantly, this second element is physically contiguous to the matrix. Our interpretation of its meaning may be unconventional but is guided by one of the most venerable and culturally valued of interpretive strategies: the convention of unity (see Berger 1972, 13 and Culler 1980, 61). By means of this convention, readers seek to unify the multiple elements any text may present. Interpretive efforts directed by this convention "are not in any sense personal and idiosyncratic acts of free association; [on the contrary] they are very common and acceptable formal strategies" (Culler 1980, 61). Although an interpretation deriving from this convention may be historically specific, it reproduces the binding force of culture itself, which according to Ott, supplies "a *unifying* . . . meaning . . . for [its] members" (1989, 50). If this interpretive strategy is accepted, then the meaning of the Tanning figure's skirt may be seen as amplifying the deconstructive and confrontational significance of her uprightness and her brambles. The link between the brambles and the skirt is more than physical: unlike conventional nudity exemplified by the Degas and sanitized in the gin ad, the lower half of Tanning's figure is not nude. As observed above, the matrix supplies such lower halves, but in a way that deconstructs the genre's preoccupation with the female torso. McNally and Wolfe find that

> the skirt extends this irony; a close look at its folds reveals them to be a
> series of concentric ovals that anatomically resemble nothing so much as
> the shape of the female orifice they simultaneously echo and hide. Thus
> the figure deconstructs male desire by gratifying it in the skirt mockingly
> and in the branches hideously. (1991, 298)

Conclusion

We have attempted in the analysis of the Degas and the ad to reveal bonds between past and present signifying practices. We see in *The Birthday* evidence of a visual consciousness that simultaneously deconstructs the patriarchal practices of yesterday and anticipates the *birth* of a new *day* when women and men, artist and art historian, teacher and student, and even advertiser and consumer have freed themselves from the brambles of patriarchal ideology. The curricular implications of this analysis may be best summarized by Jeanne Brady Giroux, who reminds us that

> schools are one of the most important sites where the construction of gender takes place, but can be challenged pedagogically. To make patriarchy visible as a form of oppression is to offer ... students [tools] they can use to criticize how patriarchal interests are produced within visual texts and social relations. (1989, 6–7)

The curriculum we envision would examine all images as an effect of those texts and social relations *and* as a catalyst for change in both future image-making and social relations. This study both exemplifies and calls for an integration of art theoretical-art historical, mass media theoretical-mass media historical, and feminist insights, methodologies, and pedagogies as a means of explaining and opposing the historical and continuing devaluation of women in image-making and in image-interpretation. Such an integration, if achieved, could serve as a model for studying the visual devaluation of other social groups, such as African-Americans and Hispanics. Perhaps one day these lines of research can be combined to generate a powerful over-arching explanation for gender-, race-, and class-biased signifying practices. Such an explanation may well be the necessary precursor to effective, multidisciplinary, multicultural, bi-gendered political action. To paraphrase a 1960s rhythm-and-blues song, that theoretical and practical project "may be a long time comin', but [we] know, a change gon' come."

Notes

1. Steeves, citing Williamson, suggests that mass communicated capitalist ideology appears to be required by capitalism, while conversely, capitalist ideology "makes people think [capitalism] is necessary" (1987, 115). Similarly, patriarchal ideology may be required to sustain patriarchy, while, conversely, patriarchal ideology makes people *think* patriarchy is necessary.

2. Whether the grievances of women and nonpatriarchal men can be redressed through work sanctioned by an institution as arguably patriarchal as the university remains to be seen. This issue, however, cannot be adequately explored in this study.

3. For example, feminist mass communication scholar Jackie Byars uses a multidisciplinary approach to study televised American family melodramas of the 1950s.

4. The authors requested permission from the gin company to reprint the ad but permission was not granted.

5. Our choice of the masculine possessive and pronoun is deliberate. To use the non-sexist form, his/her or s/he, would insult women.

6. Evidence of Schneede's belief in this discriminatory distinction may be found in his discussion of Max Ernst's painting, *The Robing of the Bride*. Schneede lauds Ernst for his "critical cultural analysis [and] technique" (1973, 72). Yet, Ernst's conventional representation of female nudity in this work is ignored.

Works Cited

Armstrong, Carol M. "Edgar Degas and the Female Body." In *The Female Body in Western Culture*, ed. Susan R. Suleiman. Cambridge, Mass.: Harvard University Press, 1986.

Berger, Arthur Asa. *Media Analysis Techniques*. Vol. 10 of *The Sage COMMTEXT Series*. Beverly Hills: Sage Publications, 1982.

Berger, John. *Ways of Seeing*. London: British Broadcasting Corp., 1972.

—, (producer). *Ways of Seeing, Part I.* British Broadcasting Corp., 1972.

Betterton, Rosemary. "How Do Women Look: The Female Nude in the Work of Suzanne Valadon." In *Visibly Female: Feminism and Art: An Anthology*, ed. Hilary Robinson. New York: Universe Books, 1988.

Byars, Jackie. "Gender Representation in American Family Melodramas of the Nineteen-fifties." Ph.D. diss. University of Texas at Austin, 1983.

Chadwick, Whitney. *Women, Art, and Society.* London: Thames and Hudson, 1990.

Culler, Jonathan. "Prolegomena to a Theory of Reading." In *The Reader in the Text: Essays on Audience and Interpretation*, ed. Susan R. Suleiman and Inge Crosman. Princeton: Princeton University Press, 1980.

Fry, Roger. *Reflections on British Painting.* London: Faber & Faber, Ltd., 1934.

Giroux, Jeanne Brady. "Feminist Theory as Pedagogical Practice." *Contemporary Education* 61 (Fall 1989): 6–10.

Goffman, E. *Gender Advertisements.* London: Macmillan, 1979.

Harris, Ann Sutherland, and Linda Nochlin. *Women Artists: 1550–1950.* New York: Los Angeles County Museum of Art, Alfred A. Knopf, 1977.

International Visual Literacy Association. *Membership Brochure.* Blacksburg, Va: International Visual Literacy Association, 1990.

Jameson, Fredric. *The Political Unconscious: Narrative as a Socially Symbolic Act.* Ithaca: Cornell University Press, 1981.

Jardine, Alice. "Death Sentences: Writing Couples and Ideology." In *The Female Body in Western Culture*, ed. Susan R. Suleiman. Cambridge, Mass.: Harvard University Press, 1986.

Katz, Elihu. "The Return of the Humanities and Sociology." *Journal of Communication.* ("Ferment in the Field: Communications Scholars Address Critical Issues and Research Tasks of the Discipline") 33:3 (Summer 1983): 51–52.

Kreiling, Albert. "Toward a Cultural Studies Approach for the Sociology of Popular Culture." *Communication Research* 5 (July 1978): 240–63.

Marcuse, Herbert. *One-dimensional Man.* London: Sphere, 1968.

McNally, Colleen, and Arnold S. Wolfe. "Deconstructing Images: Understanding the Role of Images in the Social Production of Meaning." In *Investigating Visual Literacy*, eds. Darrell Beauchamp, Judy Clark Baca, and Roberts Braden. Conway, Ark.: International Visual Literacy Association, 1991.

Millum, Trevor. *Images of Women: Advertising in Women's Magazines* London: Chatto and Windus, 1987.

Olin, Margaret. "Forms of Respect: Alois Reigel's Concept of Attentiveness." *The Art Bulletin* 71 (June 1989): 284–99.

Ott, J.S. *The Organizational Culture Perspective*. Pacific Grove, Calif.: Brooks/Cole Publishing, 1989.

Parker, Rozsika and Griselda Pollock. *Old Mistresses: Women, Art, and Ideology*. New York: Pantheon, 1981.

Pollock, Griselda. *Vision and Difference: Femininity, Feminism, and Histories of Art*. London and New York: Routledge, 1988.

—. "Women, Art, and Ideology: Questions for Feminist Art Historians." In *Visibly Female: Feminism and Art: An Anthology*, ed. Hilary Robinson. New York: Universe Books, 1988.

Scholes, Robert. *Semiotics and Interpretation*. New Haven: Yale University Press, 1982.

Steeves, H. Leslie. "Feminist Theories and Media Studies." *Critical Studies in Mass Communication* 4 (June 1987): 95–135.

Schneede, Uwe M. *Surrealism*. Trans. Maria Pelikan. New York: Harry N. Abrams, 1973.

Williamson, Judith. *Decoding Advertisements*. London: Marion Boyars, 1978.

Chapter 3

Old Maids and Helpful Husbands: Alerting Students to Gender Bias in Biography, Criticism, and Autobiography

Brenda Gross

Old Maids writing alone in their childhood rooms . . . filling their barren lives with books but wishing for home and children. Helpful husbands shaping and refining their wives' raw, unpolished talent . . . offering masculine strength and savvy to talented yet timid women who would otherwise not venture forth into the world of men.

Gender bias comes in many forms, some more easily recognizable than others. My primary concern is the ripple of subtle gender bias that runs throughout much biography, criticism, and autobiography—the less easily identifiable bias, the kind of bias that informs the way that a writer approaches his or her subject, the kind of bias that makes a male biographer structure a woman's biography differently from that of a man, the kind of bias that affects the way a theatre critic looks at a play, and the kind of conditioning that makes a highly successful woman write an autobiography that diminishes her accomplishments, her ambitions, and even her pain.

Today, most of us and most of our students recognize blatant gender bias—bias in language and conversation, conventional remarks that begin with "women can't" or "women shouldn't" or "women never have," television commercials that objectify women, and labels that degrade them. The feminist consciousness of most students is "raised" to the point where they can identify blatant sexism and will protest when their curriculum ignores women. Alerting them to more subtle forms of bias, however, is a slightly different, more complicated task. The struggle must be waged on a day-to-day basis: text by text, course by course, student by student. Unlike promoting women's studies courses or revising reading lists, creating an awareness of subtle literary bias does not require committee meetings, petitions, or votes. What it does take, however, is individual effort, commitment, creativity, and, to a certain degree, a sense of humor.

I first became interested in gender bias, particularly in biography, in 1979. During an undergraduate internship at the Feminist Press, I conducted a study of the existing biographies of women for young audiences. My objective was to discover what was available for children ages eight to fourteen when they went to the library to read or do a book report on a biography of a famous woman. I was to read as many "Young Reader" biographies as possible and then comment on their quality and quantity.

The results of a preliminary study were dismal. Not many biographies existed and those that did were so unsophisticated and uninteresting that even a highly motivated child would soon tire of them. In terms of variety, there were few breaks with convention. Although there was an occasional volume on Helen Keller or Amelia Earhart, the biographies focussed primarily on presidents' wives and on women who became military heroes because they disguised themselves as men. The most recent additions to the library collections tended to be about sports stars, such as Chris Evert and Tracy Austin. The role model choices for a young reader thus seemed somewhat limited: marry an important man, cross-dress (and wage war), or hope for the glamour of being an athletic superstar.

The available women's biographies also tended to be very bland in tone and traditional in structure. Heroine as little girl, heroine as wife and mother—heroine's split second of glory—then heroine quickly back at home, safe and secure in her traditional role. The message to young readers was clear: the ideal heroine was feminine in spite of her accomplishments, a "real" woman despite her achievements outside the feminine sphere. The Young Reader shelf of 1979 had not caught up with the women's movement. In fact, it was not unlike the biography shelf that confronted the young Carolyn G. Heilbrun in the late thirties and early forties. As she explains in *Writing a Woman's Life*,

I was profoundly caught up in biography because it allowed me, as a young girl, to enter the world of daring and achievement. But I had to make myself a boy to enter that world; I could find no comparable biographies of women, indeed, almost no biographies of women at all. (1988, 27)

Forty years later, my research indicated that little had changed. Even in 1979, a young girl seeking excitement had best pick up a biography of a man, any man, since "men had the adventures, men ran the world, men lived the better stories" (Beachy and Mathews 1989, 77).

Ten years pass. It is 1989 and I am a college professor, teaching a new class on contemporary women playwrights at a private university on Long Island. The course is unconventional in focus and content. To be honest, some students take it just to find out if there *were* (or are) any women playwrights in America. (Is it possible that "American Drama 101" might not have been as complete as the professor promised?) The class is fun and the discussions lively. We talk about a study by Judith Stephens of three decades (1918–1949) of Pulitzer Prize winning drama. The students are both outraged and amused to learn that most women characters in American drama are preoccupied with love, physically passive, more emotional than rational, and rarely professional. The class and I are "in sync" or so I think.

I assign each student a report on an individual woman playwright. The assignment sounds easy but it is difficult to find resources. Aside from Lillian Hellman and Lorraine Hansberry, few women playwrights have made it into theatre history books, anthologies, or even indexes. Until recently, the theatre press also paid little attention to plays by women dramatists. Therefore, it takes a lot of looking to come up with one or two reviews or magazines articles. But my students push on. In the end, most of them base their oral reports on one or two biographical books, often written as part of a series and almost always written by men. As they get up to speak, I am proud of their resourcefulness and persistence (it took a lot of legwork to find these sources!). As I listen to their presentations, however, I realize that I have not fully prepared them to research the lives of women.

The students are eager but not particularly sophisticated when it comes to research and interpretation. As they report I realize that they are following, in both major and minor ways, the style and structure of the authors of the biographies they have read. Like the biographers, they refer to the playwrights as "Gertrude," "Lorraine," and "Lillian," although they would never consider giving a report on "Arthur" (Miller), "Edward" (Albee), or "Tennessee." Like the biographers, they focus on the "feminine" attributes and preoccupations of the women playwrights, dwelling at length on their childhoods and marriages. (It strikes me that the playwrights, as described by my students, sound not unlike typical women characters in American drama: passive, irrational, overly emotional, and obsessed with love.) Like the biographers, they talk about the "men behind the women"—those gutsy, nurturing, good-natured guys who pushed their wives, girlfriends, and daughters into playwrighting and guided them to their success. According to my students, almost every female playwright owes her success to a man: a father, a producer, a husband, a lover, even the "man who got away." Dashiel Hammett calmed Hellman's rages and gave her direction, George Cram Cook tricked Susan Glaspell into writing plays. The playwrights' careers seem to stop and go, rise and fall, succeed and fail, based on their liaisons with men. In addition, almost every woman's life is told within the framework and chronology of her relationships with men. Like the biographers, my students assess the playwright's temperament from a non-feminist point of view, searching for "common female faults," overly masculine attributes and other character defects that help both to explain and diminish the playwright's exceptional accomplishments. Like the biographers, they ask the conventional questions: Was the playwright "shrill" or soft-spoken? vain or modest? ambitious (read masculine) or easy-going? self-centered or giving (read feminine)? What did she accomplish? Did she accomplish too much? Was she too good at what she did to be a good wife? a good mother? Did she write because she missed out on marriage? Did she miss out on marriage because she wrote? Why didn't she marry? Why didn't her marriage work? Was she too dependent on her family? too independent? too *physically unattractive*?

As the student reports demonstrate, this last attribute, physical beauty (or the lack of it) holds a particular allure for many biographers who see it as a central means of "explaining" a woman's life. For many, it is the key to analyzing a woman's happiness and success in both the professional and personal spheres. A case in point is William Wright's biography of Lillian Hellman. In *Lillian Hellman: The Image, The Woman*, Wright makes numerous references to Hellman's physical attractiveness or lack of it. His description of her early years, for example, is highlighted by successive references to her unconventional looks. For example, on page 34: an N.Y.U. classmate describes her as "very homely and very unhappy" (don't the two always go together?). On page 35, Wright himself describes her as "no beauty" but an "agreeable physical presence . . . a good figure (particularly her legs)" and on page 36, Wright notes that several people who knew the young Hellman, "both women and men, insisted she was 'ugly.'" Wright dwells obsessively on Hellman's mysterious appeal to men. Why do men (*real* men like Dashiel Hammett) fall so hard for the less-than-beautiful-but-well-legged Hellman? The biographer eventually concludes that it was the "package" that appealed: the combination of Hellman's intellect and physical attributes plus her "strong sexual aura" (1986, 36). In Wright's index, under Hellman, there are the following headings: "appearance of" (34, 35–36, 103, 111, 117, 197, 326, 347, 354, 378); "effect on men of" (36, 49, 111, 218, 280, 322, 325, 353); "flirtatious manner of" (336, 340, 347, 422); "types of men attractive to" (32, 44, 45, 267, 288). There is even a heading for "body odor as concern of." At first, I thought that Wright had been the victim of an overzealous computer indexing program. On turning to page 393, however, I discovered that Hellman had been unnerved all her life by an early lover's comment that she had an odor "down there." It turned her into an incessant bather and, Wright speculates, may have ruined her sex life (which does not seem to jive with his "sexual aura" theory—wouldn't Hellman have communicated her own misgivings about her body to men?). To give Wright his due, I must mention that he recognizes that "the body odor of a subject is [generally] outside the legitimate or relevant areas of biographical investigation" and devotes a long footnote to explaining his own deviant behavior. According to Wright, the matter warranted investigation (he did ask around) because Hellman publicly admitted the incident and may have indirectly used it in a novel (1986, 393).

Try as I might, I cannot picture William Wright asking a director or former lover about Arthur Miller's or David Mamet's body odor. Still, I try to be an empathetic reader, to understand that unconventional tactics are sometimes necessary in order to analyze a writer's life fully. In his preface, Wright vows to take us behind the scenes and document Hellman's emotional life; to give us the "real Hellman" and relate "her life as she really lived it" (1986, 14). Nonetheless, I find it difficult to believe that these issues of physical attractiveness and sexuality would be explored to this extent if Wright were creating a biography of a contemporary male playwright. In a book entitled *Arthur Miller: The Image, The Man* would the index look the same? Would Wright rate Miller's legs or any other part of his anatomy? Would he dwell on his appeal to women, asking what possessed lovely Marilyn Monroe to marry plain Arthur Miller? Can you picture an index with eleven page references for "appearance of," sixteen references to "sexuality of," five pages on "types of women attractive to"? Even if a biographer did explore these subjects, chances are that he would not explore them to this degree and that that last heading would read: "types of women attracted to" versus "attractive to," making the subject of the biography more than just a passive object of desire.

Wright's overall approach worries me despite his occasional attempts at a feminist perspective. When teaching Lillian Hellman, I find myself calling his book "readable" but cautioning my students against swallowing it whole. "Read the book," I say, "but remember that the biographer may have some knee-jerk responses to women that figure into his analysis of Lillian Hellman." Wright himself may have a somewhat confused perspective about the difference between the "image and the woman."

Although few students cannot detect blatant sexism, most undergraduates (even in nontraditional disciplines such as women's studies) still can be slow to detect more subtle gender bias. Few courses train them to question a book like Wright's, to examine critically its structure and content and see if, even in its emphasis, there is a bias at work that distorts the life of the woman in question. Undergraduate students tend to trust their sources. If, and when, they go on to graduate school, they may learn to question every uncrossed "t" and undotted "i" (of such actions are dissertations born). At the undergraduate level, however, they are generally happy to accept their sources as authoritative. If in doubt, ask a student if she has written her paper yet. "No," she says, "but I've got the books," the implication being that the big job is collecting and reading the material versus evaluating it in terms of its accuracy, relevancy, and bias. Accuracy, relevancy, and bias. I myself never really heard those words applied to research until I got to graduate school. However, if we want students to undertake quality research in nontraditional areas about nontraditional subjects (such as women in theatre), I think we need to encourage them to evaluate materials using these and other criteria.

There are, of course, some simpler solutions. In certain disciplines, it has become increasingly possible to direct students to new biographies or criticism written from a feminist perspective. In many areas, however, such as theatre, few new texts are available. Feminist scholars cannot keep up with the demand for more and better biographies of women in theatre (a previously invisible group). Therefore, we must work with what we have. Research in theatre is further complicated by the need to focus not only on the dramatic text but on the realization of that text onstage. Students need to read reviews in order to get a sense of the production, the period, the play's reception, and the playwright's expertise. Thus, even though plays by women have historically received little serious attention from the press, no scholar can completely ignore the words or impact of the theatre critics. Students need to read reviews in order to get a sense of the period, the play's reception, and the playwright's expertise. Again, we must work with what we have, whether it is a thirties review by George Jean Nathan or an eighties review by Frank Rich. What we can do, however, is to help students see the critic and his criticism in context. (I say "his" because there are still no major women theatre critics in New York.) We can point out that critics did not (and do not) write in a vacuum. They live and work in a particular time and place and, as a result, are likely to adhere to their period's predominant view of women.

To illustrate my point, I read my class some comments by George Jean Nathan, a critical powerhouse of the early twentieth century whose reviews were widely read and respected. In an essay entitled "The Status of the Female Playwright," Nathan observes that women playwrights are destined always to be inferior to men because of their "generic feminine disability or . . . disinclination" to control their emotions. This female failing turns everything women write into melodrama. Their excessive emotionality also leads women playwrights to oversimplify issues and overidentify with their characters. Again, this is a female problem, stemming from woman's inherent irrationality and lack of complexity. Since male playwrights do not have these problems (according to Nathan, men are both rational and complex), melodrama by men is intentional and artistic. The critic's conclusion: Strindberg wrote melodrama because he wanted to, Hellman wrote melodrama because she couldn't write anything else (1941, 35).

Nathan was not the first critic to see playwrighting as a male domain. Although commercially successful, Rachel Crothers had to endure confusing (and telling) remarks like that of Walter Pritchard Eaton who blamed her for not achieving the necessary "masculinity of structure" in her 1909 play, *A Man's World* (1910, 115). Other reviewers objected to the way that Crothers ended the play: they found it implausible or unfair that a woman would send away her lover simply because he supported (in both word and deed) the conventional double standard of sexual morality. Although *A Man's World* ends with the female protagonist clearly rejecting her lover, critics insisted that she would, even should, take him back. Most reviews distorted the reality of the play, ignoring its feminist content and sensibility. As Lois C. Gottlieb observes,

With the exception of [Eleanor] Flexner, very few critics, then or later, paid much attention to the larger women's issues raised by the play, and some indirectly attached the theme of independence by paying undue attention to the more traditional minor female characters. (1979, 46)

Nathan and others distorted and downplayed the efforts of women playwrights to such an extent that they became almost invisible. Susan Glaspell is only now being rediscovered as a significant contributor/founder of the Provincetown Theatre and we still await a book on American expressionism that deals not only with Elmer Rice but with the theatrical innovations of Sophie Treadwell, author of *Machinal*. Moreover, Gertrude Stein, whose concept of "theatre as landscape" profoundly influenced the avant-garde theatre of the sixties, has yet to make it into most theatre history texts.

Today's women playwrights have less of a problem being recognized and reviewed. They may not be seen as "mainstream" but most newspapers do send a critic to see their productions. These critics are generally men but some are genuinely supportive of women's work. Old habits die hard, however, and gender bias still creeps into even the most positive reviews. As Daniel Sullivan, director of *The Sisters Rosensweig*, recently pointed out, many critics have referred to Wendy Wasserstein's plays as "phenomenons," suggesting "a success beyond their worth or an inexplicable event" (Harris 1994). They imply that Wasserstein is not deserving of success and that audiences are misguided. After all, who would pay good money to see plays by and about women?

Critics and biographers help to perpetuate myths about women's work, ambitions, and sensibilities. But they are not alone. Women themselves have, historically, clouded the issue of female identity. Thus, a third relevant area for concern by both students and professional scholars is women's autobiography.

To undergraduates, autobiography can seem even more authoritative than biography or criticism. They tend not to question the author's observations or motivations. The idea that a woman might reinvent her past to make it more palatable to a publisher or to the reading public is quite foreign to most students. Zipping through the lively autobiographies of someone like film pioneer Anita Loos, they can easily miss the writer's pain, so veiled is it in jokes and one-liners. Loos uses humor to distance both herself and her audience from the sharper disappointments of her life. She gaily describes her husband's infidelities, his parasitic nature, and her failed marriage. Loos good-naturedly refers to John Emerson as a "pimp," whose "devotion was largely affected by the amount of money I earned" (1975, 17, 14). Always the entertainer, Loos never risks confronting her audience with unpleasantness, anger, or any other unsettling emotion.

"What has been forbidden to women is anger," observes Carolyn G. Heilbrun (1988, 13). As a result, they reveal little rage or pain in their autobiographies. Suffering is masked by good humor and nostalgia. Women also derogate or denigrate their accomplishments. As Heilbrun notes,

> Well into the twentieth century, it continued to be impossible for women to admit into their autobiographical narratives the claim of achievement, the admission of ambition, the recognition that accomplishment was neither luck nor the result of the efforts or generosity of others. (1988, 24)

Unlike their male counterparts, accomplished women feel the need to explain why they deviated from the traditional female roles of wife and mother. As a result, their autobiographies tend to accentuate the role of fate: they did not choose to serve but were, instead, pushed or called into service. Unlike their male counterparts, female autobiographers hesitate to draw attention to their accomplishments lest someone question their motivation or virtue.

> Goodness *is* selflessness, these autobiographies suggest; and vice versa— a notion by its nature unlikely to make for effective autobiography, since autobiographies are about selves. (Spacks 1980, 114)

After studying autobiographies by celebrated women such as Emma Goldman, Eleanor Roosevelt, and Golda Meir, Patricia Spacks concluded that highly successful women tend to diminish themselves.

> They use autobiography, paradoxically, partly as a mode of self-denial. Although they have functioned in spheres rarely open to women, their accounts of this activity emphasize its hidden costs more than its rewards and draw back—as women have traditionally done—from making large claims of importance. (1980, 132)

Biography, criticism, autobiography. Few safe havens seem to exist for students intent on researching the lives, work and ideas of women which is why we, as professors, must become skilled in alerting students to gender bias. There are several options available to us, some of which have already been mentioned. First, we can avoid or lessen the problem by steering students toward more recent biographies and autobiographies, preferably those with a feminist sensibility. Second, we can urge them to read less conventional sources such as unpublished diaries and letters for, as Heilbrun points out, "these sometimes contain less self-censorship and more of a woman's passion and ambition" (1988, 24). Third, we can train students to evaluate sources. We can train them by example, by spending time in the classroom critiquing our own choices, explaining why we choose what we choose for our courses and for our own research. We can also teach source evaluation by alerting students to contemporary scholarship on bias in biography, criticism, and autobiography. Articles and books that discuss the nature of woman's biography (such as Heilbrun's *Writing a Woman's Life*) can become a part of our curriculum. Finally, we can show students just how serious we are about source evaluation by giving them credit for critiquing and analyzing the books that they use, by letting them write papers on gender bias, and by asking them to create annotated bibliographies that discuss the value and bias of works consulted.

Integrating these practices into the curriculum is certain to be taxing. (In retrospect, alerting students to blatant gender bias may seem like a breeze.) Encouraging students actively to recognize and assess more subtle forms of gender bias is an ongoing task, one that must be updated and reshaped with each new course, each new class, and each new semester. It may be one of the last feminist academic frontiers but it is by no means the easiest because of the individual effort, commitment, and creativity it demands.

Bias is not something that we can, or will (or, on some level, even want to) completely eliminate. By alerting students to the existence and implications of gender bias, however, we can begin to shape a new generation of scholars who are more fully aware of the kinds of bias that inform their work. As biographer Phyllis Rose has observed,

There is no neutrality. There is only greater or less awareness of one's bias. And if you do not appreciate the force of what you're leaving out, you are not fully in command of what you're doing. (1985, 77).

Works Cited

Beachy, Lucille, and Tom Mathews. "The Lives of Women." *Newsweek* (November 1989): 77.

Eaton, Walter Pritchard. *At the New Theatre and Others: American Stage, Its Problems and Performances 1908–1910.* Boston: Small Maynard, 1910.

Gottlieb, Lois C. *Rachel Crothers.* Boston: Twayne, 1979.

Harris, William. "Hoping to Fill a Broadway House? Call Wasserstein." *The New York Times* (February 1994).

Heilbrun, Carolyn G. *Writing a Woman's Life.* New York: W.W. Norton and Company, 1988.

Loos, Anita. 1974. Reprint. *Kiss Hollywood Goodbye.* New York: Random House, 1975.

Nathan, George Jean. "The Status of the Female Playwright." In *The Entertainment of a Nation.* New York: Knopf, 1941.

Rose, Phyllis. *Writing on Women: Essays in a Renaissance.* Middletown, Conn.: Wesleyan University Press, 1985.

Spacks, Patricia. "Selves in Hiding." In *Women's Autobiography*, ed. Estelle C. Jelinek. Bloomington: Indiana University Press, 1980.

Wright, William. *Lillian Hellman: The Image, The Woman.* New York: Simon and Schuster, 1986.

Chapter 4

The Male-Dominated Curriculum in English: How Did We Get Here and Where Are We Going?

Charlotte Templin

It is well-known that, except for Emily Dickinson and a handful of novelists, few women who wrote before the twentieth century are included in English Department curricula. This sends a message to the students, male and female, who sit in our classes—the message that women have contributed little of importance in the field of literature and that women probably lack the abilities necessary to make contributions that will rank with men's achievements. Equally troublesome is the fact that those works that are read by generation after generation of students make an ideological statement relating to female nature and proper female roles, all the more powerful since it is never questioned or modified by women's voices. It would be an interesting exercise to make an explicit summary of this ideology by tracing it through the standard literature anthologies. I wish, however, to trace the history of the origin of this curriculum, or canon, and then to explore what possible changes may be taking place.

In discussions of the curriculum, traditionalists are quick to assert that those who wish to modify the canon are acting on behalf of special interests and attempting to circumvent the processes by which canonicity is usually established. This point was made recently by William Phillips, editor of the *Partisan Review*, who states that the works the reformers would like to substitute "have not been selected by a consensus" of the intellectual community and thus presumably are not as good because they have not passed all the tests that the classics have passed (1989, 175). In his concern about what is happening to the canon, Phillips has a lot of company, as I found when I began work on this paper. Close to Phillips' article on the library shelf, I found a similar essay by art historian Edmund Burke Feldman in the journal *Liberal Education*. In an article entitled "Ideological Aesthetics," Feldman suggests that the motivation for changing the art history canon is ideological, stemming from the psychological needs of those who wish for change. He asks,

Would the self-esteem of Latin American Spanish-speaking students of Indian origin be enhanced by the study of *Las Meninas* by Diego Velazquez? . . . Do women feel good about themselves after beholding Artemesia Gentileschi's *Judith Decapitating Holofernes*? (1989, 8)

He admits that these questions may sound like caricatures of the current debate but asserts that they are pretty close to reality.

Of course these questions do come close to reality, and the answer to both questions is yes. Women and other groups excluded from the canon do want to see their own images in art and literature as they want to study the lives and experiences of people like themselves in other disciplines. Women are told condescendingly that such desires may be natural but that the works of women are not universal and fail to qualify as great. Greatness cannot be decided by vote, Feldman says.[1]

But how is "greatness" decided? The crucial matter here is evaluation. As they deal with the question of evaluation in their defense of the canon (as they must, of course), the traditionalists typically present accounts rife with question begging. Like Feldman, Phillips asserts that the canon "has never been decided by popular vote" (1989, 176). He then explains the process of canon formation by offering this account: "figures in various fields have been perpetuated by later figures" (1989, 176). Phillips' account leaves out the contemporary dynamics that made the work visible in the first place, and since it begs the crucial questions of why and how choices are made, it explains nothing.

I propose that it is time to demystify ideas about quality—literary, artistic, and so on. Judgments about quality are made by people, and their tastes, needs, and interests determine the judgments that they make. I will deal here specifically with literary quality and assert that far from being an objective property of texts, literary quality is created by the perspective of the reader. This has certainly been my finding in my own research on literary evaluation in book reviewing. Here I draw on the theories of Barbara Herrnstein Smith, who points out that, far from being objective and eternal, literary value is characterized by mutability and diversity. Readers call a book good when they find it useful. Instead of asking "How good is it?" we must ask "Good for what?" or "Good for whom?" Judgments about quality are not the objective property of texts, but are contingent: they are the political judgments of individuals and, as such, a function of their tastes, interests, and beliefs. In the past, critics have argued that the value of a work of art does not depend in any way on its usefulness. The aesthetic realm has been declared to be separate from the utilitarian. Smith asserts, however, that to defend aesthetic value by distinguishing it from all other forms of value is to "define it out of existence; for when all other such particular utilities, interests, and sources of value have been subtracted, nothing remains" (1988, 33). Thus, one could have no opinion at all if one could divest oneself of all one's beliefs, preferences, and needs because one would have nothing left with which to have an opinion. Judgments about quality are not objective judgments, because no such thing as complete objectivity exists except as the political judgments of people, and, as such, becomes a function of their tastes, interests, and beliefs. Smith's work, which deals with the general question of value, not just with literary value, is related to a large body of theoretical work in English studies that focuses on the reader as subject rather than the literary work as object.

The present canon in literature has been established by those with cultural authority—those in positions of influence in the literary establishment and in the universities. Those persons have been overwhelmingly white, middle class, and male. Significantly, people like Feldman are quick to point out that women identify with certain art works because they see images of themselves, but are unable to see that the entire canon reflects the white, male, middle-class image of those who have chosen it.

After texts have reached canonical status—are indeed often the sacred monuments of high culture—it is difficult not to see them as unique and self-sufficient, having inherent value. But, in fact, these works have attained canonical status through a process that takes place in history and that can be traced and analyzed. There is no such thing as a work of literature that makes its own way into the canon; rather, it is placed there, or it arrives there through the agency of many persons within a historical process.

Some recent studies have documented what many of us have noted in our work as educators: it is difficult for women to achieve canonicity. Space given to women writers in American literature texts was listed as between 7 and 14 percent by Judith Fetterley and Joan Schulz in a 1982 study. The 1989 Norton edition of American literature devotes only 10 percent of its pages to women writers—about 600 pages out of 6000. This is not very different from the 4 to 10 percent given to women in the sixties and early seventies (reported in the Fetterley/Schulz study) or the 8 percent average found in anthologies of the fifties in a similar study (mentioned by Lauter [1983]). Attention paid to women writers has been minimal, perfunctory, and often condescending as examination of anthology introductions reveals.

An analysis of canon formation suggests how contingent and historical the whole process is. In both American and English literature, much of the present canon was established in this century. The list of those writers considered to be the American classics changed drastically during the first decades of this century, with some of the figures regarded today as giants—Henry David Thoreau, Herman Melville, and Mark Twain—achieving late recognition (Lauter 1983, 436). Concerning English literature, Frank Kermode reports that during his days at Oxford, Charles Dickens and George Eliot, although read by the general public, were not considered appropriate for university study, while William Blake was a marginal figure and James Joyce was not yet part of the formal curriculum (1979, 82).

In "Race and Gender in the Shaping of the American Literature Canon," Paul Lauter describes how "in the twenties processes were set in motion that virtually eliminated black, white female, and all working-class writers from the canon" (1983, 435). Analyzing American literature texts from 1919 through the 1950s, Lauter found that while the earlier texts contained works by a number of women writers, later texts did not. Those anthologized in a 1919 textbook included Harriet Beecher Stowe, Mary Wilkins Freeman, Sarah Orne Jewett, Helen Hunt Jackson, Rose Terry Cooke, Constance Fenimore Cooper, and Emma Lazarus, along with many other women and blacks. But

> by the end of the fifties, one could study American literature and read no
> work by a black writer, few works by women except Dickinson and

perhaps Marianne Moore or Katharine Anne Porter, and no work about the lives and experiences of working-class people. (1983, 440)

Lauter offers three factors that may account for this development: 1) the rise of a professional body of teachers of literature; 2) the establishment of an aesthetic theory that privileged certain texts and defined the domestic sphere as inappropriate for art; and 3) the division of American literature into the now conventional literary periods, such as "Puritanism," "The Frontier," and "The Rise of Realism," thus again defining literature as dealing with primarily male concerns, such as theology, glorification of male individualism on the frontier, and so on (1983, 440-454).

In analyzing these three factors, it would seem that the professionalization of the teaching of literature is the fundamental explanation for the decline in attention to women writers. It is professors who adopt and promote aesthetic theories and who map literary history. As Barbara Ehrenreich, Deidre English, Gerda Lerner, and others have shown, before the professionalization of medicine, women could be doctors, and before the professionalization of law and pharmacy, women could be lawyers and apothecaries. Before the professionalization of English studies, the work of women writers could be viewed as significant and read with attention and respect. As Ehrenreich and English's study of the professionalization of medicine demonstrates (1979), often both women as purveyors of services and women as clients lose during this process, the point of which, of course, is to establish the power and authority of an exclusive body of experts. I need hardly point out that the professionals we are concerned with here—the professors—were men. The contingencies of their particular needs, interests, and purposes ruled absolutely. There was nothing objective, eternal, inevitable, or universal about their choices and judgments. Instead those judgments were subjective, contingent, local, partial, contextual, personal, and mutable, as all such judgments about quality must be. Because of the complicated "dynamics of endurance" (1988, 47), in Smith's phrase, we still have most of these works in the canon. Once a work has attained visibility, it can remain in a privileged position, and once it has endured for a long time, it begins to create the cultural values that give it its worth, and thus its status as a classic is likely to be perpetuated indefinitely.[2]

Lauter shows that before American literature began to be taught in universities after the First World War, literary study was carried on in literary societies and clubs, which were mainly female. After 1920, the choice and evaluation of literature and the formation of taste were taken over by professors, who, of course, were largely male. Female professors were more common earlier in the century than later. As the profession consolidated its gains during the first half of the century, women's position was eroded. The number of female college teachers peaked about 1930, but gave rise to a perception that female English teachers were too numerous. There was also a concern that many undergraduate students of literature were female. Reorganizational efforts that restricted the role of women were undertaken in the Modern Language Association. Thus, the proportion of women in the profession and their influence were declining at the same time that the number of women writers in the canon was declining.

Those interested in this subject might also want to look at Leslie Fiedler's book *What Was Literature?* Fiedler traces the increasing professionalism and elitism of English professors from the first generation of gentleman professors coming from America's ruling class to the next generation, the New Critics—elitists who affected bohemianism, but elitists nonetheless—to Fiedler's own generation, a non-WASP generation "many of [them] the offspring of non-English speaking stock, with a veneer of Anglo-Saxon culture only a generation thick" (1982, 60). But, alas, says Fiedler, these newcomers were "elitist still, needing to prove by demonstrating their superior rigor their right to the positions they [occupied]" (1982, 62).

Women did not fare well with any of these canon makers. The New Critics "took their patriarchalism for granted" (1983, 131), Jerome J. McGann remarks in a discussion of John Crowe Ransome, one of the bright lights of that critical school. Poet and New Critic Allen Tate's writings also reveal patriarchal, if not sexist, assumptions.[3] Certainly women get short shrift in the anthologies created by the New Critics. *Understanding Poetry*, which E.D. Hirsch Jr. has called "the most influential literary textbook of our time" (1984, 372), contains 8 poems by 5 women poets out of 240 poems by over 90 poets in the first edition of 1938. One of the poems by a woman, "The Pilgrim" by Adelaide Proctor, is included as an example of horrors to be avoided. Most of the poems by women are imagist poems. Certainly none have feminist themes. (This unsatisfactory textbook figures in my own personal history in a way that illustrates its influence. It was put into my hands in a freshman course in 1959, and it was also the text that had been ordered for the first poetry course I taught as an assistant professor eleven years later.) In the textbook *An Approach to Literature*, there is also a scarcity of women writers—4 selections by women out of 161 selections in the revised edition. It is also worth noting that all the Brooks and Warren anthologies, such as the two alluded to above, are what H. Bruce Franklin calls "pure white" (1978, 277, note 3).

Influential individuals often have a great deal of impact on canon formation. We have already mentioned the New Critics, but we should also note that their choices were largely T. S. Eliot's choices. Eliot, as a poet, was evidently a very influential figure for the New Critics, poets themselves. I do not know of any study that traces the institutional and social factors that account for Eliot's extraordinary influence.

Women did not fare very well in the works of two other canon makers: D. H. Lawrence, who laid out his personal canon in *Studies in Classic American Literature*, and F.O. Matthiessen, who presented his list in *The American Renaissance*. Fiedler comments that "somehow all the novelists they praised turned out to be WASP males," and adds, "Lawrence in fact sought to define 'the spirit of the place' in which he had so briefly sojourned . . . without mentioning a single book by a woman or with a black person as a major character" (1982, 147).

Of course, the canon-makers believed and sometimes explicitly stated that their choices had nothing to do with politics. In *F. O. Matthiessen and the Politics of Criticism*, William E. Cain shows us that Matthiessen, a socialist, excluded politics from his formally oriented criticism. The New Critics were socially conservative, almost reactionary, and also considered themselves formalist critics. Recent research has shown, however, that the New Critics were responsive to social and political influences.[4] Their emphasis on formal characteristics was influenced by their efforts to make literature as prestigious a field of study as science. By positing a special relationship between form and content and establishing literary language as special in nature, they were attempting to give the study of literature the increased status necessary in those days of the growing prestige of science, an expanding arms race, and the launching of Sputnik. As has frequently been noted, New Critical theory also lent itself to the teaching of literature on a mass scale, necessary in the post-war fifties. We are now beginning to understand that we can't escape from politics. As we make judgments about quality, we are all implicated, impure, subjective, and biased. This state of affairs is natural, normal, and benign. The only problem is the failure to acknowledge it. It is by a process of complex social dynamics that the tastes and preferences of males have been institutionalized in the university to the point where even most women professors, except for feminist activists, unquestioningly accept them.

That was a brief history of where we have been. I would now like to say something about where we are going. Let me comment first on a paradox I have noticed in my field of English studies. I find it paradoxical that in 1989, feminist theory, gender theory, and women writers figure so prominently in the programs of professional English conferences while back home in the English department, feminist perspectives and attention to women writers are still so woefully inadequate. An examination of the convention program of the 1989 Modern Language Association Convention, for example, suggests that English studies have been revolutionized by the women's movement. Almost one third of the sessions deal in part or as a whole with women writers or with feminist or gender theory. It is indeed heartening to read such titles as "The Death of the Heroine on the European Stage," "Women Reading the Bible," or "The United States Latina Writer's Voice." At the local level, however, the picture looks very different. A study by the Modern Language Association in 1986 (mentioned by Graff and Cain) concludes that changes have occurred only on the fringes of the curriculum, in elective courses, while the courses that form the main body of departmental offerings remain the same. My own findings, based on my observations and on a study of women writers taught in English literature survey in Indiana, are similar.

While I am by nature an optimist who believes that people either are feminists or else will eventually become feminists, I must admit that the going is slow in the English curriculum, even in my own department, which is largely sympathetic and supportive. I believe that in the majority of our courses, we should teach half and half, female and male authors (and that our courses should reflect the racial and ethnic diversity of American culture). However, in spite of my best efforts at persuasion, in my department we teach courses with no female authors, including such recently taught courses as the graduate course in the eighteenth century, a course in science fiction and fantasy, and one in American travel literature.

In pursuing my objective of making women visible in the curriculum, I receive tremendous positive reinforcement from my students, not only the female but also the male students. When we begin focusing on women writers, the female students start choosing their paper topics. One student, whom I had in class a number of times at our small university, received her first "A" from me for a paper on Margaret Cavindish. (She learned about Cavindish, who was not in our Norton text, through a xerox I brought into the class.) Conversely, another female student won our departmental essay contest with a paper about women's poetic responses to the male *carpe diem* poem. Yet another student, now in graduate school, is doing a thesis on a woman writer she was introduced to in my class.

I observe here parenthetically that it is a matter of no small concern that women students for many years have had to deal with the disadvantage of being subjected to a curriculum produced by the tastes and interests of men. Surely their classroom performance, their achievements as scholars, and the rewards that success in school brings have all been hampered, as least for many, by the fact that they have been set to learn material remote from their own interests and concerns. Of course, many have succeeded by adopting on some level the masculinist viewpoint that still largely pervades American education.

Along with many other feminist educators, I have made it my educational mission to counter the masculinist ideology of the academy. I have come to the conclusion, however, that as an English professor, I am the exception rather than the rule. For most professors, literary quality is found almost solely in the writers they studied in graduate school. Besides, it is time-consuming to go to the library to find additional materials for class, and the available anthologies are inadequate. Even on those rare occasions when anthology editors are progressive, commercial pressures work against inclusion of women. While I approve of including in our curriculum male writers who are a part of our common culture and who are associated with the glories of our past (I indulge in a little Virginia Woolfian irony here), I believe it is perfectly feasible to teach numerous women authors as well. Of course we have to select, but selection is the "name of the game." In my two-semester novel survey I can teach only about fourteen novels, a very small selection of the hundreds of thousands or possibly millions of novels written. Typically, I choose seven novels by women and seven by men. All the novels I teach are "good" literature in the only sense the word has meaning for a person in my position: they have been judged as interesting, meaningful, and valuable by a significant number of people, as indicated by the fact that they have been passed along by a series of gate-keepers, including reviewers and academics.[5] From the many "good" novels, in this sense of the term, I choose those which I believe will be enjoyed by my class of young adults, and those which enable me to present a course with thematic coherence, those that enable me to trace the literary modes and styles of the period I am teaching, while bearing in mind that I need gender, ethnic, and racial variety.

Other colleges and universities in Indiana are in as deplorable a state as my own. In a survey I did recently of English literature courses covering the period before 1800, I found that relatively few women are taught. Of the thirty-four courses I surveyed, fifteen include no women and nine include one woman, almost always either Queen Elizabeth or Margery Kempe, an illiterate medieval woman who dictated her story to a scribe. Five of the courses I surveyed (including my own) include five or more women. Sometimes listing women writers in the course syllabus does not necessarily mean they receive much attention in class. One professor who listed seven women writers he has assigned confessed that "they don't always get covered in class." I also found that a number of people think that if their department offers a course in women's literature, there is no particular need to include women in the other courses.[6]

It is apparent that feminist scholars still have a task ahead of them. In a recent article in the *Nation*, Lillian S. Robinson makes a reference to a professor who "deplores the (dubious) fact that more undergraduates are required to read *The Color Purple* than the works of Shakespeare" (1989, 319). Questioning whether "Shakespeare is so universal we don't need others" (1989, 330), Robinson notes that Shakespeare's only treatment of domestic violence is *The Taming of the Shrew* and then continues,

> His black man is the Prince of Morocco or Othello. His black woman, aside from a single nasty remark in *Love's Labour Lost* is nonexistent. Doesn't Alice Walker have something to tell us about "incestuous sheets" that *Hamlet* hasn't already discovered? (1989, 320)

Indeed the Alice Walkers do have something to tell us, and we must continue to work to give students an opportunity to hear them.

Notes

1. Many others, from the now-famous Allan Bloom to the lesser-known who send articles to an array of scholarly and popular publications, have expressed similar views. This outcry can be viewed as a backlash from those persons who feel threatened by the attention paid to works by women and minorities.

2. Barbara Herrnstein Smith explores what she calls "the dynamics of endurance," the complex interactive phenomena that hold a work in place after it has once attained visibility.   See Chapter 3 of *Contingencies of Value.*

3. See especially "The Profession of Letters in the South" in *Reactionary Essays on Poetry and Ideas.*

4. I am indebted to Jane Tompkins' *Sensational Designs* for this account. Her final chapter explores the responsiveness of editors to social and political influences.

5. In an article entitled "The Shaping of a Canon: U.S. Fiction, 1960–75," Richard Ohmann analyzes the process of the creation of literary reputation. The stages he identifies include hard-back sales, best-sellerdom, and, a significant factor in advancing a novel to the pre-canonical state, favorable attention from reviewers in leading intellectual journals. The last stage is promotion by the academic community—assigning the work in courses and attention to the work in academic journals.

6. While I was teaching the first half of the English literature survey (from the beginnings through the eighteenth century), I surveyed thirty-four similar courses in public and private colleges and universities in Indiana. The writers included (with the frequency of inclusion) are as follows: Margery Kempe (13), Queen Elizabeth (10), Lady Mary Wortley Montague (8), Aphra Behn (6), Lady Mary Wroth (5), Fanny Burney (4), Mary Astell (4), Anne Finch (4), Katherine Philips (3), Anne Killegrew (3), and Dorothy Osborne (2). Others mentioned (once) were Lady Anne Halkett, Charlotte Smith, Margaret Cavindish, the Duchess of Marlborough, Mrs. Mary de la Riviere Manley, Julian of Norwich, Eliza Haywood, Jane Baker, and Lady Mary Chudleigh. Most of these courses were one-semester surveys of English literature through the eighteenth century, but three courses covered all of English literature in one semester, and two courses surveyed did not go up to the late 1700s. The largest number of women writers taught in any one course was twelve.

As I examine these results, on the one hand, I am appalled that so few courses include significant treatment of women authors while, on the other hand, I recognize that definite progress has been made. Without the women's movement and the burgeoning of feminist scholarship in recent years, I doubt that many of these fine writers would be taught at all.

Works Cited

Baym, Nina, et al., eds. *The Norton Anthology of American Literature.*
3d ed. 2 vols. New York: Norton, 1989.

Brooks, Cleanth, Jr., and Robert Penn Warren. *Understanding Poetry.*
New York: Holt, 1938.

Brooks, Cleanth, Jr., John Purser, and Robert Penn Warren. *An
Approach to Literature.* rev. New York: Crofts, 1944.

Cain, William E. *F. O. Matthiessen and the Politics of Criticism.*
Madison: University of Wisconsin Press, 1988.

Ehrenreich, Barbara, and Deidre English. *For Her Own Good: 150
Years of the Experts' Advice to Women.* New York:
Anchor/Doubleday, 1979.

Feldman, Edmund Burke. "Ideological Aesthetics." *Liberal Education*
(March/April 1989): 8–13.

Fetterley, Judith, and Joan Schulz. "A MELUS Dialogue: The Status of
Women Writers in American Literature Anthologies." *MELUS* 9
(1982): 3–17.

Fiedler, Leslie. *What Was Literature?* New York: Simon and Schuster,
1982.

Franklin, H. Bruce. *The Victim as Criminal and Artist.* New York:
Oxford, 1978.

Graff, Gerald, and William E. Cain. "Peace Plan for the Canon Wars."
National Forum (Summer 1989): 7–9.

Hirsch, E. D., Jr. "English and the Perils of Formalism." *The American
Scholar* (Summer 1984): 369—79.

Kermode, Frank. "Institutional Control of Interpretation." *Salmagundi*
43 (Winter 1979): 72–86.

Lauter, Paul. "Race and Gender in the Shaping of the American
Literature Canon." *Feminist Studies* 9 (1983): 435–63.

Lawrence, D. H. *Studies in Classic American Literature.* New York:
Viking, 1964.

Lerner, Gerda. *The Majority Finds Its Past.* New York: Oxford
University Press, 1979.

Matthiessen, F. O. *American Renaissance: Art and Expression in the
Age of Emerson and Whitman.* London: Oxford University Press,
1941.

McGann, Jerome J. "The Religious Poetry of Christina Rossetti."
Critical Inquiry 10 (September 1983): 127–44.

Ohmann, Richard. "The Shaping of a Canon: U.S. Fiction, 1960–75. In *Politics of Letters*, 68–91. Middletown: Wesleyan UP, 1987. Originally published in *Critical Inquiry* 10 (1983): 199-223.

Phillips, William. "Comment: Further Notes Toward a Definition of the Canon and the Curriculum." *Partisan Review* 2 (1989): 175–78.

"Program of the 1989 Convention of the Modern Language Association." *PMLA* vol. 104, 5 (1989).

Robinson, Lillian S. "What Culture Should Mean." *Nation* 25 (September 1989): 319–21.

Smith, Barbara Herrnstein. *Contingencies of Value: Alternative Perspectives for Critical Theory*. Cambridge, Mass.: Harvard University Press, 1988.

Tate, Allen. *Reactionary Essays on Poetry and Ideas*. New York: Scribners, 1936.

Tompkins, Jane. *Sensational Designs: The Cultural Work of American Fiction 1790–1860*. New York: Oxford University Press, 1985.

Chapter 5

The Nature and Effects of a Gender-Biased Psychology Curriculum and Some Suggestions for Implementing Change

Sharyl Bender Peterson

In the relatively literate culture of the United States, books play a significant role in shaping the development of human beings. Both the preschooler who is read to and the older child, the adolescent, and the adult who read both nonfiction and fiction are influenced in important ways by the explicit and implicit content of what is read. Readers learn about the world through their books and learn who, what, and how they are expected to be in that world. Moreover, a large part of the "who, what, and how" is determined by the reader's gender, as books tell readers about "appropriate" and "inappropriate" gender-related roles and behavior. This paper summarizes some of the research that has explored these issues and describes my present research, which examines gender biases in college and university textbooks for psychology courses—those courses that purport to tell students about fundamental patterns of human behavior.

A Little History

Twenty years ago, a number of feminist scholars, researchers, and educators began to describe the prevalence of sexist stereotypes in many of the books then published for children. The researchers focussed first on books for pleasure-reading, later on books used in elementary and secondary school classrooms, and most recently on textbooks assigned in college and university courses. Perhaps the best-known of the early studies was that performed by Women on Words and Images. In an excellent summary of this study, Susan Basow notes the following key findings. First, females appeared significantly less often than males—often at ratios as low as one to six. Furthermore, this differential level of appearance occurred in fictional stories about people, in stories about animals, and in biographies (1980, 148). In addition, the contexts in which females and males appeared were significantly different. Females were portrayed as weak, passive, and incompetent, whereas males were portrayed as strong, active, and competent. Girls and women watched, while boys and men achieved. This inequitable and discriminatory pattern was found again and again, in a host of subsequent studies (e.g., Engel 1981; Peterson and Lach 1990; Weitzman, Eifler, Hokada, and Ross 1972).

Not surprisingly, studies that examined the effects of exposure to such stereotyped materials on readers' cognitive and affective development found negative effects on girls' and women's development, and positive effects on boys' and men's development. In one such study, Sandra L. Bem demonstrated that gender stereotypes affect readers' perceptions of others' behavior, their memory for that behavior, and the inferences drawn from it (1981, 355). Debra B. Hull and John H. Hull reported similar findings (1986, 136). Patricia B. Campbell and Jeana Wirtenberg described several studies that examined the effects of gender-biased versus nonbiased reading materials on children's attitudes and school achievement. These studies found that gender-biased materials had negative effects on both attitudes and achievement, while the reverse was true for nonbiased materials. Specifically, children exposed to nonsexist reading materials developed more egalitarian attitudes about what girls and boys can do, and showed decreased sex-stereotyping in general (1980, 5–6). These studies, and others, have clearly shown that gender stereotypes have pervasive effects—both on several dimensions of the reader's cognitive performance, on the development of the reader's self-concept, and on the reader's potential for achievement.

Past Research on Gender Biases in College Textbooks

After a decade of growing concern over these issues, in 1975 the American Psychological Association (APA) created a Task Force to examine whether or not sex biases existed in textbooks used in graduate courses in psychology. The APA Task Force conducted a content analysis of thirteen textbooks then widely used in graduate education in psychology in the United States. They concluded that

> authors frequently fail(ed) to follow good rules of scholarship . . . either (not reporting) sex differences, or (providing) discussion . . . restricted to genetic-based interpretations, and . . . (that they) applied stereotypic terms . . . (and that) women (were) invisible in psychology textbooks as research subjects, as scientists, and as subject matter. (1975, 684)

Astonishingly, their overall conclusion was that "most of the authors were to be commended for the absence of gross sexist material" (1975, 682).

The APA Task Force did, however, note two types of concerns. First, they expressed concerns regarding sex-biased language in the textbooks and generated a set of stylistic guidelines that were subsequently incorporated into the *Publication Manual of the American Psychological Association*, which provides the procedural writing standards to which psychologists writing and publishing in their field must conform. Second, they discovered numerous methodological errors with respect to inappropriate reporting of, or failure to report, sex of research subjects and/or sex differences in research findings. To remedy these problems, the APA Task Force recommended a set of Substantive Guidelines that provided directions for reporting data. These recommendations included:

> (1) Authors should avoid generalizing from the behavior of one sex to that of the other. Specifically, when subjects are all of one sex, generalizations should not be made to people in general. It is the responsibility of each author to state the sex of the norm group for each study cited. If the sex of the norm group cannot be determined, this should be noted by the author.
> (2) When research results yield sex differences, those differences should be reported.
> (3) The author should consider all reasonable interpretations of reported sex differences, including the possibility of biases in methodology.

(4) It has been noted that women are at times underrepresented in text citations in proportion to the number of eminent women in that field. Authors should avoid such misrepresentation. (1975, 683)

So far as I am aware, these Substantive Guidelines were never incorporated into the *Publication Manual* or into any other document that regulates or describes the appropriate reporting of psychological research.

Two years after the APA Task Force report appeared, Lorette Woolsey conducted an analysis of college-level developmental psychology textbooks, and found that things had changed very little. Focusing her analysis on the coverage of gender-roles, she found that fewer than half of the thirty-five textbooks she surveyed contained any coverage of gender-roles at all, and of those that did, coverage tended to be stereotyped, and consistently to devalue the female role (1977, 71–72). The most positive comment she offered with respect to any of the books analyzed was that *one* team of textbooks authors did "appreciate that there is an issue as to *whether* (emphasis mine) the sex-role stereotypes (presented in the textbooks) should be perpetuated, changed, or completely done away with" (1977, 72).

That same year, Vicky A. Gray reported a limited content analysis of ten introductory psychology textbooks, and reached the same conclusions that the APA Task Force had reached two years earlier. She found that women were still relatively invisible in illustrations, examples, and subject and author indices (1977, 52–53). She also found that language biases still existed, and that only three of the ten books she surveyed consistently used language-neuter constructions (1977, 51). Reports or discussions of sex differences were either attributed to genetic causes or omitted altogether (1977, 50). Moreover, when sex roles were considered, they were typically traditional and stereotyped (1977, 49, 54). Yet, she, like the APA Task Force, concluded that "the examples of sexism found in psychology texts are attributable more to omission than commission" (1977, 50).

In 1982, Florence L. Denmark reported another informal study of sixteen introductory psychology books published between 1979 and 1982. Denmark reported that topics about women (e.g., sex-role development, sex-role stereotypes, and achievement motivation) were unevenly covered, and "frequently seemed to be tacked on as an afterthought" (1982, 39). She also commented that "it has become standard practice to present largely pessimistic views of women" (1982,

40), and elaborated on this point in her analysis of illustrations and descriptions of women, as they compared with the portrayals of men. To quote Denmark:

> Women are presented . . . as phobic, anxious, emotional, and mentally ill . . . (Compared to males) (f)emales are more frequently depicted as overweight, as mental patients, or as watching males conduct scientific experiments. Males, on the other hand, solve complex mathematical problems and are more often seen in the role of experimenter or psychotherapist. The significant psychologists pictured in the textbooks are more frequently male; rarely is a female psychologist featured. Thus, women continue to be depicted as sick or passive where men are depicted as intellectual, healthy, and strong. This bias in the selection of illustrative material that reinforces the culturally accepted female/male stereotype cannot be blamed on one or two texts. It was found throughout most of the books reviewed. (1982, 40–41)

In 1984, Elizabeth Percival performed a similar analysis of the eight most widely used introductory psychology texts in Canada, and reached similar conclusions. She found that the use of "generic" male pronouns seemed to be decreasing (1984, 57) and that coverage of some issues relevant to gender roles and gender stereotyping seemed to be increasing, although the raters in her study were split in their judgments about the degree to which overall sex stereotyping still existed (1984, 39). However, she concluded that there was still considerable room for improvement (1984, 41). In fact, given some peculiar patterns of rater inconsistencies in her findings, she also concluded that "perhaps a better definition and a more refined measuring instrument are needed to detect sex bias" (1984, 41).

Interestingly, with the exception of Florence Denmark, the authors of these studies all seemed to feel that the portrayal of women and the coverage of women's issues in textbooks had improved substantially since the early 1960s. Sensitivity to gender-biased language seemed to have increased, and its use to have decreased. However, given much of the data reported in these studies, and the authors' clear unwillingness to conclude that stereotyping and related problems had indeed been solved, the question remained as to whether gender biases have in fact been eliminated from textbooks. Based on my own frustrations in trying to find textbooks that I consider acceptable for teaching my own courses, I believed that they had not.

Research Goals and Findings

The primary goal of my research project was to test the hypothesis that gender biases are still prevalent in psychology texts for undergraduates. A related goal was to develop an instrument that would permit objective, empirical measurement of the types of material—with special regard to sex and gender issues—presented in introductory psychology and in human development textbooks. Earlier studies tended to rely on relatively subjective measures of stereotyping and other gender biases, which offered some leeway in the conclusions one might draw from the findings presented. I wished to develop a coding method that would offer unequivocal proof that gender biases are still pervasive, and make that case in a way that would be clear to *any* observer, regardless of his or her own particular biases or theoretical perspective.

Focusing on the issues raised by Woolsey, Gray, Denmark, and Percival, as well as my own earlier research on gender stereotypes in children's books, with the participation of an undergraduate research assistant,[1] I developed two coding scales. One was designed to be used for analysis of texts for introductory psychology; the other was designed for analysis of texts for human lifespan development courses. These scales were subsequently used to perform a content analysis of the forty-six top-selling introductory psychology textbooks and the fifteen top-selling textbooks on human lifespan development. While a discussion of the complete coding scales is beyond the scope of this paper, they are available in full from the author. For present purposes, the data obtained is more relevant and interesting than the methodology related to the development and use of the coding system, although elements of that methodology will be described whenever necessary for an understanding of the findings. Further, for the sake of brevity, only the data on the introductory texts will be described here. Data on the developmental texts is available from the author, as well as in Peterson (1992a).

General Method

Most introductory texts begin with a chapter on the history of the field of psychology, typically followed by an overview of contemporary work in the field. Because of the importance of this chapter in providing a cognitive framework for the material that will come later, the material on historical and contemporary work in psychology was coded in its entirety. In contrast, due to the very large volume of material in the remainder of these texts (the typical length is approximately 700 pages), samples of the verbal and pictorial content were coded for each of the remaining chapters in each text (on average, twelve additional chapters per text).

In the first chapter on the history and contemporary overview, three types of codes were used. A "description" meant that the treatment of a person's work or theory was three sentences or longer. A "mention" meant that two sentences or less of text were used to refer to a person's work or theory. An "illustration" included any type of pictorial depiction of a person referred to in the text or used to illustrate some contemporary domain of psychology.

In subsequent chapters, verbal content was coded for approximately 30 percent of the material in each chapter. Coding rules for "descriptions" and "mentions" were identical with those used for the first chapter. In addition, if a person of an identifiable gender was used to illustrate a concept, this was coded as an "example" under the appropriate gender. An equivalent proportion of the pictorial content of each of the twelve or so subsequent chapters was also sampled. In addition to counting the number of females and males in each coded illustration, we also coded the context of each illustration. The context was coded based on the apparent agency of the person pictured. An "Active/Agent" code was assigned if the person was clearly engaging in, and/or initiating some activity (e.g., recording physiological responses of subjects or patients, participating in an athletic event, or providing leadership for a group of people). A "Passive/Object" code was assigned if the person was behaving passively (e.g., sitting quietly, simply observing another's activity) or was the object of another person's behavior (e.g., having one's brain waves recorded).

In addition, the numbers of female and male text authors and reviewers were counted, as were numbers of women and men listed in subject and author indices. Most texts typically employ standard APA style, and provide only initials for authors' first names, so that author sex for citations was not readily identifiable. Since there are hundreds of citations per text, making it virtually impossible to check each citation for which initials only were provided, we decided only to count citations by gender for the texts that used authors' full names. Finally, based on questions raised by the earlier authors, we examined the degree to which gender-appropriate language was used in text chapter titles and subheads.

Findings

Historical Work and Overview of Contemporary Work

Looking first at the material on the history of the field, we found a large difference between the presentation of the work of women and men. As Table 1 shows, texts averaged far less than one description or mention of a woman's work or theory in the historical chapter of each text. In contrast, there were seventy-two times as many descriptions of men's work as women's, twenty-two times as many mentions of men's work as women's, and twenty-six times as many illustrations of men as of women per text. The general portrayal of the historical development of the field is clearly one that is comprised almost entirely of men. In the rare cases where women were mentioned, the two women who typically merited inclusion were Anna Freud (noted almost always as "the daughter of Sigmund Freud") and Karen Horney (usually referred to as "a follower of Freud"). In both cases, these women were described in relation to a male figure of significance. Further, only two of the texts coded had even a single illustration of a woman in the historical section.

TABLE 1
Representation in Historical Work
Average Number of Representations Per Text

	Descriptions	Mentions	Illustrations
Women	.12	.36	.24
Men	8.6	7.8	6.32

Note that all sex differences in this and the following tables, with the three exceptions noted below, were significant at the p<.001 level.

Overview of Contemporary Work

The coverage in the early chapter that provides an overview of contemporary work in the field was equally uneven. As Table 2 shows, although the difference between the number of women and men represented was not as egregiously large as in the historical treatment, it is still significant in all cases. The majority of texts contained one or fewer illustrations of women doing psychological work today, and while women's work was more likely to be included here than in the historical section, it was still much less likely to be discussed than was the work of men.

TABLE 2
Representation in Contemporary Overview Section
Average Number of Representations Per Text

	Descriptions	Mentions	Illustrations
Women	.35	.25*	.70
Men	1.7	3.3	1.6

*Difference significant at p<01.2

Verbal Coverage in Remainder of Text Material

As Table 3 shows, the coverage in the verbal material that makes up the remainder of these texts was just as lopsided as the material on history and contemporary overviews of the field. Men's work was eight times as likely to be described, and eighteen times as likely to be mentioned as was that of women. (For the sake of clarity, in this and in the following section, "women" is taken to include girls as well, and "men" to include boys. By and large, illustrative examples were of adult rather than of pre-adult persons and behaviors.) The only area approaching equity was in the use of females and males as illustrative examples of concepts; in this case, men were only 1.7 times more likely to appear than were women.

It should be noted, however, that even this apparent equity is misleading. Separate analyses showed that women were most frequently used as examples in the chapter on development, where they were often referred to specifically as mothers, whereas males were almost never described as fathers. Women also appeared frequently—both in verbal references and in pictures—in the chapters on psychopathology and therapy, as illustrative examples of various pathological conditions and as patients in therapy.

TABLE 3

Representation in Verbal Content in Remainder of Text

Average No. of Representations Per Coded Section of Each Text

	Descriptions	Mentions	Examples
Women	.68	.16	4.04
Men	5.34	2.93	6.79

Pictorial Coverage in Remainder of Text Material

Interestingly, women were represented in pictorial illustrations at somewhat higher rates relative to men than in the texts' verbal content. As Table 4 shows, women appeared about three-fourths as frequently as men (in contrast to the much larger differences in the text material described above). However, the contexts in which the two sexes were shown differed significantly.

While women were about twice as likely to be shown in active as in passive roles, men were four times more likely to be shown in active rather than passive roles. This difference becomes even more important in light of a separate analysis of the degree to which agency was related to a positive or negative evaluation. It was possible, using both the content of the illustrations and the captions, to assign a Positive or Negative evaluation code to the illustrations. An analysis of agency and evaluation indicated that Active illustrations were eleven times more likely to carry a Positive evaluation than were Passive illustrations. Thus, men were significantly (approximately twenty times) more likely to be portrayed in a positive context than were women.

TABLE 4
Representation in Pictorial Content in Remainder of Text

	Total/Text	Active/Agent	Passive/Object
Women	1.59**	2.0***	1.19
Men	2.29	3.63	.94

**Significant at p<.04
***The interaction between context (agency/passivity) and sex was significant at p<.001.

Other Representations

As shown in Table 5, women comprised only 17 percent of the total authors for the texts reviewed. They fared somewhat better as reviewers, making up nearly 25 percent of reviewers. They were more seriously underrepresented in indices, with eight-and-a-half times as many men as women cited in subject indices, and four times as many men as women cited in author indices. Even though the analyses took into account the relative proportions of men and women in psychology (as reported by APA), differences in numbers of reviewers and in numbers of citations in subject and author indices were all significantly different at p<.001. Thus, the differential in-print representation of the work of women and men that was noted by the APA Task Force in 1975 continues to occur nearly 20 years later. And, with over 13,000 citations of articles on women in the current psychology literature (Walsh 1986), this pattern would appear to be due to some factor other than simple oversight.

TABLE 5
Other Representations
Average Number Per Text Coded

	Authors	Reviewers	Subject Indices	Author Indices
Women	8*	324	54	501
Men	38	974	452	1997

*Non-significant sex difference

Language Use

Turning last to the issue of language constructions, it appears that there has been an increase in language-bias consciousness. Virtually all of the texts in the coded sample employed gender-neutral constructions or alternated the use of female and male pronouns, with appropriate gender-related references. None of the texts we analyzed contained the kinds of gender-biased titles (e.g., "The Child is the Father of the Man") that appeared in these kinds of textbooks only a few years ago.

Summary

Unfortunately, the latter data (on language use) provide scant grounds for optimism. If one examines the remainder of the evidence, it is clear that the only domain in which significant change has occurred is the relinquishing (with the exception of one very prominent text) of the "generic" male pronoun. Otherwise, very little change seems to have occurred in the past two decades. Women are still grossly underrepresented in these texts, both in descriptions of the history and development of the field, and in coverage of contemporary concepts and work. Their accomplishments in creating theory, conducting research, and engaging in practice are seldom acknowledged, much less elaborated upon as are the comparable accomplishments of male psychologists. When a woman's existence is acknowledged, it is still typically in stereotyped and/or negative contexts.

Implications

Many undergraduate students complete courses in introductory psychology and/or in human development—in fact, these courses are among the most popular at many colleges and universities. However, many of the students who complete these courses do *not* go on to complete further coursework in the field, so their knowledge about and perceptions of the field of psychology, and perhaps of human behavior in general, are significantly influenced by what they learn in these introductory courses. As Phyllis A. Bronstein and Michele Paludi note,

> The questions, issues, facts, and possible biases that students encounter in the introductory course can have lasting effects on their perceptions of both human nature and the field of psychology, as well as on their expectations as consumers of psychological services. The course may enhance their understanding of their own motivations, affect their social perceptions and attributions, shape their beliefs about mental illness, and inform their future behavior as parents. Thus, it is important that it cover not only a sufficient range of topics but also a sufficient diversity of human experience by including issues and information about sociocultural factors, ethnicity, and gender in its content. (1988, 21)

Unfortunately, current psychology texts are *not* presenting such information, and much of what they are presenting is incomplete and/or inaccurate.

One of the strongest and clearest inaccurate messages that students receive is that psychology is a profession practiced mostly by men that studies the behavior of men—not of people in general, but of males. This constitutes misrepresentation; virtually since the inception of psychology as a field, at least one-third of psychologists have been women, and, currently, that percentage has increased to nearly two-thirds, as measured by the number of students enrolled in undergraduate and graduate programs in psychology (U.S. Department of Education 1987). Yet, despite academic careers and accomplishments as impressive as those of their male contemporaries, the work of women psychologists has been omitted almost entirely from the historical record.

Further, the research that is presented in the texts includes predominantly studies using all-male samples, or studies in which sex differences are either not reported, or, if reported, are not discussed (other than the occasional default attribution of such differences to biological factors). For example, when describing the "normal" pattern of moral development, Lawrence Kohlberg's work—using all-male samples—is invariably presented as "the" current model in this domain. Carol Gilligan's work, which has suggested a quite different pattern of moral development for women, is either omitted entirely, or referred to in a brief paragraph that typically notes that her findings differ from Kohlberg's, and that fails to explain those differences or to discuss their implications.

Presenting behavioral models based largely or entirely on male data also constitutes misrepresentation, because such data only describe the behavior and/or psychological experiences of half the population (and, in fact, of far less than half, since most researchers have primarily examined Anglo-American male experiences). Nonetheless, white, middle-class, heterosexual, male behavior is presented in these texts as normative. If the behavior and psychological functioning of women are described at all, the examples chosen too frequently refer only to the experiences of white middle-class women. Further, even those limited allusions are often trivialized and, if different from behaviors or experiences of males, are labelled either implicitly or explicitly as deviant and/or dysfunctional.

It is important to recognize that these issues also apply to the depictions of many people who belong to various groups of ethnic, cultural, physical, and social "minorities" who are underrepresented and misrepresented in textbook materials, and it is as essential to correct those kinds of misrepresentations and stereotypes as it is to correct those regarding the ways in which women are currently treated in texts.

Further, this is not an issue to which only psychologists need to be sensitive and responsive. Stereotypic and denigrative portrayals of white women, African-Americans, Native Americans, Chicanas and Chicanos, Latinas and Latinos, Asian-Americans, lesbians and gay men, aged persons, and physically challenged persons apppear in books intended for and used in college and university courses in *many* academic disciplines.

To quote Phyllis A. Bronstein and Kathryn Quina (1988, 633), who speak directly to the issues confronting psychologists,

As individual teachers, we have an intellectual and ethical responsibility to provide our students with the most current and accurate information possible, a responsibility underscored in Principle 1.e of the "Ethical

Principles of Psychologists" (APA, 1981, 5): "As teachers, psychologists recognize their primary obligation to help others acquire knowledge and skill. They maintain high standards of scholarship by presenting psychological information objectively, fully, and accurately.

These ethical principles apply in the general sense not only to psychologists, but to all who teach. The responsibility is even broader than this, however. We must help all students understand that their own personal experiences are valid and valuable; that because they are female, bisexual, African-American, or physically challenged, others do not have the right to devalue them, nor should they devalue themselves. However, that is tremendously difficult in a society in which people who are not middle- or upper-class able-bodied heterosexual white males are repeatedly made to feel that they are flawed and deserve to be treated badly. We must help students understand, appreciate, and respect the tremendous diversity of all human beings. While this is an enormously difficult task, there are steps we can take.

The first is to continue to work on becoming ever better informed. It is difficult (although becoming less so) to find information about women (and members of other "minorities") in psychology. Resources like Phyllis Bronstein and Kathryn Quina's *Teaching a Psychology of People* are invaluable, both in discussing issues that should be of concern to us as teachers, and in offering a list of resources and exercises that may be useful in our teaching. The advent of new informational technology, like the WMST-L electronic network, provides a virtual world-wide array of colleagues who can provide assistance and suggestions for additional resources.

Second, we must not only be willing to share those materials with colleagues, but actively encourage them to transform their courses. When I talk with my colleagues about revising the material they cover in their sections of the general psychology course, they sometimes indicate that they would include more information about women if they knew whom to include, and where to get information about those women. One could argue that we as concerned feminists and educators should not have to assume the primary responsibility for being knowledgeable in this domain, or the related responsibility for providing assistance to our colleagues who are perhaps less motivated than we would wish to seek this information as avidly as they seek other kinds of material that they consider "important" to cover in their courses. While I agree with that argument, it is nonetheless true that if we do not provide such assistance, most of our colleagues will not make the required effort on their own. Providing colleagues with copies of texts like Agnes N. O'Connell and Nancy Felipe Russo's *Models of Achievement* (*Vols. I* and *II*), Gwendolyn Stevens and Sheldon Gardner's *The Women of Psychology* (*Vols. I* and *II*), Elizabeth Scarborough and Laurel Furomoto's *Untold Lives*, or Robert V. Guthrie's *Even the Rat Was White* may provide the informational foundation and/or impetus to alter the way they are presently teaching their courses.

Third, we must write and publish appropriate textbooks ourselves. Fewer than 20 percent of the authors of the current textbooks we surveyed are women. If existing textbooks are seriously flawed (which they indeed are), we must replace them with better texts. That is not an easy task, however. Traditionally, in all fields, women have had more difficulty getting their work into print than men have had. Nonetheless, it is essential that we create new texts if we wish to alter the current gross misrepresentations.

Finally, we must begin to make more demands on those who provide textbooks to us. I recently completely a survey of publishers in the United States who produce textbooks for introductory psychology and developmental psychology courses (Peterson, 1992b). Among other findings was the fact that reviewers of manuscripts raise specific concerns about content biases and stereotypes much *less* frequently than they raise concerns about breadth of coverage of topics, lack of currency of reported research, or concerns with reading level (although the first two of those three are often related to stereotyping and bias). Interestingly, when reviewers do raise concerns about content biases, gender biases are the most frequently mentioned (followed by concerns about racial/ethnic biases, age biases, and occasionally biases about disabilities). Also interesting was the finding that only half of the publishers surveyed have policies prohibiting gender-biased language use, and only three-fourths have policies prohibiting overtly discriminatory content. If these concerns are important to us, it is essential that as reviewers, and as potential users of textbooks, we make it clear to publishers that we do not approve of current editorial policies, and insist on appropriate changes. Perhaps the ultimate statement we might make to publishers would be a refusal to use biased, inaccurate materials.

If we do not attempt to accomplish these goals, "the future of our past" will be a continuation of our past. Women (and many others) will continue to be misrepresented, and to be discriminated against because of that misrepresentation. If we truly believe in and want a different future, then we must take action to create change.

Notes

1. The author gratefully acknowledges the assistance of Traci Kroner with the research described in this paper.

Works Cited

American Psychological Association (APA) Task Force on Issues of Sexual Bias in Graduate Education. "Guidelines for Nonsexist Use of Language." *American Psychologist* 30 (1975): 682–84.

Basow, Susan. *Sex-Role Stereotypes: Traditions and Alternatives.* Belmont, Calif.: Brooks-Cole, 1980.

Bem, Sandra L. "Gender Schema Theory: A Cognitive Account of Sex Typing." *Psycological Review* 83 (1981): 354–64.

Bronstein, Phyllis A., and Kathryn Quina. *Teaching a Psychology of People.* Washington, D.C.: American Psychological Association, 1988.

Bronstein, Phyllis A., and Michele Paludi. "The Introductory Psychology Course From a Broader Human Perspective." In *Teaching a Psychology of People,* eds. Phyllis A. Bronstein and Kathryn Quina. Washington, D.C.: American Psychological Association, 1988.

Campbell, Patricia B., and Jeana Wirtenberg. "How Books Influence Children." *IRBC Bulletin* 11 (1980): 3–6.

Denmark, Florence L. "Integrating the Psychology of Women Into Introductory Psychology." In *The G. Stanley Hall Lecture Series,* eds. C. J. Scherere and A. R. Rogers, vol. 3. Washington, D.C.: American Psychological Association, 1982.

Engel, Rosaline E. "Is Unequal Treatment of Females Diminishing in Children's Picture Books?" *The Reading Teacher* (March 1981): 647–52.

Gray, Vicky A. "The Image of Women in Psychology Textbooks." *Canadian Psychological Review* 18 (1977): 46–55.

Gray, Vicky A. "The Image of Women in Psychology Textbooks."
   Canadian Psychological Review 18 (1977): 46–55.
Guthrie, Robert V. *Even the Rate Was White: A Historical View of
   Psychology.* New York: Harper and Row, 1976.
Hull, Debra B., and John H. Hull. "A Note on the Evaluation of
   Stereotypical Masculine, Feminine and Neutral Behaviors of
   Children." *Journal of Genetic Psychology* 147 (1986): 135–37.
O'Connell, Agnes N., and Nancy Felipe Russo. *Models of
   Achievement: Reflections of Eminent Women in Psychology*, vols. I
   and II. New York: Columbia University Press, 1983, 1988.
Percival, Elizabeth. "Sex Bias in Introductory Psychology Textbooks:
   Five Years Later." *Canadian Psychology* 25 (1984): 35–42
Peterson, Sharyl Bender. "Survey of Publishers: Report and Implications
   for   Publishers' Roles Regarding Mainstreaming Gender and
   Diversity into Psychology Textbooks." Paper presented at the 100th
   Annual Meeting of the American Psychological Association,
   Washington, D.C. (1992b).
Peterson, Sharyl Bender, and Mary Alyce Lach. "Gender Stereotypes in
   Children's Books: Their Prevalence and Influence on Cognitive and
   Affective Development." *Gender and Education* 2 (1990): 185–197.
Peterson, Sharyl Bender, and Traci Kroner. "Gender Biases in
   Textbooks for Introductory Psychology and Human Development."
   Psychology of Women Quarterly 16 (1992a): 17–36.
Scarborough, Elizabeth, and Laurel Furomoto. *Untold Lives: The First
   Generation of American Women Psychologists.* New York: Columbia
   University Press, 1987.
Stevens, Gwendolyn, and Sheldon Gardner. *Women in Psychology:
   Vol. I: Pioneers and Innovators.* Cambridge, Mass.: Schenkman
   Publishing Company, 1982.
—. *Women in Psychology: Vol. II: Expansion and Refinement.*
   Cambridge, Mass.: Schenkman Publishing Company, 1982.
U.S. Department of Education, Center for Statistics. "Earned Degrees
   Conferred in 1984–85 by U.S. Colleges and Universities." *Chronicle
   of Higher Education* 15 (July 1987): 34.
Walsh, Mary Roth. "The Psychology of Women's Courses: A
   Continuing Catalyst for Change." *Teaching of Psychology* 12 (1986):
   198–203.
Weitzman, Lenore J., Deborah Eifler, Elizabeth Hokada, and Catherine
   Ross.   "Sex-Role Socialization in Picture Books for Preschool
   Children." *American Journal of Sociology* 77 (1972): 1125–50.

Woolsey, Lorette. "Psychology and the Reconciliation of Women's Double Bind: To be Feminine or to be Fully Human." *Canadian Psychological Review* 18 (1977): 66–78.

Women on Words and Images. *Dick and Jane as Victims*. Princeton N. J.: Author, 1972.

Chapter 6

The Personal is Professional is Political: Feminist Praxis in a Graduate School Counselor Training Program

Eleanor Roffman

> For the Master's tools will never dismantle the Master's house. They may allow us to temporarily beat him at his own game, but this will never allow us to bring about genuine change. (Lorde 1981)

These words of Audre Lorde have as strong an impact on me today as they did when she first wrote them over ten years ago. They express my belief that in order to bring about significant and lasting change, we need to develop new ways of doing things. I know that my behavior as an educator needs to be substantially different from the way I was educated. *How* I do things matters as much as *what* I do. Paying attention to process is an invaluable tool that I have learned from feminist thinking. Another valuable feminist insight for me has been the thought that the "personal is political." What this means to me is that how we live our daily lives, the choices that we make, and how we treat others is the basis for our political postures.

As a feminist I know that power inequity is the core issue in many women's struggles, whether it be economic, political, social, educational, or psychological. One of my goals as a teacher of psychology is to encourage others to feel their power as a positive and creative force, a tool for change. My responsibility is to examine how I use my power as a teacher, especially how I model power sharing.

As those of us who have been engaged in struggles know, people do not give up power readily. In my work as a teacher of feminist counseling, my effort as a role model is motivated towards empowering others by helping them master the task at hand through guided self-exploration, feedback, and peer support. I work at translating my feminist commitment of a just, equitable, and democratic distribution of power into quality education, critical thinking skills, and increased self-awareness. This article explores my efforts to integrate my theoretical convictions with practice, and examines the impact that this has had on my students' sense of self as women and as mental health professionals.

It is limiting to discuss feminist theory without discussing women's differences as well as women's bonds. Issues such as sexism, racism, classism, and homophobia affect our daily lives. The manner in which we approach these issues determines our practice and effectiveness as teachers and outspoken feminists. "Survival," Audre Lorde says, "is not an academic skill." It is not something we learn in the comfort of the academy without taking risks, to be willing to stand alone, to place ourselves on the margins of society, or to take an unpopular position. Lorde beckons us to "make commonsense" with others outside the mainstream, and to create a world where we all can live with respect, dignity, and care (1981, 99). Lorde makes the distinction between academic skill and teaching. She acknowledges that teaching is both a survival skill and the only way real learning can take place. She succinctly describes the interactional nature of the teaching process when she says, "I was examining it and teaching it at the same time I was learning it. I was teaching it to myself out loud" (1981, 88). In this generative dynamic spirit, I perceive my relationship in the academy.

"Counseling Women: Applying Theory to Practice," is the second part of a two part course, of which "Psychology of Women" is the first in the sequence. In the first semester, students explore major issues that affect women's lives from a women centered perspective. We read works by women and discuss the relationship of feminist theory to mainstream psychology. Students are asked to think about how they are assimilating the information presented in the course. They are encouraged to explore their feelings. They write about what emerges for them as they encounter material that challenges self-perception, beliefs about psychology, and perceptions of the world they live in. Each week students are encouraged to talk about their reactions to the readings, and they are required to submit short response papers. Response papers allow students to express feelings, ask questions, and to express in writing how they are affected by feminist thought regarding their inner and outer worlds. Through my responses to their papers, and our continuing dialogue, the students further their explorations in these areas. In the classroom, we examine the impact of new knowledge, as well as the effect of new processes for learning.

Students in my classes are mostly women who range in age from about twenty-four to sixty. With slight variation, most of my students have reached graduate school feeling like frauds or incompetents. This is not uncommon for women students, and, in my class, we discuss self-image, especially that of learners, from a feminist context. I evoke these feelings intentionally, because I believe that women need to give voice to their concerns about themselves and their intellectual capacities. Women need to contextualize these impressions from within a social political framework that helps them make sense of their feelings. The investigation of the ways we understand reality and its impact on self-esteem is one of the connecting threads of this two-course sequence. However, before I present how I teach the skills course and its impact on the students, I would like to focus on the theoretical bases that influence my work.

I believe that in order for learning to take place, the relationship between student and teacher needs to be honored. In our capitalistic and patriarchal system, the relationship has been one of dominant to subordinate as defined by gender and class. A critical progressive educational theory is committed to altering that relationship by creating models for societal change. Our educational system not only determines what education is available to us, but how gender shapes our sense of self and our relationship to knowledge. Critical education theory explores the relationship of class and race to education, but substantially ignores the role of gender.

Kathleen Weiler (1988), integrates the work of important critical education theorists with that of significant feminist theorists. Weiler focuses on major educational and feminist theorists who concern themselves with the ways that social class and gender are produced and reproduced in schooling under a capitalist, patriarchal system. Weiler illuminates the weakness of critical educational theory that fails to recognize the significance of sexism in education.

Crucial to critical educational thought is the belief that change becomes possible through an understanding of our subjective experience. A major theorist committed to the conviction in the individual's capacity to change is Paulo Freire (1970), who examines the dynamics of the relationship between teacher and student as the breeding ground for constructing and reconstructing meaning. Freire encourages peasants to learn how to read by examining their own lives through the written word. As a teacher, I am committed to creating a classroom environment in which students can articulate their understanding of self, other, subjective reality, empathy, and the surrounding environment through the critical lens of a feminist framework. As we recognize our experiences, we become capable of making changes.

Like Kathleen Weiler, I am influenced by the work of Antonio Gramsci, an Italian revolutionary, who wrote in the 1920s about politics and culture. Hegemony, according to Gramsci, is the control of ideology and socialization through institutions. Gramsci believes in people's ability to contest this control. He asserts that the working class can create intellectuals who have their fingers on the pulse of their communities and that schools are a place where the rich and creative discourse of teacher and student can bring about change. My efforts are guided towards making my classroom such a place, in part, by recognizing that what I teach and how I teach are intimately related.

A critical feminist educational theory stresses the relationship between class structure, schooling, capitalism, and the gendered nature of relationships. We need to be aware of the monocultural control of patriarchy, racism, and homophobia and how these controlling ideologies have silenced discussion. Raising these issues in the classroom allows us to talk about the limitations, inquiries, and fears that our culture generates. A feminist lens helps us to understand that social relations are always in process; that schooling reproduces gender inequities; that we have the capacity to make meaning out of our lives; that we can resist oppression; and that this capacity to comprehend is shaped by class, gender, and race (Weiler, 1988). Feminist teaching engenders self-conscious analysis that can oppose the hegemony of the existing order and build a new base for an understanding and transformation of society.

The Course

"Feminism is taught through process as well as formal content. To reflect feminist value in teaching is to teach progressively, democratically, and with feeling" (Schniedewind and Davidson, 1983). As feminist teachers we are challenged to create meaning in a world that denies our subjectivity, and we are challenged to create value out of what is devalued. We bring to the classroom and say out loud what has been, until this time, repressed and unavailable for discussion. "Counseling Women: Applying Theory to Practice" attempts to foreground the woman's viewpoint.

I assume as a psychologist and as a teacher that the ability to understand the needs of others is rooted in efforts to understand the self. Before we can witness, guide, and explore with others their inner realities, we need to experience this journey ourselves. Toward this end, I require my students to keep a journal. Ira Progoff, in his approach to journal keeping, agrees that the process of growth in a human being, the process out of which a person emerges, is essentially an inward process (1975). Journals are thus the starting point for students to explore their inner world, to write down thoughts and feelings that occur to them as they experience this course. Students do not have to hand in their journals, share them with anyone, or feel that they have to judge or control the content or the form their writing takes. The journal assignment allows students a safe space in which to become more intimately aware of how they think and also allows them to observe what it is like to engage in this process. I believe that journal writing can be a healing process. Like expressing things verbally, writing things lends power to our beliefs and feelings. By recording them we make them visible and tangible.

In addition to journal keeping, students are required to respond in writing to a series of exercises in *Women and Self-Esteem* (Sanford and Donovan, 1984) and *The Courage to Heal*, (Bass and Davis, 1988). These exercises help students focus on the personal aspects of issues that affect women's lives. They also encourage memory retrieval, self-reflection, introspection, and the working through of painful experiences. Because these exercises are personal, students are not required to submit their responses. However, they have an opportunity to share this material with an assigned counseling partner with whom they work throughout the semester.

Students are paired with another class member in a counseling dyad that meets weekly. They share the class hour allowed for this assignment by alternately being client and counselor. Although students take roles, they are encouraged to "real play," not role play. They are not required to share their personal experiences if they do not choose to. However, they are encouraged to focus on how dealing with these issues with clients makes them feel, and, consequently, how their feelings might affect the counseling relationship. This experience parallels the "real life" counseling relationship by encouraging the client to set the agenda and to focus on her feelings. There is a wide range of stimuli for students to respond to, including journal writing, the assigned readings, and classroom discussion, as well as any ongoing life experience. I act as a consultant, checking on the dyads, listening for difficulties and impasses. When I encounter a dyad that seems to be having a hard time, I help them to focus on their difficulties by exploring with them what their feelings are about the topic, their interactions, and how the counseling process and their roles are affecting their ability to participate in the task.

At the end of the individual counseling period, students gather in peer supervision groups. In these groups of about four students, class members decide collectively how to use their time. As in other supervisory experiences, the focus is on learning how to be a better counselor, to give and receive feedback, and to sharpen skills. Each week I meet with a different supervision group, as a consultant. I help the students develop a topic of concern that seems appropriate to share with the whole class. As their consultant, I assist them in clarifying concerns and framing questions. The group that I consult with is then responsible for choosing a topic for the whole class to discuss in the last section of the class time. I place emphasis on peer supervision because I believe, from my own experience and that of my colleagues, that this is an important avenue of professional growth. More continuous meaningful discussion occurs among peers than in almost any other modality. In addition, I believe that the consultation role that I play provides an opportunity for the students to experience a supervisory relationship in which they can trust a mentor, an experienced therapist, whose purpose is to foster their expertise as therapists.

The structure of this course allows students to explore their internal worlds through the response sheets and journals; they then shift from awareness of the inner self to an opportunity to learn about self in relation to another, especially within a professional role. They practice counseling in a laboratory setting that emphasizes the giving and receiving of feedback as a vital learning tool. The counseling dyads, as well as the peer supervision groups, are models for generative and collaborative work. The time that students spend in the peer education aspects of the course encourages them to take responsibility for their own learning. The skills that I model as a consultant are designed to introduce the students to consultation as a valuable professional tool, as well as to offer leadership about ways to ask for help. When we meet together periodically as a large group to evaluate how the course is going, students are encouraged to think about how the different processes and configurations of the course have contributed to their learning about counseling women.

Student Responses

> I leave the course empowered, with a heightened sense of direction, having made new sense of my life experience in the world as a woman, from and through the perspective of feminist theory and practice . . . I was able to make my own egalitarian core that runs through feminist theory. (Janet Norman, student, 1989)

Evaluation of the course is continuous. Each day at check-in time at the beginning of the class, students are invited to raise issues that have surfaced for them during the week and to address whatever concerns they might have. At mid-term, we focus our check-in time specifically on how students are feeling about their progress and the ways the course is facilitating their growth. At the end of the semester, we engage in a more summative evaluation of the course experience. Students are required to submit a final paper that includes a self-evaluation of themselves as counselors, an analysis of their counseling partnership, their thoughts about the process of change, and an evaluation of the supervision groups and other class experiences. Below is a summary of their evaluations.

Student Evaluations

Students have responded very enthusiastically to journal writing. One student commented on how, "the experience helped me to connect thought to feeling, and to take more time to reflect on what happened in the various segments of the class." She reported that

> being able to explore the topics in depth, helped me make connections to important material. How I counsel is a lot like how I was mothered! The associations between my behavior in class and my experience of my family has really made me take notice of what I need to work on.

This student's awareness of what she needed to do to change herself is an example of the power that can be generated through journal writing.

Another student wrote, "practicing her inner voice," in the journal was, "like singing in the shower."

"The private exploration that the journal affords has helped me to accept and let go of some of the pain from past injuries. This has been a process of bringing back the locus of control to myself," one student wrote on her evaluation form. Through journal writing, students have learned to take words and make them their own. From this experience they have learned to abstract knowledge and link their experiences and thoughts with their personal interests and concerns. They are aware of the counseling program's focus on 'self as instrument,' and see journaling as a way to sharpen that sense of self. Examining one's own experience is a legitimate avenue of intellectual and emotional exploration, a crucial element of feminist pedagogy.

Students experienced working with a partner as a vehicle for gaining confidence as a professional. In the words of one student, the partnership helped "create a space to work on issues of self-disclosure and empathy." Another student commented, "becoming more aware of women's issues in the counseling dyads helped me to develop a greater awareness of boundaries." Several members of the class remarked that self-disclosure seemed to deepen their understanding of the role of authenticity in a counseling relationship. They valued being able to help each other learn and discover in a noncompetitive environment. This experience seemed to emphasize the importance of allowing for the recognition and expression of feeling, being able to identify the nameless emotions attached to anxiety. "I had a heightened sense of anxiety, that I would fail my client. At least I was able to talk about it," said one of the class participants. Students became much more aware of the self-defeating roles of the perfectionist and the rescuer. "I learned to sit with the pain, not problem solve," commented another class member. One student wrote that "the power of listening encouraged the expression of voice."

It was interesting to observe the shift in attitude towards gender-linked qualities associated with the role of counselor. At the beginning of the semester, students talked about their ambivalence towards traditionally female traits in terms of their value in the counseling process. We discussed this as another way that women are devalued. During the course of the semester, they began to feel more comfort with one of the most obviously gender-linked qualities, that of nurturance. In the voice of one of the students, "I felt more o.k. about myself as a mothering person, this time with skills." The counseling dyads stimulated each woman's understanding of her relationship to traditional female roles. One woman wrote about her "newly developed understanding of authority by seeing the therapist as fallible and the client as powerful." In classroom discussion, students perceived this idea as a challenge to the social constructs that define women and the therapy process. Understanding the gender linked issues that surface in the counseling process and how they reveal themselves in the therapist/client relationship is crucial to understanding therapy from a feminist perspective.

The students valued the supervision group as a place where they could see how other counseling partners approached relationships and issues. They were able to bring to the peer group their concerns about perception of self as therapist. One student drew the parallel between the experience of being the client and the feelings associated with getting feedback in the peer supervision group. She felt "respect translated into acceptance and skillful attending."

One woman talked about how powerful it was to learn about empathy in a woman-centered environment. She shared with the class, "Being able to share my own issues about self-esteem in this environment felt very companionable. I felt like I was with people who really cared and understood. They were able to understand without being the same. This felt like heightened empathy."

Within the small group context, students were able to examine the value of working together as well as learning an appreciation for difference. Group members were able to experience each other's contribution to another's learning as an important self-teaching tool. Being able to clarify feelings, especially those related to boundaries and empathy exemplified the parallel process between therapy and learning. The women created a working environment in which they felt control and relatedness.

In the peer education portion of the class, students learned to view mistakes as opportunities to learn. They brought to the foreground issues that are usually hidden because of fear of devaluation. They understood more clearly the role of denial, grief, and anger when working with oppressed people. One woman spoke of the sense of power she felt when "I could let from the inside out what I really thought about the attitudes that foster racism and sexism." Another women spoke of this class time, "being like making a collage. The individual, social, personal, and political aspects of our lives seem to come together as we use the information gleaned from the different levels of experience."

Feedback about my teaching style and the focus on integrating theory and practice was essentially very positive. One student valued my ability to "encourage students and provide sound criticism." Another student stated that, "her attentiveness and her ability to make a person's contribution even clearer was an important strength."

"Her teaching skills and her listening skills are good. I bet she is a good therapist." This student's comment was very important to me. I felt like I had accomplished what I set out to do. The safe environment I worked to create encouraged students and inspired me. I was able to create an environment where skill, safety, the value of intellectual challenge, and the sense of community were integrated. All of our experiences mattered.

In summary, I believe that the educational environment allowed students to understand what is particularly significant about counseling women, especially from a feminist perspective. Students learned how the concerns of developing professionals can be addressed within a feminist context. Students felt recognized; they were convinced that their experiences were honored; and they believed that they had developed a deeper understanding of women's potential to be healing agents with each other. Moreover, many of the students continue to meet in peer supervision groups, and they still comment to me on the value of the classroom experience, especially as it relates to internship or work experience.

The motivating force of this feminist pedagogy is twofold. I want to use the classroom as a vehicle to challenge the social construction of gender as well as challenge the nature of education in our society. Schools, as reproductive institutions in our society, contribute to our personal and political identities. Exploring social realities and power relationships are vital to the development of a feminist perspective. I encourage students to bring their voices into the classroom, to value their subjective experience, and to expand beyond their personal experience in a way that lets them recognize the reality of another person in an appreciative way. In this classroom, being introspective and self-critical, speaking in one's own voice, being heard, and "being there" for others are all essential features of a feminist learning experience. Being able to examine one's self critically, being able to affirm self and others, and being able to act in nonoppressive ways that support change and growth are fundamentals of the feminist counseling experience.

This course thus allows me, as a progressive feminist, to explore the relationship between theory and practice within the context of the stated class goals. I find myself open to reexamining in a new and critical light my beliefs about women's power and strength. As feminist teachers, we increase the dialogue not only among the students, but among ourselves. The opportunity to write about my experience is an opportunity to strengthen this dialogue.

Works Cited

Bass, Ellen, and Laura Davis. *The Courage to Heal—A Guide for Women Survivors of Child Sexual Abuse*. New York: Harper and Row, 1988.

Cully, Margo, and Catherine Portuges, eds. *Gendered Subjects: The Dynamics of Feminist Teaching*. Boston: Routledge and Kegan Paul, 1975.

Freire, Paulo. *Education for Critical Consciousness*. New York: Herter and Herter, 1973.

—. *Pedagogy of the Oppressed*. Trans. Myra Bergman Ramos. New York: Seabury Press, 1970.

Gramsci, Antonio. "The Prison Notebooks." In *Selections from Prison Notebooks*, eds. Quinton Hoare and Geoff Nowell-Smith. New York: International Publishers, 1971.

Harding, Sandra, ed. *Feminism and Methodology*. Indiana: Indiana University Press, 1987.

Lorde, Audre. "The Master's Tool Will Never Dismantle the Master's House." In *This Bridge Called My Back: Writings by Radical Women of Color*, eds. Cherrie Morago and Gloria Anzaldua. Watertown, Mass.: Persephone Press, 1981.

Nin, Anais. "Lectures, Seminars, and Interviews." In *A Woman Speaks: The Lectures, Seminars, and Interviews of Anais Nin*, ed. Evelyn Hinz. Chicago: Swallow Press, 1975.

Progoff, Ira. *At a Journal Workshop: The Basic Text and Guide for Using the Intensive Journal*. New York: Dialogue House Library, 1975.

Sanford, Linda, and Mary Ellen Donovan. *Women and Self-Esteem*. New York: Penguin Books, 1984.

Schniedewind, Nancy, and Ellen Davidson. *Open Minds to Equality: Learning Activities to Promote Race, Sex, Class, and Age Equality*. Englewood Cliffs, N. J.: Prentice-Hall, 1983.

Smith, Dorothy. "A Women's Perspective as a Radical Critique of Sociology." In *Feminism and Methodology*, ed. Sandra Harding. Indiana: Indiana University Press, 1987.

Stanley, Liz, and Sue Wise. *Breaking Out: Feminist Consciousness and Feminist Research*. London: Routledge and Kegan Paul, 1983.

Tong, Rosemary. *Feminist Thought*. Boulder, Colo.: Westview Press, 1989.

Weiler, Kathleen. *Women Teaching for Change: Gender, Class, and Power*. South Hadley, Mass.: Bergin and Garvey, 1988.

Chapter 7

Woman as Witch: The Renaissance and Reformations Revisited

Judith Ochshorn

> History is not written today for people of past times but for people of our own times. The antiquarian understanding of history is not only epistemologically impossible but also historically undesirable. What needs to be recovered is the understanding of history not as artifact but as "historical consciousness" for the present and the future . . . (Fiorenza 1985, 51)

> Thus far, historians have spent a little time and energy explaining the role of women in the history of witchcraft but have paid no attention to the role of witchcraft in the history of women . . . from 1480 to 1700, more women were killed for witchcraft than for other crimes put together. (Monter 1977, 132–3)

> Until the twentieth century, it could be argued plausibly that the witch craze was the most sustained and statistically the greatest instance of mass persecution in Western history. (Klaits 1985, 18)

> I believe that the sudden rise in prosecutions for witchcraft that began in Europe c. 1560 was related in part to attempts to take away women's control of their sexual and reproductive lives. (Barstow 1988, 8)

Attempts to recover women's history are not entirely new. What is new is that the 500-year exclusion of women from European and American universities came to a close in the nineteenth and twentieth centuries. In the past two decades, there has been a confluence of some of the latest of several generations of educated women and the reemergence of feminism, in which the former were, in part, products of a movement whose questions and challenges they helped to articulate. One important aspect of this process has been a serious revision of women's history, placing in the foreground of scholarly inquiries what formerly comprised a silent, unobtrusive background.

Like the recently emergent fields of social and family history, women's history looks at the past "from the bottom up," focusing on ordinary, anonymous, historically marginalized people and their everyday activities that helped to shape the past but were assigned no importance by most historians, and therefore were rendered invisible. But beyond all that, historians of women assert that a study of gender and the significance attached to it must be added to all other basic categories of analysis. Feminist historians argue that one characteristic of androcentric, male-dominated societies has been that the historical experiences of women have most often been different from those of men. Hence, historical accounts that ignore female experiences are only partial, less accurate and comprehensive than those that include them. Indeed, they are accounts only of elite groups of men. In addition, most feminist scholars contend that gender is socially constructed, and historians of women have assembled a rich and complex body of data that counter assumptions about the "nature" of women and the inevitability of their social status. Among the effects of this conceptual shift has been a fundamental challenge to historical periodization itself, or how we understand what transpired in the past (cf. Cott and Pleck 1979, 24; Lerner 1986, 3–6).

Other than commemorating its victims, why return to the witchcraft trials of early modern Europe? Beyond Santayana's well-worn admonition that those ignorant of their history are doomed to relive it, most simply, the experiences of European witches are our own insofar as these women were able to be savaged specifically because they were female. Also, knowledge and reevaluation of our past might help those of us who have spent years studying, explaining, putting into proper context, and excusing the problematic ideas of those great men whose thought undergirds much of the Western intellectual tradition and who were, simultaneously, misogynistic, indeed those whose theoretical outposts lie squarely in our own heads. We have become experts on the difference between the baby and the bath water.

What I propose to outline are the following: 1) some of the assumptions that I and others make about the past; 2) the nature and extent of the witchcraft trials in sixteenth- and seventeenth-century Europe; 3) why those trials were not only an integral part of the Protestant and Catholic Reformations (as has recently and persuasively been argued by some), but also an integral part of the Renaissance (which has been somewhat more difficult for many to accept given our identification of the latter as the age of Leonardo and Shakespeare); 4) the enormity of the silence of theologians, philosophers, and historians—then, subsequently, and now—about the witch hunts; 5) a number of scholarly explanations of the witch craze; and 6) by implication, the enormity of the task of recovering our past, and the cost if we do not.

Like others, I assume that even if women's historical experiences have been different from those of men, and even in male-dominated societies, the activities of women have had as much historical significance as those of men. I also assume that women, like men, have been central rather than peripheral to the creation of culture. However, in the narrations and interpretations of the past and in the assignment of greater historical significance to male rather than female activities, the latter have been displaced from the center of Western history (cf. Plaskow 1990; Lerner 1986; Fiorenza 1983; Brooten 1982).

Also, prevailing ideologies about the significance of gender and gender differences have always been fundamental to the structure of society and thought. In short, the mentality that accounted for the experiences of accused witches in the sixteenth and seventeenth centuries both reflected and, in important ways, was central to the content and course of the Renaissance and Reformations.

No account of the past is totally objective, unmediated by the values and language of past times and places as well as those of our own. As Elisabeth Schussler Fiorenza aptly phrases it, history is not only "of" certain events in the past but is also written "for" a particular audience of one's own time. It is never wholly value-neutral or nonideological, nor should it be, but rather it expresses "our experiential presuppositions or institutional interests." Indeed, it is what enables us "to make the causal link between the past and our world" (1985, 50, 52).

As a student, one of the first things I learned about doing historical research, and what I have taught my own students endlessly, is that one must not project contemporary values and judgments on an earlier and different world. Lately, I have come to believe that just as linear causality does not entirely explain our past, except retrospectively, so there have been very influential leaps of consciousness—e.g., in our century, in the thinking of Albert Einstein and Simone de Beauvoir—that are so original and take such risks, that, in some ways, they transcend the explanatory context of their own time. In other words, historical context, while usually staking out the parameters of our imagination, does not irrevocably determine the ideas or behavior that emerge out of it, ideas and behavior that, in turn, comprise part of any historical context.

Furthermore, aspects of traditional scholarly detachment, even if possible, often lead to a sense of historical functionalism, i.e., "that whatever was was right." This alleged objectivity fails to distinguish among varieties of human experiences, and tends to discount what they meant to those who experienced them. For example, I think that slavery was as onerous in the ancient world as in the nineteenth century when viewed from the vantage point of the slave, whether or not there was a fully developed belief in the value of the individual in ancient Greece and Rome. Likewise, I believe that the rape and torture of women accused of witchcraft was as difficult for them to endure in the sixteenth and seventeenth centuries as it would be for us today, regardless of how those accusations were philosophically justified, and whether or not lower-class women were valued at that time. In short, when we try to understand our past and its significance through the eyes of members of oppressed groups, we get quite a different assessment than that conveyed by the articulate and powerful, remembering that one constant throughout most of Western history, at least since the twelfth century, has been the educational deprivation of most women.

Turning to the witch trials, the numbers are staggering, given that estimates of women accused of witchcraft (in the absence of complete or accurate sources) range from ca. 100,000 (Monter 1987 213–14, 203–04; Barstow 1988, 7) to over eight million (Gimbutas 1989, 319). The trials, peaking from ca. 1560 to 1670, extended across Europe from England and Scandinavia through France, Germany, Switzerland, Italy, Spain, and the borderlands between them, moving to New England in the seventeenth century and to Poland and Russia in the eighteenth. The last witch was burned in Europe in the 1780s, ca. 210 years ago.

On average, 80 percent, in some areas more than 90 percent, of those accused, and 85 percent of those executed, were women. They were often lower-class, and/or widows, and/or old, often midwives and healers (either because they were especially valued or especially vulnerable, and the arguments for both are plausible, cf. Klaits 1985, 92–103; Barstow 1988, 17). Often the accused were independent and unattached to men (Monter 1977, 132–33; Barstow 1985, 41; Klaits 1985, 95).

For example, in Spain, where the Inquisition was relatively mild, its full force was directed against the beatas of Seville, the most celebrated of them madre Catalina de Jesus. Charismatic, visionary mystics at the forefront of an inward-looking religious revival, these women took vows of poverty and chastity, prophesied, prayed, and criticized traditional religion, all of this outside of the jurisdiction of convent or husband. Amassing a large following among women and men who acknowledged their spiritual authority over them, the beatas ended up publicly degraded and imprisoned by the Holy Office, isolated from their followers in strict enclosure, and trivialized and vilified in legend as weak, hysterical women (Perry 1990, 97–117). When forced to participate in an *auto de fe*, "Often gagged, these women paid with silence the penance demanded of audacious females" (Perry 1990, 5).

Beyond these "facts," all that we know about the content of the witchcraft trials and confessions, the Sabbats and pacts with the Devil, come from the records of inquisitors, judges, and prosecutors–and frequently the last two roles were merged–as well as the writings of learned men who confirmed the necessity for inquisitorial proceedings and the "truth" they yielded. With rare exceptions, e.g., when the accused were upper-class men and had the means to have their letters smuggled out of prison (cf. the letter of Johannes Junius, Burgomaster of Bamberg, to his daughter in 1628, in Kors and Peters 1984, 253–59), the alleged witches themselves left no written records of their experiences, beliefs, feelings, perceptions of reality, or ordeals. Therefore, it is a bit tricky to assert *anything* about the accused witches or their states of mind; however, this has not deterred scholars (cf. Russell 1972, 285, 287).

Despite all the diversity in the trials—in their frequency, the incidence of torture used in interrogations, the ecclesiastical or secular nature of the courts, the numbers condemned to die compared with those given milder sentences or freed—there were some commonalities.

Since witchcraft was considered an "exceptional" crime by the authorities once it became associated with arch-heresy, ordinary legal safeguards for the accused were suspended and a judicial system evolved, particularly in Germany, which itself became conducive to witch trials. For example, contrary to precedent, false or unproven accusations no longer could result in punishment for the accuser. Very young children could denounce or bear witness against the accused or, in the Basque country, were themselves confessed witches (Klaits 1985, 169; Kors and Peters 1984, 341). With the exception of England, torture was routinely administered as the interrogatory method of first choice, always, according to the judges, for the good of the accused's soul (cf. Klaits 1985, 73, 128–58; Russell 1972, 287). Since the torture of suspects would not cease until the desired answers were given (cf. Klaits 1985, 128–59), it is not surprising that what the records most often show are similar responses to formulaic questions. Also, judges and scholars have not counted the rape of the accused by jailers as torture (Barstow 1985, 42; Daly 1990, 201–02). Those trials, in fact, were paradigms of power and powerlessness, initiated and presided over by the most educated men in Europe who prosecuted mostly lower-class women.

According to Joseph Klaits, the witch craze developed and flourished only when educated people (read men) connected rural, lower-class beliefs in supernatural forces, and their ability to cause suffering, with heretical activities and Devil worship:

> Elite groups—lawyers and judges, theologians and other clerics, physicians and philosophers, rulers and wealthy landowners—were the ones who vigorously asserted the reality of cults devoted to Satan. By transmitting their fears to the uneducated majority, the authorities transformed the traditional popular suspicion of harmful magic into terror of devil worshipers. (Klaits 1985, 16–17; see too Kors and Peters 1984, 10)

The witch craze and the specific identification of women with the practice of witchcraft embodied male animosity toward women, translated it into sexual terms, and acted it out violently. Indeed, the increasing association of eroticism with violence by the sixteenth century, the denunciation of the accused as whores and witches, the belief in the explicit sexual servitude of the witch to the Devil through her pact with him, the enduring belief that women are more carnal than men and have great power over male sexuality, all of these expressed not just fear of the Devil but of female sexuality and its power (Barstow 1985, 41; Klaits 1985, 65–77; Russell 1972, 73–75, 76–78, 284–85; Kors and Peters 1984, 127, 151).

Both Catholic and Protestant churches kept their hands "clean." When the trials took place in ecclesiastical rather than secular courts, while church officials encouraged denunciations, interrogated suspects, and authorized torture to get at the "truth," once the victims' guilt was established they were "relaxed" to the secular arm of the government for punishment. The churches did not burn one witch.

E. William Monter does not find it strange, given the misogyny in European literature, philosophy, and religion, that it was overwhelmingly women who came to be accused of committing *malefice*, all sorts of foul and destructive acts. What he questions (a query less susceptible to a clear, uncomplicated answer), is *why* these accusations of witchcraft became widespread and lethal in the sixteenth and seventeenth centuries (Monter 1977, 133). Obviously, many factors contributed to their spread. Among these were: 1) the durability of the double standard and the strengthening of the patriarchal family in the sixteenth century, when women's status reached a nadir in the social relations of the sexes; 2) economic hard times during the development of proto-capitalism, beset by recurrent plagues and famines, and the search for scapegoats to explain inexplicable disasters; 3) a belief, across classes, in the intervention of the supernatural in everyday life; 4) a centralizing church and state and the involvement of each in the affairs of the other; 5) the missionary zeal of elite Protestant and Catholic reformers in their attempts to complete the Christianization of Europe by stamping out paganism, exemplified by what they viewed as the sexual immorality of lower-class rural women; and 6) the revival of works by misogynistic classical writers whose ideas about women were merged with Christian misogyny in Renaissance humanism (cf. Stone 1975; Agonito 1977, 43–56, 69–90; Stuard 1987, 153–72; Bell 1973, 17–21; Cantarella 1987; Pomeroy 1975).

Since the nineteenth century, the Renaissance and Reformations have been seen as watersheds in European history. The first, marked by genius in the arts and the "rebirth" of ancient Greek and Roman masterpieces, also saw the emergence of concepts precious to modern western culture, e.g., individualism, and rewards for talent and accomplishment rather than for birth alone (cf. Burckhardt 1961). The second, marked by a belief in "the priesthood of all believers," sanctioned the right of individual access to the divine independent of ecclesiastical hierarchies and, presumably, of sex. Protestantism articulated an "ethic" of individual responsibility that legitimized and facilitated the development of a "spirit" of capitalism based, of course, on individualism, in a process of development characterized by reciprocity and mutual reinforcement between the two (Weber 1930). Hence, it is with some discomfort that many scholars have danced around the possibility that the ideology and practices of the witch hunts not only flared during the Renaissance and Reformations but were, in fact, deeply embedded in their very fabric. But it was more than that, as Joan Kelly argues:

> . . . the moment one assumes that women are a part of humanity in the fullest sense . . . the set of events with which we deal takes on a wholly different character or meaning from the normally accepted one. Indeed, what emerges is a fairly regular pattern of relative loss of status for women precisely in those periods of so-called progressive change. (Kelly 1984a; and cf. Lerner 1969)

More specifically, Kelly demonstrates that the women belonging to the "normative" upper and middle-classes that established the character of the Renaissance did not have the same experiences as the men of their own classes but, instead, suffered a relative loss of status, i.e., relative to the men and the earlier period (Kelly 1984b, 19–50). What I am contending here is that the Renaissance, the Protestant Reformation, and the Catholic Counter-Reformation, all were, most profoundly, male enterprises.

Prior to the twelfth century, cultural pluralism and social diversity, e.g., with regard to Jews, homosexuals, even religious nonconformists, usually were easily accepted (Klaits 1985, 19–21). At a time of decentralized political power, before the separation of the public and private spheres, women were able to exercise considerable political and economic power through their family roles and, across classes, through their economic productivity (Stuard 1987, 154–58; McNamara and Wemple 1977, 104–09; Herlihy 1962, 89–120). In the less formally and academically structured frontier societies of the earlier Middle Ages, brilliant women were publicly influential and honored in the expansion and consolidation of the church and state (McNamara and Wemple 1977 96–100; Labalme 1984, 3; Wemple 1987, 140-1; Eckenstein 1896). After the twelfth century, institutional structures gradually evolved that supported the development of capitalism and the centralization of church and state, both reflecting and sanctioning the gradual increase of emphasis on the significance of gender differences and gender hierarchy. They, in turn, played themselves out in institutional arrangements relating to dowries and marriages, perhaps particularly in the middle and upper classes (cf. Stuard 1987, 160–72). Medieval beliefs about the roughly similar capacities of women and men came to be replaced, in the by then all-male universities of the twelfth and thirteenth centuries, by Aristotelian notions of the absolute polarity and "natural" hierarchy of the sexes. In addition, neo-Platonism, which tended to spiritualize and objectify women colored the thought of many

male humanists (Kelly 1984b, 36–47). Over time, the ideas of Aristotle
and Plato were dispersed among the sons of the ascendant middle class
who were being educated like their noble brothers, so that the High
Middle Ages experienced what Susan Stuard named "the dominion of
gender" (Stuard 1987, 153–72). In other words, the high value placed
on individualism and the rewards for talent regardless of birth were
applicable primarily to Renaissance men.

Italy provides a prototype of this crucial change in attitude. In
Renaissance Italy, the most influential groups prized learning; indeed,
the latter became a cultural requirement for the *true* Renaissance man.
At the same time, learned women's lives took a totally different
trajectory. Educated women, all upper-class, were subjected to hostility.
They were considered (and often considered themselves) deviant,
compelled to choose between a convent and a "book-lined cell" in their
parents' homes, variously seen as asexual blocks of ice, or literally men
because of their intellect, or as engaging in incest or promiscuity (King
1978, 807–31; King 1984, 66–90; Anderson and Zinsser 1988, 89–96;
Labalme 1984, 4). The experience of Elena Lucrezia Cornaro
exemplifies the "sea change" in attitudes from the twelfth century on,
as Italy moved through the stages of the Renaissance. The Venetian
prodigy, Elena Lucrezia Cornaro, when pushed by her father to redeem
the glory of her family, qualified in 1677 to be examined for a doctorate
in sacred theology but (since that would have enabled her to teach
future theologians and priests) instead had to accept a doctorate in
philosophy. Famous for her erudition, she nevertheless ordered most of
her writings destroyed and left little of real consequence. She always
denied her femininity, and said of herself and all women: " . . . the
highest ornament of woman is silence. They are made only to stay at
home, not go abroad" (Labalme 1984, 140–43). In general, in the
encompassing masculine milieu of the Renaissance, even when women
achieved prominence in economic, professional, or political life, they
usually were denied or themselves refused leadership roles (Smith 1976,
97–114; Casey 1976, 224–49; Kelly 1984b, 19–50).

The same kind of marginalization typified the lives of working-class
women in the early modern economy, whose labor on the land, in towns
and cities, and at home, all contributed heavily to the growth of
capitalism. But though their economic productivity was indispensable,
the prevailing ideology, as in the case of the marginalization of learned
women, diminished the importance of that productivity and ultimately
helped determine the character and perceived valued of women's work.
Increasingly, the gulf between women's work and men's work widened,

so that the work women did, certainly within the home as well as elsewhere, came to be devalued as was, by implication, the worker herself (Wiesner 1987b, 221–49; Wiesner 1987a, 64–74).

The downside of the Protestant Reformation involved, among other things, the disestablishment of communities of women as well as the dethroning of Mary both as icon for women and mother of God. Despite the priesthood of all believers, the presumed equal right of women to read the Bible did not always guarantee their systematic education (Monter 1987, 201–02). Martin Luther's belief that women were naturally made for domestic work and rearing children (Luther, 1524, in O'Faolain and Martines 1973, 196–97), and John Calvin's assertion that God imposed the necessity of marriage on men to remedy their lust, as well as his strong opposition to women assuming priestly functions (Calvin, 1560, in O'Faolain and Martines 1973, 199–200, 202–03), all suggest that, with the exception of dissident sects (e.g., the Anabaptists and Quakers), while Protestants believed in the equality of souls, on this earth women were to be subordinated within the family and society. Unremarkably, few individual women converted to Protestantism in the sixteenth century and, when they did, it was most often in the company of male kin. As for the Catholic Counter-Reformation, it continued to meet the wishes of nuns to engage in community service with the requirement of strict enclosure (Monter 1987, 205–11; Davis 1975, 65–95).

Thus, with the political, intellectual, economical, and religious marginalization of women during the Renaissance and Reformations, it becomes more apparent why the witch mania could have occurred. The extreme masculine perspective of this period might not have been necessary, but it was certainly a sufficient condition for the creation of the soil in which the woman-hating witch hunts took root and flourished.

The ways in which the witchcraft trials have (or have not) been explained beggar the imagination. The most enlightened contemporaries, e.g., Montaigne, expressed doubt that the fanaticism of Inquisitorial methods could lead to knowledge of the truth (Kors and Peters 1984, 332–37). However, the silence of the rationalists and empiricists of the time was deafening. As Mary Daly sees it (and I believe she is correct):

The acceptability of witchburning in Renaissance society is evident in the absence of objections to the massacre in the writings of such prominent and prolific thinkers as Bacon, Grotius, Selden, and Descartes, who "flourished" in the early seventeenth century, the peak period of the witchcraze. (Daly 1990, 202)

Even when a few, like Montaigne in the sixteenth century, had reservations, there was no real challenge to the trials or their underlying misogyny. Likewise, recent analyses of Enlightenment views of women (Kleinbaum 1977, 217–35; Fox-Genovese 1987, 251–77) indicate that, while seventeenth- and eighteenth-century philosophers relied on reason as a means of detecting and remedying social injustice, none of them analyzed the very recent treatment of women as witches as particularly unjust. Many of them attacked the church as superstitious and backward and believed that all institutions ought to be scrutinized in the light of reason, but most of them neither attacked the churches' view of women's inferiority as particularly superstitious or backward, nor scrutinized beliefs about the nature of women held by the Inquisition, nor even disputed those views prevalent in their own time. For the most part, generalities about women's nature remained untouched and unchallenged.

Perhaps just as important, eighteenth-century thought promoted a belief in the value of individualism and the equality of individuals, but most of the latter were understood to be male. Most Enlightenment philosophers (with notable exceptions, e.g., Mary Wollstonecraft and the Marquis de Condorcet) continued to see women as polar opposites of men, and tended to view women more than men primarily in terms of their sex and sexuality. It is doubtful that philosophers' "elevation" of middle-class mothers to a "pedestal" represented progress for those women or any others, and that view tended to reinforce the deep ambivalence toward women in modern Europe. In short, the new cosmology of the seventeenth and eighteenth centuries, frequently credited with bringing an end to the witch hunts, had little to do with challenging assumptions about the nature of women or with improving their lot. It remained for later feminists to appropriate Enlightenment ideas and modify them to include women in the category of the human.

In our own time until the 1960s, although there had been local documentation of the witch trials, there was no scholarly interest in or comprehensive explanation of witchcraft, except for Margaret Murray's now-discredited earlier theory of surviving pagan cults (Monter 1972, 38–9). By 1972, the issue of why the majority of the accused were women had not yet been examined (Monter 1972, 450). By 1988, despite unquestioned evidence to the contrary, "historians have for the most part not dealt with the persecutions as an attack on women" (Barstow 1988, 9). Indeed, it is perfectly possible to write a social history of early modern Europe and not mention witchcraft at all (cf. Huppert 1986).

There is a dearth of straightforward discussion by scholars about the etiology and content of the witch hunts. First, there is silence or denial about witchcraft or that the accused witches were women. Next, there is a curious shift of responsibility so that culpability is shared by the accuser and the accused who, in this scenario, collaborated on the accusations and confessions given under torture: "Each for their own reasons, then, the learned and the illiterate combined to prosecute and burn thousands for witchcraft" (Klaits 1985, 17; see too Larner 1981, 156; Russell 1972, 286). Then there is the claim that some confessions were voluntary rather than offered under fear of torture (cf. Ginzburg 1983). There is the approach that focuses on the sincerity and idealism of the inquisitors, ever ready to save errant souls (cf. Russell 1972, 287; Klaits 1985, 78; Baroja 1973, 256–57).

Finally, blame is placed entirely on the witches, on the theory that these women were simply mentally ill, hysterical, delusional, neurotic, or, alternatively, more devoted than men to heresy and therefore more attached to witchcraft (cf. Russell 1972, 282–83; Szasz 1970; Zilboorg 1969).

It may be that these intellectual contortions spring not only from a denial of the existence of misogyny but also from scholarly detachment. Here, for example, is one reputable scholar of witchcraft:

> . . . though the female sex in general was blamed for witchcraft, little girls in particular were not. If their mothers had exposed them to the evil, they were sometimes flogged and forced to witness the execution of their parents [sic], but only seldom was a prepubertal girl herself executed. Perhaps the authorities had some pity for children. . . (Russell 1972, 284)

And then, accepting the *inquisitors'* testimony about the activities of witches, he compares "the orgiastic elements of the witches' revels" to the rites of Tantric Buddhism! (Russell 1972, 284).

There are references to the sixteenth-century Jean Bodin, a " . . . learned and humane scholar and statesman, and one of the earliest defenders of toleration in a century of religious hatreds and bloodshed" immediately followed by: "On the subject of witchcraft, however, Bodin was a traditionalist and an implacable enemy of all who would question the justice of the witch-hunt-and-execution" (Kors and Peters 1984, 213). Thus are wedded, in our own time, learning, humaneness, statesmanship, defense of toleration, and the widespread hunting and execution of women as witches.

This is the stuff of high rhetoric. But as Monter accurately maintains: "The sad truth is that, in women's 'real' social history, the pedestal is almost impossible to find, but the stake is everywhere" (Monter 1977, 135). If we do not reconceptualize our past so that we understand the witchcraft persecutions as part of the history of women, the Renaissance, and the Reformations; if we do not question the great silences and distortions about the lives of lower-class women, the past will be rendered meaningless to the present and future. We shall have become complicit in denying, discounting, and trivializing the lives and pain of those women as well as our own.

Works Cited

Agonito, Rosemary, ed. *History of Ideas on Women: A Sourcebook.* New York: G. P. Putnam's Sons, 1977.

Anderson, Bonnie S., and Judith Zinsser. *A History of Their Own: From Prehistory to the Present.* New York: Harper and Row, 1988.

Baroja, Julio Caro. *The World of Witches.* Trans. O.N.V. Glendinning. Chicago: University of Chicago Press, 1973.

Barstow, Anne Llewellyn. "Joan of Arc and Female Mysticism." *Journal of Feminist Studies in Religion* I (Fall 1985): 29–42.

—. "On Studying Witchcraft as Women's History: A Historiography of the European Witch Persecutions" *Journal of Feminist Studies in Religion* IV (Fall 1988): 7–19.

Bell, Susan Groag, ed. *Women: From the Greeks to the French Revolution.* Belmont, Calif.: Wadsworth Publishing Co., 1973.

Boxer, Marilyn J., and Jean H. Quatert. *Connecting Spheres: Women in the Western World, 1500 to the Present.* New York: Oxford University Press, 1987.

Brooten, Bernadette. *Women Leaders in the Ancient Synagogue: Inscriptional Evidence and Background Issues.* Brown Judaic Studies 36 (1982), Atlanta: Scholars' Press.

Burckhardt, Jacob. 1860. Reprint. *The Civilization of the Renaissance in Italy,* ed. Irene Gordon. New York: Mentor Books, The New American Library, 1961.

Cantarella, Eva. 1978. *Pandora's Daughters: The Role and Status of Women in Greek and Roman Antiquity*, trans. Maureen B. Fant. Baltimore: Johns Hopkins University Press, 1987.

Casey, Kathleen, "The Cheshire Cat: Reconstructing the Experience of Medieval Women." In *Liberating Women's History: Theoretical and Critical Essays*, ed. Berenice Carroll, 224–49. Urbana: University of Illinois Press, 1976.

Cott, Nancy F., and Elizabeth H. Pleck. *A Heritage of her Own: Toward a New Social History of American Women*. New York: Simon and Schuster, 1979.

Daly, Mary. 1978. Reprint. *Gyn/Ecology: The Metaethics of Radical Feminism*. Boston: Beacon Press, 1990.

Davis, Natalie Zemon. *Society and Culture in Early Modern France*. Stanford: Stanford University Press, 1975.

Eckenstein, Lina. *Woman under Monasticism*. Cambridge, Mass.: Cambridge University Press, 1896.

Fiorenza, Elisabeth Schussler. *In Memory of Her: A Feminist Theological Reconstruction of Christian Origins*. New York: Crossroad Publishing, 1983.

—. "Remembering the Past in Creating the Future: Historical-critical Scholarship and Feminist Biblical Interpretation." In *Feminist Perspectives on Biblical Scholarship*, ed. Adela Yarbro Collins. Chico, Calif.: Scholars Press, 1985.

Fox-Genovese, Elizabeth. "Women and the Enlightenment." In *Becoming Visible: Women in European History*, eds. Renate Bridenthal, Claudia Koonz, and Susan Stuard. 2d ed. Boston: Houghton Mifflin, 1987.

Gimbutas, Marija. *The Language of the Goddess*. San Francisco: Harper and Row, 1989.

Ginzburg, Carlo. *The Night Battles: Witchcraft and Agrarian Cults in the Sixteenth and Seventeenth Centuries*. Trans. John Tedeschi and Anne Tedeschi. Baltimore: Johns Hopkins University Press, 1983.

Herlihy, David. "Land, Family, and Women in Continental Europe" 701–1200. *Traditio* 18 (1962): 89–120.

Huppert, George. *After the Black Death: A Social History of Early Modern Europe*. Bloomington: Indiana University Press, 1986.

Kelly, Joan. 1976. "The Social Relation of the Sexes." In *Women, History, and Theory: The Essays of Joan Kelly*. Chicago: University of Chicago Press, 1984a.

—. 1977. "Did Women Have a Renaissance?" In *Women, History and Theory: The Essays of Joan Kelly*. Chicago: University of Chicago Press, 1984b.

Kelso, Ruth. *Doctrine for the Lady of the Renaissance*. Urbana: University of Illinois Press, 1956.

King, Margaret Leah. "The Religious Retreat of Isotta Nogarola (1418–1466): Sexism and its Consequences in the Fifteenth Century." *Signs: Journal of Women in Culture and Society* (Summer 1978): 807–31.

—. "Book-lined cells: Women and Humanism in the Early Italian Renaissance." In *Beyond their Sphere: Learned Women of the European Past*, ed. Patricia Labalme, 66–90. New York: New York University Press, 1984.

Klaits, Joseph. *Servants of Satan: The Age of the Witch Hunts*. Bloomington: Indiana University Press, 1985.

Kleinbaum, Abby. "Women in the Age of Light." In *Becoming Visible: Women in European History*, eds. Renate Bridenthal and Claudia Koonz, 217–35. 1st ed. Boston: Houghton Mifflin, 1977.

Kors, Alan C., and Edward Peters. *Witchcraft in Europe 1100–1700: A Documentary History*. Philadelphia: University of Pennsylvania Press, 1984.

Labalme, Patricia H. *Beyond their Sex: Learned Women of the European Past*. New York: New York University Press, 1984.

Larner, Christina. *Enemies of God: The Witch-Hunt in Scotland*. Baltimore: Johns Hopkins University Press, 1981.

Lerner, Gerda. "The Lady and the Mill Girl: Changes in the Status of Women in the Age of Jackson." *Midcontinent American Studies Journal* 10 (Spring 1969): 5–14.

—. *The Creation of Patriarchy*. New York: Oxford University Press, 1986.

McNamara, Joann, and Suzanne F. Wemple. "Sanctity and Power: The Dual Pursuit of Medieval Women." In *Becoming Visible*, eds. Claudia Bridenthal and Renate Koonz, 90–118. 1st ed. Boston: Houghton Mifflin, 1977.

Monter, E. William. "Inflation and Witchcraft: The Case of Jean Bodin." In *Action and Conviction in Early Modern Europe: Essays in Honor of E. H. Harbison*, eds. Theodore K. Rabb and Jerrold E. Siegel. Princeton: Princeton University Press, 1969.

—. "The Historiography of European Witchcraft: Progress and Prospects." *The Journal of Interdisciplinary History* II (1972): 435–51.

—. "The Pedestal and the Stake: Courtly Love and Witchcraft." In *Becoming Visible*, eds. Renate Bridenthal and Claudia Koonz, 119–36. 1st ed. Boston: Houghton Mifflin, 1977.

—. "Protestant Wives, Catholic Saints, and the Devil's Handmaid: Women in the Age of Reformations." In *Becoming Visible*, eds. Renate Bridenthal and Claudia Koonz, 203–11. 2d ed.Boston: Houghton Mifflin, 1987.

O'Faolain, Julia, and Lauro Martines, eds. *Not in God's Image: Women in History from the Greeks to the Victorians*. New York: Harper Torchbooks, 1973.

Perry, Mary Elizabeth. *Gender and Disorder in Early Modern Seville*. Princeton: Princeton University Press, 1990.

Plaskow, Judith. *Standing Again at Sinai: Judaism from a Feminist Perspective*. San Francisco: Harpercollins, 1990.

Pomeroy, Sarah. *Goddesses, Whores, Wives, and Slaves: Women in Classical Antiquity*. New York: Schocken Books, 1975.

Russell, Jeffrey Burton. *Witchcraft in the Middle Ages*. Ithaca: Cornell University Press, 1972.

Smith, Hilda. "Gynecology and Ideology in Seventeenth-Century England." In *Liberating Women's History: Theoretical and Critical Essays*, ed. Berenice Carroll. Urbana: University of Illinois Press, 1976.

Stone, Lawrence. "The Rise of the Nuclear Family in Early Modern England: The Patriarchal Stage." In *The Family in History*, ed. Charles Rosenberg, 13–57. Philadelphia: The University of Pennsylvania Press, 1975.

—. *The Family, Sex, and Marriage in England, 1500–1800*. New York: Harper Torchbooks, 1979.

Stuard, Susan. "The Dominion of Gender: Women's Fortunes in the High Middle Ages." In *Becoming Visible*, eds. Renate Bridenthal, Claudia Koonz, and Susan Stuard, 153–72. 2d ed. 1987.

Szasz, Thomas S. *Ideology and Insanity; Essays on the Psychiatric Dehumanization of Man*. Garden City, N. Y.: Anchor Books, 1970.

Weber, Max. *The Protestant Ethic and the Spirit of Capitalism*, Trans. Talcott Parsons. New York: Scribner's, 1930.

Wemple, Suzanne F. "Sanctity and Power. In *Becoming Visible*, eds. Renate Bridenthal, Claudia Koonz, and Susan Stuard, 131-151. 2d ed.Boston: Houghton Mifflin, 1987.

Wiesner, Merry E. "Women's Work in the Changing City Economy, 1500–1650." In *Connecting Spheres*, Marilyn J. Boxer and Jean H. Quatert, 64–74. New York: Oxford University Press, 1987.

—. "Spinning Out Capital: Women's Work in the Early Modern Economy." In *Becoming Visible*, eds. Renate Bridenthal, Claudia Koonz, and Susan Stuard, 220–49. 2d ed. 1987.

Zilboorg, Gregory. *The Medical Man and the Witch during the Renaissance*. New York: Cooper Square Publishers, 1969.

Part II

How does a feminist perspective influence *how* we teach in the classroom?

Chapter 8

Hyper-feminisms: Poststructuralist Theories, Popular Culture, and Pedagogy

Lisa S. Starks

The "departmentalization" of feminism in academic institutions has resulted in a strange phenomenon: stereotypes of the "feminist" and of "feminism." "Feminism," which has become synonymous with "women's studies," is often characterized as a monolithic discourse that is fixed and rigid in its ideological/political straightjacket, separated and disassociated from the patriarchal discourses that surround it. Hence, academic feminism or women's studies feminists have inherited an image supported by the media and perpetuated by many women's studies professors and college students alike, an image of which many feminists may be unaware. The image of the women's studies teacher as an "asexual women's libber" who condemns pornography, censures heterosexual desire, and prohibits any traditionally "feminine" pleasure; who lacks both a sense of humor and an open mind; and who retreats into an ascetic existence to avoid the world she scorns may seem antithetical to what one may define as a "feminist." However, this image would be recognized as the portrait of a feminist in contemporary American culture.

Whether one wishes to acknowledge it or not, this image saturates popular art and dictates opinion. Television shows such as "Star Trek: The Next Generation" and "Saturday Night Live" have attempted to question and satirize the assumptions underlying this rigid "feminism," and in doing so have further solidified this concept of the American feminist. The 1991–92 season of "Star Trek: The Next Generation" included an episode entitled "The Outcast" (Piller 1992), which depicts a planet of asexual, non-gendered beings (who sport "butch" lesbian attire and haircuts, the popular conception of a "feminist uniform"). On this planet, these beings are forced to erase any traces of heterosexual desire or gendered identity. Those who adopt feminine or masculine behavior or heterosexual preference are brainwashed and conditioned to be genderless, like everyone else. This episode criticizes the treatment of homosexuals in contemporary culture, while simultaneously attributing this narrow-minded perspective to a species who enforce androgyny. In a more humorous vein, "Saturday Night Live" (Michaels 1991-92) satirizes the idealization of "androgyny" attributed to feminism in the character of "Pat," an extremely unattractive androgynous person whose gender is ultimately undeterminable. "Pat" is so popular that s/he appeared in the 1992 Emmy awards presentation in a skit with two perfect stereotypes or human caricatures of femininity and masculinity: Burt Reynolds and Loni Anderson. "Star Trek" and "Saturday Night Live" are two examples among many that illustrate the popular conception of the kind of world "feminists" advocate: one devoid of gender difference or difference of any kind—bland, humorless, pleasureless—the economy of the same.

The problem seems to stem from confusion over the term "feminism." As those with a background in feminist theories know, there is no one "feminism," but rather many "feminisms." However, most people outside these discourses are completely unaware of diverse feminist ideas that have taken shape in the last couple of decades and that are presently taking place in various countries, especially France. The popular conception of feminism fuses attitudes from different phases of feminist thought. What results is an image of the feminist as an androgynous, genderless woman who has denounced men and heterosexuality and labels anything that is contrary to her lifestyle as "patriarchal." Briefly, this image is made up of assumptions derived from both the first and second waves of feminism in its second phase (fifties to present). First-wave feminists, for the most part, attempted to search for the origins of women's oppression; whereas, second-wave feminists argued for a "woman-centered" perspective (see Eisenstein 1983, xi–xx). To those outside of these discourses, the first-wave feminists became the bra-burners who "wanted to be men," and the second-wave feminists became radical lesbians who desired nothing more than to eliminate men and live in a women's utopia. When conflated through the media, this dichotomy presented a paradoxical view of the feminist: she hated men, but ultimately wanted to be one. The second-wave perspective does appear to offer a reversal of the first, advocating a view of women as essentially caring, nurturing people who are superior to men, while simultaneously working towards political and economical equality for women. This contradiction does present a problem, one that many contemporary feminists are now tackling.

I, along with many other feminists, have attempted to redefine "feminism" to rid it of the essentialism that has led to the either pro-masculine woman or pro-feminine woman fallacy. In my view (which is greatly influenced by continental feminism, feminist appropriations of poststructuralist theories, and the views of feminists like Judith Butler and Sandra Harding), a feminist is one who studies gender in order to demystify the essentialist mythologies that trap men and women into determining gender identity as "natural." Rather than policing desire and prescribing "politically correct" behavior (sexually and otherwise), the feminist strives to open up the range of possibility in terms of gender and sexuality and to encourage others to respect differences in particular personal choices about one's "style" of gender and sexual preference. This goal requires work from many perspectives within various academic fields and an awareness of our contemporary culture—how it shapes our reality and subjectivity.

Unfortunately, this is often not the way feminism is taught. In fact, poststructuralist feminisms are often completely neglected, except perhaps in a few graduate fine arts, English, or philosophy courses. In contrast to classic feminism, poststructuralist feminisms—including the work of feminists like Julia Kristeva, Luce Irigaray, Hélène Cixous, Gayatri Chakravorty Spivak, Judith Butler, Sandra Harding, and many others—rarely enters the classroom. Working on the "borderlines" of linguistics, literature, psychoanalysis, philosophy, and science, these feminists are not easily "departmentalized" in the mainstream discourses taught in American universities. Therefore, an awareness of the multiplicity of feminist perspectives escapes the typical college student. Both women's studies courses and courses focusing on women's issues taught through the social sciences or other departments are often limited to first- or second-wave feminist thought. Therefore, students emerge without even an inkling that other kinds of feminist perspectives exist. They learn what I will label as "classic feminism," a conflation of the first- and second-wave feminisms (depending on the field of study, some prefer one attitude over the other). Most students are familiar with this position; in fact, it informs their concept of what their "feminist" teacher should look and act like and what "feminism" is all about. Classic feminism, for all its insights and positive work to change the lives of women, often fails to address our contemporary culture and to work out the contradictions in its own essentialist assumptions, because it functions on an outdated model of culture and subjectivity.

I was forced to acknowledge this situation when given the monumental task of teaching (as an underpaid adjunct, no less!) a course entitled "Feminist Perspectives." This particular course was offered at a college that had no women's studies department per se, but did offer a women's studies minor and women's studies electives within particular disciplines. Only this specific course, "Feminist Perspectives" (for undergraduates, junior level), was prefixed as women's studies. I saw this course as a wonderful opportunity to introduce students to those feminisms that are not often taught, especially continental feminisms, third-world feminisms, and feminist film theory. However, I also had to provide them with some background on both waves of the second phase of feminisms. How was I to achieve such a feat in a fifteen-week semester? I decided to begin with a review of the first two waves, and then I introduced a new topic each week—women and history, women and film, and so forth. Rather than attempting to provide the students with everything they could possibly know about each topic, I decided to introduce them to new ideas using textual references with which they were already familiar—popular culture.

Before we discussed film theory or women and representation, I devoted some time to elaborating on the cultural context within which these representations circulate. Appropriating some theories of Jean Baudrillard (in much the way that Arthur and Marilouise Kroker do in *Body Invaders: Panic Sex in America*), I exposed my students (and myself) to fascinating new approaches in reading contemporary culture, ideology, and thus the construction of gendered subjectivity. Being products of the television world and MTV, the students felt these theories to be appropriate and relevant to their experiences and ideas. Employing Baudrillard's theories, the Krokers argue that our world, the Real that now exists, is made up of fragments of dead Western culture—signifiers devoid of meaning, creating discourses that contradict each other (*Playboy* and fundamentalism, Hallmark and Betty Crocker Goodness combined with Bud Light and pop music sex ads, "just say no" and "safe sex" along with sex and wealth as the ultimate gratification). Religion, democracy—these discourses still contain the trace of past meanings, and combined with other cultural "excrement" (as the Krokers call it), create the "mediascape" wherein the "real" of our culture can be found. As Baudrillard theorizes in "Simulacra and Simulations," representation can be ordered into four phases:

1. It is the reflection of a basic reality.
2. It masks and perverts a basic reality.
3. It masks the *absence* of a basic reality.
4. It bears no relation to any reality whatever: it is its own pure simulacrum. (1988, 170)

According to Baudrillard, the contemporary world is operating in the fourth phase; it has become a "hyperreal," high-tech, mediaconstructed world, in which the images that are constantly produced and consumed no longer have a clear referent. The "hyperreal" is the only reality, for

Abstraction today is no longer that of the map, the double, the mirror or the concept. Simulation is no longer that of a territory, a referential being or a substance. It is the generation by models of a real without origin or reality: a hyperreal. (1988, 166)

According to Baudrillard, this simulacra is now the "Real," a surface creating and recreating its own simulated reality. As Mark Poster comments on Baudrillard, "Culture is now dominated by simulations, . . . objects and discourses that have no firm origin, no referent, no ground or foundation" (1988, 1). Within this hyperreal, "a potentially infinite play of signs is thus instituted which orders society while providing the individual with an illusory sense of freedom and self-determination" (Poster 1988, 2). The simulacra employs seduction through its endless production of

consumer objects [that] are like hysterical symptoms; they are best understood not as a response to a specific need or problem but as a network of floating signifiers that are inexhaustible in their ability to incite desire. (Poster 1988, 3)

Baudrillard uses Disneyland and Southern California as an illustration of the "hyperreal." Baudrillard argues that the amusement park itself, with its simulations of America, has become the "Real" that masquerades as illusion in order to make its surrounding area of Southern California—a hyperreality—appear to be more "real." Examples of Baudrillard's simulacra are ubiquitous. At the center of

American culture—the mall—the "hyperreal" creates and recreates consumer desire, and through identification and representation it acts as an appendage to the mediascape in shaping subjectivity through seduction.

I witnessed a striking example of Baudrillard's theories last Halloween (1991) in Tampa, Florida, at a festival called "Guavaween." Guavaween is a street party in the spirit of Mardi Gras, when crowds of people, all in Halloween costumes, drink beer and roam the streets of Tampa's historic district, Ybor City. The experience became an enactment of the hyperreal for me as I witnessed people wandering about in outfits exaggerating the highlights of the mediascape—the simulacra on parade. I counted twenty-four various Madonnas and five Jimmy Swaggerts alone. Moreover, in true Baudrillard fashion, there appeared an actual and an imitation Hare Krishna band. Ironically, the spectators assumed that the imitators were the real Hare Krishnas, for the simulated band was more believable than the actual band itself. The visual language of the mediascape—especially highlighted in music videos, advertisements, popular films, and TV—has become the residue and the core of contemporary culture. This "mediascape" is our culture, from whence emerge our constructs of reality, morality, and, my particular interest, gender identity.

I found the mediascape an effective place to start because although a student may not be "well-read" in written texts, she will probably be well versed in the visual texts of contemporary popular culture. I am not arguing that popular art is better, or that we should just give up the written words of the past in favor of MTV. On the contrary, I think that through analyzing visual texts, along with exposure to written texts (those inside and outside the canon), our student will learn to read her culture, including both MTV and Milton, in a much more sophisticated way. When the ideological meanings are made visible, the mediascape will no longer have its mystifying effect; our student will understand (as much as one can) why the remnant signifiers of Western culture still remain, what they possibly did mean and what they could mean, and how that has helped to make her who and what she is.

In dealing with the topic of women and representation and women and film, I decided to use both written and visual texts as an introduction to these theories and how they can relate to feminist concerns. In this lesson, I used a particular situation as a text, and explained different feminist readings of it, in order to contrast the perspectives of classic and poststructuralist feminisms. As an illustration through which students could see the various approaches, I chose the topic of women and fashion, because of its relevance to every student's day-to-day life in today's hyperreal culture. In addition, feminist dialogues about fashion comment on and critique the stereotypical "feminist" described above.

First, I assigned "A Tale of Inscription/Fashion Statements" by Kim Sawchuck, and I discussed various other positions (indicated below) in class. Sawchuck describes the different feminist positions on fashion. Classic feminism takes an anti-fashion stance. Women who wear make-up and love clothes are "buying into" the ideology transmitted by the media, the monster that has distorted the "natural" person into an "unnatural" female. Susan Brownmiller epitomizes this position in her book entitled *Femininity*, in which she claims that wearing skirts is an "artificial gender distinction," and that "the nature of feminine dressing is superficial in essence" (1984, 234). Therefore, a classic feminist must scorn fashion and its industry as a statement against its capitalist and sexist machinery, because fashion oppresses women and forces them into the position of object in relation to men.

In contrast to the classic feminist view on fashion, contemporary feminists like Jane Gaines, Elizabeth Wilson, and Kim Sawchuck challenge the assumptions and logic underlying this standpoint and offer alternative strategies in interpreting and coping with women and fashion. Gaines points out that feminism has changed from the anti-beauty and fashion culture position to one that seeks to interpret the image of woman as a construct. This theoretical position entails an awareness that any image is a construct—including that of the "stereotypical feminist in dungarees and Dr. Martens boots," as Elizabeth Wilson describes her (1990, 32). There is no "natural" self or style, and, as Wilson rightly comments, the so-called "zero-degree" or "anti-fashion" dressing of feminists has gone through many changes in style. Therefore, the "natural" anti-feminine look described by Brownmiller above is no more natural than any other look; it is just another style. After all, feminist style is a part of a larger fashion discourse (Wilson 1985, 240–43). In addition, pants (that Brownmiller argues are "natural" for women to wear) are designed for men, who do not have to remove them when urinating. Tight or ill-fitting pants can cause vaginal irritation and infection, as well. In many ways, it could more easily be argued that dresses are more comfortable for women—and even for men.

Wilson also argues that "fashion-haters," who condemn the materialism of the fashion industry and thus people (mostly women) who "buy" into it, see nothing wrong with compiling other material objects like VCRs, books, cars, and so forth. However, in both the discourses of classic Marxism and feminism, there remains a vehement, moralistic condemnation of beauty and fashion. Their argument would be that unlike the material objects noted above, beauty and fashion are employed solely for the pleasure of men. Several of my students had a particular problem in relating this logic to their own experience as women, for they felt that men were anti-make-up and fashion, and that women had to fight for their "right" to indulge in it. According to these students, puritanistic fathers and possessive boyfriends or husbands have often tried to control their daughters' or wives' flamboyance as expressed through cosmetics and clothes. Many women, like these students, do tend to associate the voice of classic feminism and Marxism with that of the "Law-of-the-Father," the patriarchal prohibitory voice that seeks to restrict and police their desires and pleasures.

I then asked my students if they were acquainted with any other "anti-fashion" discourses.   Yes, they remarked, fundamentalist Christianity. As Kim Sawchuck explains, fundamentalist Christianity, along with Western Platonic and nineteenth-century utilitarian philosophies (see Wilson 1990, 28–29) are tied into a long history of discourses that condemn fashion, acting on the same assumptions as classic feminists: fashion distorts the "pure," essential self. In the Christian tradition, the "painted woman" is the temptress out to hoodwink man, deceitfully covering up her "true" sinful nature. Another anti-fashion tradition emerged from literary satire, especially from the eighteenth and nineteenth centuries.   Jonathan Swift's poems, for example, characterize women's love of fashion as an indication of their frivolity, stupidity, and vanity.

In reacting to these ideas, one student remarked that some male professors still judge women who fail to adopt a stereotypically "feminist" dress as silly and unintelligent. She has sensed that women must be "frumpy" or plain to be considered intellectual because only silly women think too much about their appearance. These academics, she noted, wear tweed suits and sport a pipe for that "professor" look, or adopt a more bohemian, "young intellectual" look, obviously taking great care in fashioning their own appearances. Virginia Woolf mocks such hypocrites beautifully in *Three Guineas*. She describes a legal case in which a judge chastises a woman for her love of fashion, her "weakness" as a woman. The judge explains that although women cannot be expected to abandon fashion since it is "'one of nature's solaces for a constant and insuperable physical handicap'" and the "'psychology of the matter must not be overlooked,'" the woman's excessive ornamentation must not be allowed, for "'the rule of prudence and proportion must be observed'" (1938, 228–29). Woolf points out that

> The judge who thus dictated was wearing a scarlet robe, an ermine cape, and a vast wig of artificial curls. Whether he was enjoying 'one of nature's solaces for a constant and insuperable physical handicap,' whether again he was himself observing 'the rule of prudence and proportion' must be doubtful. But 'the psychology of the matter must not be overlooked'; and . . . the singularity of his own appearance together with that of Admirals, Generals, Heralds, Life Guards, Peers, Beefeaters, etc., was completely invisible to him so that he was able to lecture the lady without any consciousness of sharing her weakness . . . (1938, 229)

The judge in question made these remarks completely unaware that he was also a "fashion monger."

On the issue of fashion, classical feminism aligns itself, as it does on the issue of pornography and censorship, with the conservative right. I argue that this contradiction arises because classic feminism employs the same model of the "self" as does misogynist ideology. Hence, feminism can benefit from appropriating poststructuralist theories of subjectivity, for these concepts call into question this notion of the natural, essential being, this whole person as a prelinguistic self. As Sawchuck reminds us, fashion or "inscriptions of the social take place *at* the level of the body, not *upon* it" (1987, 65). There is no natural "self," either metaphysical or physical. Even the nude body is stylized. In fact, as Anne Hollander insists in *Seeing Through Clothes*, painted nudes throughout the centuries have mirrored the female body according to vogue concepts of femininity, beauty, and fashionable undergarments, proving that "nakedness is not universally experienced and perceived any more than clothes are" (1978, xiii). Fashion is more than a "reflection of the social onto the body"; it is the writing of the body. There is no escape from fashion, only an awareness of its all-encompassing construction of the body and the fictive "self." We are always already inscribed into the discursive realities of gender and style, as theorists like Michel Foucault and Judith Butler posit. In *History of Sexuality*, in opposition to our traditional view of sex as essential and prediscursive, Foucault described sexuality as a construct. Extending this view, Butler argues in *Gender Trouble* that gender (which includes "biological" sex) becomes, ultimately, a surface that "performs" a non-essential gendered subjectivity.

How do these new perspectives change an evaluation of fashion in the lives of women? Certainly a feminist would not advocate a "fashion freak" response, the reversal of "fashion prohibition." Perhaps, as Wilson asserts, fashion can be described and analyzed as "an art form and a symbolic system" (1990, 31). Sawchuck also notes that women (and men) should freely derive gratification from fashion—the joy of the return, the bond between people—without guilt or shame (1987, 69). With an awareness of fashion "as an art form and a symbolic system" it is also possible, as Sawchuck reminds us, to "perform" fashion in a way that dramatizes how the image of woman is constructed and radically redefines the mediascape's consumerized fashion product. Like a performance artist, one can use fashion and change meanings self-consciously to create one's own image or style. Like the postmodern designer, Jean-Paul Gaultier, one can create an image that exaggerates the construction of the female (or male) body at different cultural moments, for example, by incorporating the fashions of the fifties—pointy bras, Jestson hairdos—transformed with futuristic, hi-tech flair. In no way, however, should one style be considered more "morally correct" than another, but merely another style, one's own signature.

After reading written texts on the subject and engaging in a lively class discussion, my next step was to illustrate these concepts through an example, a familiar text that most of my students knew and felt they could relate to—a video by the popular artist Madonna. Madonna's self-conscious manipulations of her own media image illustrate what I explained about the proliferation of meanings, symbols, and fashion. Hyperreal consumer culture gobbles up her image, so she continues to transform it to stay new, emphasizing the stylization and nonessential quality of the hyperreal "self." She employs and exploits as intertexts punk, glamour film stars from old movies, Marilyn Monroe, and so forth. In appropriating these cultural icons, she then transforms their images, sometimes drastically changing their meanings as symbols. She redefines the passive, vulnerable sex appeal of Marilyn Monroe into a revised version of the "woman on top," who is active and in control of her own sexuality and relationships. In her videos, she (and her directors) use intertextuality of other films and images, constantly referring to other textual meanings.

To illustrate postmodern perspectives on fashion, I showed the music video "Vogue" (directed by David Fincher). "Voguing" itself originated in the Harlem "ball circuit" (performance competitions in exclusively gay male clubs) in the late eighties, as fully documented in the film *Paris is Burning* (Livingston 1990). In Harlem's "ball circuit," where gay male contestants perform gender identities (both masculine and feminine, in every possible degree and style), "voguing" is an intense dance competition between two opponents who attempt to "out-vogue" one another. The dance itself combines poses from models in *Vogue* magazine to pantomime, with an emphasis on perfect lines and the maintenance of awkward positions. "Voguing" celebrates glamour by enabling the dancer to feel a part of the *Vogue* world of the rich, beautiful, and famous.

Incorporating this dance as an intertext, Madonna's video "Vogue"—like the "ball circuit" itself—demonstrates fashion as a performance of the "self," dramatizing how one is constructed and can artistically re-construct oneself. The video emphasizes the fabrication of the body through other textual images of both masculine and feminine beauty and glamour. It points out the relevance of fashion and style to both genders, but especially it hones in on the image of the woman's body. In one clip, the camera focuses on the back of Madonna's body, which is clad in a corset, pointing to the exaggerated ideal waist of the nineteenth century. Simultaneously, the song lyrics repeat, "let your body move to the music. . . let your body go with the flow." At another moment, the camera zeros in on Madonna wearing a famous Gaultier "cone" bra, an exaggeration of the ideal breast, of the fifties. Fragments of the cultures of the twenties to the fifties, corresponding to the icons she names—Jean Harlow, Bette Davis, Fred Astaire, Jimmy Dean, et al.—illustrate the various, changing representations of beauty and sex appeal. The importance is on the surface, on style, and on the pleasure of "dressing up."

I encouraged the students to respond, and they did. In fact, many of them related these ideas to the work of other theorists and to other issues relevant to contemporary feminism. I know I did not succeed in teaching these students everything there is to know about "Feminist Perspectives," but I am sure that I found an effective method through which to introduce and expose them (and me) to new, invigorating ideas and to challenge their preconceived notions about "feminists" and "feminism."

Works Cited

Baudrillard, Jean. *Selected Writings*, ed. Mark Poster. Stanford: Stanford University Press, 1988.

Brownmiller, Susan. *Femininity*. New York: Linden Press, 1984.

Butler, Judith. *Gender Trouble: Feminism and the Subversion of Identity*. New York: Routledge, 1990.

Eisenstein, Hester. *Contemporary Feminist Thought*. Boston: G. K. Hall, 1983.

Fincher, David (director). "Vogue." In "Madonna: The Immaculate Collection." Warner Video, 1990.

Foucault, Michel. *The History of Sexuality*. Trans. Robert Hurley, vols. 1–3. New York: Pantheon, 1978.

Gaines, Jane. "Introduction: Fabricating the Female Body." In *Fabrications: Costume and the Female Body*, ed. Jane Gaines and Charlotte Herzog. New York: Routledge, 1990.

Harding, Sandra. *The Science Question in Feminism*. Ithaca: Cornell University Press, 1991.

Hollander, Anne. *Seeing Through Clothes*. New York: Viking, 1978.

Kroker, Arthur, and Marilouise Kroker. *Body Invaders: Panic Sex in America*. New York: St. Martin's Press, 1987.

Livingston, Jennie (producer). "Paris is Burning." Off-White Productions. Prestige: Miramax films, 1990.

Michaels, Lorne (producer). "Saturday Night Live." NBC. 1991-1992.

Piller, Michael (producer). "The Outcast," television episode. In "Star Trek: The Next Generation," created by Gene Roddenberry. Independent Network, 1992.

Poster, Mark. "Introduction." In *Baudrillard: Selected Writings*, ed. Mark Poster. Stanford: Stanford University Press, 1988.

Sawchuck, Kim. "A Tale of Inscription/Fashion Statements." In *Body Invaders: Panic Sex in America* ed. Arthur Kroker and Marilouise Kroker. New York: St. Martin's Press, 1987.

Wilson, Elizabeth. *Adorned in Dreams: Fashion and Modernity*. Berkeley: University of California Press, 1985.

—. "All the Rage." In *Fabrications: Costume and the Female Body*, ed. Jane Gaines and Charlotte Herzog. New York: Routledge, 1990.

Woolf, Virginia. *Three Guineas*. New York: Harcourt/Brace, 1938.

Chapter 9

Navigating in a Brave New World: Teaching Feminist Literary Criticism

Sara Munson Deats

Six years ago—it seems six decades—the Director of the Graduate Program in English asked me to teach a graduate course in feminist literary criticism, after female graduate students had petitioned that the course be offered with me as the teacher. My response to this request was ambivalent. On one hand, I was flattered that the students had asked for me to teach the course. On the other hand, I had fifteen years of experience teaching graduate and undergraduate courses in Elizabethan and Jacobean drama and I realized that this would be a major new preparation and one outside of my area of scholarly research. I was, however, sorely tempted. Ever since my radical student days in the sixties I had been a dedicated feminist: I was a member of the National Organization for Women (NOW); I had demonstrated for Pro Choice; I had electioneered for female political candidates; and I was fully committed to feminist causes. Furthermore, the prospect of focusing on the image of women in literature was most intriguing. Of course, I ended up saying, "Yes." Six years and some hundred books and countless articles later, I am aware that teaching a course in feminist literary criticism involves much more than merely examining the image of women in literature. It involves an entirely new perspective on literature, criticism, society, and oneself. For a tyro in contemporary critical thought, preparing for this particular course was almost equivalent to earning a second doctorate—this one in the contemporary zeitgeist.

Feminist literary criticism is a familiar enough term; we hear it all the time. But what does it mean? I soon realized that each of the constituent words in this title is highly problematic, and this ambiguity poses a problem for the teacher of a course covering this topic. First, the teacher must clarify the meaning of the word "feminist." To which of the many "feminisms," ancient and modern, does this term refer? Does it refer to the first wave of the feminist revolution dating roughly from 1837 to 1930, a revolution that concentrated on economic, political, social, and educational reform, without, as many feminists believe, successfully attacking the patriarchal assumptions with which women and men are unconsciously indoctrinated? Or, does it refer to the second wave of the feminist revolution, emerging in the 1960s and continuing until today? This revolt, unlike the first revolution, concentrated primarily on the psychological assumptions underlying our patriarchal social system. Does it refer specifically to the feminism dominating the early 1970s, which identified the socially constructed difference between the sexes as the chief source of female oppression and thus wished to minimize these differences? Or does it refer instead to the feminism appearing in the late 1970s and 1980s, which valorized the socially constructed divergences between the sexes, affirming "Vive la difference"? Does the term, therefore, describe the feminism that minimizes sexual differences and seeks androgyny, or the feminism that glorifies the feminine, or the feminism that states categorically that "Woman cannot be; Woman is something that cannot exist." A class in feminist literary criticism should introduce the student to all of the faces of feminism.[1]

Well, feminism is a controversial term, we may all concede, but at least we all know what literature is. Or do we? I soon learned that contemporary literary theory, and particularly feminist theory, sought to dissolve the boundaries between what has traditionally been considered literary and what has traditionally been regarded as popular or folk. Furthermore, the same theory refuses to separate literature from the culture to which it belongs, viewing history and politics as texts, even as literature is a text. Lastly, the feminist enterprise is committed to dissolving boundaries not only between literature and history but also between literature and other disciplines, including philosophy, psychology, anthropology, sociology, art, even science; for after all, boundaries and categories belong to the hierarchies and restrictions of the patriarchal ideology that feminism is committed to subverting. It follows, therefore, that a course in feminist literary criticism should introduce the student to feminist scholarship across disciplines.

With some trepidation I approach the final term. Surely, many of you will say, we all know what criticism is. Or do we? When I entered the profession I had a clear concept of my role as critic. My function as critic was either to evaluate the aesthetic or moral value of a literary work or to illumine aspects of that work that had heretofore gone unnoticed or been neglected. From this perspective, therefore, literature is seen as a kind of treasure chest in which the author places beautifully crafted jewels of wisdom. The critic's function is to open up this cache and share these precious jewels with the reader.

However, contemporary theory views the role of the critic very differently. Contemporary theory sees the critic as co-producer of the text, each produced text being a dialogue between text and critic. Thus, the word "criticism" may be used in the traditional sense to refer to a variety of discursive practices used to elucidate and evaluate works of literature, or it may be employed in the more contemporary sense to describe a discourse that uses literary texts only as occasions for further theorizing. In this second sense, criticism itself becomes a primary mode of writing, like poetry and fiction, and the boundaries between criticism and fiction, like those between literature and popular culture and those between literature and history, are dissolved.

In summary, therefore, a course in feminist literary criticism should make students aware of the many different types of feminism noted above; it should also introduce students to the varieties of feminist scholarship in a number of different disciplines; lastly, it should familiarize students with both traditional and contemporary attitudes toward criticism and the role of the critic. Also, after the student has achieved some understanding of the implications of the term "feminist literary criticism" and mastered some of the strategies and approaches associated with this term, she or he should have the opportunity to apply these methodologies to specific literary texts. This is a tall order for a one-semester course. In the remainder of my essay, I shall share with you some of the strategies and methodologies I have used to cover this terrain, or, to develop the nautical metaphor I employ in the title of this essay, to navigate this body of water. I use a nautical metaphor partially because fluids—tears, milk, blood, but particularly water—have traditionally been identified as the feminine element, and partially because this metaphor expresses the fluid nature of my own course which is still in the process of development, a kind of subject in process.

My most daunting challenge was the vast expanse to be covered, because for many of my uninitiated students, feminist literary criticism offered an endless ocean of knowledge to be explored. In my navigation through this ocean, I sought to avoid both the whirlpool of total chaos and the sharp, hard rocks of patriarchal inflexibility. Of course, as all teachers know, the easiest way to communicate substantial amounts of knowledge is to lecture. Yet the lecture, with its affirmation of authority and its distancing of the teacher from the students, reinscribes the very patriarchal values of rigid authority and hierarchy that feminism seeks to subvert. I thus decided to sacrifice control for creativity and, whenever possible, to jettison the lecture for class participation and the podium for a communal seating in a semi-circle, partially because the circle dissolves privilege and priority and partially because the circle is a traditional feminine symbol.

This strategy worked brilliantly during the first couple of sessions, which were devoted to the defining of key terms—such as sex, gender, androgyny, gyandry, misogyny—necessary for a fruitful dialogue. Many of my students had never questioned the equation of biologically determined sex and socially constructed gender; many further accepted as natural and universal certain stereotypes of femininity and masculinity. Thus, during the first two sessions, we engaged in a most valuable inductive exercise to identify and denaturalize the qualities traditionally associated with the two socially constructed, asymmetrical genders. These early sessions of introduction and definition were followed by a discussion of the origin and history of misogyny, in which students participated actively in identifying examples of misogyny in the literature of all periods from the classical and medieval to the modern and contemporary. Since I have taught this course to graduate students only, each class has offered a wide spectrum of literary expertise, and the examinations of misogyny in literature have proved to be most informative to everyone in the class, including myself.[2]

Thus far, all had gone swimmingly. However, my attempt to introduce my students to feminist scholarship in other disciplines offered the first substantial obstacle to our progress. I had identified eighteen texts by eighteen feminist commentators that, in my opinion, epitomize some of the best and most influential scholarship in a number of different fields (see Appendix 1)—Gerda Lerner in history, Sherry Ortner and Michelle Rosaldo in anthropology, Jean Baker Miller and

Nancy Chodorow in psychology, Mary Daly in theology, Angela Davis in political science, Riane Eisler in archeology, to mention only a few. But how could I ask harassed, overworked graduate students to read eighteen texts in a half-dozen different disciplines? One solution would be to assign reports with each student responsible for one of the feminist texts. But reports too often degenerate into mini-lectures, complete with papers read from a podium. I thus decided to experiment with one of the techniques associated with feminist pedagogy—role playing. I asked each student to select one of the eighteen texts to read (I cap my classes at eighteen so that I can indulge in active class participation), to learn something about the author's life, and then to play the role of the selected critic. The scenario went as follows. We are holding a conference on gender studies, and we have invited a number of distinguished feminist scholars from a wide range of different disciplines to participate in a panel discussion. The conference covers two three-hour sessions. During the first session, I introduce each visiting scholar and provide some background on her scholarly achievement (in my script all of the scholars were female, but this need not always be the case). Each scholar is then allowed five minutes to outline her critical focus and methodology. After the introductions, the group as a whole is invited to debate *in character* a number of questions critical to feminist theory, including such queries as the following: "What, in your opinion, is the origin of female subordination?" "What methods can feminists use to combat the patriarchy and achieve greater equality for women?" "What solutions do you advance for the amelioration of society?" This debate constitutes the majority of the two sessions. During the second session, at the end of the debate, each scholar is allowed a few minutes to summarize her position on these issues before the hypothetical conference is concluded.

This performance strategy has been one of the most successful pedagogical techniques I have ever employed. Students, males as well as females, have universally thrown themselves into their parts and debated the convictions of their assigned characters with logical rigor and emotional ardor. This role-playing strategy accomplishes a number of objectives: first, the students have always prepared rigorously for their parts and learning has certainly taken place; second, adopting a perspective that may not be their own has provided them the experience of seeing reality from multiple perspectives; third, and most important, they have been learning about feminist ideology while actually enacting this ideology. I would recommend this role-playing technique to anyone teaching courses in womens studies and I have even adapted this technique to my teaching of Shakespeare. There is, however, one danger inherent in this strategy. The volley of fervent debate—and the debates have sometimes become very heated—can become confusing. So that students can later—through emotion recollected in tranquility—sort out scholar with thesis, I have asked each participant to furnish members of the class with a one or two page abstract delineating the central focus and thesis of the critical text discussed. Thus, the class has avoided the chaotic whirlpool of Charybdis while also maneuvering successfully around the sharp rigid rocks of Scylla.

I have been less successful in navigating around the second obstacle to our feminist journey, the crucial necessity of introducing the class to the basic tenets of contemporary critical thought—Structuralism, Marxism, Lacanian Psychoanalytic Theory, and Deconstruction. Frequently, my students have no background in these critical perspectives that are absolutely vital to the understanding of contemporary feminist theory. I would prefer to try another role-playing experiment with students assuming the parts of the "Great White Fathers"—Saussure, Bakhtin, Althusser, Barthe, Lacan, and Derrida—but this would require a critical sophistication my students have rarely achieved. Anyway, to date, I have been reduced to lecturing on these figures, while attempting a dialogical interchange whenever possible.

After maneuvering around Structuralism, Marxism, and Post structuralism, all was relatively smooth sailing. Guided by Virginia Woolf's *A Room of One's Own* (1929), Elaine Showalter's "Feminist Criticism in the Wilderness" (1985), and an excellent collection of essays, *Making a Difference* (Greene and Coppelia 1985), collaboratively we were able to evolve a definition of feminist literary criticism and even to derive some understanding of feminist critical methodologies and what has been identified as a "feminine" literary style.

The last section of the course was devoted to applying some of these strategies to literary works. The last two times I taught this course, I selected six fictional texts (see Appendix 2) and during the final six weeks of the semester we experimented with analyzing these works from a number of different feminist critical perspectives. Again, I experimented with techniques in collaborative learning. Three students were involved with me in the teaching of each of these six texts. For example, in the teaching of *Wuthering Heights*, I assigned one student a critical essay using a gynocentric approach to the text, another an essay adopting a Marxist feminist reading, and a third an essay exemplifying the feminist strategy referred to as revisionary mythopoetics. The three then took turns interpreting the work from these three perspectives after which I moderated a debate that included the class as a whole. This collaborative approach, with different critical perspectives, was adopted for each of the six texts we studied.

Navigating in the brave new world—or perhaps I should say the brave new sea—of feminist theory does, however, offer other dangers. One of the most threatening barriers is the term paper, the *sine qua nom* of the English graduate class. One of the most heated debates in feminist literary theory concerns the question of a feminine style, as critics argue the question, "Is there a specifically feminine sensibility and, if so, is it reflected in a distinctively feminine style?" I do not have the space in this essay to explore the intricacies of this debate but only to summarize some widely accepted conclusions. Feminist theorists from Virginia Woolf to Rachel Blau Du Plessis have argued that because of their social conditioning, women have developed a specific sensibility that is reflected in a distinctively feminine style. French feminists Julia Kristeva and Hélène Cixous have also identified a distinctively feminine mode of writing, while insisting that it is not sex specific, in other words, men as well as women can manifest this feminine style. Most commentators agree that this feminine style deliberately ruptures traditional grammar, syntax, and punctuation and defies traditional concepts of logical development and orderly organization. After having discussed feminine style for half a semester, how can a teacher assign students a traditional term paper that observes accepted rubrics of grammar, syntax, and punctuation? On the other hand, how can a teacher, trained in the patriarchy of academe, evaluate a work of critical analysis that ignores or, worse still, defies these traditional grammatical standards? This is the dilemma that faces the teacher of feminist literary criticism.

The solution I have devised again tries to navigate between the whirlpool of chaos where all standards are abrogated and the rigid reefs of patriarchy on which all creativity is smashed. Following the paradigm offered by Kristeva (see Appendix 3) I have assigned a very short critical essay to be written in both styles, juxtaposed as illustrated by Kristeva. In the right hand column (right is conventionally masculine and patriarchal) will appear the traditional version of the essay penned in standard English, observing accepted rubrics of grammar, syntax, and punctuation. In the left, sinister column (left is conventionally associated with the feminine and the subversive) the same essay will be rewritten in the flowing, discursive, rhythmic style identified by Cixous as *écriture feminine*, by Luce Irigaray as *Parler femme* and by Kristeva as the semiotic. Of course, I emphasize to my students that they are not expected to write like Cixous, Irigaray, and Kristeva (who can?) and that they will not be evaluated on the creativity of their *écriture feminine* but only on the degree to which their essay shows their knowledge of what attributes have been identified as characteristic of feminine style.

Having circumnavigated the spacious material on the subject, while successfully avoiding the threatening shoals of lecture (which can ground any course, however dynamic the teacher) and the dangerous rapids of uncontrolled discussion (which can carry a class over the brink into anarchy) and having maneuvered around the perilous crag of the term paper (on which many a student has floundered), I have generally been able to steer the course smoothly into its final haven. My primary goal in this course has been to incorporate into the study of feminist theory some of the innovative pedagogical strategies generated by the feminist movement—collaborative learning, role-playing, personal interaction—so as to transform a traditional university course into a first-hand experience of the brave new world of feminist liberation. I believe that this course has liberated and empowered my students; I know that it has been a liberating and exhilarating experience for me.

My students and I may not have reached the perfect safe harbor, but we all shared an exciting voyage.

Appendix 1*

1970 Kate Millet, *Sexual Politics.*
1970 Mary Jane Sherfey, "The Theory of Female Sexuality."
1970 Shulamith Firestone, *The Dialectic of Sex.*
1971 Elizabeth Janeway, *Man's World, Women's Place.*
1972 Phyllis Chesler, *Women and Madness.*
1974 Juliet Mitchell, *Psychoanalysis and Feminism.*
1974 Sherry Ortner, "Is Female to Male as Nature is to Culture?"
1974 Michelle Rosaldo, "Women, Culture, and Society."
1975 Susan Brownmiller, *Against Our Wills.*
1976 Jean Baker Miller, *Toward a New Psychology of Women.*
1977 Dorothy Dinnerstein, *The Mermaid and the Minotaur.*
1978 Nancy Chodorow, *The Reproduction of Mothering.*
1978 Mary Daly, *Gyn/Ecology.*

1979 Gerda Lerner, *The Majority Finds Its Past.*
1981 Susan Griffin, *Pornography and Silence.*
1981 Angela Davis, *Women, Race, and Class.*
1982 Carol Gilligan, *In a Different Voice.*
1987 Riane Eisler, *The Chalice and the Blade.*

Appendix 2*

Texts for the Class:
Emily Bronte, *Wuthering Heights.*
Charlotte Bronte, *Jane Eyre.*
Jean Rhys, *Wide Sargasso Sea.*
Charlotte Perkins Gilman, "The Yellow Wallpaper."
Margaret Atwood, *Surfacing.*
Alice Walker, *The Color Purple.*

Appendix 3*

Julia Kristeva, "Stabat Mater." In *Contemporary Literary Criticism; Literary and Cultural Studies*, 2d ed., eds. Robert Con Davis and Ronald Schleifer. New York: Longman, 1989.

*(See Works Cited for complete citation.)

Notes

1. For a cogent discussion of the many faces of feminism, see Hester Eisenstein (1983); see also Kate Millet (1970).
2. The definitive study of misogyny in literature is probably still Katherine Roger's, *The Troublesome Helpmate* (1966).

Works Cited

Cixous, Hélène. "The Laugh of the Medusa." Trans. Keith Cohen and Paula Cohen. *Signs* 1 (Summer 1976): 875–93.

Du Plessis, Rachel Blau. *Writing Beyond the Ending: Narrative Strategies of Twentieth-Century Women Writers.* Bloomington: Indiana University Press, 1985.

Eisenstein, Hester. *Contemporary Feminist Thought.* Boston: G. K. Hall, 1983.

Greene, Gayle, and Coppelia Kahn, eds. *Making a Difference: Feminist Literary Criticism.* New York: Methuen, 1985

Irigaray, Luce. *The Sex Which Is Not One.* Trans. Catherine Porter and Carolyn Burke. Ithaca: Cornell University Press, 1985.

Kristeva, Julia. "Revolution in Poetic Language." In *The Kristeva Reader,* ed. Toril Moi. Oxford: Blackwell, 1986.

Millet, Kate. *Sexual Politics.* Garden City, N.Y.: Doubleday, 1970.

Rogers, Katherine. *The Troublesome Helpmate.* Seattle: University of Washington Press, 1966.

Showalter, Elaine. "Feminist Criticism in the Wilderness." In *The New Feminist Criticism; Essays on Women, Literature, and Theory,* ed. Elaine Showalter. New York: Pantheon Books, 1985.

Woolf, Virginia. *A Room of One's Own.* New York: Harcourt, Brace, and World, Inc. 1929.

Chapter 10

The Centrifugal Classroom

Linda Woodbridge

To what extent can feminist teaching strategies inform our pedagogy when feminism, women's issues, and gender are *not* the primary subject matter of the course? I want to show how a postmodern, feminist approach might be adapted to the teaching of *any* class.

The postmodern: a decentered world where hierarchical, central authority yields to the power of the people, where the official feast succumbs to the anarchic, centrifugal forces of carnival—the decentering, antihierarchical perspective of feminism has contributed a good deal to the construction of that world. The modern city with its centralized skyscrapers and its Central Park is dissolving into the unfocalized postmodern landscape whose democratic suburbs and shopping malls refract each city's center into many centers. Cubism, though quintessentially "modern," in fact heralded the postmodern in its democratic sameness from corner to corner of the canvas, an art without central focal point; what such art replaced was painting (in a direct line from the Renaissance) whose architectural vanishing points, foreshortened floor tiles, lances, rays of sunshine, and spectators' gazes all directed the beholder's eye to a focal point emphasized by color and lighting. Our classrooms used to be like that: the audience-like arrangement of student chairs, the lectern or podium reminiscent of a pulpit, the gaze of student spectators focussing on that central point, the instructor. Just as we are beginning to listen, in literature, to marginalized voices, to argue that what the soldier Williams says about the ethics of war may be as important and as valid as what King Henry V says, so we are starting to uncrown the instructor as the classroom's voice of wisdom, to seek postmodern teaching strategies wherein many voices are heard and the instructor is no longer King Henry. A rebellious, anti-authoritarian feminism has taught us to let the silenced be heard. But to believe in postmodern pedagogy is by no means as hard as to practice it.

[B]ell hooks [sic] voices the disenchantment of a black female student with politically radical professors who still wear their crowns in the classroom:

> Whether one took courses from professors with feminist politics or Marxist politics, their presentation of self in the classroom never differed from the norm. This was especially so with Marxist professors. I asked one of these professors, a white male, how he could expect students to take his politics seriously as a radical alternative to a capitalist structure if we found Marxist professors to be even more oppressively authoritarian than other professors. Everyone seemed reluctant to talk about the fact that professors who advocated radical politics rarely allowed their critique of domination and oppression to influence teaching strategies. (1989, 100)

But it isn't only that as feminists or Marxists we are naturally domineering and/or hypocritical, though we may be so: it is partly that learning to teach undomineeringly is hard. Creating a cubism of the classroom calls forth intellectual and pedagogical sweat.

Take the difficulty of creating a physical space appropriate to decentered teaching. The 1960s saw alternative classrooms constructed on many campuses; replacing the proscenium arch with a theater-in-the-round, putting students in a circle facing each other instead of in rows facing the teacher, didn't necessarily decenter the teacher, who now became the center of a circle unless s/he deliberately sat among the students; but insofar as it enabled students to see each other and talk to each other, it was a centrifugal move. However, those bear-pit alternative classrooms constructed in the sixties have, on many campuses, now been deconstructed. Physical discomfort was one problem—often such classrooms had no chairs, since sixties students preferred to sit on the floor, and I fear that 1990s students lack the moral fiber we had in those early days, or perhaps with the advance of anorexia they simply lack the requisite adipose cushion. At any rate, one seldom encounters classrooms-in-the-round now. Some of us still try to create them, in rooms where chairs are movable and the class isn't too large, but it's a running battle with janitors and other instructors who use the room—the chairs have to be rearranged afresh daily, students begin to grumble about being furniture-movers, and one begins to suspect that the students don't care quite so much about decentering and marginalized voices as one does oneself. The latest problem is the battery of electronic equipment installed across the front of classrooms: an instructor stands behind a long counter that bristles with overhead projectors and sound equipment. When I teach in our Business Building (the business faculty is wealthy and business professors apparently put their every word on transparencies for overhead projection), I'm stuck peering out at my class from behind an electronic barricade, all wired into the floor and immovable, and I can't easily come out and walk around the room because the floor is booby-trapped with plugs and wires to which TV monitors on wheels are hooked up. The instructor in such a setting is being constructed as TV anchorperson, the pedagogue of an electronic age. Our Humanities Centre is somewhat better, because the equipment is movable, but (humanitarians being assumed to be thieves) it is chained to tables at the front of the room, and I have to enlist the aid of a couple of students every day to move equipment-laden tables so that they don't separate me from the students. Some of the chains, for obscure institutional reasons, are covered with rubber, and one day while dragging away at chains and rubber hoses, one of my students muttered, "There's something kinky about this." Such are the physical difficulties encountered in the quest to decenter oneself.

In a more purely pedagogical sense, decentered teaching is hard, much harder than an old-style dictatorial lecture. If we simply abdicate sovereignty without having something in its place, the classroom will be like a country that has had a revolution but has no democratic institutions in place. A teacher must forge such institutions, from the beginning of each course. In what follows I talk mainly about Shakespeare and Renaissance literature, but courses dealing with other subject matter have provided a few examples.

On the first day of every course, I begin the process of helping students get to know each other. In a graduate seminar or other very small class, we simply go around the room and introduce ourselves and talk about our background, our present research interests, and something personal. In a larger class, I pass out a brief questionnaire asking students what name they want to be called, where they grew up, what their major is, what other English courses they have taken, and why they are taking this course. I take these home and use them to divide students into four groups (most of our classes have around thirty-five students). I spend a long time trying to create a mix in each group—of gender, academic background (mixing English majors with non-English majors, more advanced with less advanced students), personal background (mixing local with foreign students, city students with small-town students), and attitude (mixing those who are keen on taking the course with those who were forced to take it by circumstances beyond their control—something they usually are not shy about mentioning). At the next class meeting, I tell students about the group system, list membership of all groups on the blackboard, and send students off to sit with their groups in the four corners of the room. I give them an hour-long ice-breaking exercise that involves each person telling the group what they were doing for the 48 hours before the course began and then engaging in an exercise wherein each person in the group imagines what each other would do in a particular circumstance, and then tells the group about the imagined scenario, focussing on each person in turn. This gets the students in each group to know each other and gives everyone the idea that each person's experience is of interest. Each person gets a chance to talk while others listen, and each person has the experience of being the center of the group's attention. This begins the work of creating thirty-five "centers" in the classroom, not just one. I drift around the room during this hour, eavesdropping on the groups so that I get to know the students too. Students really enjoy this exercise, and throw themselves into it, and ever after they are (with some lonely exceptions—inevitable, I fear) bonded together into a group with considerable esprit de corps.

I keep these groups together all year now—in a full-year course I used to scramble them into completely new groups at mid-year, to give each person close contact with another seven or eight people in the class, but I noticed that they still continued to sit in the classroom with members of their first group, and I would see them around campus, having coffee with members of their first group. It seems that students get imprinted on their first group, like ducklings imprinted on the first object they see, and this is no bad thing—on a large, impersonal campus of some 30,000 students, it can mean a lot to students to have a few close friends.

I give groups a variety of activities during the year. The most important are debates: Group One debates Group Two; Group Three debates Group Four. We also act out scenes from plays—usually one group provides enough actors to do a scene. Sometimes groups do close readings of paired poems on the same topic; I drift around eavesdropping again, putting in a question here and there. (Once I heard a group discussing "The Hock-Cart, or Harvest Home" and concluding that harvest takes place in spring—clearly I hadn't been successful enough in mixing urban with rural students in that group.)

Debate topics are carefully chosen—I make sure there is plenty of evidence in the text to support both the affirmative and the negative. For example, here is a topic I have used in a senior Shakespeare course: *Resolved that "Henry V" is a jingoistic play that glorifies war, asserts England's national pride, and treats King Henry as a national hero of almost epic stature.* Of course, much in the play supports the affirmative—particularly the Chorus, with its omniscient air of privileged commentator on the action; but much in the play questions the ethics of war in general and reveals the suspect motives of this particular war; much looks askance at nationalism, and shrewdly plays up Henry's wily foxiness, rationalization, and habit of scapegoating others. Both sides in the debate have plenty of ammunition, and they arrive with their texts marked up in red ink and stuck all over with yellow Post-it™ notes, and go at it hammer and tongs. This introduces students to a central poststructuralist project, the problematizing of literary meaning. It is also a feminist project since feminism endorses the multiple rather than the unitary. Deconstructionists (as I will tell students sometime after the debate) maintain that irresolvable conflicts between different camps of critics signal irreducible inconsistencies in the text—*Henry V*, they argue, is (like most texts closely read) a text divided against itself. What, then, is the source of meaning? Does authorial intention stand behind the text's meaning, and if so, how (especially in the case of inscrutable, reticent Shakespeare) do we find out what it was? Or does reader response determine meaning? If it is possible to disagree so profoundly as the students find themselves doing in the debate, not on grounds of uninformed opinion but on the basis of carefully assembled evidence from the text, then which reader response is "right?" The very idea of *one* right meaning is a centralizing notion—debate is a perfect vehicle of decentered teaching because it makes real to students the possibility that meaning may be plural and conflicted, and ultimately undecidable. A further way of opening up this unsettling possibility is a strategy I usually employ during the first debate: I set a time limit for the debate, and when it is over I ask students to resume their seats in the classroom (during the debate they have been sitting across the front, coping as best they can with projectors, chains, and rubber hoses). I tell them that now the debate is over, they are not limited to the side they were on, but can argue what they personally believe about the text. Almost invariably they stay on the same side they were on during the debate, and at the end of the session I point this out to them: they were put on one side or the other by the flip of a coin, and then they talked themselves into believing in that position while preparing to argue it in public. At this point, the slippery basis of literary meaning begins to grow palpable. In keeping with this poststructural insight, and in line with my feminist view of competition as pernicious, we do not take a vote on who won the debate; but we do talk about the extent of ego investment in any argument, and about what that says about determining literary meaning. (In olden days I used to fret that my tendency to leave debates unresolved signalled a basic wishywashiness in my character; now, happily, I see that I'm just postmodern.)

Decentered debate is *not* an anarchistic free-for-all. Students choose a moderator (from a group not involved in the debate) who keeps order and apportions time equally between the sides, and students meet as a group outside class time to plan the debate, parcel out which arguments are to be made by which person, and so forth. (I don't require this—they do it spontaneously, usually with the aid of alcohol and rock music, I believe.) My only instruction to them is to give everybody a chance to talk.

Some would argue that debate, as a conflictive, agonistic mode, is opposed to the ideals of feminism, which values cooperative learning. I respect that view, and yet I know that to make her way in a tough world, a feminist often needs to know how to argue effectively. I try to get students to avoid an obsession with scoring off each other in the debate, and I work to instill a sense of spirited but courteous debate, of respect for each other's arguments and feelings. I tell students that learning to argue effectively on your feet is one of the life-long benefits of an English course, and that besides, arguing well is one of life's pleasures.

Care is necessary, though, to ensure that the combative atmosphere of a debate does not work to the disadvantage of women students. As Catherine Krupnick notes,

> talkativeness studies in general have concluded that men dominate mixed discussion groups everywhere. . . . Numerous studies have demonstrated that in mixed-sex conversations, women are interrupted far more frequently than men are. (1985, 19–20)

She cites a study involving numerous videotapes of actual classrooms, which showed that

> comments of women students often were confined to 'bursts' lasting only a few seconds, while male students typically kept on talking until they had finished. Moreover, once interrupted, women sometimes stayed out of the discussion for the remainder of the class hour. (1985, 19–20)

Defending women students from interruption, in my experience, is more often necessary in graduate seminars than in undergraduate classrooms; I attribute this to the fact that in English classes, women students typically outnumber men at the undergraduate level, while at the graduate level the numbers are more nearly equal and sometimes women are outnumbered. I quite often find myself in graduate seminars saying "Wait a minute, Ted—Janice has been waiting for a turn to talk." It is heartening to know that just having a woman instructor can be a help to female students: in the study, Krupnick describes,

> the presence of female instructors apparently had an inspiring effect on female students. They spoke almost three times longer under instructors of their own sex than when they were in classes led by male instructors. (1985, 19)

(That word "under" is not very feminist or postmodern, is it?)

As a follow-up to the *Henry V* debate, I get students to read Norman Rabkin's "Rabbits, Ducks, and *Henry V*" (1977), which argues that similar to a Renaissance "perspective" drawing, which reveals rabbits if one focusses on the black spaces, ducks if one focusses on the white spaces, *Henry V* contains evidence that points in two directions, toward mutually exclusive views of the action. I have also shown scenes from Olivier's *Henry V* side-by-side with scenes from Branagh's *Henry V*, to demonstrate how in the theatre or on film, wildly divergent interpretations can arise from the same words—dramatic texts lend themselves even better than non-dramatic texts to opening students' minds to the instability of meaning and to the idea of meaning as an interpretive act rather than a discoverable entity.

One of my favorite essay assignments in a senior Shakespeare course is to get students to find two critics who strenuously disagree with each other on some Shakespearean topic and to try to judge, on the basis of a close reading of the text, which one (if either) is "right." This is a viable topic with Shakespeare because such a vast secondary literature exists, and critics are so cantankerous and so damned positive about their views that it's easy for students to find material. And again, the fact that two professional critics can find in the same play plenty of evidence to support mutually exclusive arguments can be an eye-opener to students who have always unreflectingly accepted that there's one discoverable right meaning to any text, or even that opinions they see expressed in print must be "true."

Theatricality is built into the act of teaching, and again I try to move it into the classroom rather than letting it remain at the level of The Teacher As Ham or in the relatively passive activity of students as film viewers. I like to begin a Shakespeare course with a student production of Act V of *A Midsummer Night's Dream*; because this scene is about bad acting, even if the student acting isn't very competent, the worse it is, the funnier it is. Students love acting that scene; I've never known it to fail. Once a bearded giant of a student turned up in a pioneer dress to play Thisbe; the following year, I was telling my new class about him—I said he was certainly a man with no hang-ups about his masculinity. The young man who had just volunteered to play Thisbe in the new class said rather aggressively, "you make that sound like a challenge—either we appear in drag or we have hang-ups about our masculinity," which filled me with remorse for having made the remark. He turned up for the production in a stylish evening gown and three inch heels.

In a first- or second-year literature survey, I've had students act out *The Creation and the Fall of Lucifer* (the mystery play), scenes from *Everyman* or *The Second Shepherd's Play*, scenes from *1 Henry IV* and/or *Dr. Faustus*, from *The Way of the World*, and so forth. Sometimes I make a script out of a scene from a narrative poem or novel—I have had students read the Lady Bercilak/Sir Gawain seduction scene and the Lady Booby/Joseph Andrews seduction scene, which make a nice pair for comparison—a good exam question. I don't require students to rehearse or wear costumes or use props, but they always do; we always have devils with red capes and cardboard pitchforks, a generous amount of transvestism, and blackboards decorated with "Welcome to Hell—Burn Lotion, $1,000,000 a Bottle." The men in the class, it must be said, quite enjoy the role of God. One year during a performance of *The Creation and the Fall of Lucifer*, God stood up on a table (next to the overhead projector) and turned his back to the audience to reveal a hockey shirt sporting the player's name of "GOD, #1." Several weeks later, another group was presenting *Everyman*, and another actor stood up on the same table and whirled around to reveal, on the back of his bathrobe, the words "GOD 2: THE SEQUEL." The seduction scenes are always popular—at the end of one of these, a particularly vampish Lady Booby went back to her seat in the classroom which was right next to the seat of the young man who had played Joseph, and after the enthusiastic applause died down, the young man turned to her and said "Take your hand off my knee!" Without missing a beat, she replied, "Was that your knee?" I think it was five minutes before the class stopped laughing.

The main purpose of the theatricals is joy: awaking a sense of the pure fun of literature is, I think, our pleasantest and not our least important task. But one thing that fascinates me is the way that, once students have acted a few scenes, the debates become theatricalized. The first debate is rather sober and nervous; by the second debate, students are nearly always in costume. (I never suggest this, but it almost always happens.) Second-year students debating the topic *Resolved that Satan is the hero of "Paradise Lost"* came attired in red for the Satanic side and in black Puritan garb for the negative, more godly side. They wrote "TOWN MEETING 8:00 TONIGHT" on the blackboard and debated the effects on their community of the shocking text recently published, *Paradise Lost*, which gave so much play to what could only be called a Satanic cult. Students debating the topic *Resolved that in "As You Like It" Shakespeare treats country folk as bumpkins and holds country life up to contempt, affirming urban values as the true values of civilization* came attired in business suits on the affirmative side and in straw hats on the negative; the negative side decorated the whole classroom with flowers, handed out daisies to the rest of the class, and ended their rebuttal with a round dance. In our postmodern, poststructuralist age, New Historicism has argued for the theatricality of power and the theatricalized nature of meaning; students engaged in both debates and amateur theatricals teach themselves about the theatricality of debate and persuasion, an insight which loops back into what they have been learning about the slipperiness of literary meaning. It opens the door, too, to strategically placed discussions of essentialism versus the social construction of gender: students who, in a debate, have presented themselves and their opinions as a dramatic persona (sometimes in drag) will be more ready to understand notions such as Judith Butler's idea that gender is a performance in everyday life.

I suppose an instructor has to make clear that she welcomes incursions of theatricality, because not all instructors do. There are problems—I have had neighboring instructors complain about the noise, and once I responded to this by inviting the neighbour class to a performance; unluckily the neighbour class was a course in "Fundamentals of Writing for Engineers," and *The Interlude of Youth* seemed to leave the young engineers cold. I have given up playing a tape of *Dr. Faustus* in a darkened classroom on Halloween, and welcoming students to class that day dressed in a floor-length hooded black cape, because several classes seemed to find this unendurably embarrassing. But if one has a reputation for welcoming the slightly off-beat in the classroom, there can be wonderful moments, like the day in "Literature and the Other Arts" when a student presentation, rather than comprising the standard comparison of a motet with a sonnet or a painting with a play, took up the art of dance. The student making the presentation had enlisted the aid of belly-dancing friend, who swept into the room jangling her bells and swirling her veils. When she had finished her sensuous dance, she swept out of the room (surprising a couple of my colleagues in the corridor), whereupon the student resumed her presentation, solemnly comparing the belly dance to a religious poem by George Herbert. Stunned at first by this yoking together by violence of two such disparate works of art, class members and I only gradually recognized that the presentation itself was meant to be a metaphysical conceit.

In group work of various kinds, it is fascinating to watch students structuring their discourse by the genres of television and other modern media (right down to *The National Enquirer*). In one debate on *Henry IV*, students put Falstaff on trial, configuring the two sides as opposing attorneys and witnesses, advancing their literary evidence in the form of testimony under oath, and couching their arguments in the language of TV lawyers—the genre and language were perfectly familiar to everyone. In the *Paradise Lost* debate, several students sprouted southern accents and took up the oratory of televangelists; one student cried out to her opponent, "Oh, hush your mouth now, Tammy Faye." Two students reporting back to the class on their group discussions of poems by Donne and Jonson adopted the lingo and accents of two sports commentators in a post-game show. Graduate students do this too: one student making a presentation on criticism of *King John* set himself up as a game show host, distributed a quiz, and sent rapid-fire questions at his fellow students. Another, presenting on the history of criticism of *Henry VIII*, made a tape of his voice in different accents and talked against it, positioning himself as a talk show host. "Hi!" the tape would boom; "this is G. Wilson Knight phoning from 1933." The presentation even featured (with the help of an echo chamber) an impressive call from the play's first and most negative critic: "This is God phoning. *Henry VIII* is a terrible play, I hated it. Who do you think hurled the thunderbolt that burned down the Globe while *Henry VIII* was being performed?" (There's God again—that ever-popular role. Does the Deity's popularity in the classroom hint at a nostalgia for the metaphysical grounding of literary meaning?)

In approaching canonical (and rather old) literary texts through familiar models of the mass media, students are doing what Ernst Gombrich says the human mind always does when approaching the unfamiliar—assimilating the unfamiliar to the familiar. But they are also engaged in a decentering, uncrowning project of their own: bridging the gap between "their culture" (television, rock music, tabloids) and "our culture"(canonical literature). In line with our postmodern project of decentering literary study by uncrowning the old classics of the canon, studying marginalized texts by women, working class writers, and non-Europeans, we should also welcome opportunities to approach the old classics of the canon through their continuity with popular culture. A book I've found helpful in this project is Harriett Hawkins's *Classics and Trash* (1990) (with chapters like "From King Lear to King Kong"), which makes links between Shakespeare and "trashy" films of the twentieth century.

Both feminism and postmodernism advocate the dissolution of boundaries. If one of the hallmarks of the postmodern is the permeability of boundaries, especially the boundary between outside and inside, then students who approach canonical texts through schemata provided by television or tabloids are making a postmodern move in effacing the boundary between academic and popular/commercial discourse. Postmodern architecture brings the outside inside—students here at the University of Alberta are intimately familiar with one of the world's largest malls, West Edmonton Mall, inside which on the bitterest winter day one can swim in artificial surf, visit a galleon in a lagoon, play golf, watch live dolphins sport in a pool, admire strutting peacocks, or contemplate the Bakhtinian carnivalesque at an amusement park which brings to the center of Alberta's placid prairies two of the most terrifying carnival rides on earth, the Drop of Doom and a lethal, beautiful red rollercoaster, the Mind Bender. Our students are happily habituated to such inside-outness; helping the exterior discourses of TV and tabloid to penetrate (and even to make sense of) the inner sanctums of academic literary study is an intellectual mind bender to which they take like dolphins to a fake lagoon.

The group system works better than anything I have tried for getting every student involved in debate and discussion. Even quieter students can be drawn into discussion this way, partly because they have the moral support of friends in their group. Mine is a large university in a city of about 600,000, but many of our students come from small rural communities and feel quite lost at first; putting them at ease and making them feel important as people is something we can do in English classes, as instructors in science and social sciences—condemned to classes of 500 students—too often cannot. Here is a geographical decentering—helping to bestow a sense of validity on opinions that come from little country towns rather than always valorizing city outlooks. The *As You Like It* debate on "bumpkins," of which I spoke above, actually took place not at my university but at the Centre for Shakespeare Studies in Ashland, Oregon, where I spent a week this past summer teaching twenty-five high school teachers from all over the United States. When dividing them into groups, I had paid particular attention to mixing geographical regions and to mixing city folk with country or small-town folk. In the debate, one speaker on the "city slicker" side pointed to Orlando's statement, "I thought all things had been savage here," noting that although Orlando's interlocutors are *not* savage, this is only because they happen to be courtiers exiled in the Forest of Arden; this debater held that the play still paints the countryside as dangerous and inhospitable. At this point, a quiet woman from upstate Maine made an impassioned speech from the "country" side of the debate: she said that the speaker's remarks reminded her of the attitude of New Yorkers or Bostonians who come to Maine—they are always double-bolting their doors and activating alarms on their hub caps. "They act as if they are coming to a savage hinterland," she said; "but the truth is, they are projecting city dangers onto the countryside. They bring their fear with them. So it is with Orlando." It is this kind of eloquent voice from the margins, the periphery answering back to the center, that true decentered/decentering pedagogy can foster.

Decentered teaching can operate in day-to-day class discussions too, as well as in more formal debates. My own abilities as a discussion leader improved after an experience (oddly enough) with administration—the experience of chairing large meetings when I was Department chair. The first thing I had to learn was to keep my mouth shut, and this shocking experience brought home to me how hard a thing it is for an English professor to keep her mouth shut. My initial impulse, during Department discussions, was to make some response to every speaker, and it didn't take long for me to realize that this was very inappropriate: not only is a meeting chair supposed to stay out of debate, but also, it seems presumptuous for one professor to keep putting her oar into discussion at a meeting of peers—why is she worth hearing from any more frequently than others? Therefore, I learned to keep track of the order in which people put up their hands and to call on them to speak in that order. The discussion proceeded on its lurching course—in a multi-sided discussion, few speakers are directly responding to the person who spoke just before; most are responding to something said two or three speeches back. There was no input from me except if somebody asked me a question. Going directly from such a meeting to the classroom provoked reflection: why didn't I consider my students peers, as I considered my colleagues peers? Why should I respond to everything they said, noting whether I agreed with it or not, or rephrasing their comments into what I considered a more coherent argument? Why should I be worth hearing from more frequently than others? I tried keeping my mouth shut. It was great. I called on speakers as they raised their hands, and the discussion proceeded lurchingly on its way, students responding to each other rather than to me. Before, discussion used to go from Instructor to Student A to Instructor to Student B to Instructor to Student C, etc.; now it went from Instructor to Student A to Student B to Student C, etc. The sight lines centering on the instructor now bounced around the room; it was like the shift from focal-point to Cubist painting.

This kind of discussion-leading isn't easy, however. It depends on preliminary spade-work—the work of getting the students to know each other, to trust and respect each other, that the group work has been fostering. It depends on asking good questions, open-ended questions that will provoke disagreement and not regurgitory questions that will simply boomerang the conversation back onto the instructor. Day-to-day classroom experience gradually culls out the questions that cause discussion to fall lifeless to the floor and lie there among the electrical cables, rather than soaring.

This kind of teaching is hard because a truly open discussion is unpredictable in its direction. If a teacher is to give it shape by gently leading, nudging, making connections between ideas advanced by different speakers, she must constantly be on her toes, living by her wits, rather than dragging the conversation safely back to the points she had planned to cover that day and set down firmly in her notes. As I grow more experienced (or maybe just older) I find that the days on which I am under-prepared go much better than the days I enter the room with a packet of points to be got through at all costs. To let a discussion wander aimlessly is dreary and destructive: what is needed is the kind of *bricolage* for which postmodernism is renowned—the centrifugal teaching experience demands skill in improvisation. It is a little like riding a spirited horse—control remains essential, and there aren't many times when one gives a class its head completely; but there are occasional exhilarating gallops when you let discussion go in a completely unanticipated direction, because you suddenly see it's a brilliant direction to go in, better than any of the directions you foresaw when you entered the classroom. For me, some of the best classroom moments are those when I can honestly say to a student or the whole class, "You've convinced me; you've changed my mind."

Does your feminist, postmodern, decentered teacher quit lecturing altogether? No! We're paid to know more than the students know and to share our knowledge with them—why else do we read all these books and essays and attend all these conferences? Students expect to profit from our expertise and they grow restive if they find themselves listening only to each other's opinions. I lecture about a third of the time, periodically in hour-long background lectures, but more frequently in ten- or fifteen-minute segments interspersed with the discussions, debates, and theatricals—I do some lecturing in almost every class meeting. Even posing a good question sometimes involves a mini-lecture: the "problem of evil" is not a concept familiar to all, and one frequently finds it necessary to stop and elaborate before posing the rest of the question. Decentered teaching does not or should not mean total professorial abdication.

What about grades? There is definitely a tension between decentered classroom teaching and the necessity to re-invoke our hegemonic power when judging students' work; this past year, a student visited me in great puzzlement after failing her first essay, saying "You're not like this in class—you say 'very interesting' even if what the student said was very stupid, but now you're failing me on my essay." She had a point—I had been telling students, too, that studying literature was joyful and fun, and there's nothing very joyful or fun in failing an essay. Are grades by nature unfeminist and unpostmodern? Maybe they are, but they're likely here to stay. The many 1960s experiments with grade-free programs and even grade-free universities like Evergreen have thinned out considerably in more recent times; eventually, they will probably go the way of the bear-pit classroom. One thing is certain—we cannot simply wish our students into caring about the subject matter rather than the grade; we have to earn that sort of caring by making the subject matter compelling. I never give grades for debates, theatricals, or reports on group discussions; yet so much do students enjoy those activities that in years of using them in the classroom I can never remember a complaint about the out-of-class effort required for a non-graded activity. I do give grades on reading quizzes every week; I am quite shameless in using those to bludgeon students into getting their reading done, and if that's unfeminist or unpostmodern, I don't care, because it works, and they *must* get their reading done if they are to learn anything about literature and if discussions are to go anywhere at all.

Can there be such a thing as feminist, postmodern marking? That there can, and is, is suggested by the virtual disappearance from our parlance of the phrase "correcting papers," with its implication of one right answer, in the possession of the teacher, who can enforce the parroting of the one right answer by sheer force of red ink. Such an old-style view of marking was always paradoxical—a hegemonic discourse operating literally on the margins; and students were, of course, always free to treat a professor's peremptory marginalia as marginal stuff is so often treated—just ignore it. To me, feminist, postmodern marking consists not in grade-free marking but in putting one's money where one's mouth is when one tells students (as I always do, on the first day of class) that I don't expect or want them to agree with me, and that I'll always take their interpretation seriously as long as they argue it logically and support it with evidence from the text. They never believe this. I have to earn their belief, earn their trust, by treating their views with respect every day in the classroom, even (or especially) when they disagree with mine. I have to follow through with what I promise and threaten at the outset—that I give high marks for a well-argued original interpretation even when it disagrees with mine and low marks for an unthinking regurgitation of my own views.

Finally, both feminist and postmodern pedagogy need to press students to articulate the ideological commitment behind their own reading and their critical stances. Students these days, spooked by charges of political correctness and under pressure from a conversative outside world, are often gun-shy about encountering ideology—when I make clear at the beginning of a course that I'm a feminist, a certain number of students nowadays (male and female) react as if they've been slapped. They need to be asked to reflect on their own ideology, to understand that the fact that they don't express it or acknowledge it doesn't mean it doesn't exist. We are often doing this with other critics—a hallmark of poststructuralist theory is its insistence that no reading is ideologically innocent, that all criticism grows out of entrenched world views. But how often do we practice this with students, especially undergraduates? I like to use a discussion of *Othello* as one vehicle for getting students to lay bare the underlying assumptions governing their own reading.

When I'm pressing a class to uncover their own hidden ideological commitments, I like to give them Alan Sinfield's essay "Give an Account of Shakespeare and Education . . ." (1985), which protests against examination questions that ask students to describe their "personal" response to Shakespeare, without recognizing the extent to which this response is institutionally conditioned and subject to the pressures of students' social class, economic circumstances, race, education, and historical moment. Sinfield is talking about English O-level and A-level examinations, but his essay always rings bells with students who have come out of high schools in my Canadian province, where "personal response" questions on provincial exams are very common. I try to move the class to question how "personal" a personal response really is, to think about what societal pressures have helped form the person making that response. In a graduate seminar, I use Catherine Belsey's *The Subject of Tragedy* (1985) to get students thinking about the instability and constructedness of the individual subject; in an undergraduate course, I use *King Lear*, a play that unmasks all too disturbingly the evanescence of any individual character beyond socially assigned roles such as Father and King.

Part of the postmodern academic experience, and certainly part of every feminist critic's experience, is the pervasiveness of critical theory. How much theory should we do in class? After one deeply discouraging attempt to teach Eagleton's *Literary Theory* (1983) in a first-year course, I have settled for trying to introduce theory, at the first-year level, rather sneakily and without identifying it by naming its various schools—I get students talking about the difficulty of knowing whether Chaucer's narrator is being ironic when he says of the worldly monk "I said his opinion was good"; even if we historicize Chaucer and talk about medieval moral and religious values, how do we know Chaucer wasn't a renegade in his own age? But I don't couch this in philosophical abstractions dealing with indeterminacy of meaning—I just set them thinking about it. In senior courses, I used to start out with a couple of theory lectures to provide a framework, but that came to seem too top-down an approach—the instructor as Henry V again—and too much like the articles and books that madden one by their heavy front-loading of abstract theory which they seldom succeed in bringing to bear very well on the literary criticism that follows. In recent years, I've been trying to let theory emerge inductively, as it were: when students are beginning to unmask their own ideological commitments, I begin to give names to their positions. One (to his astonishment) learns that he is a reader-response critic, and another finds that her view of language is enmeshed in linguistic disputes, and that she could articulate her position better if she read some Saussure and learned about signifiers. Theory is less scary if it seems home-grown, rather than an exotic import from Paris. If it's a matter of giving names to ideas class members are capable of coming up with on their own, it quickly becomes domesticated.

In my graduate seminars of the last several years, I have asked students to "pick a theory," from deconstruction to feminism to New Historicism to semiotics, and give a (highly condensed) 20-minute presentation on it to the seminar, and to hand out to fellow students a one- or two-page list of essential readings on their theory; their second presentation is then an application of one of these types of theory to a piece of literature, say a Shakespeare play. This reflects my feeling that the quickest way to learn something is to have to teach it to someone else. Also, I myself learn a tremendous amount from these presentations, which is important because (like other members of my generation) I didn't grow up with theory, and have had a lot of catching up to do. I think it's good for graduate students to know that their teacher is learning from them and alongside them; it's another decentering/uncrowning, but it's also another kind of deterrorization: students who see that learning is a life-long process are less likely to fall into the trap of thinking they have to know everything before they have finished their Ph.D., which can be a most paralyzing deterrent to finishing the Ph.D. Another benefit of the "pick a theory" strategy is that it allows one to capitalize on the expertise of one's colleagues—in any given English department, many kinds of theory are being taught in various seminars and supervisory situations, and students draw liberally on what they have learned from other instructors when doing their theory presentations. Thus again, in good feminist, postmodern fashion, boundaries dissolve—the boundary that made my seminar room a little kingdom now becomes permeable and all the good ideas of my colleagues come flowing in.

Unmasking is vital to centrifugal learning. The classroom experience is deeply theatricalized, and students (by putting on costumes in amateur theatricals or in debates) are learning something about the fact that stances adopted in arguments are often a matter of putting on intellectual costumes—of acting out the roles culture has taught us to play. But finally, the classroom experience must also be a matter of taking off costumes, the unsettling experience of laying bare the naked gooseflesh that is the quivering ground on which our opinions rest, on which literary meaning rests.

Some years ago at the end of a course I received a gift from an older student; she was an art major, an excellent print maker. It was a two-inch by three-inch print, a self-portrait expressing how she often felt during the course. She was crouching totally naked except for a large pair of spectacles, with the knuckles of one hand pressed hard into her mouth and a fiercely contemplative glare on her face. The print was entitled "THINK!" The postmodern classroom experience is often uncomfortable and taxing, what with all its unclothings and uncrownings. But it can be as exhilarating as it is unsettling. Paradoxically, for all its arguing and its conflicts, such a classroom offers a sense of feminist community: here is no solitary drowse of note-taking but a communal effort at learning. Even at its worst, such learning at least builds survival skills. When it is moderately successful, it hones the wits, raises questions about meaning and evidence and logic, and helps bring texts alive as conflicted (rather than safely mapped) territory. And, at its best, it is fun. If the tigers of wrath *are* wiser than the horses of instruction, it must follow that to "take" a course, to "have" an instructor, to "get" a degree—dully acquisitive activities—is less dangerous, less exhilarating, less beautiful, than to ride the mind bender of postmodern, feminist pedagogy.

Works Cited

Belsey, Catherine. *The Subject of Tragedy: Identity and Difference in Renaissance Drama*. London and New York: Methuen, 1985.

Bradley, A. C. *Shakespearean Tragedy: Hamlet, Othello, King Lear, Macbeth*. Greenwich, Conn.: Fawcett, 1965. First published 1904.

Butler, Judith. *Gender Trouble: Feminism and the Subversion of Identity*. New York: Routledge, 1990.

Eagleton, Terry. *Literary Theory: An Introduction*. Minneapolis: University of Minnesota Press, 1983.

Gombrich, E. H. *Art and Illusion: A Study in the Psychology of Pictorial Representation*. New York: Pantheon, 1960.

Hawkins, Harriett. *Classics and Trash: Traditions and Taboos in High Literature and Popular Modern Genres*. Hemel Hempstead, N.Y.: Harvester, 1990.

hooks, bell. *Talking Back: Thinking Feminist, Thinking Black*. Boston: South End Press, 1989.

Krupnick, Catherine. "Women and Men in the Classroom: Inequality and Its Remedies." In *On Teaching and Learning*, 19–25. Cambridge, Mass.: Danfort Center for Teaching and Learning, 1985.

Rabkin, Norman. "Rabbits, Ducks, and *Henry V.*" *Shakespeare Quarterly* 28 (1977): 279–96.

Sinfield, Alan. "Give an Account of Shakespeare and Education. . ." In *Political Shakespeare: New Essays in Cultural Materialism*, eds. Jonathan Dollimore and Alan Sinfield. Ithaca: Cornell University Press, 1985.

Shakespeare, William. *Complete Works*, ed. David Bevington. 3d ed. Glenview, Il.: Scott, Foresman, 1980.

Chapter 11

Valuing the Personal: Feminist Concerns for the Writing Classroom

Carol Mattingly

Writing that incorporates retelling and reflection about events or experiences of personal significance has most commonly been called personal experience writing, or simply personal writing. Composition scholars use the terms personal and personal experience widely, often implying that the terms have a singular definition that is universally understood, and rarely defining the exact nature of writing assignments using the personal. In fact, when teachers speak of personal experience in writing, they may mean anything from expressive accounts of intimate personal occurrences to more general narratives or descriptions, a retelling of something observed. Furthermore, while William E. Coles Jr. and James Vopat found that teachers most often chose autobiographical writing as "good" writing, especially that which exhibited "honesty" and "integrity," none addressed the fact that assessing such honest, intense autobiographical writing might be problematic (1985).

Feminists, too, have long valued personal experience writing. Ironically, perhaps inevitably, inclusion of personal experience has become problematic for feminists, in spite of their history of support for the personal. Especially in the composition classroom, some difficulties have evolved because teachers have often transposed practices that had proven successful in earlier, more homogeneous settings onto the more diverse writing classroom.

Feminist theory's interest in personal experience evolved from the women's consciousness-raising groups of the late 1960s and early 1970s. Feminists continued to emphasize the personal in women's studies programs, in literary theory classes, and within feminist journals. Students in women's studies classes and subscribers to feminist journals were primarily women, very often mature and academically sophisticated. Students in literary theory classes were generally upper division English majors or graduate students who were sympathetic supporters of the feminist cause. These users and shapers of early feminist theory and pedagogy represented a uniquely coherent group.

Elizabeth Flynn has described composition studies as a "feminization of our previous conceptions of how writers write and how writing should be taught" (1988, 423), but she bases this assertion on the fact that composition studies have "been shaped by women" (1988, 424), not necessarily by feminists. She further acknowledges that "the fields of feminist studies and composition studies have not engaged each other in a serious or systematic way" (1988, 425). Indeed, no conscious, systematic adjustment of the theories and applications previously implemented by rather elite, homogeneous groups accompanied the acceptance of these theories in composition classes, although students constituting such classes are commonly younger, more diverse, and often unsympathetic or even hostile to the feminist ideals. The subsequent use of practices previously geared to more homogeneous groups has raised issues for feminists in composition. These feminists are now beginning to question and to alter some feminist theory and practice in an effort to achieve a more appropriate fit with the diverse composition classroom. The issues are complex because of the acknowledged importance of personal discourse for women and because of the increasing awareness of problems inherent in some practices connected with the personal.

Although feminists feel a great need to validate the personal because of women's long association with the personal and private, the volatile issues arising from inclusion of the personal threaten to disrupt the delicate balance achieved in relation to other concerns significant for women. A number of feminists are beginning to fear that the protective practices surrounding much personal writing may diminish its validity. Others worry that some methods actually romanticize problematic differences or promote hegemonic notions. Perhaps the most troublesome concern for feminists is the possible emotional and physical danger for students inherent in practices that promote "emotionally intense" personal writing.

Few feminists deny the overpowering importance of personal experience for women. Because women have traditionally been "other" (their selfhood defined in relation to others), identity recovery (a reformulating of what it means to be women retrieved from women's lived experience) is crucial. Proponents see dismissal of the personal and the concomitant emphasis on the objective and abstract as a patriarchal exclusion of those things most closely associated with women; they argue for incorporation of the personal as a means of making education more relevant to women.

Personal writing in feminist classrooms most often takes the form of journal writing. For example, feminists often use journals as a means of allowing students to express themselves in order to validate personal experience. Journals are often valued because they provide a "safe place" where students can "critically examine their world" (Perry 1987, 152). Teachers seeking to use journals in this manner often promise confidentiality and may even use a system, such as identification by social security number, to insure a student's comfort with that confidentiality (Reimer 1987, 159), or they may suggest that students staple or clip pages that they don't want the teacher to read (Perry, 1987, 152). In these cases, journals are used to encourage personal introspection and to give students an opportunity to share the private thoughts they feel uneasy about sharing in class.

This very personal journal writing, or expressivist recounting of experience, has been valued by feminists because women have been silenced in the past. Women needed to give voice to their experience in order to reclaim it, to validate it, and to construct their own reality and identity apart from that categorized for them by men. More recently, to support this validating of the personal, feminists have drawn upon studies by Mary Field Belenky, Blythe McVicker Clinchy, Nancy Rule Goldberger and Jill Mattuck Tarule, which define the cognitive development of women in a number of different learning situations. Belenky et al. have defined five perspectives from which women perceive knowledge. Because the first of these perspectives is silence, some feminists continue to promote the value of expressivist writing, although Kathleen Dunn's and Frances Maher's studies seem to show that few, if any, women in college remain in this first stage.

Although feminists often claim that women in college classrooms are silenced, they are using the term in a sense different from that established by Belenky et al. References to women's silencing in classrooms generally refer to the privileging of responses by male students and the preferential attention and unequal amount of discussion time extended to men. Belenky et al.'s term refers to a deeper, psychological muting. Few composition teachers confront truly "silenced" women in composition classrooms, and there has been greater emphasis in recent years on going beyond the merely expressivist inclusion of personal experience. Even though feminists who use primarily expressivist writing in the classroom often cite *Women's Ways of Knowing* as justification, Belenky has noted the "danger in a narrow focus on private journal writing and private freewriting that doesn't broaden into a more extended and hard-nosed kind of dialogue and thus keeps a person lodged in the subjectivist mode" (Ashton-Jones and Thomas, 1990, 289). A variety of measures may prove to be of benefit to silenced students, but any attempt to remedy such problems must address the specific nature of the silencing. Any solution must also account for its possible exclusionary effect upon both men and women in classrooms that demand writing about very personal experiences.

While silence has traditionally been seen in a negative light, Deirdre Mahoney has recently called for a revision of past theories of silence in favor of one that reconsiders its importance as potentially empowering. Mahoney suggests that "silence plays a crucial role in helping women hear their most distinctive feminine voices" and warns against a continued reinforcement of women's oppression related to silence (1991, 6).

Like personal experience, the term silence has often been used as though its definition is commonly agreed upon. That we may misread women's silence, as Mahoney suggests, is a likely possibility. For example, Ann Lavine has expressed concerns regarding differing male and female responses toward a personal writing assignment. The assignment asked for a narrative highlighting a distinctly male or female experience. Lavine found that while men were "embarrassingly confessional," an excellent woman writer hid "behind platitudes without delving into any kind of meaningful specifics" (1987, 136). For Lavine, an obvious explanation for the difference in resulting narratives might be that women and men have become attuned to the different receptions accorded to writing about male (accepted) and female (unaccepted) experiences. While women may have learned that "to be well received, women must avoid writing about topics which point out the femaleness of the author" (1987, 140), it seems possible also that a woman may choose not to reveal very personal experiences. Many women may have learned both the power and the protection implicit in silence. More complete studies of silence may provide a greater understanding of the nature of silence with regard to women's writing.

The potentially marginalizing effect of validating simple recounting of personal experience has become even more problematic. Moving beyond the expressivist is vitally important to women of color, for example. These feminists believe that personal narratives are much too complex for simple readings and celebrations. Marian Schiachitano (1990) points out that "voices, histories and stories *need* to be legitimated, valued, and celebrated—but unless they are linked to a socio-historical context we run the continual risk of ignoring the very real lived pain and damage these narratives come out of," and bell hooks [*sic*] has warned of the need to move the emphasis in "the personal is political" away from the "personal." Because cultures of domination are necessarily narcissistic, hooks warns, taking women in white-supremist, capitalist patriarchy as the starting point is risky (1989, 105).

Feminists are also beginning to address the concern that while personal experience has increasingly been included in writing pedagogy, it is often taken less seriously than traditional, "objective" writing. Some feminists are seeking a restructuring of methodology using personal experience in an effort to validate its importance and to emphasize the need to change the model of what powerful language is. The most viable suggestions for accomplishing this goal demand more rigorous use and consideration of personal experience.

Journals were rarely graded during their early use, and feminists seldom questioned the curricula that almost always moved from narrative during the early part of the semester to argument in the latter, as students became more experienced and more proficient at academic writing. In questioning the values and messages communicated to students when grades are based solely on "formal," "objective," expository writing, Jerilyn Fisher insists that in order for personal experience writing to be taken seriously and thus for real support to be given to feminist pedagogy, students' journals must be graded (1987, 92). Pamela J. Annas further avoids the implicitly negative messages that composition teachers promote by their efforts to "wean" students from subjectivity into objectivity by making the last assignment of the semester a position paper based on a topic of "intense interest" to the students, and derived at least as much from their own personal experiences as from more traditional forms of information. Annas believes that traditional treatment that moves from narrative toward expository and argumentative writing questions the real value of the personal. She warns also against examining journals, sketches, and response papers less critically than other writing (1985, 360). However, Annas does not focus entirely on the personal. She believes that women writing the political is especially important since women have been discouraged from using public forms (1985, 369). She hopes, therefore, to guide her students toward an ability to bring the two together, giving equal significance to both.

The recent concern that the feminist emphasis on a subjectivity based on gender posits a "universal" experience has led to further re-examination of women's epistemological position and its significance for feminist theory. Feminists are concerned that such positions belie the varying conditions of women based on race, class, age, sexual preference, and geographic location. But in recognizing the importance of context for individual women, feminists have often taken a pluralistic position that, in effect, supports the patriarchal culture. Many feminists are attempting to assimilate a theory that avoids the essentializing claim to a uniquely feminine and superior position from which women experience life, while at the same time, recognizing the complexity of women's subjectivity and the problematic nature of dealing with women's experience in a manner that denies determinism and allows for agency (Grant 1987, Hawkesworth 1989, Alcoff 1988, Lauretis 1987).

In an effort to apply new feminist theories to rhetoric and composition, Teresa L. Ebert has called for a rewriting of the "difference within." In a *College English* article, Ebert suggests a resistance theory that allows for intervention and social change, a postmodern materialist feminism that permits "intervention in the structure of oppression: both at the macrolevel of their structural organization of domination and at the microlevel of different and contradictory manifestations of oppression" (1991, 902). In a similar effort, Susan Jarratt has challenged the use of the expressivist relating of personal experience, and, more specifically, Peter Elbow's unquestioning acceptance of voiced experience in groups as essentially value-free (1991, 109–10; 116–17).[1] Jarratt opposes this simplistic validation because many class members may feel violated by others' writing about personal experience. Jarratt points to examples that she has collected: narratives by heterosexual male students about sexual conquests; a fictional account of violence committed against a female teacher written by a white male student; writing by a white male student in which blatant sexism is overlooked because of its honest voice. Jarratt calls for a "productive conflict in feminist composition pedagogy" that acknowledges difference and challenges domination (1991, 118–21).

Nevertheless, relatively little work has been done with regard to feminist use of personal experience in the writing classroom. The latest *Bedford Bibliography for Teachers of Writing* lists only seven entries under "Gender and Writing," several of those only tangentially related to writing and none dealing with the use of personal experience. Yet, use of personal experience presents a problem for feminists because they are committed to the personal, but they also wish to create critical consciousness and to allow for difference.

Should feminists, then, like bell hooks, insist that students share experiences with one another so as to validate those experiences? Should they encourage students to express their feelings and opinions, "to work at coming to voice in an atmosphere where they may be afraid or see themselves at risk" so that all are "empowered in a rigorous, critical discussion," not just an assertive few? Or should they provide opportunities for students to express feelings and thoughts without fear of exposure, permitting them to opt out of class discussion and providing safe places with anonymity? If feminists insist that students go beyond the expressivist relating of feelings and experiences, what are the specific connections they wish to encourage students to make? More importantly, whether they try to provide a "safe place" for students or to push them toward participation, doesn't the success depend largely upon the ethos of the teacher, an element few feminists mention in connection with today's writing classroom except with regard to the maternal, nurturing model, a model that is increasingly acknowledged as problematic? And finally, even if the teacher's ethos encourages students' trust, isn't there danger in students' revelations of very intimate personal experiences?

Many feminists have begun to seek answers by taking a more critical look at what appear to be admirable classroom practices. In her article "On the Subjects of Class and Gender in 'The Literacy Letters,'" Linda Brodky has shown how the "unacknowledged tension over the control of subject positions contributes to rather than alleviates" antagonisms inherent in the hierarchical structure of a male constructed system (1989, 133). Brodky's study of the use of the personal both supports and moves beyond Robert J. Connors' notion that the "curious discomfort in English teachers' attitudes toward students writing from personal experience . . . [leads to] a subordination of personality to information for practical purposes" (1987, 178).

For Brodky, the problem goes beyond the usual discounting of the "merely" personal. In order to permit the empowerment of students through the personal, teachers must "learn how to 'read' the various relationships between writer, reader, and reality that language and discourse supposedly produce" (1989, 125). Brodky insists that this requires confronting the hierarchical structure of educational discourse that places authority in the teacher. She believes that we must re-examine not only overt methods, such as setting topics, determining the direction of discussion, and allocating turns, but also covert practices that place teachers in subject positions, even when the use of the personal is deemed to be of value. Regardless of the admirable intentions generating "the literacy letters," in which interested teachers shared narratives with Adult Basic Education students for the purpose of providing a "real" reason for writing, the hegemonic nature of the teachers' control determined acceptable subjects for narrative and decided the direction and intensity of the discourse, confirming teachers as subjects, students as objects. Even more problematic, subsequent writing implicitly validated white middle-class experience while invalidating experience of members of lower socioeconomic backgrounds.

We must also question whether the very personal recounting of experience that was meant to give voice to silenced women in early consciousness-raising groups is an appropriate technique for writing classrooms. Writing teachers are not trained psychotherapists. Encouraging students to reveal their most private feelings, as in the manner of Anne, the first year college student in Thomas Newkirk's "Anatomy of a Breakthrough" (1983) who "comes to voice" about her father's tragic shooting of her mother, may entail risks that composition teachers are unprepared to cope with properly. Perhaps more important for feminists, there is a hint of voyeurism in encouraging students to write about personal matters inappropriate to the very limited relationship between a college professor and a first-year student. When feminists search for a "safe place" for students to write, strive to empower students by accepting the worth of the students' experience, and attempt to relate to and value student writing by encouraging intimate personal expression, the teacher's ethos must be a defining ingredient. Journals can never be a safe place for students, regardless of clips and staples and promises of confidentiality, unless there is implicit trust and acceptance between student and teacher.

The notion of acceptance and validation comes into question even though teachers may consciously wish to empower students by validating their experience. Patrocinio Schweickart has noted that we are

> subtly undermining . . . [the] sense of self worth of minority students while we imbue [mainstream students] with the confidence that the experiences, concerns, and perspectives of people like them constitute what is valued by the culture, (1988, 25)

making them unconcerned for the voices of others

As Brodky has pointed out, unless teachers explicitly resist and consciously confront the nature of the hegemonic discourse hidden within the hierarchical structure of society and the institution, the results are certain to be marginally effective at best and may even serve to work against espoused intentions. Dale M. Bauer further speaks against the expressivist model because she believes that it reinforces the dominant patriarchal culture (1990, 390), and she insists that we must not return to the politics of the personal (1990, 387). But, for many composition teachers, there has been no escape from the personal, and Bauer would agree that a public-private split is no solution. For Bauer, the answer is to foreground the issues of dominance in classroom discussion, and she initiates this primarily by her choice of material selected for use in her classes.

Perhaps the greatest need is for a closer examination of implicit messages that teachers impart in classroom teaching with reference to personal experience. If Linda Brodky is correct in her assessment of the middle-class discomfort with experiences that are not a part of the dominant culture, it is imperative that teachers examine their unconscious valorizing of the dominant culture's experience. When classroom discussion incorporates personal experiences, if the examples used are always ones that validate the dominant culture, some students are again marginalized even though use of the personal is intended to empower.

While writing teachers draw from a broad variety of theorists in their use of personal experience, they sometimes fail to acknowledge differences specific to writing classrooms. (B)ell hooks, for example, who insists that all students share and participate in her classes, teaches courses in which students choose to enroll. First-year writing courses are almost always mandatory, however, and therefore significantly differ from hooks' classes.

We must take into account other differences as well, such as the differences between women's studies and composition classes. Many practices have evolved from women's studies classes that are uniquely homogeneous, and there are a number of dangers involved in transposing the same pedagogy onto the composition classroom. Basil Bernstein has noted the significant amount of control implicit in situations with weak framing. That is, when pedagogy becomes less explicit, more open, and apparently more free, as in "nurturing" classrooms in which validation of the personal is important, often very specific expectations exist, although they may be hidden. Many students become attuned to expectations, however implicit, and strive to produce whatever will gain the teacher's acceptance; thus, the teacher unconsciously exercises considerable control over the student. If honest, emotional, revealing writing is the weakly framed expectation, students may try to provide more and more intimate details, information that may be inappropriate for the composition classroom and dangerous for the students. Aside from the fact that too much encouragement to expose the personal might create situations for which teachers are not properly prepared, as Bernstein points out, this seemingly free, accepting atmosphere actually makes maximum surveillance possible. The vulnerability of students and the possibility for control become much greater than in the more apparently controlling classroom that registers overt, strong framing. Where the pedagogy is visible, the hierarchy is explicit, and any infringement on boundaries is obvious. Weak framing, on the other hand, "encourages more of the child to be made public and so more of the child is available for direct and indirect surveillance and control" (Bernstein 1977, 235). Certainly, encouraging writing about personal, often intimate, experiences exposes students to possible manipulation and exploitation in ways traditional objective writing does not.

Feminists must decide how intimate personal experience in writing may become and still remain appropriate for the writing classroom. Teachers' understanding of the implications of their use of personal experience within the writing classroom is important because the teacher determines the degree of intimacy achieved in the classroom by making assignments and by directing class discussion. The teacher sets the tone for dealing with attitudes toward difference, decides the direction of critiques, and through the overall pedagogical methodology, communicates messages regarding the value of the personal. Since the teacher so obviously determines how theory is translated into practice, composition scholars might want to refocus attention on teachers, a neglected group in recent years.

One problem is that compositionists have tended to conflate the personal with the autobiographical and the intimate. Students may write about matters that are very personal without revealing intimate secrets.

In reexamining the use of the personal, we may wish to take another look at narrative and description as ways of including the personal, perhaps in a less intimate manner, a manner suggested by Ira Shor. Shor suggests studies of various aspects of mass society, for example fast food, as a means of bringing the personal to students. Students do find personal meaning in numerous features in their society, especially from within popular culture.

Narrative is a form of personal writing that has been undergoing re-examination. For instance, David Jolliffe has noted the increased questioning of the continuum that always moves in complexity from expressive to transactional writing based upon James Britton's study that defines expressivist writing as less complex than other writing.[2] Moreover, Debra Journet's work with narrative has shown that narrative, rather than being a "simple" form of writing, may instead offer a powerful means of communicating and understanding that traditional academic or expository writing is unable to provide. Journet's study shows the importance of narrative for two neurologists and their patients in their attempts to create a more clearly defined reality.

Greg Sarris also urges use of narrative for its value as a classroom tool to gain understanding of difference. Sarris uses storytelling as a means for encouraging critical discourse and as a method for bridging the split that he, like Dale Bauer, has found between the life experiences of students and critical thought in the classroom. Sarris finds storytelling effective in forcing culturally diverse students "to negotiate the discrepancies between home life and that which is found in the classroom" (1990, 173). By engaging students in classroom narratives, Sarris helps make them aware of how their assumptions are based upon their own cultural experience.

We are finally undertaking a serious, systematic examination of pedagogical practices. In a profession that has, as Stephen North observes, devalued practitioners and by extension pedagogy as well, this diligent look at a common classroom practice is inspiring. The myriad questionings concerning the incorporation of personal experience into the writing classroom exemplify a renewed interest in improving the pedagogical applications of feminist and composition theories. Since the 1963 watershed that initiated a greater emphasis on research, and subsequently a declining interest in practice, there has been an imbalance between theory and pedagogy, especially in composition journals. Practitioners have generally gone outside the field of composition and rhetoric to discover their methodologies, as exemplified by the widespread reference to Paulo Freire and the dependence upon the fields of educational psychology, women's studies, and feminist theory. While keeping abreast of pertinent information in other, relevant fields is valuable, scholars within rhetoric and composition may be able to improve the effectiveness of classroom methodology by re-emphasizing the practical applications of theory. In valuing our own "personal" classroom experience, we might allow for a dialectic between theory and practice that permits practice to inform theory, displacing the overwhelming privileging of theory as the shaper of practice.

Notes

1. Compositionist Peter Elbow proposes an introspective approach to writing that encourages students to seek insights from within and to express them openly as the most productive means of writing. Many scholars believe this approach ignores the importance of social context.

2. Britton suggests that writing difficulty may be measured according to a continuum that begins with self-expression and narrative and progresses in difficulty toward transactional writing, or writing whose purpose is to communicate information.

Works Cited

Alcoff, Linda. "Cultural Feminism Versus Post–Structuralism: The Identity Crisis in Feminist Theory." *Signs* 13 (Spring 1988): 405–36.

Annas, Pamela J. "Style as Politics: A Feminist Approach to the Teaching of Writing." *College English* 47 (April 1985): 360–71.

Ashton-Jones, Evelyn, and Dene Kay Thomas. "Composition, Collaboration, and Women's Ways of Knowing: A Conversation with Mary Belenky." *Journal of Advanced Composition* 10:2 (Fall 1990): 275–92.

Bauer, Dale M. "The Other 'F' Word: The Feminist in the Classroom." *College English* 52 (April 1990): 385–96.

Belenky, Mary Field, Blythe McVicker Clinchy, Nancy Rule Goldberger, and Jill Mattuck Tarule. *Women's Ways of Knowing: The Development of Self, Voice, and Mind.* New York: Basic Books, 1986.

Bernstein, Basil. *Class, Codes and Control: Towards a Theory of Educational Transmissions*. Vol. 3. 2d ed. Boston: Routledge, Kegan, and Paul, 1977.

Britton, James. "The Composing Processes and the Functions of Writing." In *Research on Composing*, eds. Charles Cooper and Lee Odell. Urbana, IL.: NCTE, 1978.

Brodky, Linda. "On the Subjects of Class and Gender in 'The Literacy Letters.'" *College English* (February 1989): 125–41.

Buzzell, Patricia, and Bruce Herzberg. *Bedford Bibliography for Teachers of Writing*. New York: Bedford Books of St. Martin's Press, 1991.

Coles, William E., Jr., and James Vopat. *What Makes Writing Good.* Lexington, Mass.: Heath, 1985.

Connors, Robert J. "Personal Writing Assignments." *College Composition and Communication* 38 (May 1987): 166–83.

de Lauretis, Teresa. *Technologies of Gender: Essays on Theory, Film, and Fiction*. Bloomington: Indiana University Press, 1987.

Dunn, Kathleen. "Feminist Teaching: Who Are Your Students?" *Womens Studies Quarterly* vol. 15 (Fall/Winter 1987): 40–45.

Ebert, Teresa L. "The 'Difference' of Postmodern Feminism." *College English* 53 (December 1991): 886–904.

Elbow, Peter. *Writing Without Teachers*. New York: Oxford University Press, 1973.

Fisher, Jerilyn. "Returning Women in the Feminist Classroom." *Women's Studies Quarterly* XV (Fall/Winter 1987): 90–95.

Flynn, Elizabeth. "Composing as a Woman." *College Composition and Communication* 39 (December 1988): 423–35.

Grant, Judith. "I Feel Therefore I Am: A Critique of Female Experience as the Basis for a Feminist Epistemology." *Women and Politics* 7 (Fall 1987): 99–114.

Hawkesworth, Mary E. "Knowers, Knowing, Known: Feminist Theory and Claims of Truth." *Signs* 14 (1989): 533–57.

hooks, bell. *Talking Back: Thinking Feminist, Thinking Black*. Boston: South End Press, 1989.

Jarratt, Susan. "Feminism and Composition: The Case for Conflict." In *Contending with Words: Composition in the Post-Modern Era*, eds. Patricia Harkin and John Schilb. New York: Modern Language Association, 1991.

Jolliffe, David. *The Content of Composition: Subjects and Genres in College Writing Instruction*. Forthcoming.

Journet, Debra. "Forms of Discourse and the Sciences of the Mind: Luria, Sacks, and the Role of Narrative in Neurological Case Histories." *Written Communication* 7 (April 1990): 171–99.

Lavine, Ann. "Subject Matter and Gender." In *Teaching Writing: Pedagogy, Gender, and Equity*, eds. Cynthia L. Caywood and Gillian R. Overing. Albany: SUNY Press, 1987.

Maher, Frances. "Pedagogies for the Gender-Balanced Curriculum." *Journal of Thought* vol. 20 (Fall 1985): 48-64.

—. "Classroom Pedagogy and the New Scholarship on Women." In *Gendered Subjects: The Dynamics of Feminist Teaching*, eds. Margo Cully and Catherine Portuges. Boston: Routledge and Kegan Paul, 1985.

Mahoney, Deirdre. "A Woman's Solitude, Silence, Interruptions and Work: Negotiating a Self." Paper presented at the Wyoming Conference on Rhetoric. Laramie, Wyoming (June 1991).

Newkirk, Thomas. "Anatomy of a Breakthrough: Case Study of a College Freshman Writer." In *New Directions in the Composing Process*, eds. Richard Beach and Lillian Bridwell. New York: Guilford, 1983.

Perry, Donna M. "Making Journal Writing Matter." In *Teaching Writing: Pedagogy, Gender, and Equity*, eds. Cynthia L. Caywood and Gillian R. Overing. Albany: SUNY Press, 1987.

Reimer, James D. "Becoming Gender Conscious: Writing about Sex Roles in a Composition Class." In *Teaching Writing: Pedagogy, Gender, and Equity*, eds. Cynthia L. Caywood and Gillian R. Overing. Albany: SUNY Press, 1987.

Sarris, Greg. "Storytelling in the Classroom: Crossing Vexed Chasms." *College English* 52 (February 1990): 169–85.

Schiachitano, Marian. Letter to the author (September 1990).

Schweickart, Patrocinio. "The Challenge of Diversity." *ADE Bulletin* 88 (Winter 1988): 21–26.

Shor, Ira. *Critical Teaching and Everyday Life*. Boston: South End Press, 1980.

Chapter 12

Evidence and Ideology When College Students Write About Gender

Virginia Nees-Hatlen

Writing Assignments *Beyond* Academe

In recent years, American universities have sponsored energetic efforts to demystify academic writing, prompted by new theoretical insights and facilitated by new methods for studying the hidden processes of which the written text is only the outward and visible sign. The field of rhetoric and composition, in which I was trained, has recently built a dynamic new academic community (and it has arguably improved the status of university writing instructors, many of them traditionally part-time women). This new scholarship has supported practical curricular reform in English, writing, and communication programs in which these scholars teach. But the topic of academic writing doesn't belong just to the teachers of rhetoric/composition. Many scholars from other disciplines have been retrained through the Writing-across-the-Curriculum movement to assist students learning to write in their fields. They, too, are writing teachers. Together, writing specialists and their colleagues are producing new classroom approaches and textbooks to implement the vision of Writing-across-the-Curriculum (or, in its alternative designation, "Writing in the Disciplines").[1]

But despite our new knowledge and collaborative approaches to teaching writing in academe, we have not solved all of our problems nor examined all of the implications of our work together, work of supreme importance to our society as well as to our academies. While we labor to reproduce ourselves, that is, to mentor new generations of academics, we also have a chance to teach generations about the public arts of language that citizens in a democracy need to maintain that fragile enterprise.[2]

Several years ago, when I was directing the one-semester first-year composition course on my campus and teaching a literature course called "Gender, Race, and Class in American Literature," I became haunted by two questions. The first question was a rather local and academic concern: Is there a useable carry-over between general composition classes and the subsequent fate of our college writers in later academic courses? The second question concerned me as a citizen and member of society at large: When college graduates have occasion to produce written argument in nonacademic settings, is there a useable carry-over from academic learning?

I have since come to believe that this latter question is perhaps the great begged question of academic life. We assume lasting results from the quality and rigor of our work, but we rarely make such results the subject of systematic inquiry. My paper focuses on this question of carry-over into our common social life; it reports on a research project that I conducted to explore the question in relationship to a vital issue affecting women in academe and in our society at large: gender equity in the workplace, especially in connection with the principle of Affirmative Action.[3] I wanted to see if students taught about gender issues in the academy and introduced to academic methods for assessing that information would use academic information or methods when addressing a nonacademic public. That is, would the academy seem useful to them and be accessible to them in a public rhetorical situation?

On my campus, the community most concerned with Affirmative Action and most committed to academic inquiry about other issues affecting women is a multidisciplinary project, designated "Women in the Curriculum," which sponsors colloquia, study groups, and women's studies courses. Women in the Curriculum (or WIC) funds grants to help faculty in all disciplines infuse recent scholarship about and by women into their classes. Over the past ten years, the WIC project has given out over forty grants to revise existing courses in history, literature, philosophy, political science, sociology, psychology, education, etc. The grants were awarded to help faculty read new material in their disciplines about and by women and by feminist scholars, to acquire library resources, and to provide stipends for time spent revising course materials. No specific provisions were made to link new writing tasks or pedagogies to the curricular changes funded by these grants. I wanted to look at what happened when students involved in such revised classes were called upon to write about the question of Affirmative Action to an audience and in a situation identified as nonacademic, specifically what happened as they chose their evidence and marshalled their arguments. I hoped to learn whether their classroom experience appreciably affected their writing strategies or their beliefs and assumptions as articulated in a working or public context. As a writing teacher, I was most curious about the effects of academic experience on the rhetorical complexity of their arguments. As a feminist, I was most interested to see if they could discourse theoretically (with conscious awareness and acknowledgment of feminist or other systematic principles and allegiances), or if their discourses would express personal or mass ideologies whose grounds were not consciously acknowledged and accounted for as principles and allegiances. I designed the research to probe both issues.

Methods: Writing Prompt and Rating

I gave the same writing task (or "prompt") to over 500 students at the University of Maine in 1987 and 1988, half of whom were first-year college students and half of whom were students in the revised courses funded by WIC. Respondents wrote for fifty minutes. I adapted the prompt from one used in a 1979 study by Charles R. Cooper and others of first-year college writers at SUNY Buffalo (1984), because that earlier study had validated the task as eliciting a range of writing abilities in a college population. Here is the prompt I used:

> At the place where you work, a woman has just quit her job, leaving vacant the company's only executive position ever held by a female. The Board of Directors have stated their preference that a woman replace her in order to fulfill an Affirmative Action quota. As a member of the Hiring Committee, it is your job to help choose a successor to the post. The only woman who has applied for the job seems competent and meets all of the written qualifications for the job, but the two men she is competing with have stronger credentials in some areas.[4] Members of the Hiring Committee disagree about what should be done: some say hiring a woman is absolutely necessary for breaking down employment discrimination; others say hiring a less qualified person would be foolish

as well as unfair to those working under the new executive. To have a full hearing of all views on this critical issue, the Hiring Committee has asked each member to prepare a carefully written statement to be distributed in advance of the meeting to discuss the issue. Write a statement which represents your position on the matter, making it as logical and persuasive as possible. Your writing task is to persuade the Committee to adopt your own view and to vote on the job candidates in accordance with your view.

A random sample of 140 scripts was culled from these 500+, and accompanying data about the writer's gender, age, year in school, and enrollment in the WIC classes was set aside. Anonymous and unidentified as to the writer's gender, age, or experience with academic material on women, each script was then rated by a team of seven readers. Raters were asked to describe the scripts on ten scales in terms of their recommendations to the Hiring Committee, their argumentative strategies, and the sources of their evidence and reasoning.

The rating team was trained for four hours before the reading, and in the end we achieved inter-rater reliability ranging from 55 to 95 percent on the scales, the former number too low to set much reliance on, the latter a very high index of rater reliability. The scales appear in Table 1. We had trouble attaining reliability on the rating categories E and F, which I designed to measure the complexity and maturity of argument. However, I will be reporting in this essay on findings with high inter-rater reliability, those derived from categories designed to gauge the writers' allegiances, methods of analysis, assumptions, and evidence (Categories A and H-J, Table 1.). Fortunately, among these findings are the issues most likely to be of interest to people concerned with Affirmative Action and gender. I will now briefly summarize some of the results.

Rating Category A: Hiring Recommendation

Of those writing, 50 percent recommended hiring one of the two men, whereas 35 percent recommended hiring the woman. No significant difference was found between males and females, or between first-year students and students in revised courses. Of the remaining group, 2.9 percent made no recommendation, 10.2 percent made an unclear recommendation, and one person recommended that the committee extend the search.

TABLE 1
Writing about Gender Equity: Rating Categories

A.	Hiring recommendation
B.	Audience addressed
C.	Invention of specific candidates' job histories/credentials
D.	Response to prompt assertion that males'credentials are "stronger in some areas"
E.	Mode of reasoning (in support of recommendation or another claim)
F.	Concessions to other points of view
G.	Corporate values used as argumentative warrants
H.	"Affirmative Action" used as argumentative warrant
I.	Evidence from personal experience or gender identity (include "As a Man/Woman, I")
J.	Evidence from academic experience

Rating Category H: Affirmative Action Used as an Argumentative Warrant

Of those surveyed, 16.1 percent of the students cited Affirmative Action as a warrant for hiring the woman (see Table 2). If this percentage is representative of larger demographic trends among the college generation, those of us committed to Affirmative Action policies need to engage in a defensive, "catch-up" fight to change minds. Furthermore, 19 percent of the sample categorically rejected Affirmative Action as a viable principle in hiring or social policy. It is striking that 44 percent never used the term (neither affirming nor challenging the principle), although it was provided in the task wording as a policy of the company. Thus, this 44 percent never systematically *critiqued* the principle; they simply treated it as irrelevant. Neither gender nor experience in a WIC revised course was a significant variable here. By contrast, 71 percent of the students surveyed cited profit and productivity (referred to in Table 1.G as "Corporate Values") as either the most important goal of the hiring process or one of several goals for the hiring process.

TABLE 2

H. "Affirmative Action" Used as Argumentative Warrant

	1.	No response; fragment.
44.5%	2.	The term "Affirmative Action" is never used.
9.5%	3.	The term "Affirmative Action" is used, but its value or viability as a concept is not clear.
16.1%	4.	"Affirmative Action" is cited as a warrant for hiring the woman.
10.9%	5.	"Affirmative Action" is cited as a once useful or sometimes useful concept, not appropriate to this hiring decision.
19.0%	6.	"Affirmative Action" is categorically rejected as a viable concept.

Rating Category J: Evidence from Academic Experience

Only five writers in the entire sample (3.6 percent) cited academic information or experience, which we construed to include any reference to class lectures, class activity, or reading, or to any published academic authority or theorist, statistic or illustration (Table 3). Again, experience in the classroom seemed to be an insignificant source of rhetorical tactics for our student writers.

It is interesting to note that personal experience and family experience, too, were avoided as sources of arguments by the writers, only eight of whom (5.8 percent) talked about themselves or their relatives' or friends' experiences (see Table 3).

TABLE 3

I. Evidence from Personal Experience or Gender Identity (includes "As a Man/Woman, I")

	1.	No response; fragment.
94.2%	2.	Personal experience (of self, family, friends, or community) is not cited as evidence or illustration.
5.8%	3.	Such personal experience is cited as evidence or illustration.

J. Evidence from Academic Experience

	1.	No response; fragment.
96.4%	2.	Academic information or experience (disciplinary constructs, texts, research, lectures, or classroom activities) is not cited as evidence or illustration.
3.6%	3.	Such academic information or experience is cited as evidence or illustration.

Evaluation of Results

So, what does all this mean? Let us look for a moment at the category involving the use of personal experience as evidence or illustration and ask what the findings imply about how these students were bringing their academic work to bear on the performance of a public rhetorical art, the position statement. Since our first-year writing course celebrates the value of the personal example, I must infer that our writing advice has been found irrelevant in our writing task's "real-world" rhetorical situation. And since many of the WIC courses celebrate the feminist axiom that "the personal is political," I must also infer that these college writers are not conscious feminists who value the life experiences of themselves, their mothers, their female friends, etc.—or if they do value women's experience as significant evidence, they do not believe it is useful to enact that value in a persuasive writing situation in the public arena. But more disturbing implications lurk in the category for academic experience as evidence. Clearly, students had not found academic approaches to women's issues relevant to this great public question—or else they judged their academic knowledge and methods to be inappropriate argumentative ammunition in a nonacademic situation.

Implications

As we academics contemplate these results, how do we feel? What are our vested interests? Do we not wish to have a greater impact on the content and standards of public, corporate, and private discourses that our students will create over the next forty years of their lives than these results suggest we will have? Or will we be content to limit our influence to the sometimes naive or jejune apprentice papers our students write during the few years we have contact with them? In their influential study of British secondary school writing, James Britton et al. (1975) problematized the narrow range of audiences addressed in school writing and termed the going-nowhere-but-school paper a "dummy-run." They concluded that language arts curricula were paying inordinate attention to success in school-only genres like the examination essay, the like of which most general students and many university graduates will never again see in their lives, whereas little time seemed devoted to helping students practice forms of discourse and engage in literate practices which public life, work life, and private life would repeatedly call on them to employ during their adult lives. My study suggests that American universities might want to follow the lead of Britton and examine themselves along these lines.

The study prompted me to change my goals and many of my writing assignments in advanced English classes, and it is guiding my planning for a women's studies course I will teach in the spring. In both courses, I am trying to give students practice in the genres of power and persuasion, and show them ways to articulate their academic learning for nonacademic audiences. I believe it is necessary to develop this sort of bridge-making as an alternative to standard academic papers. To truly profess what I know, I have to enable my students to profess what the university has taught them after they have left it.

As an example of the kind of assignment I now believe is most valuable in a women's studies course, I offer the writing task that I asked our students to address in this study. It is keyed to the sorts of audiences our students will need to address in their lives after graduation; it asks students to bring their academic experiences in women's studies to bear upon a gender-related question that divides contemporary Americans; it offers possibilities for role-playing the hiring committee and developing skills in oral communication; and it allows me as the instructor both to evoke and examine the pre-course ideological premises of the students, working with them as collaborators.

By thus discussing with students the various issues and interests implicit in the task as they draft and revise their position statements, and by specifically guiding them to scrutinize their theoretical or ideological presuppositions in the classroom context, I hope to achieve results with my own students quite different from those reported on in this paper. I will be satisfied as a first step to have students use things learned at the university to make a principled argument against Affirmation Action; as a second step, I will attempt to use reason and better evidence to change their minds.

Notes

1. Writing teachers and "content" teachers at all college levels can now teach with composition textbooks and readers that offer disciplinary-specific tasks and advice. For example, the Heath *Writer's Guide* series, whose muse is Toby Fulwiler, specifically links writing to the special methods of a discipline in chapters with such titles as "Learning Biology Through Writing" (Biddle 1987, 29–78) and "Approaches to Writing and Learning History" (Steffens 1987, 33–58). Another such enterprise, the Sociology Writing Group's *A Guide to Writing Sociology Papers*, discusses specific features of "the sociological imagination" that participate in framing questions and arguments in sociology (Giarrusso 1991, 7–23).

2. I am indebted to Paul Connolly, Director of the Bard College Institute for Writing and Thinking, for highlighting the phrase "public arts'" for me. He has a vision: Academics can and must train college students to address themselves to America's present and future social problems by articulating curricula and pedagogies in the public arts. His efforts to place listening skills, tolerance, and commitment to fair argument at the center of the Bard College workshops in Language and Thinking have given me new classroom goals to contemplate for the next decade.

3. I had the help of a small grant from the Women in the Curriculum Program at the University of Maine to pilot this project, and a 1987 grant from the National Council of Teachers of English Research Council to complete it.

4. Our prompt departed from the Cooper et al. wording here: "The only woman who has applied for the job seems competent and meets the written qualifications for the job but she is clearly less qualified than both of the men she is competing with" (1984, 22). This original categorical language seemed to skew reactions to the three job candidates, threatening to flatten the range of responses we would get. I felt, too, that in many situations, a woman's credentials were weighed as if all such qualifications were a matter of no debate, instead of valorized assessments themselves tied to ideologies of gender (such as the notion that unpaid work or childrearing were not related to abilities or qualifications of paid work).

Works Cited

Biddle, Arthur W., and Daniel J. Bean with Toby Fulwiler. *Writer's Guide: Life Sciences*. Lexington, Mass.: D. C. Heath and Co., 1987.

Bizzell, Patricia. Review of "What Can We Know, What Must We Do, What May We Hope: Writing Assessment." *College English* 49, no. 5 (September 1987): 575–84.

Britton, James, et al. "The Development of Writing Abilities." In *Schools Council Research Studies Report*. London: Macmillan Education, 1975.

Britton, James N., Nancy C. Martin, and Harold Rosen. *Multiple Marking of Compositions*. London: Her Majesty's Stationery Office, 1966.

Cooper, Charles R., ed. *The Nature and Measurement of Competency in English*. Urbana, Il.: National Council of Teachers of English, 1981.

Cooper, Charles R., et al. "Studying the Writing Abilities of a University Freshman Class: Strategies from a Case Study." In *New Directions in Composition Research*, 19–52, eds. Richard Beach and Lillian S. Bridwell. New York: The Guilford Press, 1984.

Giarrusso, Roseann, et al. (The Sociology Writing Group, University of California, Los Angeles). *A Guide to Writing Sociology Papers*. 2d ed. New York: St. Martin's Press, 1991.

Griffin, Gail B. *Calling: Essays on Teaching in the Mother Tongue*. Pasadena, Calif.: Trilogy Books, 1992.

Harkin, Patricia, and John Schlib. *Contending with Words: Composition and Rhetoric in a Postmodern Age*. New York: Modern Language Association, 1991.

Kaufer, David S., and Cheryl Geisler. "Novelty in Academic Writing." *Written Communication* 8 (1989): 236–311.

Lanham, Richard A. "The Extraordinary Convergence: Democracy Technology, Theory, and the University Curriculum." *South Atlantic Quarterly* 89 (1990): 27–50.

Lawson, Bruce, Susan Sterr Ryan, and W. Ross Winterowd. *Encountering Student Text: Interpretive Issues in Reading Student Writing*. Urbana, Il.: National Council of Teachers of English, 1989.

Lloyd-Jones, Richard. "Primary Trait Scoring." In *Evaluating Writing: Describing Measuring, Judging*, 33–66, eds. Charles R. Cooper and Lee Odell. Urbana, Il.: National Council of Teachers of English, 1977.

Mellon, John C. *National Assessment and the Teaching of English.* Urbana, Il.: National Council of Teachers of English, 1975.

National Assessment of Educational Progress. *Writing Achievement, 1969–79. Results from the Third National Writing Assessment.* Denver, Colo.: Education Commission of the States, 1980.

Solsten, Judith W. *Literacy, Gender, and Work: In Families and in School.* Norword, N.J.: Albex Publishing Company, 1993.

Steffens, Henry J., and Mary Jane Dickerson with Toby Fulwiler. *Writer's Guide: History.* Lexington, Mass.: D. C. Heath and Co., 1987.

Sternglass, Marilyn S. "Applications of the Wilkinson Model of Writing Maturity to College Writing." *College Composition and Communication* 33 (1982): 167–75.

Takalan, Sauli, Alan Purves, and Annette Buckmaster. "On the Interrelationships between Language, Perception, Thought and Culture and Their Relevance to the Assessment of Written Composition." *Evaluation in Education: An International Review Series* 5, no. 3 (1982): 317–42.

Chapter 13

Woman to Women: Understanding the Needs of Our Female Students

Mary Ann Gawelek, Maggie Mulqueen, and Jill Mattuck Tarule

In conferences and in most major works about gender in the academy, questions about what should be taught and about transformations of the disciplines are conventionally addressed. *How* teaching itself, and pedagogy generally are influenced by gender differences is rarely considered. This paper presents three theoretical perspective—epistemological development, female sex-role identity and competence development, and intimacy and autonomy drives—and shows how these perspectives have influenced our teaching.

We acknowledge the significant biases that guide our thinking. We enter into this study recognizing the critical importance that socio-cultural context plays in all human development. This is especially important in understanding women's development, as evidenced by the now documented negative impact of sex-role stereotyping and oppression experienced by women in our society. Given this fundamental premise, three essential assumptions follow: Women enter the academic experience with particular learning needs; women, particularly feminist professors, enter the teaching experience with distinctive competencies, attitudes, and feelings; and, an emphasis on the relationship between the teacher and students is fundamentally important to the learning experience of women (and probably men as well).

We wish to acknowledge that our formulations are based on our educational backgrounds (both in the accumulation of discipline-based knowledge and in our process as learners), our professional experiences as psychologists, teachers, and researchers, and our experiences as women. The theoretical perspectives that each of us brings to the understanding of gender in academe are a result of both our personal experiences and our professional practice.

Currently, we teach in a Counseling Psychology masters program of at Lesley College that has a predominately female, nontraditional age population. In addition, the counseling psychology faculty is composed of five women and three men. Women participate in all levels of administrative leadership at the college—Dean of the Division, Dean of the Graduate School, and President of the College. Thus, the presence of women, both in numbers and in positions of power, impacts how we experience the academic environment and how our students experience both their learning and themselves as women.

The writing of this paper began as the three of us discussed our particular perspectives. Each of us then drafted our perspective and shared those drafts with graduate students from our Counseling Psychology Program. Each of the students who responded to the presentation had experienced us as instructors in one or more classes, although none is currently enrolled in classes that we teach. We then asked these students, in a small group discussion, to respond to the theoretical materials and reflect on how their own experiences either verified or differed from what was presented. Following that discussion, we redrafted the paper and added the students responses. In that form, the paper was presented at the "Gender in Academe" conference where audience reactions further clarified the issues presented. The current paper includes all of these conversations.

We came to understand that each of the three theoretical perspectives has important implications concerning our understanding of the developmental needs of our women students, as well as implications for how best to create learning environments that are sensitive to these needs and foster growth. In our examination of the students' development from each of our perspectives, we came to appreciate how each of the theories is a part of the same whole and how each is necessary to our broader understanding of women's development.

Connected-Separate Learning

The first perspective is epistemological. One of us has done other research focusing on women's experience as learners (Belenky et al. 1986). From this research, three ideas emerged that are critically important in shaping the experience of and practice as a teacher: (1) The role of gaining and having a voice and its impact on the experience of being a student; (2) connected learning and the relational emphasis in learning; and (3) collaborative learning endeavors.

Voice—Voice has become a core concept in work about women's development. First, Carol Gilligan (1982) used voice as a metaphor for a strand of ethical and moral decision making that not only had been silenced but had been judged morally inferior. Moreover, the informants studied in Mary Belenky's *Women's Ways of Knowing* (1986) expressed that their sense of their own voice is deeply entwined with a sense of self and of efficacy in the world. Thinking about *voice* in teaching leads one to be concerned with how students feel about speaking up in class, about sharing their thinking out loud. Voice is the "currency" of the academy—in lectures, writing, discussions, doctoral committees, and in faculty meetings. If the only voice heard is the instructor's, students are deprived of a primary and critical way of knowing: "How do I know what I think until I hear what I say" is how one student expressed it. Talking is a narrative, explorative mode of learning that many learners require.

Each of our theoretical perspectives identifies particular forms of dialogue as a critical factor in our work with students. Opportunities to weave dialogue and conversation into learning must be provided. The simplest method is having students work in dyads or small groups. A second strategy is making it possible for individuals to speak in class without having to ask questions. Most classroom dialogues consist of student question/teacher answer. Creating a norm of identifying and speaking what Fritz Perls called "the statement behind the question" encourages students to wonder out loud about how they are thinking, to dare to state their half-formed idea. Equally important in establishing this norm is the use of writing as a way of locating and articulating one's ideas *and* one's doubts and confusion. As one of our student participant/researcher explained, "I can get the ideas in my little room by myself, but the life is in the discussion."

Connected and Separate Learning—One of the core findings from *Women's Ways of Knowing* is a definition of "connected learning" and "separate learning" as two different strategies for analysis. To characterize the strategies, separate learning is the "majority culture" way to learn what is traditionally taught and expected in higher education. Separate learners look for what is wrong, they play "devil's advocate." In contrast, connected learners begin critical analysis by caring about the other person's perspective, whether that other person is an author or a co-student, and argument is constructed out of this real or imagined relationship. Connected learners prefer learning environments that recognize the importance of relationships in learning.

Prevalent "majority culture" theory about learning has always been the basis for educational design and practice. Dominant descriptions, ethos, and practices about cognitive development and educational practice emphasize the developing learner as separate—isolated, solitary, and, usually, competitive. Connected learners, on the other hand, describe nondominant characteristics of the learning environment as providing them with appropriate challenge and support, characteristics that emphasize affirmation, dialogue, and collegial efforts. Connected learners need to know that their analysis is not surreptitious and faulty reasoning but legitimate and productive thinking, and that the core of thinking, itself, consists in constructing relationships among ideas and between experience and theory.

As women professors, we were all well trained as separate thinkers, so understanding connected learning can produce a profound and transformational impact on one's teaching. It now seems critical, both as a political act and a personal conviction, to emphasize strategies that assure the connected learners that their thinking is valid. Whether referring to hypotheses as "hunches" or referring to feeling passionate about ideas, each strategy attempts to introduce new terms into old constructs. A sensitivity to the relational emphasis also prompts a reassessment of relationships in the classroom, ushering in collaborative learning as a pedagogical strategy.

Collaborative Learning—Collaborative learning is a national movement (Whipple 1987; Landa 1989) with a complex, multifaceted definition. Here, two ideas will be discussed: (1) Collaborative learning assumes that learning occurs through relationships and dialogue; and (2) collaborative learning assumes the learner to be active in her or his own meaning-making and to be a knower in her or his own right. Both of these assumptions and their related practices are informed by social constructionist theory (Bruffee 1986) that argues that all knowledge is produced in community within paradigmatic frames that transform over time (Kuhn 1962). Collaborative learning thus emphasizes interdependency and co-creation (co-labor) of knowledge. True collaboration reconnects the individual's experience with his or her education. That is, experience-in-education is like the notion of self-in-relation (Miller 1976; Surrey 1983), the entwining of each component is critical to the development of both. In collaborative classes, much of the class time is often devoted to group work. A basic assumption underlying collaborative pedagogy is that students have "related" knowledge and that within a very short period of time, they will be asking questions of the discipline that either have not been asked or have not been answered by the scholars. The students' confusion and doubt, and the use of dialogue as a way of learning are all celebrated. Students are asked to pay attention to each others' ideas, to "think together." Collaboration is antithetical to the learning paradigm that rewards only individualistic thinking and accomplishment. A constant renegotiation also occurs in regard to authority in the classroom. With an emphasis on student/teacher collaboration, authority is lodged less in the teacher and more in the discipline and the discourse of the classroom.

Undertaking gender-sensitive research about learning has led to teaching differently. It has also led to change in the definition of scholarship, the disciplines, and the nature of knowledge. In short, the research and subsequent experience has led to a "deconstructing" of pedagogy in which difference (connected and separate learning) is respected, language and voice are honored, and collaboration is expected. As in the next two perspectives, the challenge is to find a balance between separate and connected learning strategies, so that all learners can feel good about themselves and challenged to think more, think together, and question old concepts and create new ideas. Hearing and acknowledging students' epistemological needs often creates an environment in which female students can explore their own competence. In addition, their relational needs for intimacy or autonomy can often be satisfied as well. The following sections address these aspects of women working with women.

Competence and Sex-Role Identity Development

This research considers competence motivation theory, since females' sense of competence is constructed through sex-role identity formation and both their sense of competence and their sex-role identity influence self-esteem. Generally, femininity and competence are considered to be mutually exclusive (Barnett and Baruch 1978;

Broverman et al. 1972). Since both a positive sense of competence and a positive sex-role identity are important components of self-esteem, women are at a disadvantage in developing high self-esteem. A wealth of data confirms that women consistently score lower than men on self-esteem measures (Sanford and Donovan 1984). Accepted female competencies—i.e. nurturance, child rearing—are devalued in the same way that connected learning is denigrated as an epistemology. Traditional models of competence motivation theory (White 1975) fail to address the power of sex-role socialization as it shapes development. Therefore, women are confronted with the dilemma of trying to achieve competence (in male sex-role identified activities or definitions) or successfully fulfilling female sex-role expectations (usually undervalued behaviors and attitudes). The resolution of this dilemma for women is to integrate both sex-role identity and sense of competence into a personality whose healthy, esteem-building features are not determined by gender. The precursors for mastering this integration involve redefining both femininity and competence. The only understanding of femininity that makes sense is to realize that if a woman does something, it is feminine.

Competence motivation can be understood as our pursuit of competence in all aspects of our lives, not just in those ways or tasks that the environment characterizes as competent. For example, maintaining a rich childhood friendship through adulthood can be seen as both competent and feminine and thus positively contributing to overall self-esteem. Through redefining both competence and femininity, the opportunity exists for women to pursue both and increase their self-esteem.

Pursuing both a sense of competence and a positive sex-role identity presents a new model for developing self-esteem defined as "balancing" (Mulqueen 1992). Women who are balancing are attempting to create new patterns for living that reflect their own interests and desires rather than attempting to fulfill prescribed societal expectations. Attempting to achieve balance necessitates learning how to reinforce oneself for behavior that is either not supported or not valued by society. For most women, this is nothing less than swimming upstream without a life jacket, especially since most women are keenly tuned in to issues of approval.

Applying the concept of *balancing* in the educational process is critically important for women. It is important to note that graduate education in any discipline is still a nontraditional pursuit for women. Therefore, when women students enter graduate study, the tension between their sex-role identity and competence issues are heightened. This may be especially true for women returning after years at home with their children or women who have been in the work force full-time. (Given current demographics, this is a particularly important population to consider.) In addition, these women may be entering their studies with little or no support from their families or friends. Many female students are struggling with issues of identity and anxiety about their ability to perform academically. They are confronting a potential crisis in their sense of competence, in their ability to balance, and in, as will be discussed later, their capacity to form satisfying relationships.

Although school supposedly is a learning environment where one's sense of competence should grow, more often than not, women students seem to experience it as a place where their sense of competence diminishes. Becoming competent is some mysterious process that students are supposed to acquire on their own through readings and assignments, but the classroom itself is actually the environment where competence is tested. Especially for women students who are enculturated not to speak, who may feel out of place to begin with, engaging in a conversation about theory may feel overwhelming. It is essential to think about what is needed to create an environment that will encourage growth and manage anxiety. At the same time, it is essential for the professor to avoid being so attentive to women's fears of incompetence that she alters her expectation of women's ability to be scholars. Such a lowering of standards reduces the potential for growth.

Creating a classroom environment that promotes competence and femininity is difficult and challenging; this is especially true when teaching a theory course. One example that illustrates attention to the need for balancing follows. At the end of the "Theories of Counseling and Psychotherapy" course, students are required to submit a paper that presents their own theory of counseling. The expectation is an assignment that even the most seasoned clinician might find challenging. For many women students it can be terrifying. Formulating an opinion in writing and making a commitment to an idea, both of which this assignment requires, are not typically comfortable positions for a woman to take, or if she does, she may experience an imbalance, perhaps feeling competent but not feminine.

Some specific pedagogical strategies to promote competence development and encourage the redefinition of femininity are as follows. First, echoing the importance of dialogue, students throughout the course are encouraged to comment on the material, not just raise questions. For many students, needing to take the critical stance involved in raising a question silences them, whereas if they are encouraged to comment on the material they often feel more comfortable speaking in class. Competence is seen as the ability to ask the penetrating question, while femininity includes not challenging another, but conversation marked by care. The opportunity to comment exemplifies a balance of femininity and competence. Second, since many students are quite anxious about being in school, as well as about the task of writing a theory paper, naming this anxiety and helping students to strategize how to manage it, rather than setting up the expectation that it can be eliminated or that competent people do not feel anxious, can help to dispel self-doubt, paving the way for a balancing approach to the problem.

Encouraging students to see themselves as knowers, not simply passive, receptive learners, helps students with the task of understanding theory and thinking of themselves as novice theorists. For women, beginning with the personal is often a freeing and novel experience. They then see how they can connect that information to help them become critical thinkers, replacing the belief that academic thinking is different and alien to them. Challenging women students to move beyond the personal to the theoretical empowers them to own and feel pride in their opinions rather than discounting them as merely their own ideas or experiences.

Throughout the course, each theory is presented without articulating the instructor's theoretical bias. Otherwise, it may be difficult for students to challenge the authority of the teacher and take a different stance. At the end of the class, after the students' papers are submitted, the professor's theoretical orientation is presented and illustrated with case examples from clinical practice. Case examples, successes and failures, are used to underscore the notion that competent people are not always perfect.

Given the aforementioned importance of balancing femininity and competence, the female professor has a wonderful opportunity to serve as a role model. It is essential that women who have managed to achieve in higher education commit themselves both to changing the alien environment many women experience during school and to encourage them to pursue degree opportunities that may seem "beyond" them, outside of their expectations for themselves. Remembering that many women, especially older students, often may receive little support or even face outright opposition from their family and friends for such aspirations, we intentionally try to help them develop insight into themselves as both competent and feminine as they pursue their education.

In conclusion, women students' sense of competence is increased when they are encouraged to complete difficult but worthwhile academic tasks in ways that strengthen their femininity rather than threaten or denigrate it. Women students may then develop what can appropriately be called feminine analytical thinking. The most important factor in supporting women students to be feminine *and* competent in their academic endeavors is providing them the opportunity to increase their self-esteem by creating academic environments that are welcoming to this important population.

Intimacy and Autonomy Drives in Women

Traditional personality theory has continually emphasized the drive toward autonomy as the healthy achievement of adulthood. From Freud onward, personality theorists have valued mature development as represented by separateness, independence, and achievement in the environment. These traits have been consistently associated with the male experience. More recent theorists have placed greater emphasis on relational aspects of psychological development; however, they continue to recognize the importance of separateness as the goal of a mature, autonomous self.

Women began to be recognized as more than a "nuisance variable" in psychology in the late sixties. Although women thinkers were not new to the field, at this time theorists began to realize that the experience of women might be significantly different from their male counterparts. Jean Baker Miller dramatically highlighted the centrality of relationship to women's experience (1976). Miller's work was soon followed by a wave of feminist thinking: Nancy Chodorow (1978) addressed the impact of mothering on women's drive for intimacy and closeness, and Carol Gilligan (1982) presented the moral development of women from a responsibility orientation or ethic of care, in which all normal choices are made in the context of relationship. The central concept presented by these theorists is that a woman's identity is defined by her capacity for relationship and a consistent striving for intimacy. Theorists at the Stone Center of Wellesley College have continued to study and reflect on the importance of intimacy in women's lives. Their work has stressed the centrality of mutuality, empathy (Jordan 1991), intersubjectivity, connectedness, differentiation, and self-in-relation theory (Surrey 1983). Significant challenges have been raised by feminist theorists regarding the emphasis on intimacy and empathy as key components of women's development. The most dramatic criticism occurs in the realm of ethnic and racial myopia. It is argued that what is being presented as woman's developmental theory is really white, middle-class women's development theory. Moreover, the characteristics proposed as central to women's development are the same as those commonly identified among oppressed people in general (Freire 1970; Espin et al. 1989; Espin and Gawelek 1992). If this is true, then what appear to be unique and positive aspects of women's personalities may in fact be by-products of their subordinate societal position.

Thus, there is a significant difference in emphasis between traditional psychological theory and feminist thinking on the importance of intimacy and autonomy in healthy development. The theoretical emphasis, revealed in our socially constructed (*man-made*) language reveals conventional judgments. "Autonomy" is associated with thoughts of maleness, separateness, dominance, self-governance, maturity, and adulthood; "intimacy" is associated with femaleness, closeness, merger, infancy, dependence, and neediness. The now-famous Broverman study (1972), in which mental health practitioners assessed traits associated with maleness (autonomy) as being healthy adult traits and those associated with femaleness (relational or affective) as being less healthy or immature, empirically demonstrated the value system masquerading as scientific objectivity.

A group of psychologists, all psychotherapists, have chosen to examine intimacy and autonomy as a dualistic drive for women (Gawelek et al., forthcoming). Since their experience and the life stories of their clients reflected that one drive could not exist without the other, the goal was to value equally the relational aspects of personhood and the more independent, self-defined aspects of the self. These drives can then be understood as having a figure/ground relationship to the total picture of a person. That is, the urge for intimacy is always shaped by the urge for autonomy; hence, there is a depth and breadth to the experience provided by both drives and an additional dimension that results in the interaction between the two drives. From this perspective, neither intimacy nor autonomy is seen as the primary drive or valued as a more mature/developed stance. It can also be assumed that the drives for intimacy and autonomy are equally present at each developmental phase. A constant dynamic process exists that allows the individual to move towards another (or the environment) or to move away from others into the self. Thus, in a healthy state, the person is comfortable with either posture, realizing that he or she will experience both the urge for autonomy or intimacy simultaneously or at different times and with different people.

Since both drives, intimacy and autonomy, carry strong socio-cultural meanings, correlating one drive with a gender, i.e., autonomy with men, intimacy with women can create enormous sex-role limitations. Given the positive attributes associated with autonomy, however, men may be limited in the recognition of their need for intimacy, but are not likely to receive strong negative reinforcement for this lack of recognition. On the other hand, women, if they satisfy their need for intimacy, may be deemed immature and are thwarted in their attempts toward autonomy, being judged as "pushy", "castrating", or "unfeminine."

One may wonder what the recognition of these dualistic drives has to do with the academic experience of women in higher education. If women who teach women pay attention to these drives in students, the students ability to learn and grow should be enhanced. This attention is also important for male students, but does not seem quite as critical to their overall well-being. A female professor, being conscious of her own posture towards intimacy and/or autonomy can better understand the dynamics that occur in the classroom. This sensitivity illuminates the teacher/student dynamic, which is a central relationship and plays a critical role in constructing a successful learning experience.

An example will help to illustrate this concept. In a large lecture class, one female student is quite vocal. Her verbal expressions in class often take on an aggressive tone. Although she seldom argues with the content presented, she seems to be stretching to find a greater truth or a more important reality than that presented by the professor. Outside of class, she consistently seeks out her female professor for feedback on her assignments and needs assurance that her thinking is solid. She illustrates one woman's urge for intimacy and autonomy. For her, the need to feel and be experienced as separate is very apparent in her classroom behavior. Her way of being separate demands that she be adamant and aggressive in tone. Thus, many *female and male* faculty members might experience *her* as antagonistic and abrasive. In reality, she has demonstrated a behavior that is often associated as male, independent, or autonomous. It is critical, as the professor, to be able to appreciate her position and to respond to her need for this autonomous stance. As a woman, this need to be separate, to be different from a professor, may be difficult if the professor needs a more intimate posture with this student; or, if owing to the professor's own needs for autonomy and power, she wants to have control of the conversation. Outside the classroom, this student is more vulnerable. Alone with the professor, the student seeks reassurance that her thinking is valid and that her presentation is appreciated. This posture represents a drive toward greater intimacy and may signify some degree of neediness. Again, it is essential to be able to meet this need with respect and to relate to the student's posture so that her learning is enhanced. If a professor can only tolerate the student's position of autonomy and cannot validate her need for support, the professor will not be able to affirm the student's more dependent/vulnerable self.

Similarities Across Theoretical Perspectives

Our joint theoretical perspectives frame the educational experience in several significant ways. First, we believe that dividing women's experience into dichotomies is highly significant: connected versus separate learning, femininity versus competence, intimacy versus autonomy. Second, it is critical to recognize that each pole of these dimensions has attached socio-cultural values—i.e., autonomy, separate thinking, and competence are characteristics that are valued in the culture, resulting in a rendering of the companion characteristics (intimacy, connected thinking, and female sex-role identity) as weaker and less valuable. In short, the conditions for prejudice and oppression are evident.

Pedagogically, we each see teaching as a socio-political activity and see ourselves as responsible for actively combating the results of the aforementioned oppression that our women students (and we ourselves) bring into the classroom. We seek pedagogical approaches that affirm the use of one's personal experience as a foundation for learning, and validate the broader context of women's lives (not just their identity as students). We seek to "name" or "rename" the experiences of the learner in ways that are inclusive and "balancing" of the dual drives, rather than continuing the exclusivity and imbalance that has characterized educational practice. We see the importance of finding ways to enact and demonstrate that women are capable of productive and creative work, competent in thinking, acting, and relating. The encouragement of dialogue that is inclusive and explorative in content is critical. The recognition and renegotiation of power and authority in relationships allow for an increased sense of self-esteem, as students explore becoming authoritative knowers themselves. Each perspective insists that, as "new words" (Woolf 1929) are found, each student locates her capacity as a learner together with her other crucial identity pursuits. We work to associate feminity—for our students and for ourselves—with redefined conceptions of what constitute critical thinking, competence, and the capacity for satisfying interpersonal relationships. The challenge as women educators continues to be, at least, threefold: Redefining our notions of a mature, educated human being; creating pedagogical practices that manifest this redefinition; and recognizing that we are women teaching women, and the continual assessment of the roots of our own assumptions becomes, itself, both role modeling and a subtext in all our work with students. We cannot ask of students that they recognize and struggle with being feminine and empowered if we are not also willing to do so within our own academic endeavors and institutional policies.

Students' Experience and Theory

Current second-year students and some alumni were invited to respond to the presentation materials. (Eight women were originally asked to participate in this study; six women agreed to participate, three attended the small group discussion.) It is important to note that the women were quite positive in their response to our request to participate. Scheduling prevented the nonparticipants from joining; those who were unable to join the group discussion sought out one of us to express their disappointment and share their reactions. They all commented that sharing with them draft copies of our papers communicated our willingness to dialogue about partially formed thoughts and ideas. They found this empowering.

We began the discussion by sharing with the participants our philosophical assumptions regarding the education of women (women having particular learning needs, female professors possessing unique competencies and the importance of relationship in education). The women uniformly stated that they did not enter their academic experience with the conscious notion that because they were women, they had unique learning needs. However, as they described their past learning experiences and talked about what they were looking for in the graduate school experience, all identified an environment that valued the person and emphasized experiential learning. The women did not correlate their wishes for such an environment to their sex but rather to their appreciation of humanistic education. They also clarified that they had not chosen this academic institution because of the high number of women students or faculty. Furthermore, that they did not feel a particular desire to seek out women faculty as professors. Thus, on the surface our participants did not share our own assumptions regarding women learners. However, during the course of the discussion the following acknowledgments were made:

> I knew what I wanted, but didn't assume they were based on being a woman; I never thought that I could have needs, . . . they were my needs, but I didn't identify it as a woman's needs.

We then asked the women to identify any similarities they noticed in all of the theoretical presentations. The strands that were discussed during the general discussion included: The role of questions in the classroom, the importance of connected learning, experiential and theoretical versus traditional perspectives, the reality of feminine and masculine characteristics existing in each individual, centrality of relationship in the classroom, importance of role modeling, critical need to have an expectation of excellence, and the valuing of safety in the learning experience.

We have categorized these topics into three major themes: The role played by the female professor as an authority or expert, the fostering of excellence in an environment of safety, and the centrality of affirmation as women. We explore these themes, in part, by using the students' descriptions of their experiences. However, as researchers, we actively engaged in the discussion with our participants since we believe in feminist methodological designs that recognize the intersubjectivity of the researcher/participants phenomenological responses (Gergen 1988). Thus, we include our own reactions as part of the discussion of the student participants' responses.

1. Female Professor as Authority or Expert. The students were impressed that we professors paid so much attention to our relationships with students in the classroom. Since all of the participants had shared an academic experience with at least one of us, we asked the students to address how the concepts we had articulated had affected their experiences. One of the participants shared the following, which exemplifies the importance all of us place on the teacher as role model.

> I had classes with all of you my first semester at Lesley. There was a tremendous amount of role modeling. Vulnerability, I think there's a big difference in the way men say, 'Let me tell you about a little something that went on in my practice.' Generally speaking, they're kind of removed from it. There is a way in which all of you at one

time or another spoke about failures in your professional life that was
not self effacing but was a way of being vulnerable, as a way of
teaching and connecting. Which I experienced as very empowering
and also made me feel connected with all of you and at the same time
though, it wasn't, 'now we're going to share our experiences', as if
there won't be any boundaries. It was real clear that you were
modeling, coming from your position as authority, but that was a way
of opening things up. And, I experienced that as a very gentle way of
teaching; that was different from what I had experienced before.
Especially since (participant pondered) how come the boundaries are
still there?

The students affirmed our conviction that as women teachers, our
responsibility is to model an integrated person connected to the student
and able to acknowledge our own expertise and our role as evaluator of
their learning. The women reacted strongly to our willingness to be
vulnerable and critical, available and judging.

Another participant offered:

> Role models are vital, but it became a part of me here because there
> are so many women around . . . I just don't assume I can't do it, they
> (women professors) are doing it so, therefore, I must be able to.

A third participant voiced her experience:

> You certainly are one of my role models of feminine competence, and
> I only expect my feelings to increase as you become a mother.

Thus, participants expressed the important role played by women
models, not only in their learning, but also in their developing identity
as women professionals.

Another important factor addressed by the participants was the ways
each of us attended to students' voices. It was clear that the participants
appreciated our eliciting their thoughts during classroom discussions. In
the words of one participant:

> To be able to hear the student's voice on her own terms and respond
> whenever it's appropriate to respond, whether that's to encourage
> someone that, 'Yes, I'm hearing you and I hear your question' or
> saying, 'I hear where you are and I think you're able to accomplish
> more than you think you can.'

Each described her own personal security or anxiety in relation to voice (i.e., greater security in writing, speaking being easier than listening, and fearfulness about challenging the instructor or peers), and then shared her feelings that the attention given to her participation was helpful. As such, we validated the importance that we placed on the interactive process in the classroom environment. The participants acknowledged that this emphasis on what they thought about material presented was not always reassuring or welcomed. They recognized that this style of learning eliminates the possibilities of "hiding" and is often more difficult and challenging to the student. We began to understand that allowing students to enact the compliant, silent role constitutes lowering standards for them, while supporting them (and ourselves) to be vulnerable and demanding seemed to communicate effectively the dual message of high standards and expectations grounded in trustful explorative dialogue.

2. Excellence in Safety. Each of the theoretical perspectives places a great deal of emphasis on creating an environment in which the women feel safe to be who they are and to grow. This emphasis on security was noted by the student participants. All of the participants identified connected learning as a safe experience. However, they were not as able to see this style of learning as rigorous or as "real" learning. In the same vein, the participants felt that the expansion demanded by the "Theories" course, the movement from the personal to the theoretical, did not always feel safe. However, it became clear as the discussion continued that the participants equally valued the demand for excellence and the creation of a safe environment, although it seemed difficult for them to recognize the experience of safety and the achievement of excellence in the same experiential frame. In this, we heard the students echoing the dilemma of equally valuing both of these goals. Thus, the students asserted that both the inclusion of their experience as knowledge and the affirmation of them as knowers challenged feelings of safety. However, these were often seen as interpersonal pedagogical "tricks" and thus unrelated to what they identified as academic achievement and competence. It was somewhat troubling to encounter this compartmentalization because it suggested to us that, despite our theory and teaching, the students had internalized traditional pedagogical values.

3. Affirmation of the Female Experience. What was most striking and most disturbing to each of us was the student's rejection of the

gender of professor as significant. Several times during the discussion, a participant would describe a female-identified characteristic as pathological. In addition, the women seemed almost frightened to admit that as women they might have particular needs or desires. The following example illustrates this point:

> There were more women here (at Lesley) and it felt better, easier . . . to be me it comes back to the safety issues. I don't associate it with being female but my experience is that it happens more often in settings with women than with men (Discussion group laughter).

And, as is standard in gender studies, the participants felt a need repeatedly to assure us of the worth of our male faculty counterparts. One participant describes this phenomenon:

> In many ways it's safer for me with a woman instructor, but I'm not sure that this is valid, because it's probably because of the baggage I'm bringing into it from my background . . . Clearly, I learned from the male instructors here.

Only in veiled terms were these women able to correlate what was positive in their classroom experience with the fact that they were being taught by women who were sensitive to women.

As researchers, we were faced with interpreting this information in two ways: (1) The students were telling us that gender was not important, or (2) although they spoke to the importance of gender, the societal devaluation of the feminine is still so strong that the women refused to acknowledge the salience of the gender variable. Obviously, as feminists, we believe the latter. However, this certainly has raised for us questions about context. Since our program is women identified, with large numbers of women faculty and students, and since we as instructors attend to the women students' needs in ways that we believe are essential to providing a healthful learning opportunity for women, do the women benefit from the experience without realizing that it is feminist and therefore affirming of their womanhood? How do women students themselves feel about feminist teaching? How can we affirm intimacy, connection, and femininity and yet maintain the more traditionally valued styles? How critical is it to have a conceptual scaffold that defines one's learning approach? These questions can only be answered as we continue to articulate how and why we teach our women students the way we do and to ask these same women students what their experience is as students.

Summary

We believe that women students thrive in an academic environment that fosters connected learning, but the learning environment must also recognize and acknowledge to women students that false dichotomies exist—femininity versus competence, safety versus rigor, and intimacy versus autonomy. First, the identification naming of these tensions allows women to feel grounded in their learning environment, and second, the recognition that the dichotomies require balance, not choice, enables students to confront the challenges of education as full human beings. As women professors who are feminist, we face the important challenge of modeling the integration of these dualities, creating an environment for students where this integration can be experienced, encouraged, and celebrated such that it makes it possible for all students to continue to grow.

Finally, our own scholarship has developed and thrived in environments like those we attempt to create for our students. Nor do we think that our ideas or theories would have been possible were this not the case. So, we understand that what we know is inextricably entwined with how we know it. Thus, our pedagogy—*how* we teach is entwined with *what* we teach. In the end, we learned that this fundamental association of knowledge and process was less firmly asserted by our students and that the snag seemed to be a lack of understanding on their part that their own femininity was a valued feature in the project of becoming educated. We close this exploration with concerns that there is more to be done on the level of description and definition than we originally imagined. We are committed to exploring both feminist theory and pedagogy, and we are hopeful that our students, too, will learn that they can be competent learners, effective professionals, and feminists.

Works Cited

Barnett, Rosalind, and Grace Baruch. *The Competent Woman: 6 Perspectives on Development.* New York: Irvington, 1978.

Belenky, Mary, Barbara Clinchy, Nancy Goldberger, and Jill Tarule. *Women's Ways of Knowing: The Development of Self, Voice and Mind.* New York: Basic Books, 1986.

Broverman, Inge, Susan Yogel, Donald Broverman, Frank Clarkson, and Paul Rosenkrantz. "Sex-role Stereotypes: A Current Appraisal." *Journal of Social Issues* 28 (1972): 5–78.

Bruffee, Kenneth. "Social Construction, Language, and the Authority of Knowledge: A Bibliographical Essay." *College English* 48 (1986): 773–90.

Chodorow, Nancy. *The Reproduction of Mothering.* Berkeley: University of California Press, 1978.

Espin, Oliva, and Mary Ann Gawelek. "Women's Diversity: Ethnicity, Race, Class and Gender in Theories of Feminist Psychology." In *Theories of Personality and Psychopathology: Feminist Reappraisals*, eds. L. Brown and M. Ballou. New York: Guilford Press, 1992.

Espin, Oliva, Mary Ann Gawelek, Louise Christian, and Eileen Nickerson. "Intimacy and Autonomy: A Stereoscopic View of the Psychology of Women." In *Association of Women in Psychology Newsletter* (1989).

Freire, Paulo. *Pedagogy of the Oppressed.* New York: Seabury Press, 1970.

Gawelek, Mary Ann, Eileen Nickerson, Oliva Espin, and Louise Christian. "Intimacy and Autonomy in Women: A Stereoscopic Vision." Forthcoming. Gergen, Mary McCanney, ed. *Feminist Thought and the Structure of Knowledge.* New York: New York University Press, 1988.

Gergen, Mary McCanney, ed. *Feminist thought and the Structure of Knowledge.* New York: New York University Press, 1988.

Gilligan, Carol. *In a Different Voice.* Cambridge, Mass.: Harvard University Press, 1982.

Jordan, Judith. "Empathy and Self Boundaries." In *Women's Growth and Connection*, eds. Judith Jordan, Alexandra Kaplan, Jean Baker Miller, Irene Stiver, and Janet Surrey. New York: Guilford Press, 1991.

Kuhn, T. *The Structure of Scientific Revolutions.* Chicago: University of Chicago Press, 1962.

Landa, A. "Setting the Context for Theory." *Lesley College Collaborative Project Newsletter* I (1989): 1–2.

Lyons, Nona. "Two Perspectives: On Self, Relationships and Morality." *Harvard Educational Review* 52(2) (May 1983): 125–145.

Miller, Jean Baker. *Toward a New Psychology of Women.* New York: Basic Books, 1976.

—. "The Development of Women's Sense of Self." In *Women's Growth and Connection*, eds. Judith Jordan, Alexandra Kaplan, Jean Baker Miller, Irene Stiver, and Janet Surrey. New York: Guilford Press, 1991.

Mulqueen, Margaret. *On Our Own Terms: Redefining Competence and Feminity*. Albany: SUNY Press, 1992.

Sanford, Linda, and Mary Ellen Donovan. *Women and Self-Esteem: Understanding and Improving the Way We Think and Feel About Ourselves*. New York: Penguin, 1984.

Surrey, J. "The 'Self-in-Relation': A Theory of Women's Development." *The Stone Center Work In Progress Papers* 13 (1983): 1–9.

Whipple, B. "Collaborative Learning: Recognizing It When We See It." *AAHE Bulletin* (October 1987): 3–7.

White, R.W. *Lives in Progress: A Study of the Natural Growth of Personality*. New York: Holt, Rinehart and Winston, 1975.

Woolf, Virginia. *A Room of One's Own*. New York: Harcourt Brace, 1929.

Part III

How does a feminist perspective influence *what* and *how* we teach outside the classroom?

Chapter 14

A Study in Feminisms: Organizing A Gender Conference

Lagretta Tallent Lenker

Imagine the opportunity to create your ideal professional two and one-half day conference—hour upon hour of stimulating presentations and discussions highlighted by the participation of some of the brightest minds in academe. Imagine the opportunity to provide a forum for voices too seldom heard and works too long unrecognized. Finally, imagine the opportunity to make a real difference on your own campus—to confront perceptions about gender stereotypes. The manifestation of this fantasy, at least for me, is the University of South Florida's Gender in Academe Conference. With two such conferences completed and plans for the third underway, I realize that, yes, the starry-eyed goals of a feminist Don Quixote are attainable and that these conferences provide the vehicles for the realization of that dream. However, a realistic assessment of our work reveals that my "Doña Quixote" more accurately resembles a long-suffering "Mother Courage," and, I must admit, I much prefer the latter analogy. The organization and nurture of this conference entails managing the tensions as well as the euphorias inherent in this process, for, indeed, such a conference provides a microcosm for the real-world macrocosm of that growth industry known as gender studies. This chapter chronicles the genesis of the "Gender in Academe" conference as a method of engaging in the debate on contemporary feminisms.

Interestingly, developmental parallels exist between the evolution of contemporary feminism and that of this conference. The first conference was a recognition of women's place (or lack of it) within traditional academic settings and an evaluation of how the past could shape the future. The second conference sought to continue the momentum garnered by the first, to move our study still further by considering both male and female perspectives, and to showcase the various viewpoints included within the feminist agenda. This last point—feminism's multiple perspectives—perhaps forms the most distinctive characteristic of feminism today. Arguably, the feminist agenda is more accepted today than ever before, with great strides for women's equality being made in fields as diverse as theology and medicine. Significantly, the 1992 political season has been labeled the "year of the woman." At last, the sexist gridlock in the U.S. Senate will be broken. Perhaps relatedly, women's concerns are becoming more central in health issues from National Institute of Health heart studies to Centers for Disease Control AIDS initiatives. Yet, I write this essay at a time in which these gains are juxtaposed with Marilyn Quayle's call for a rededication to the "essential nature of women" and Camille Paglia's derision of Gloria Steinem and company as representatives of a feminism "out of touch" with contemporary women. How can one assess contemporary feminism in light of the disparate messages sent by those supposedly intimately involved in assessing and even in pioneering new roles for women?

Perhaps the answer lies in the plural, as gender studies moves from a dual stance of *describing* women's oppression and *prescribing* remedies to alleviating that inequality (Jaggar 1978, xi) to a more open position, one that encourages disparate, even contradictory, voices. Scholars note the complex fabric of the historical solidarity of feminism. For example, Alison Jaggar contends that suffrage, temperance, and birth control have all dominated the feminist agenda. Nevertheless:

In the two or three centuries of its existence, organized feminism has not spoken with a single voice. The most recent resurgence of feminism occurred in the late 1960s with the rise of what came to be known as the women's liberation movement. This movement surpassed all earlier waves of feminism in the breadth of its concerns and the depth of its critiques. *It was far less unified than previous feminist movements, offering a multitude of analyses of women's oppression and a profusion of visions of women's liberation.* (Jaggar 1978, 4; italics mine)

Judith Butler offers a related but varied observation about the "universal" truths of feminism:

> The political assumption that there must be a universal basis for feminism, one which must be found in an identity assumed to exist cross-culturally, often accompanies the notion that the oppression of women has some singular form discernible in the universal or hegemonic structure of patriarchy or masculine domination . . . (I)t may be time to entertain a radical critique that seeks to free feminist theory from the necessity of having to construct a single or abiding ground which is invariably contested by those identity positions or anti-identity positions that it invariably excludes. Do the exclusionary practices that ground feminist theory in a notion of "women" as subject paradoxically undercut feminist goals to extend its claims to "representation"? (1990, 3–5)

In their pioneering work *Making a Difference*, Gayle Greene and Coppelia Kahn localize the polarity that exists within the feminist camp in a critique of two respected feminist scholars: Annette Kolodny's "playful pluralism" versus Elaine Showalter's "theoretical consensus." The following passage summarizes this schism:

> [Kolodny] is not willing to discard the variety of approaches she discovers in feminist criticism in favour of a single theoretical model. She advocates a "playful pluralism," responsive to the possibilities of multiple critical schools and methods, but "captive of none," a recognition "that many tools needed for our analysis will necessarily be largely inherited and only partly of our own making" (Kolodny 1980, 19). Showalter, however, is uneasy about the notion of "playful pluralism", and answers . . . [with] a call for a "theoretical consensus" . . . (1985, 54)

Thus, leading feminist scholars themselves differ on the appropriate "role and scope" of the feminist agenda. Similarly, our own "microcosm"—the USF Gender in Academe Conference—also has produced its own pressure points. As we have found, even a relatively innocuous activity, such as staging a conference to discuss the role of gender in the academy, can create potentially controversial issues that threaten to undermine the effectiveness of that enterprise. The question of who "owns" gender studies illustrates this point. Several academic departments each can lay plausible claim to being the rightful home of gender-based scholarship. On our own campus, the English, psychology, philosophy, and art departments all offer strong curricula in this area, in addition to the comprehensive program of the women's studies division. How to incorporate all of these areas becomes a formidable challenge, for all are vital to this truly interdisciplinary topic and all are extremely busy with their own agendas. I can only raise this issue as a cautionary warning to others considering a similar program, for each campus and/or academic body is different and each negotiates its own delicate balance of power in this area.

While attempting to integrate a balance of perspectives into the program, one must also consider how to involve in this process both men and those women who are wary of the feminist label. Often, this "outside" clientele forms the very audience that such a conference should reach in an attempt to highlight the values and opportunities afforded by a feminist ethic to women and men alike. Using promotional literature that stresses that multiple points of view will be considered at the conference offers an avenue for approaching those who are interested in the subject but are not committed to a particular philosophy. Also, by assembling a conference planning committee that represents various departments and specialties, a more balanced, less threatening agenda can be purposed.

In the programming planning area, how to avoid the confessional/anecdotal forms a major problem that must be addressed. While the maxim "the personal is political" serves as a rallying cry for many feminists, and women's struggles against an oppressive system are important individually and collectively, too many retellings of personal battles for equality can reduce a meeting of scholarly minds to just another gripe session, one fraught with bitterness and disappointment. The "trick" to achieving the proper balance and tone for such meetings lies in discerning when someone's own saga can be representative of those of many or when a personal experience breaks new ground in gender-related areas. An example of an effective presentation of a meaningful case history was Linda Brodky's talk at our 1991 Gender Conference. Ms. Brodky's "Trouble at Texas" chronicled her attempt to introduce gender and ethnic diversity into the traditional curriculum of a southwestern university. Her efforts were met with resistance on many levels, and her subsequent presentation was effectively designed to offer a model for attempting change rather than to use this forum to rail against her own critics. Other well-meaning presentations evidently have not been as successful. The reviews of a recent conference honoring a well-known and respected feminist scholar upon her retirement were mixed. An article in *The Chronicle of Higher*

Education reported that while the program was well-received in many camps, at least one attendee noted a tone that illustrates my point:

> Many of the women speaking are very fortunate academics. They are relatively privileged—tenured at the country's top institutions, paid enormous salaries—and yet there was this parade of complaining and shocked women and horror stories about how badly they and their women colleagues had been treated. All scholars have such stories. (1992, A18)

"Parades of complaining and shocked women" (and/or men) spell disaster for most conferences—especially when the topic is even mildly controversial. Screening panels and conference committees should guard against inviting papers and presentations not grounded specifically in research, and should include those talks of a personal nature only when a clear indication is present to suggest that this experience relates to the experiences of others in some singular way or offers pioneering advice useful to many.

These "pressure points" notwithstanding, a successful conference is possible, even probable, with sufficient planning. Few academics can spare the time necessary for organizing a conference single-handedly. A well-chosen conference planning committee comprised of five or six people can strengthen program content and decrease the burden on the conference coordinator. For maximum effectiveness, choose committee members representing disparate disciplines, with diverse talents such as marketing and scheduling, and assign people to perform tasks according to their strengths. Any of the core planners desiring to present papers at the conference should have first choice of topics and time-slots in order to keep commitment at a high level. Working closely with a university's continuing education or conferences unit will involve professionals in the planning of meetings and thus will reduce the work load of the individual or committee responsible for the conference content.

The foremost task of the conference committee will be to identify the exact topic or focus of the conference. Once chosen, the conference topic will dictate the composition of the audience both for the meeting and for any subsequent publications resulting from it. Interdisciplinary conferences such as Gender in Academe are particularly suited to the conference-publication scenario. The beauty of such an interdisciplinary topic is that this wide focus broadens the audience and then provides the opportunity to present creative, innovative approaches to the subject, a combination attractive to contributors and publishers alike. The potential for cross-fertilization of ideas in disparate fields of studies is the special bonus of an interdisciplinary conference that should not be underestimated, although this diversity, too, presents challenges of its own. Furthermore, the publication of presentations can extend the message of the conference, yield a wider audience, and even provide vehicles toward tenure and promotion for the academics involved. The multiple perspectives offered by such a conference lend an appealing diversity to such a publication, provided that a skillful editor has crafted a focus and unity for the volume while preserving the individuality of the essays.   This editorial guidance is no small task, requiring consummate tact and a discerning sense of stylistic integrity. Yet the end result can prove the crown jewel of an already worthwhile effort.

In summary, as a result of my experiences with the gender conferences, I have come to advocate something akin to a chaos theory of feminism—a theory that does not seek monolithic order or structure but rather celebrates and affirms the infinite variety of "isms" that belong under the feminist umbrella. This theory seemingly conflicts with the near-sacred caveats of conference organization that demand systemization and efficiency—no one wants to attend a conference where the guiding principle is chaos! Yet, in this case, the two disparate systems—the chaos and the systematization—are compatible. There is a place for everyone and every point of view.   Once again, the microcosm mirrors the macrocosm—the acceptance of diversity is the strength of both the larger feminist community and our gender conference.

Works Cited

Butler, Judith. *Gender Trouble: Feminism and the Subversion of Identity*. New York: Routledge, 1990.
Chronicle of Higher Education. (November 1992): A18.
Greene, Gayle, and Coppelia Kahn, eds. *Making a Difference: Feminist Literary Criticism*. New York: Methuen, 1985.
Jaggar, Alison. "Feminist Politics." In *Feminist Frameworks: Alternative Theoretical Accounts of the Relations between Women and Men*, eds. Alison Jaggar and Paula Rothenberg. New York: McGraw-Hill, 1978.

Chapter 15

Feminist Journals: Academic Empowerment or Professional Liability?

Judith Worell

Within the past fifteen years, we have seen the birth of a new breed of scholarly journal that is frankly feminist in policy and content. The appearance of feminist publications on the academic scene raises at least two important questions. First, how do these journals influence the direction of research in relevant fields of inquiry, and second, what is the impact of feminist journals on the professional lives of the academic people who are both creators and consumers of the new revisionist scholarship?

I want to explore these two questions within the context of the journal that I represent as Editor, *Psychology of Women Quarterly*, which is the major journal of feminist theory and research in psychology. I will conclude, as my title suggests, that there appear to be both positive and negative consequences of this revisionist movement. On the positive side, feminists gain voice, visibility, and empowerment from these journals. We receive validation of ourselves as creative scholars exploring new paradigms, and we proclaim the primacy of women's experiences. At the same time, those of us who publish in feminist journals face the risk of academic stigma, devaluation of our professional competence and status, and segregation of our scholarship into feminist publication ghettos.

Feminist Journals and Academic Empowerment

The first question regarding academic influence will be discussed in the context of the structure and publication policies of the *Psychology of Women Quarterly*. As a feminist journal, this publication is singular in the field of psychology in at least three major ways: structure, content, and process.

Structure

At the structural level, the operation of the journal is unique to our field, in that it is managed almost exclusively by women. The Editor and the five Action Editors are women, as are the majority on the board of thirty-eight Consulting Editors; most of the ad hoc reviewers are also women. Diversity of women is also recognized at the editorial level, with women of color and differing sexual orientations specifically included. This structure reflects the primacy of women as recognized experts in the psychology of women and gender. As well, the majority of published articles in the Journal are also authored or co-authored by women.

By redefining expertise, the feminist journal provides professional visibility and voice to women, most of whom are housed in academic positions. Many of these authors, because of their gender and minority status, as well as the content and methods they address, are less likely to find publication outlets in the major scholarly journals of psychology. As M. Brinton Lykes and Abigail J. Stewart have documented (1986), women scholars are less likely to be published in mainstream scholarly journals; their works are cited less often than those of men, and fewer women than men are listed as first authors in mainstream psychological journals.

Content

At the content level, all feminist journals address issues of concern to women. These include topics that have been previously ignored in the literature, or that have been interpreted in ways that are damaging to women. For example, feminist journals publish research on factors influencing women's achievement and career development; on women's experiences in family and work settings; on the effects of sexism, discrimination, sexual harassment, and sexual violence on women; and on media portrayals of women and the effects of stereotyped or violent role images on viewers' attitudes and behaviors toward women. Feminist journals also encourage new research on the societal and personal factors influencing women's mental and physical health status, and on the variables affecting women's satisfaction and well-being in close relationships. These examples embrace only a few of the topics concerning women that were previously invisible in the psychological research literature.

In contrast to mainstream publications, then, studies in feminist journals routinely include women as research participants and as legitimate targets of scientific inquiry. Such research reframes psychology as the study of the behavior of *people* rather than the study of men. Feminist publications are also more likely than mainstream journals to include studies that examine only the female experience, thereby redressing the scientific imbalance of attention to women as feeling, thinking, and enacting individuals. In attending to the experience and impact of sex and gender, feminist journals have also encouraged exploration of diversity among women. The complex intersects in women's lives of ethnicity, color, sexual orientation, and poverty, for example, receive increasing attention in the feminist research literature. In meeting the feminist challenge to research and thought, these journals have reintroduced women into the heritage of many disciplines and have forged new inroads into previously ignored scientific and epistemological territories.

Process

Finally, at the process level, feminist journals have focused our attention on emergent conceptions of theory and scholarship that challenge the traditional and urge us to create new realities. I see the development of feminist psychology as an emergent process rather than as an accomplished revolution.

Traditional research criteria. Established forms of research that serve heuristic purposes are not discarded, but are integrated into an evolving paradigm. Thus, in determining the quality of submitted manuscripts, we remain traditional in insisting on certain criteria that ensure high levels of communication, clarity, and scientific validity (Worell 1990). These criteria are similar to those that might be used in any major psychological research journal. For purposes of comparison with emergent feminist research criteria, Table 1 displays these traditional standards for the presentation of psychological research to the professional community.

TABLE 1
Traditional Scholarly Research Criteria

1. Presentation of theory and rationale underlying the research
2. Recognition of relevant previous research
3. Appropriate sample of respondents, carefully selected and described
4. Control group relevant to hypothesis-testing
5. Instrumentation that is reliable and valid
6. Procedures carefully described and replicable by others
7. Statistics appropriate for hypothesis-testing
8. Hypotheses and results discussed in context

Emergent research criteria. In reconstructing our conceptions of science, we remain aware of the legacies of our discipline, but we begin to ask challenging questions and to expand our methodologies. Early voices in the feminist revolution confronted and critiqued traditional experimental research paradigms; Carolyn W. Sherif and Mary Brown Parlee were pioneers in the evolution toward setting an agenda for research with women and insisting on the study of women within the relevant context of their lives. Subsequently, other voices further questioned the mirage of a "value-free" science, pointing to the ways in which sex bias in traditional research has framed our conception of "reality" (Grady 1981; Unger 1983; Wallston 1981). From within the discipline of psychology (e.g., Lott 1985; Peplau and Conrad 1989), as well as from neighboring disciplines (e.g., Harding 1986; Keller 1985) researchers proclaimed support for revisions in both our conceptions of science as well as affirming the legitimacy of alternative modes for studying human experience. The transformation to innovative modes of theory and method is a continuing journey. Alternative research strategies can augment our perspectives on the lives of all women; in particular, they can be helpful in examining important contextual issues, such as variations in group memberships, lifestyles, socialization, or gender arrangements that signify hierarchy and power. Mary Crawford and Jean Marecek (1989) have pointed out that feminists of all persuasions recognize that doing psychological research is inevitably a political act and that our values always "contaminate" our research. We want those values to be feminist.

To further articulate and clarify the aims of a feminist science, I am proposing a set of ten emergent criteria, displayed in Table 2, that can form the basis of a reconstructed psychology. These criteria do not replace the standards outlined on Table 1, but provide expanded dimensions for addressing the feminist agenda. The criteria are intended to be illustrative rather than exhaustive; they may well be modified or expanded as we evaluate their outcomes. In designing a revisionist process of evaluating scientific effort, we provide women in academia with many tools: alternative perspectives, new understandings, exciting materials for infusion into their teaching, and stimulation for their own research efforts.

In the process of producing a reconstructed science, we work to infuse its methods and outcomes into mainstream psychology as well as into psychology of women curricula. Materials drawn from mainstream journals are most likely to be referenced in the journals of other disciplines, and may receive attention from public media such as newspapers and magazines. Media displays then lead to public awareness, and public policy decisions may then be influenced indirectly by feminist insights. Thus, we anticipate that the persistent visibility and dissemination of feminist research may gradually influence the direction of public policy actions that affect the lives of women (Worell 1990).

Review procedures. A final consideration in a feminist publication process concerns review and feedback procedures. We strive to ensure prospective authors that their manuscripts will receive a fair and constructive review. In contrast to many mainstream research journals, feminist journals insist on "masked" reviews. In a masked review, authors' names are deleted, so that manuscript reviewers are not informed of author identity. Masked reviews reduce the possibility that biases due to gender and academic prestige may influence the evaluation process. This constructive approach to manuscript reviewing seeks to assist authors to improve and revise, rather than tear down and destroy their work. Encouragement and the ethic of mentoring replace discouragement and the ethic of elitism.

TABLE 2
Emergent Feminist Research Criteria

1. Challenges traditional views of women: Presents women in a range of roles, free of prescribed sex-role constraints.
2. Uses alternative methods of inquiry: Expands the boundaries of accepted methodology to explore the personal lives of women.
3. Looks at meaningful contexts: Considers women in the natural settings in which they function.
4. Collaborates with research participants: Enters into a partnership with participants to explore personally relevant variables.
5. Solicits diverse samples: Looks at women who vary by age, socioeconomic class, partner preference, minority or ethnic group, etc.
6. Compares women and men contextually: Replaces "sex differences" research with meaningful sex comparisons.
7. Avoids blaming victims of violence and injustice: Considers victim behavior in the context of power imbalance and gender-related expectations.
8. Empowers women and minorities: Looks at the positive characteristics and contributions.
9. Examines structure and power hierarchies: Considers women's behavior in the context of social structure and patriarchy.
10.Includes implications for social change: Is proactive.

In summarizing the contributions of feminist journals to academic life, I would insist that these publications can result in the empowerment of women. This empowerment can occur both within their professional disciplines as well as in the general academic community. Feminist scholars can achieve voice and visibility in otherwise neglected areas in their academic disciplines as well as having a potential impact on the media and public policy.

Feminist Journals and Academic Risks

On the negative side, I recognize that there are risks for academic women who publish in feminist journals. At least three factors may contribute to this risk—mainstream invisibility, loss of collegial status, and jeopardy to professional advancement.

Invisibility

According to a recent analysis by M. Brinton Lykes and Abigail J. Stewart (1986), authors who publish in *Psychology of Women Quarterly* are as likely to cite equally authors from feminist journals as those who publish in mainstream journals. In contrast, authors in mainstream journals seldom cite their feminist counterparts. Thus, the risks of publishing in feminist journals include professional invisibility and lower citation rates. Since documented citation rates are frequently used by academic administrators to evaluate the quality of individual faculty, programs, or departments, the possibility of risking one's professional citation rate is indeed a realistic concern. The professional dilemma here is that the types of articles that appear in feminist journals may receive rejection in mainstream publication outlets. For some authors, the choice becomes one of segregation into feminist publications versus invisibility within the discipline as a whole.

Collegial Status

Since one's status within academia is determined by multiple factors, assigning a role to publishing in feminist journals is probably a questionable practice. However, feminist research itself may be suspect at some institutions of higher learning, and may result in isolation of the researcher by other colleagues (Hatton et al. 1993; Kimmel et al. 1993). In a qualitative interview study with seventy-seven feminist professors, Judith Worell and Faye J. Crosby (1992) reported that some university teachers felt isolated and ignored by their psychology colleagues, and found more acceptance and status with women's studies professors from other disciplines. On the other hand, many professors also reported feeling valued and accepted for their feminist research, and believed that their feminist work was well supported by colleagues.

Academic Advancement

Perhaps the most damaging effects of feminist publishing may be on one's academic status within the college or university. When departmental evaluation time rolls around, administrators may be less likely to take women's journals seriously, and may regard them as unacceptable for credit toward tenure, promotion, or salary increments. As an editor, I have been called more than once by a department chair facing a faculty tenure and promotion decision to inquire about the rejection rate of *Psychology of Women Quarterly*. The implication here, of course, is that rejection rates in an authors' publication outlet reflect either positively or negatively on the quality of the author's work.

I recognize both the potential rewards and risks involved in doing feminist research and publishing in feminist journals. I have no easy answers. At one level, I might suggest that authors divide their work between mainstream and feminist journals. However, if their research is primarily feminist in scope and content, they may experience rejection from the traditional reviewer. Do we negate our identity in order to survive? Worell and Crosby found that in their sample of feminist college professors, the sense of personal feminist identity was an important source of self-esteem and empowerment for many of these women (1992).

In closing, I want to re-emphasize the role of the feminist journal in stimulating and supporting the intellectual life of the academic community. Without contrast and challenge, our science remains static, androcentric in its attention to issues of interest primarily to men, and neglectful of the lives of women. In addressing the feminist agenda with revisionist research criteria, we provide visibility and voice to the emergent scholarship on women. But women who choose to publish in the feminist forum are cautioned to recognize that there are risks involved in challenging the academy. In doing so, they make a personal decision to follow their hearts and to let their values be their guide.

Works Cited

Crawford, Mary, and Jean Marecek. "Psychology Reconstructs the Female 1968–1988." *Psychology of Women Quarterly* 13 (1989): 147–165.

Grady, Kathleen E. "Sex Bias in Research Design." *Psychology of Women Quarterly* 5 (1981): 628–37.

Hatton, Billie Jo, Susan Jones, Judith Worell, and Patricia Atkins. "The Experience of Feminist Professors of Psychology." Paper presented at the annual meeting of the Eastern Psychological Association, Washington, D.C., April 1993.

Harding, Sandra. *The Science Question in Feminism.* Ithaca, N.Y.: Cornell University Press, 1986.

Keller, Evelyn F. *Reflection on Gender and Science.* New Haven, Conn.: Yale University Press, 1985.

Kimmel, Ellen, Judith Worell, Judith Daniluk, Mary Ann Gawalek, Cathy Lerner, and Geraldine Stahley. "Process and Outcome in Feminist Pedagogy." Paper presented at the First National Conference on Education and Training in Feminist Practice, Boston, Mass., July 1993.

Lott, Bernice. "The Potential Enrichment of Social/Personality Psychology through Feminist Research and Vice Versa." *American Psychologist* 40 (1985): 155–164.

Lykes, M. Brinton, and Abigail J. Stewart. "Evaluating the Feminist Challenge to Research in Personality and Social Psychology: 1963–1968." *Psychology of Women Quarterly* 10 (1986): 393–412.

Parlee, Mary Brown. "Appropriate Control Groups in Feminist Research." *Psychology of Women Quarterly* 5 (1981): 637–644.

Peplau, Ann, and E. Conrad. "Beyond Non-Sexist Research: The Perils of Feminist Methods in Psychology." *Psychology of Women Quarterly* 13 (1989): 379–400.

Sherif, Carolyn W. "Bias in Psychology." In *Feminism and Methodology*, ed. Sandra Harding. Bloomington: Indiana University Press, 1987.

Unger, Rhoda Kessler. "Sex as a Social Reality: Field and Laboratory Research." *Psychology of Women Quarterly* 5 (1983): 645–53.

Wallston, Barbara Strudler. "What are the Questions in the Psychology of Women? A Feminist Approach to Research." *Psychology of Women Quarterly* 5 (1981): 597–617.

Worell, Judith, "Feminist Frameworks: Retrospect and Prospect." *Psychology of Women Quarterly* 14 (1990): 1–7.

—. "Gender in Close Relationships: Public Policy vs. Personal Prerogative." *Journal of Social Issues* 49(3) (1993): 203–18.

Worell, Judith, and Faye J. Crosby. "The Feminist Teaching Project: Interim Report." Preliminary report submitted to the Women's College Coalition, Washington, D.C., November 1992.

Chapter 16

Building an Effective Model for Institutional Change: Academic Women as Catalyst

Gloria DeSole and Meredith A. Butler

Overview

The overall agenda for women in higher education remains relatively unfulfilled in many significant areas in spite of twenty years of struggle for equity. One reason for this lack of progress is that insufficient attention has been paid to the context in which change for women in higher education must occur. If women are to be successful in transforming the environments in which they work to make them more inclusive and more responsive to diverse clienteles, they must create structures which support and foster institutional change. Women who wish to create a climate that actively supports the goals of affirmative action and a spirit of collectivity, which welcomes diversity and recognizes difference as a strength, must build an institutional network in which these feminist values can be realized. The authors discuss the process of structuring an effective network of women's committees to serve as a vehicle for the integration of feminist values into the academic institution to enhance women's lives and support women's participation in the life of the institution. In so doing, they identify the factors that are essential to the process of institutionalizing social change in higher educational organizations.

Introduction

As we look at the results of the past twenty years of struggle for
equity for women in higher education, we can see that some successes
have been achieved and some improvements have been made. Women
are entering colleges and universities in greater numbers as students, as
faculty members, and as professional employees and administrators.
Today, women comprise more than half of the undergraduate and
graduate students enrolled in colleges and universities. More women
than ever before are receiving graduate and professional degrees and
women are an increasingly larger percentage of new faculty and
professional hires at many institutions. Women now hold 26.4 percent
of all full-time faculty positions (American Association of University
Professors 1989, 19). However, despite the obvious gains in education,
career choices, and employment opportunities (and to a lesser degree in
salary, tenure, and promotion), most feminists would agree that the
overall picture for women in higher education remains relatively
unchanged (Simeone 1987, 141).

Shavlik, Touchton and Pearson argue in their recent *New Agenda
of Women for Higher Education* (1988) that one reason for this lack of
progress is because very little attention has been paid to the context in
which changes for women occur (Agenda 1). Because there has not
been sufficient change within institutional structures to encourage,
support, and maintain women or the new roles they have developed,
change has been individual, not collective or systematic. These
researchers also agree that the agenda for women in higher education
and in society in general has not been met and that the needs, concerns,
and issues of women and other historically underrepresented groups in
higher education are often low on the priority list of most institutions.
As a result, it is often difficult for women to develop their own
collective sense of vision and to articulate and attend to their own needs
(Agenda 3).

In this paper, we will review the status of and climate for women
in higher education today. These conditions present a case for creating
a strong, carefully constructed, and integrated institutional network of
women's committees as one way to foster institutional change and
create more diverse and responsive educational and work environments
that actively support, nurture, and empower women. Although women's
committees and women's networks are not new in the academic
environment, it is rare to find a consciously structured interlocking
network of women's committees woven into the fabric of campus life

and supported by the institutional framework. Such a structure integrates and amplifies the separate and collective voices of individual committees and groups working for social change. It also fosters and strengthens social activism and enhances the climate for all people within the university. Such a model exists at the State University of New York at Albany—a network of women's committees, consciously created and integrated within the institutional context. This network serves as an effective vehicle for social change and provides the foundation for a strong, active, and effective women's community at the University. In this essay, we will discuss the factors that are essential to the process of continuing successful social change in the institutional setting and propose strategies for applying the Albany model to other higher educational institutions.

The Current Status of Women in Higher Education

There is a general societal notion, a myth promoted by the popular press and repeated in the academic media, that equality for women has been achieved, that women have "made it" in higher education. The common perception is that most barriers have been removed, that discrimination has been eliminated, and that women are being hired in great numbers to fill the ranks of the professorate and at all levels of administrative positions. The reality is far different as even a cursory glance at recent literature on the topic shows. In higher education for the past fifteen years there have been fewer job opportunities as budget crises and cutbacks became commonplace at many universities and colleges. Although women are getting an increasingly larger share of advanced degrees compared to past years (in 1972, 16 percent of new doctorates went to women; in 1986, 35 percent went to women) (Chamberlain 1988, 257), and have made substantial gains in the attainment of professional degrees in many fields, they remain significantly underrepresented among college and university faculty, holding only 26.4 percent of full-time faculty positions in 1989. Moreover, women are particularly underrepresented at the higher academic ranks (53 percent of male faculty are associate or full professors compared to 11.8 percent of women faculty) (American Association of University Professors 1989, 19). The percentage of women faculty who are full professors has not changed significantly in twenty years (Chamberlain 1988, 259). More women faculty also tend to be employed at two-year public institutions. In fact, at two-year colleges without academic ranks, 37.7 percent of all full-time faculty are women (American Association of University Professors 1989, 19). With respect to tenure, women continue to experience inequality. In the mid-1970s, 64 percent of all academic men compared with 46 percent of academic women were tenured (Chamberlain 1988, 262). In 1989, 71 percent of men were tenured compared with 49 percent of women (American Association of University Professors 1989, 15). In research universities, the comparison is even more pronounced: 73 percent of men are tenured compared with 46 percent of women. Similarly, at research universities, 93 percent of male academics are on tenure-track appointments compared with 79 percent of female academics (American Association of University Professors 1989, 16).

Similar disparity exists when we look at current information about average salaries for men and women academics. At research universities, women's salaries are on average 85 percent of men's salaries. For all types of academic institutions, women earn on average 86 percent of what their male counterparts earn (American Association of University Professors 1989, 11). Comparison with earlier salary information shows that the dollar gap between men and women faculty actually widened in the 1980s (Chamberlain 1988, 259). It is safe to say that in 1992, at every rank, in every field, at every type of institution, women faculty earn less than male faculty.

The picture for women of color in higher education is similarly disturbing but harder to draw because women of color are often not recognized as having unique needs. Therefore, separate data on them are very difficult to find and historical comparisons are difficult to make (Chamberlain 1988, 54). More Ph.D.s are being awarded to women of color, but they have made little progress in terms of faculty appointment and tenure. In 1975, women of color composed 11 percent of all women faculty; in 1983, they represented 11.5 percent of all women faculty or 2.8 percent of all full-time instructional faculty (Chamberlain 1988, 54). Where researchers have been able to chart the progress of women of color, they are finding that women of color have made much less progress in higher education than men of color and considerably less progress than white women.

The status of women in higher education administration has been studied extensively over the past fifteen years and all studies agree that while some small progress has been made, women administrators are still clustered in professional (nonacademic) and middle management positions in areas of the university concerned with student and external affairs, human resources and services, and traditionally "women-centered" academic areas such as librarianship, social welfare, and nursing (Tinsley, Secor, and Kaplan 1983, 17). Women of color are a microscopic proportion of the administrative structure (Chamberlain 1988, 54). Women of all races are unlikely to be department chairs and are even less likely to be deans, and the national average for the number of women in top administrative positions in universities is 1.1 persons (Shavlik and Touchton 1988, 240).

What does all this information tell us about the status of women in higher education today? Quite simply, we see that not only have the issues of full and equitable participation of white women and of men and women of color in higher education been largely unresolved, they have barely begun to be addressed in a serious and sustained way despite twenty years of individual and collective pressure for social change. In the 1960s before colleges and universities developed institutionalized responses to the pressure for social change through programs for disadvantaged students, affirmative action, women's studies, Afro-American studies, minority recruitment programs, and the like, activists for social change in higher education often lobbied and exerted pressure through grass roots organizations that were external to their institutions. They were members of civil rights organizations such as the National Association for the Advancement of Colored People (NAACP), the Congress for Racial Equality (CORE), the Student Nonviolent Coordinating Committee (SNCC); of women's rights organizations such as the National Organization for Women (NOW), the National Women's Studies Association (NWSA), women's political caucuses; or of task forces and caucuses in professional associations that focused on equity issues for women and minorities. Today, we can still find a weak echo of these lobbying activities within professional associations and in faculty and professional unions.

This "activist/outsider" lobbying model is problematic in the current academic environment. Younger faculty and professional staff often lack the political awareness, frame of reference, and commitment of their older activist colleagues. They don't want to be perceived as powerless and don't want to operate outside the institutional setting. Often they have no experience participating in a constituent group particularly in an academic setting.

Institutions of higher education have changed as well. They now have structural mechanisms specifically set up to accommodate the needs of underrepresented groups. They have plans and policies in place. They have taken the necessary first steps to address issues of equity and representation and, if their plans are less ambitious than they might be and the results less effective than they could be, the answer, they believe, lies not within the institutions and their lack of energetic commitment, but rather in external impediments to progress such as lack of resources, unavailability of qualified minorities, societal sexism and racism, and the like.

Activists and lobbyists for social change in higher education have been co-opted by partial success. Misled by messages in the popular press proclaiming that women and minorities have "made it," and lulled by over-enthusiastic generalizations about the success of a few offered by those who wish to preserve the status quo, many protected class people do not fully realize the growing disparity between what they are told has happened to underrepresented groups in higher education throughout the last twenty years and what they observe to be the real degree of change. They mistake the partial change discussed earlier, e.g. new academic programs for women and minority studies, new administrative policies and programs, enrollment of more women and minorities in graduate and professional degree programs, the hiring of more minorities, and the increasing visibility of white women on university campuses, for the promised change of full and equal participation in society and higher education. Many people, including many individual women, believe that campus discrimination against women has ended. Fewer people are aware of the realities of the "glass ceiling" for women, or of the revolving door for many white women and both men and women of color. And, when they find the climate of many higher educational institutions a chilly one indeed, they often feel a sense of personal failure rather than a sense of failed institutional climate.

Fostering Institutional Change—The Role of Women's Committees

Given the reality we have just described, what can women and persons of color do to energize their institutions and move them more rapidly toward substantive social change? For any plan of action to be successful, it requires that the people who stand to benefit the most from social change be organized within the institutional structure. University, college, departmental, and divisional groups and committees provide many opportunities for women to participate in governance and, increasingly, to take leadership roles. Faculty unions also provide an avenue for women to exert leadership and influence the decision making process. However, these groups and committees have many different agendas and purposes and must serve a broad constituency. Many members of these constituencies may be indifferent or even hostile to changing the status quo. Some groups, such as university senate committees, may be too broadly or too narrowly focused to address adequately the concerns of women and minorities. Others, such as faculty unions, exist outside the institution and by their very nature are in an adversarial relationship with the institution. Their programs must address the concerns of the entire membership rather than specific interest groups and their activities are limited to the terms of the contract they negotiate. In short, these groups and committees are concerned with different things and their commitment to social change is only as strong as is the commitment of the collective membership.

Women interested in transforming the environments in which they work to make them more inclusive and more responsive to diverse clienteles, and women interested in creating a climate that actively supports the goals of affirmative action and welcomes diversity and recognizes difference as strength must build an institutional network in which these feminist values can be realized. Women's committees in such a network can work directly on issues of interest to group members, garner popular participation and support, influence policy formulation and revision, and, by working collaboratively, have far greater impact than individual groups working independently.

As administrators at the University at Albany, the authors have for many years been actively building and participating in a strong women's community supported by an effective institutional network of women's committees. The principles used to create this network, the processes of its development, the model developed, and the lessons learned from its ongoing evolution can serve as an inspiration and a template for other activists for social change. These topics are discussed below. The factors that are essential to the process of institutionalizing social change in higher education are identified and strategies for applying the "Albany Model" to other educational institutions are proposed.

The Albany Model

In the late 1960s and early 1970s, many women at the University at Albany, SUNY, and in its surrounding community were active participants in the rebirth of feminism. As the Women's Movement gained momentum, Albany women created the Caucus for Women's Rights. Its stated purpose was to promote opportunity in education and employment for women at the University, and to further the common interests of university women. Its membership was open to all persons

employed by or enrolled in the University with an interest in the rights
of women. The Caucus was typical of the excellent organizations active
in feminism at that time. Again, typically, its reality was far different
from its ideals. In theory, everyone was welcome to participate and
there were to be no barriers of race, class, or gender. In reality, without
much ado, the Caucus was very quickly taken over by women
academics. These women were actively engaged in the reading and the
research, as well as thinking and talking about theoretical issues and
practical ideas of the reemerging social movement. Problems concerning
style and trust developed between the more activist faculty women and
women from other areas of the institution. People in the caucus had
different interests, different levels of political awareness, and different
agendas, and they sought different outcomes. Over time, the group
became self-selecting and specialized in its range of interests and
activities. The few who remained and emerged as leaders had many
successes in effecting social change within the University. But because
the task was so enormous and they were so few, and because they were
not part of a self-renewing larger network of people organized to carry
on their work, the leaders of the caucus could not sustain their
organizational effort. They burned out after half a dozen years and the
group dissolved.

What Albany women learned from that initial effort is that the real
challenge comes in sustaining the pressure for social change over time.
To do this successfully requires vigilance, endurance, excellence of
goals, commonality of purpose, strength in numbers, renewal of energy,
and, perhaps most important of all, an organizational framework that
unifies and strengthens its members and amplifies and extends their
collective power. Recognizing the lessons learned from the past,
women at the University at Albany set out quite self-consciously to
design and create a *carefully constructed interlocking network* of
women's committees and groups drawn together in a loose
confederation and placed within, but not controlled by, the institution.
The structure is loose enough to allow group independence and
autonomy. It is flexible enough to permit the creation and evolution of
new groups and the demise of moribund groups. It is broad-based
enough to accommodate the varied interests of diverse women. It is
inclusive enough to "take people where they are," because the model
acknowledges that different women are comfortable in different settings
and have different contributions to make depending on their stage of
personal development and social and political awareness.

However, the model requires more than simply "taking people where they are"; it requires real affirmative action. All campus women must be informed of the possibilities for them in this interlocking network, and made to feel that their needs will be served. Women from underrepresented groups, including women of color and women from segments of the workforce often overlooked in academic social change projects such as secretaries, must be actively recruited. Equally important, they must be encouraged to take leadership positions (co-chairs work well and send a very strong message), to ensure that their issues are on the agenda.

Because the Albany model is structured within the institution, it has legitimacy, recognition, and visibility. It is empowered by the continuing grass roots organizing that sustains it and the representativeness of its component parts. Over time it has proven to be a most effective vehicle for enabling those lobbying for institutional change at the University and for moving the social change agenda forward. Its success is guaranteed by its strength. As committees are successful in accomplishing their goals, the members are inspired by their experience and accomplishments. They grow in number because their accomplishments bring campus recognition and attract new members interested in being involved in the work of the committees. It is this feeling of empowerment and this collaborative effort which form the basis for the sense of community, a sense which extends beyond the actual numbers of women who are active in committees.

As we stated earlier, the Albany Model depends on an interlocking tripartite network of separate but related women's committees to which other committees may be added or subtracted as they are founded or become extinct. The foundation and center of the collective network is the Council of Women's Groups, a representative body of women from every organized women's group in the University. All women who care to be affiliated can have a part in the collective voice through the Council. The current Council is comprised of two representatives from fourteen different groups: the Women's Studies Program, Women in Student Affairs, the Day Care Center, Feminist Alliance (a student group), the President's Task Force on Women's Safety, the Clerical/Secretarial Council, Women in Athletics, the Women's Concerns Committee of the Commission for Affirmative Action, the Classified Women's Colloquium, the Affirmative Action Office, the Institute for Research on Women, the Center for Women in Government, Community Relations, and Women Professionals.

Gender and Academe

The functions of the Council of Women's Groups are various. First, it provides a network for women's groups to come together once a month to share news, plan events, request advice and cooperation, plan strategies, work on common concerns, etc. Second, it serves as a forum for discussion of issues of general interest to campus women. Third, it sponsors campus-wide events such as an annual reception for new women faculty and professionals and an awards ceremony to recognize campus men and women who have promoted women's equity at the University. Fourth, it serves as the organizing force for women's groups to come together each year and prepare an agenda for the annual meeting with the University President on the state-of-the-campus for women. And finally, but no less important, the Council serves as a vehicle for professional and leadership development for the women who co-chair it and serve on it for the academic year. On this last topic, it is important to underline a point noted above: Leadership development for both white women and women of color has been an important goal of our women's community at the University at Albany. Many of our committees are co-chaired and every effort is made to provide diverse leadership, e.g., a faculty woman serves with a woman from the professional or classified staff, a white woman and woman of color serve together, an experienced leader and a novice serve together. These assignments rotate yearly to give many women opportunities to lead in a supportive, nurturing, and empowering environment.

The second building block of the University at Albany women's collective network is the Women's Concerns Committee (WCC), an officially constituted committee of the University Commission for Affirmative Action (UCAA). Because of its affiliation with the Commission, the WCC is tied to the institutional structure and receives official recognition. It draws women from across the University from all employment categories including faculty, professional, secretarial/clerical, and students. Hence, it cuts across departmental and friendship networks and assists women to develop new and broader based networks within the University.

The WCC was created as an independent subcommittee of the UCAA to advise the Affirmative Action Office and the Commission on policy for women at the University and to identify and work on issues of common concern. Its broad charge and flexible structure have permitted the WCC to grow and change with the years, to respond to the interests of its members and the changing concerns of campus women. A primary focus of the WCC is its lobbying and advocacy function. Members of this committee have been instrumental in assessing the needs of campus women, documenting the results of the survey, publicizing the results in both public forums and written reports, and distributing these findings to university administrators for further action. A second focus of the group is professional development and, in particular, leadership development. The WCC provides many opportunities for women to take on leadership responsibilities within the committee and its various subcommittees, to develop and sponsor programming for women, and to engage in projects that expand the individual's experience and network of contacts.

The WCC's consciously flexible design promotes both wide representation and accountability. The main body meets monthly throughout the academic year to establish priorities for action, discuss issues and ideas, and determine directions. However, much of the ongoing work of the WCC is done through its subcommittees, which change annually as women identify new projects and issues they want to work on. It is this loose structure that fosters broad participation of diverse women at the grass roots level and ensures the WCC's effectiveness and generativity over time. In this academic year, WCC subcommittees are working on issues such as hiring affirmatively, mentoring of faculty and professional women, sexual harassment, concerns of women of color, creating a more diverse campus, and women and tenure. Members of the WCC also publish a twice yearly newsletter for campus women called the *Women's Connection*, now in its eleventh year.

The third building block of the Albany model is the Women's Studies Program, an interdisciplinary academic program of undergraduate and graduate courses taught by over forty faculty in disciplines throughout the University. The women faculty and students from the Women's Studies Program and its research arm IROW, the Institute for Research on Women, comprise a third crucial element in the design. They are necessarily reading, writing, and talking about the status of women and issues of particular concern to women. They move curricular and institutional reform by their very presence as a formal unit of the faculty. Not infrequently their expertise provides the analysis for institutional occurrences. Of course women faculty and most especially women's studies faculty are often members of the Council of Women's Groups and the Women's Concerns Committee, but they do not control the agendas nor are they consistently the dominant voices.

One final ingredient present in all of these groups is the pleasure that the participants feel in working with other women on issues of real concern to committee members as developing professionals and as members of the campus community. We do not mean to suggest that another set of meetings is an undiluted pleasure, or that there is no strain involved in working with women. However, it is often the case that there are too few opportunities in university life for collective efforts of real significance to university citizens and particularly to university women. We base this assertion on personal experience at these meetings over years of activity, where we have found a consistent and focused effort to support the individual woman's dignity and development in all groups. The tone of these meetings is relaxed and informal, but not unserious. Similarly, there are planned and unplanned good times, social gatherings at work and occasionally at someone's home, that reinforce the groups's sense of solidarity and offer comfort in an impersonal environment.

As we noted at the beginning of this essay, the agenda for women in higher education has not yet been met. Women labor under the additional burden of the commonplace notion that as the decade ends, everything is fair and fine, and that the woman who feels otherwise is herself out of step. In this climate, it is the responsibility of the community of women themselves to develop their own collective sense of vision and articulate and attend to their own needs. The central point is that the community of women can move forward in those tasks most steadily and joyously if they have considered the organizational structure that will:

1. Allow the individual woman to locate a committee base where she feels that her voice can be heard on the issues of importance to her.
2. Encourage the balanced and thoughtful response of the major interest groups of women however those interests are defined in a particular institutional setting.
3. Insure that through affirmative action women of color are included in their own groups, in all groups, and in leadership positions.
4. Present the voice of campus women as a clear and coherent collective voice to the larger institution on issues of importance.

Although we have offered one model, we believe that the very process of inventing the one that suits the character of the institution is both instructive and constructive for the planners. The opportunity to adjust the model so that it fits and adapt it as necessary over time so that it continues to meet the needs of campus women is part of the value of a consciously articulated structure.

Waiting for the campus climate to change, working through one's job and regular committees, and cooperating with colleagues of good will to hasten that change remains part of the daily endeavor for campus women concerned with equity and affirmative action. In fact, the greatest foe to affirmative action for women and persons of color in the next decade may be complacency, a feeling that the battle is over when it has simply entered a new phase. It is now time to reaffirm and reassert the principles, to continue analysis and monitoring, and, above all, to support those who continue their untiring efforts to put theory into practice (Chamberlain 1988, 187).

Notes

This essay previously apppeared in *Initiatives*, vol. 53, no. 2, 1990. Premission to reprint is granted by the National Association for Women in Education.

Works Cited

American Association of University Professors. "The Annual Report on the Economic Status of the Profession, 1988–1989" *Academe* 75 (March-April 1989): 11, 15, 16, 19.

Chamberlain, Mariam K., ed. *Women in Academe: Progress and Prospects*. New York: Russell Sage Foundation, 1988.

Shavlik, Donna, and Judith Touchton. "Women as Leaders." In *Leaders for a New Era*, ed. M. Green. New York: Macmillan 1988.

Shavlik, D., Judith Touchton, and Carol Pearson. *New Agenda of Women for Higher Education*. Washington, D.C.: American Council on Education, 1988.

Simeone, Angela. *Academic Women: Working Towards Equality*. South Hadley, Mass.: Bergin and Garvey, 1987.

Tinsley, A., C. Secor, and S. Kaplan, eds. *Women in Higher Education Administration*. San Francisco: Jossey-Bass, 1983.

Chapter 17

The Politics of Gendered Sponsorship: Mentoring in the Academy

Gary A. Olson and Evelyn Ashton-Jones

Olson:

Mentoring is a subject discussed in the professional literature of quite a few academic disciplines, and much of this scholarship assumes a stable, universally agreed upon definition of *mentor*. Yet, as Sharan Merriam points out in her extensive critical review of the scholarly literature, a precise, universal definition is impossible, and thus there is considerable confusion: "Mentoring appears to mean one thing to developmental psychologists, another thing to business people, and a third thing to those in academic settings" (1983, 169). Even in the academic literature, definitions will slip and slide—so much so, for example, that one set of researchers had to point out that there is significant difference between a mentor and a graduate advisor.

One attempt to make distinctions between the various terms often used interchangeably for "mentor" is offered by Eileen Shapiro, Florence Haseltine, and Mary Rowe. Their often-cited continuum works like this:

Peer pal—Someone at the same level as yourself with whom you share information, strategy, and mutual support for mutual benefit.
Guide—Someone who can explain the system but who is not usually in a position to champion a protégé.
Sponsor—Someone less powerful than a patron in promoting and shaping the career of a protégé.
Patron—An influential person who uses his or her power to help you advance in your career.
Mentor—An individual who assumes the role of both teacher and advocate in an intense paternalistic relationship. (quoted in Merriam 1983, 164)

Two recent attempts to clarify the role of mentor are even more useful. In discussing the mentor in graduate education, William Lyons, Don Scroggins, and Patra Bonham Rule argue that the mentor "plays an almost spiritual role in the life of the graduate student" (1990, 277). Citing R. Thomas, et al., they write,

> While mentoring *can* lead to success in business and the professions, having a mentor is absolutely *essential* for success in graduate school. Graduate school mentors and their protégés share a comradeship of such extraordinary intensity that it transcends the normal teacher/student relationship. They are intimately concerned with one-on-one instruction and the individual needs of their students. (1990, 279)

John W. Kronik adds that

> by tradition the mentor is protective, knowing, trustworthy, caring. The mentor-mentee relationship includes but goes well beyond teaching and advising. It stems from a freely chosen mutual attraction that involves friendship and that provides guidance and nurturing of a broadly professional sort while bearing on the private dimension as well. (1990, 53)

Thus, the mentoring relationship in graduate education is a very complex and special relationship.

The professional literature cites numerous advantages of mentoring for the protégé. Here is a list from Roberta M. Hall and Bernice R. Sandler:

- individual recognition and encouragement
- honest criticism and informal feedback
- advice on how to balance teaching, research and other responsibilities and set professional priorities
- knowledge of the informal rules for advancement (as well as political and substantive pitfalls to be avoided)
- information on how to "behave" in a variety of professional settings
- appropriate ways of making contact with authorities in a discipline
- skills for showcasing one's own work
- an understanding of how to build a circle of friends and contacts both within and outside one's institution
- a perspective on long-term career planning (1983, 3)

Other benefits, according to Hall and Sandler, are that the mentor might

- involve the protégé in joint projects or get support for a protégé's research
- introduce the protégé to top authorities in the field
- "talk up" the protégé's research to senior colleagues
- nominate the protégé for awards or prizes
- support the protégé for promotion or tenure (1983, 3)

Ashton-Jones:

Gary, I should point out that not all mentoring advantages accrue to the person who is being mentored. In fact, the literature suggests that as a mentor, you yourself probably:

- have enhanced your own professional standing as a direct result of your students' achievements
- have gained a wider network of professional contacts, largely through your students
- have been relieved by mentees of some of the more mundane burdens of your research, scholarship, and teaching

Certainly, though, the benefit balance tips toward the person being mentored. I know I have benefitted greatly from your mentorship, starting when I was working on my Ph.D. and continuing first in my position on the faculty at the University of Idaho and then in my present position at the University of Southern Mississippi.

Olson:

No doubt you're also familiar with the *disadvantages* of mentoring that researchers have noted. C. E. Weber cautions that

> mentors may be unfulfilled individuals who try to live through an alter-ego in an attempt to gain some sort of immortality. Protégés, on the other hand, may be compensating for an unhappy childhood. Neither relationship is likely to lead to a healthy relationship. (Merriam 1983, 163)

And Merriam points out that

> Fury (1979) lists five dangers protégés in the business world must be aware of: (1) the mentor could lose power or influence in the organization; (2) the protégé is limited to one other person's perspective; (3) the mentor could leave the organization; (4) the male mentor could want sexual favors from his female protégé; and (5) the protégé could become attached to a "bad" mentor. (1983, 170)

So, right from the start we can see that the mentoring relationship is much more complex than it might appear.

Ashton-Jones:

The subject of mentoring becomes even more complex when you introduce the factor of gender. There's been a considerable amount of published research and scholarship on the role of gender in mentoring relationships, and, as you might guess, scholars are far from agreement on anything. Some researchers have suggested that while it may be especially important for young women to have mentors, the same may not be true of young men (Halcomb 1980). Apparently, this is also true of women outside the academy. According to Merriam,

> Perhaps the strongest evidence for the importance of mentors to women in business comes from Hennig and Jardim's (1977) study of 25 top-level women executives. Through in-depth interviews, Hennig discovered that all had had a mentor—in each case, a male boss. Relationships were emotional, intense, but not sexual; all continued to depend on a mentor for support until age 35. Their findings led the authors to advise women pursuing management careers to "look for a coach, a godfather or a

godmother, a mentor, an advocate, someone in a more senior position who can teach . . . support . . . advise . . . critique." (1983, 166)

While it may be crucial for women to have sponsors, G. Sheehy and many others have complained that there is a distinct lack of mentors for women. Women, thus, are at a disadvantage compared to men. First, the literature confirms that many men hesitate to take on women protégés. In addition, the comparatively low number of females on graduate faculties complicates the situation. The Carnegie Commission on Higher Education suggests that

the small number of appropriate female role models available to female students may adversely affect their entry and subsequent success in graduate school and their later professional development. (Gilbert, Gallessich, and Evans 1983, 598)

Other researchers found that "more women than men believed that mentors were not generally available to members of their sex" (Atcherson and Jenny 1983, 1).

The lack of available female mentors is particularly disturbing in light of research indicating that same sex mentoring relationships are the most productive. Elizabeth M. Tidball (1973) reports that there is a direct relationship between the number of "career successful women" and the number of women faculty at these students' undergraduate institutions. And Elyse Goldstein (1979) found that protégés from same sex mentorships are likely to publish significantly more than others.

Nevertheless, other scholarship suggests that males might be the *most* effective mentors of female protégés. Angela Simeone reports that some women felt that a male mentor was "better able than a woman would have been to negotiate for his female students within the male system" (1987, 105). And according to Merriam, Quinn discovered that "females with male mentors made a significantly greater number of positive statements about the mentor's influences on the integration of their feminine and professional self concepts" (1983, 168).

Furthermore, although numerous earlier studies hypothesized that males are mentored to a greater degree than females, a study published in 1990 reports that while "it is clear that doctoral students who had experienced a close working relationship with a faculty member had a fuller education than their counterparts who had not," the researchers found no evidence "that males are more likely to be mentored than females" (Lyons, Scroggins, and Rule 1990, 277). Other studies confirm this, while still other scholarship tends to dispute it.

As you can see, there's a great deal of disagreement over exactly *how* gender affects the mentoring relationship.

Olson:

The work of Judith Long Laws is particularly revealing about the role gender plays. She analyzes what she calls the "psychology of tokenism" in the academy, where men constitute the dominant class and women comprise the "deviant class." As we all know, there's been considerable pressure on the dominant class to share privilege and power, especially in universities, where historically, says Laws, "all but a tiny fraction of faculty members are male, as is the case in the graduate faculties and professional schools, where persons are accredited for the academic profession" (1975, 55). Therefore, certain members of the deviant class must be selected and socialized to undergo this "interclass mobility." However, this "flow of outsiders into the dominant group must be restricted numerically, and they must not change the system they enter" (1975, 52). Therefore, this process must be regulated and "the mechanism for regulation" is a partnership between the token, or protégé, and a sponsor, or mentor. Thus, the aspiring academic woman is, according to Laws' analysis, a "double deviant": being born female in a patriarchical society already makes her a member of the deviant class, but "aspiring to the attributes and privileges of the dominant class," in this case the male-inscribed university, makes her a "double deviant" (1975, 53).

Ashton-Jones:

I understand what you're saying, although Laws' terminology makes me a little uncomfortable—I'm not sure I would depict myself as "deviant." What you and Laws are getting at, I think, is Simone de Beauvoir's conception of the One and the Other—with men representing, to borrow the vocabulary of psychology, the "norm" and women representing that which is not the "norm." That is, the patriarchal society establishes the male as the normal, the standard, and, therefore, the female is other than the norm, a deviation from the norm. To clarify Laws' framework, we might also say that this relationship between mentor and mentee is hierarchical by definition—the mentor is a member of the world that the mentee, either male or female, aspires to. But in a male mentor/female mentee configuration, this hierarchy is duplicated on another plane; that is, embedded in the given mentoring hierarchy is the socially authorized hierarchy of gender, which casts the male as authority on another level and the female as novice on another level as well. But what else does Laws have to say?

Olson:

Laws notes that through the mentor's tutelage, the protégé adopts the standards and value system of the dominant, that is *male*, group; and given the momentum of this upward mobility, her self-esteem is likely to be directly proportional to the degree to which she succeeds in embracing those values. As Laws points out, "All of the traditional professions are dominated by men, as is the training process by which one enters these professions," and "men have the power to reward the double deviant for performances and attributes she is developing"—the very same attributes the men themselves have determined should be privileged (1975, 55, 56).

Now, to be fair, the reproduction of ideology is not confined to gender hierarchies. Carol Berkenkotter and her co-authors (1988) describe how a graduate student is brought into the discourse community of the field—that is, how the student is socialized into accepting its values and operating assumptions—despite initial resistance and serious questioning of the methodological assumptions underlying that particular graduate program's privileged mode of scholarly inquiry. Berkenkotter and her colleagues report on this process with great satisfaction, positing that what they describe is a natural process of intellectual and cognitive maturation. But what we're really witnessing, suggests John Schilb, is systematic indoctrination. Now, there's no doubt that every teaching situation is a kind of indoctrination. Noam Chomsky writes in the *Journal of Advanced Composition* that intellectuals, academics, are the "most indoctrinated part of the population" simply because to get to where we are, we all have had to be submissive and obedient and to pass through numerous gates and filters—mechanisms that filter out those of us not basically supportive of the status quo: "You allow yourself to be shaped by the system of authority that exists out there and is trying to shape you" (1991, 19).

However, the cross-gender mentoring relationship is especially insidious because it entails, as you say, a *double* hierarchy and, thus, a double bind for the protégé. Not only must she undergo the typical indoctrination of the academic/intellectual with all the associated postures of submissiveness and obedience, but she must play out that

role within the further indoctrination of the patriarchical university with
all *its* associated male-inscribed values.

I should make it clear, too, that just as Chomsky points out that some
people are able to resist indoctrination, at least partially, Laws argues
that not all "double deviants end up as tokens in a male establishment."
Some will not "enact the token role adequately," either because they are
overly idealistic and "fail to observe the limits" set by their deviant
status as female, or because they become cynical and call into question
key basic premises. That is, "the cynical recognize and reject the role
of token" (1975, 57).

Ashton-Jones:

But now you're trapped in Chomsky's gender blindness, and you're
misconstruing Laws to suggest that women can, in fact, resist tokenism
and still gain entry into the academy—that among the *exceptions*
(women who aspire to be members of the dominant class) there are yet
more *exceptions*—those very special women who succeed without
colluding in their own oppression. But the key to Laws' point is that
women *must* acquiesce to tokenism to gain entry and to survive. She
says, "To survive in the academic profession . . . the Token must not
only be qualified to enact the professional role, but must succeed in the
very special role of Token" (1975, 57). According to Laws, the
idealists and cynics that you allude to don't gain entry into the dominant
class that constitutes the academy. And this is a very real dilemma for
women seeking change and transformation in the academy and society
at large.

Olson:

Well, Evelyn, since *you've* gained entry into that world—presumably
as a token—let's explore how Laws defines *our* tacit agreements about
your role as mentee. First, we—I as mentor, you as mentee—both
agree that the token is unusually competent. That is, you exhibit "to a
minimal degree the disvalued attributes of the primary-deviant class, and
to an exceptional degree the highly valued attributes of the dominant
class" (1975, 58). However, as a token you will interpret your
exceptionalism quite differently from how others do. Undoubtedly, you
believe that you have "escaped membership" in the deviant class, that
your "exceptionalism clearly justifies inclusion in the dominant class"
(1975, 58). In fact, you may even believe that gender plays no role at

all. As a mentor, I continually reinforce this notion of your exceptionalism.

A second dimension of our relationship is a firm belief in individualism, a belief that "effort leads to payoff in terms of achievement and success," a belief that all outcomes are the result of your own efforts (1975, 59). A third dimension is our firm belief in meritocracy, a belief "(1) that membership is achieved, not ascribed, (2) that the group's high standards justify its exclusivity, (3) that both must be upheld by members, and consequently, (4) that excellence will be rewarded" (1975, 60). The final point that we tacitly agree on is the necessity of "boundary maintenance," those procedures that maintain distance between the two classes and "foster the legitimacy of the social system" (1975, 60).

Ashton-Jones:

Perhaps, Gary, we should think about what Laws says about *your* role as mentor. Because you play the central role in bringing me into "membership" in the dominant class, you are of course a champion of women and women's rights. And, of course, I'll defend you against attacks by other women (and vice versa). But while you are a "liberal" on the "women's question" in that you participate in bringing selected tokens into the "group," you can't be a radical—that is, a feminist. As Laws points out,

> Radicalism would mean attack on the structure of the profession, particularly the prevailing sex ratios. As a radical, the Sponsor would make claims on behalf of all women not just the exceptional Token. (1975, 61)

Clearly, this process of mentoring is "an eminently conservative practice" in that both the roles of mentor and protégé support the status quo (1975, 64). And if change ever does occur, it is likely to be with me, the protégé, than it is with you, the mentor.

As Laws points out, for all your good will toward me, the protégé, you have much more to lose by "turning traitor" to your class than I do by coming to class consciousness. You, like all mentors, are likely to "follow the outlines of tolerable liberalization rather than radicalization" (1975, 65). In fact, you are instrumental in alleviating the pressure that the male-inscribed university is under to open its doors to "deviants," but doing so in such a way that the university's structure and values remain unchanged. That is, as a mentor, you actively shape your mentees as tokens, instructing them in the proper behaviors that will at once diminish or highlight their deviancy as appropriate, and you are directly implicated in the reward and reinforcement system that encourages these accepted behaviors, in this case the values and attitudes of the dominant class.

I think it's clear that the mentoring relationship is integrally implicated in perpetuating the university as a patriarchal system, that both the mentor and the mentee collude in unwitting ways to reproduce the ideology of the profession and the hierarchy of gender. But I'd like to bring this discussion down to a more pragmatic level for a moment, working from the assumption that despite their ideological implications, mentoring relationships are *essential* for successful entry into the academy and that they provide, perhaps, the only avenue for women into that world.

On a practical level, it's clear why a woman would agree to participate in a mentoring relationship with a male professor. Hall and Sandler are explicit on this point, saying that

> insufficient informal guidance and sponsorship has been cited as especially damaging for women graduate students, who are at the point of transition between student and professional, and must begin to build a professional identity. (1983)

They also observe that women "consider individual faculty encouragement and support to be more important than men do" (1983, 3). And although Simeone, Kronik, and countless others note that more and more women are joining faculties and that more and more women students are thus choosing to work with women mentors, they don't acknowledge that the male/female ratio is still incredibly imbalanced and that many women on faculties cannot mentor graduate students because they are occupying lower positions and may not even be officially credentialed for advanced graduate sponsorship. Even though Gilbert et al.'s study suggests that women graduate students who work with women faculty "viewed themselves as more career oriented, confident, and instrumental" than did those working with male faculty, women don't often have much choice about the gender of their mentor (1983, 604). In fact, when I was a student here, only about 20 percent of the faculty in the English department were women, although in our specialization, rhetoric and composition, a field where many women in English work, that percentage was 40 percent. But even in this specialized area, not a single woman was officially credentialed to sponsor Ph.D. work.

Now, I'm not trying to say that you became my mentor because you were my only choice. Rather, I'm trying to establish that it makes sense for a woman to agree to participate in a mentoring relationship with a male professor. But Laws' ideological critique of mentoring relationships doesn't (and doesn't intend to) explore why, in practical terms, a male professor would agree to mentor a woman student in the first place. But because scholarship on mentoring is rife with clues about why male professors might hesitate or even refuse to sponsor woman students, we can't gloss over or ignore the day-to-day problematics of mentoring as we wait for ideological change.

Daniel J. Levinson et al. note that "being a woman's mentor is hardly imaginable to many men" (1987, 238). Hall and Sandler suggest that "members of professional peer systems tend to choose persons most like themselves as protégés—but to overlook (or actively exclude) newcomers who are 'different'" (1983, 2). Clearly, some men will refuse to sponsor women because they believe that women are incapable of real thinking, real scholarship. As Hall and Sandler say, "Men faculty have tended to . . . see men—but not women—as capable of exceptional work" (1983, 4). But let's assume that as a "liberal," as Laws describes you, you do believe women are capable of exceptional work—in fact the *exceptionability* that you see in certain women is precisely what sets into action your participation in the education of a woman as token. Given this, why would you agree or, perhaps, hesitate to take on a female protégé?

Olson:

That's something we do have to consider, especially since the institution of mentoring itself, as Hall and Sandler remark, is "a history of relationships between men" (1983, 4). In fact, we can begin back in the mythic origins of mentoring, in the story of Homer's Mentor and Telemachus. As Kronik observes, "it was not a woman but a young man who became the first beneficiary of such a relationship," and "the concept of mentor conjures a paternalistic figure" (1990, 53). The factor of gender in a mentoring system, he says, is articulated in the metaphor of "women in a world of fathers."

But mythic origins aside, the scholarship does, as you say, suggest reasons why males may hesitate to sponsor females. For example, Hall and Sandler point out that women's "'over-visibility' may lead senior persons to avoid the risk of choosing a woman as a protégé." That is,

> While a male protégé may fail without anyone's noticing, "a woman's mistakes are often loudly broadcast"; consequently, to protect their own reputations, men may "maintain higher standards for female protégés," or exclude women altogether. (1983, 4)

In an extreme version, you might find male professors gauging their success by the number of male graduate students they attract as mentees—rather like celebrating the arrival of a new boy baby. Another concern appears so consistently in the scholarship on mentoring as to constitute a kind of trope: the issue of sexuality. Hall and Sandler observe that

> because women may be viewed *primarily* as sexual partners rather than professional colleagues, mentoring relationships may be viewed by some as sexual liaisons rather than genuine helping relationships. (1983, 9; emphasis added)

There's no doubt that the mentoring relationship is typically very intimate and the dangers of that intimacy transforming into sexual intimacy is ever-present; but, what I am most concerned with here is how social *perceptions* play out in the cross-gender mentorship.

Thus, the high *visibility* that a woman's *difference* brings to the mentoring relationship is a key factor. The mentoring relationship of a male professor and a female mentee is *observed, noticed, remarked upon*—and that isn't always a comfortable phenomenon. A woman's gender—her "deviance"—is, to return to Laws, her "master status"—at least so far as others are concerned. As Laws elaborates,

> The Token is likely to believe that she has escaped membership in the deviant class. . . . [But] for the Sponsor, as for most of those . . . with whom the Token comes into contact, her ascriptive status is still visible. For most persons, it is the master status. (1975, 58)

Kanter (1977) describes this phenomenon in another way. She says that in the male context, a woman becomes Woman: "All her acts grow more visible and carry extra symbolic weight. Any woman may represent all womanhood in stereotypical form" (Simeone 1987, 78). In a nutshell, when you're a male professor mentoring a male, you're a professor mentoring a *student*; when you're a male professor mentoring a female, you're mentoring a *female* student.

Ashton-Jones:

I think I see what you mean. Considering the stereotypical roles most often ascribed to women, then, as Rosabeth Moss Kanter elaborates, a woman in this context will be perceived as Mother, Seductress, Cheerleader, or Iron Maiden. Obviously, the female mentee cannot be constructed as Mother to the male mentor, the male mentor at once appropriating the roles of both Father *and* Mother (the nurturing, guiding hand). And the Iron Maiden cannot adequately fulfill the role of Token. So, the role options for a woman mentee—insofar as she is perceived—narrow considerably: in the eyes of the dominant class, she is construed and constructed as either Cheerleader or Seductress, perhaps both. Laws explains this situation well: my gender—my "deviance"—remains invisible to me. Tokens are by definition blind on this issue or they wouldn't be tokens at all—while to others, both women and men, my gender is a most salient characteristic. So, as a woman, I become Woman and am constructed in the ways that Woman is constructed.

Olson:

When we consider such problems as these, when I reflect on Laws' observation that neither the mentor nor the mentee "can be expected to improve the lot of women in academia or to increase the proportion of women in academia" (1975, 64), I begin to think that mentoring for women students is a conundrum, so problematic that perhaps we're best not establishing mentoring relationships at all. As your mentor, I've played into the hands of the patriarchal system; as a mentee, you've been tokenized and will not find a niche in the profession until you successfully adopt one of the stereotypical roles for women—most likely now as Mom in your department. This is all very discouraging. If mentoring relationships themselves are instrumental in obstructing the entry and progress of women in the academy, then where are we to go? What are we to do? Do we just have to wait for the transformation of society, until such a time as being a woman is no longer being "different," until a woman's gender is no longer her "master status," until a woman no longer is automatically reconstructed as Woman in

academic circles—in short, until sexism is rooted out of our social and
cultural value system?

Ashton-Jones:

Given Laws' ideological critique, it does seem as though there's
nowhere to go. But even Laws wouldn't suggest that mentoring should
be dispensed with. Clearly, we have to work with what we have, and
short of the kind of cultural and social transformation that would resolve
these problems, there *are* some things that we can do at least to ensure
that women students are mentored, that they have access to this
essential experience. Hall and Sandler offer numerous suggestions for
making sure women receive productive mentoring, both traditional and
newer approaches to mentoring. What's urgent is that we see that
women are not only mentored, but mentored successfully, and that their
mentoring relationships are perceived for what they are. For example,
workshops on mentoring for both faculty and students would go a long
way toward highlighting the importance of mentoring, educating faculty
and students on how to initiate and sustain a productive mentoring
relationship, and bringing to light some of the gender inequities in
mentoring. I think we need more mentoring for women students and
more discussion of the goals and configurations of mentoring.

Olson:

But certainly we can't stop there. Won't enacting these suggestions
actually *extend* the complicity of mentoring in excluding women from
the academy? I can understand your concern about working with what
we have, but I think we also need to continue to address this issue from
an ideological perspective. Quite frankly, there is no easy solution to
this problem, at least not until we change the root problem: sexism. It's
a paradox, but a paradox we must be conscious of and must make our
students and colleagues conscious of. Perhaps through increased
awareness, we may someday be able to reconfigure the mentoring
relationship in a more equitable arrangement—one that attempts to
balance the various complexities discussed here.

Works Cited

Atcherson, Esther, and Joanna Jenny. *What About Mentors and Women in Academe?* Educational Resource Information Center (ERIC), 1983. ED 242 642.

Berkenkotter, Carol, et al. "Conventions, Conversations, and the Writer: Case Study of a Student in a Rhetoric Ph.D. Program." *Research in the Teaching of English* 22 (1988): 9–44.

Carnegie Commission on Higher Education. *Opportunities for Women in Higher Education.* New York: McGraw, 1973.

Gilbert, Lucia A., June M. Gallessich, and Sherri L. Evans. "Sex of Faculty Role Model and Students' Self-Perceptions of Competency." *Sex Roles* 9 (1983): 597–607.

Goldstein, Elyse. "Effects of Same-Sex and Cross-Sex Role Models on the Subsequent Academic Productivity of Scholars." *American Psychologist* 34 (1979): 407–10.

Halcomb, R. "Mentors and the Successful Woman." *Across the Board* 26 (1980): 13–18.

Hall, Roberta M., and Bernice R. Sandler. *Academic Mentoring for* ✓ *Women Students and Faculty: A New Look at an Old Way to Get Ahead.* Educational Resource Information Center (ERIC), 1983. ED 240 891.

Kanter, Rosabeth Moss. *Men and Women of the Corporation.* New York: Basic, 1977.

Kronik, John W. "On Men Mentoring Women: Then and Now." ✓ *Profession 90* (1990): 52–57.

Laws, Judith Long. "The Psychology of Tokenism: An Analysis." *Sex Roles* 1 (1975): 51–67.

Levinson, Daniel J., et al. *The Seasons of a Man's Life.* New York: Knopf, 1987.

Lyons, William, Don Scroggins, and Patra Bonham Rule. "The Mentor ✓ in Graduate Education." *Studies in Higher Education* 15 (1990): 277–85.

Merriam, Sharan. "Mentors and Protégés: A Critical Review of the ✓ Literature." *Adult Education Quarterly* 33 (1983): 161–73.

Olson, Gary A., and Lester Faigley. "Language, Politics, and Composition: A Conversation with Noam Chomsky." *Journal of Advanced Composition* 11 (1991): 1–35.

Schilb, John. "Ideology and Composition Scholarship." *Journal of Advanced Composition* 8 (1988): 22–29.

Shapiro, Eileen, Florence Haseltine, and Mary Rowe. "Moving Up:
Role Models, Mentors and the Patron System." *Sloan Management
Review* 19 (1978): 51–58.
Sheehy, G. "The Mentor Connection: The Secret Link in the Successful
Women's Life." *New York* (April 1976): 33–39.
Simeone, Angela. *Academic Women: Working Towards Equality.* South
Hadley, Mass.: Bergin, 1987.
Tidball, M. Elizabeth. "Perspectives on Academic Women and
Affirmative Action." *Educational Record* 54 (1973): 130–35.
Weber, C.E. "Mentoring." *Directors and Boards* (1980): 17–24.

Chapter 18

Gender Patterns in Faculty-Student Mentoring Relationships

Kathleen Day Hulbert

While teaching responsibilities provide the foundation for faculty-student relationships, faculty members typically assume other roles with undergraduate and graduate students-advisor, role model, sponsor, mentor. Gender patterns appear to affect faculty awareness of these roles and their attempts to fulfill them in their interactions with students. Moreover, these gender patterns reflect the traditional gender roles that we all have been and continue to be socialized to accept, in which men are primarily achievers and women are primarily nurturers. Despite efforts to modify traditional gender roles, there is substantial evidence that today's educational system, including higher education, still reproduces these gender patterns through the ways that many of us as faculty relate to our students, particularly outside of formal teaching duties. I am not implying that these are absolute differences; instead, my description is based on what Nancy Chodorow identifies as "the reproduction within each generation of certain general . . . differences that characterize masculine and feminine personality and roles" (1978, 43–44).

Using the concept of mentoring, this paper will focus primarily on faculty-student interactions beyond the classroom and the ways in which such interactions shape students' self-perceptions, achievement motivation, and academic and career goals. My analysis will include the following: a review of the theoretical concepts related to mentoring; the changing nature of American higher education; mentoring in higher education; and the need for institutions of higher education to recognize and support the mentoring functions of faculty members.

Mentoring and Related Theoretical Concepts

The concept of mentoring originates in Greek mythology. When Odysseus left to fight the Trojan war, he entrusted to Mentor, his friend and advisor, the education and upbringing of his son, Telemachus. In guiding the development of Telemachus, Mentor's responsibilities involved nurturance and empowerment.

Daniel H. Levinson's *The Seasons of a Man's Life*, a study of midlife American men, is the catalyst for the recent interest in mentoring. In his developmental model, based only on men's experiences but supposedly applicable to women, the mentor plays a critical role in facilitating a man's Dream and eventual occupational achievement. Levinson describes a young man's Dream as

> a vague sense of self-in-adult-world . . . an imagined possibility that generates excitement and vitality . . . poorly articulated and only tenuously connected to reality . . . a young man has the developmental task of giving it greater definition and finding ways to live it out. (1978, 91)

The mentor "fosters the young adult's development by believing in him, sharing the youthful Dream, . . . helping to define the newly emerging self in its newly discovered world" (1978, 99). The mentor-protégé relationship is viewed as advancing the careers of both.

> The mentor is doing something for himself. He is making productive use of his own knowledge and skills in middle age . . . He is maintaining his connection with the forces of youthful energy in the world and in himself. He needs the recipient of mentoring as much as the recipient needs him. (1978, 253)

His psychodynamic scenario proposes that the protégé outgrows his mentor, necessitating a more or less traumatic termination of the relationship, similar to a son's breaking away from his father, during a stage Levinson terms "becoming one's own man." One of the criticisms of Levinson's analysis is that relationships are regarded as something to be terminated after they have served their purpose or when they are no longer useful in advancing a man's Dream.

Male theorists such as Levinson (1978) and George Vaillant (1977) have suggested that mentoring is an expression of Erik Erikson's concept of generativity. In Erikson's theory of psychosocial development, the task of midlife is to develop a sense of generativity, a concern for establishing and guiding the next generation or, in other ways, creating or producing something as one's contribution to society (e.g., artistic works). If one fails to develop and express this concern for the next generation, the negative outcome is described as stagnation, feeling lifeless. Thus, according to Erikson, the virtue of midlife is care, "a widening commitment to take care of the persons, the products, and the ideas one has learned to care for" (1985, 67).

Women theorists such as Carol Gilligan, however, question Erikson's placement of generativity as the task of midlife, noting that "from a woman's perspective . . . the bearing and raising of children take place primarily in the preceding years" (1982, 171). Gilligan points out that while Erikson's original conception of generativity includes parenting and other activities involving nurturance, Vaillant's conception of generativity tries to exclude parenting and nurturance, refocusing generativity more on occupational productivity and achievement— "responsibility for the growth, leadership, and well-being of one's fellow creatures" (1982, 202). Thus mentoring, as an expression of generativity, becomes a valued form of "leadership," in which the "best and brightest" of the younger generation are "mentored" up the career hierarchy. Note that mentoring in this conception is not altruistic or nurturant from the mentor's perspective. A senior professional person selects protégés who are clearly among the "best and brightest," attractive as protégés because of demonstrated abilities, skills, personality characteristics, and often connections. As the relationship develops, "the focus is on the mentor's agenda . . . . The protégé can advance the mentor's goals by doing the kind of legwork that makes the mentor look good." (Keele 1986, 65).

This conception of mentoring assumes that the potential protégé has already arrived at some level of visibility and demonstrated potential to be chosen as a protégé and to be provided with opportunities to advance up the professional hierarchy. To draw an analogy to the days of King Arthur and his knights, only the most promising youths were "tapped" as pages, becoming knights in training, who then had to accomplish glorious and chivalrous deeds to be subsequently knighted by the king. Thus, the person with unrealized or untapped potential will not be selected. The same is true of the person who has had limited opportunity for visibility—to be seen, heard, and taken seriously—in other words, not only in today's society but in almost all historical societies, most women and minorities.

Assuming, however, that one has the good fortune to be chosen as a protégé, Levinson describes the course and outcome of the mentoring relationship. According to Levinson, the protégé, because of his developmental need for autonomy and independence from the mentor, terminates the relationship, in the stage called "becoming one's own man." This certainly happens in some cases (e.g., the Freud-Jung relationship); however, the empirical literature does not seem to acknowledge the reverse, in which the mentor "drops" the protégé, when the protégé's abilities, efforts, or commitment do not meet the mentor's expectations or objectives. However, there are instances in which a protégé is abandoned, even fired, after a major blunder of some type or even when the mentor needs a scapegoat, former White House aide Oliver North offering a prominent example.

To summarize, the concept of mentoring has evolved to associate mentoring primarily with career achievement. However, in its original mythological conception, Mentor's responsibilities were closer to those of a parent than to an organizational superior and he did not "select" his protégé. Instead, Odysseus entrusted to Mentor the nurturance of his son.

There has been some controversy over the definition of mentoring and what associations qualify as "mentoring" relationships (Merriam 1983; Speizer 1981). According to Levinson, "mentoring is defined not in terms of formal roles but in terms of the character of the relationship and the functions it serves" (1978, 78). In research of my own that included mentoring, the following definition was used:

> a professionally centered relationship between two individuals, in which
> the more experienced individual guides, advises, and assists the career of
> the less experienced, often younger protégé. (Hulbert 1988, 5)

Here the term is used in a fairly broad sense, to encompass a continuum of mentoring functions, a variety of ways in which time may be invested in the development of a younger or junior person.

Mentoring may be conceived as representing a continuum of functions, from achievement-oriented to nurturant, reflecting to some extent the range of possibilities Erikson intended in his original conception of generativity as the guiding of the next generation.

Drawing on the work of Chodorow and Gilligan, I will show how the gender patterns through which men are socialized to be achievers and women are socialized to be nurturers are reflected in different patterns of mentoring by male and female faculty members. Thus, the research literature based on the lives of men (Levinson, Vaillant) views mentoring as an achievement-related function, undertaken to advance the careers of both the mentor and the protégé and to benefit the organization. However, there is some evidence from studies of higher education that mentoring by women is more nurturant, more supportive, and less focused on career achievement (Berg and Ferber 1983; Hall and Sandler 1983) with little or no benefit to the mentor other than the sense of generativity. It appears then that mentoring by women tends to represent the nurturant side of the continuum of possible functions accomplished through mentoring.

Faculty members have a comparable continuum of activities and a considerable degree of autonomy and flexibility in their choice of activities, among the three major faculty functions of teaching, research, and service. Some faculty responsibilities related to teaching and research are achievement-oriented activities that produce measurable outcomes—number of credit hours generated, number and dollar value of grants, number of scholarly publications, page lengths of manuscripts, and number of citations to one's publications in the citation indices. Other faculty responsibilities, such as advising and committee work, rarely produce measurable outcomes. As an example, faculty are required to be advisors, but advising, particularly of undergraduates, is typically a pro forma obligation—three office hours per week, an appointment sign-up sheet on an office door, a scrawled signature on next semester's course registration form.

The gender-based patterns of socialization of men to be achievers and women to be nurturers are reflected to some extent in the activities of male and female faculty and in the activities that are rewarded and are most valued in academic settings. Male faculty are more likely to devote their time to achievement-oriented activities, leading not surprisingly to higher "productivity," as measured by grants and publications. Female faculty are more likely to teach larger, lower-level courses less compatible with scholarly productivity and to spend more time advising and talking to students (Chrisler 1989). There are no easily measured, achievement-oriented outcomes for time invested in informal, out-of-class relationships with students who are trying to clarify their competencies, values, and interests to define realistic educational and career goals, whether they are adolescents in the stage of identity development or adult students confronting major life transitions or career changes. Serious, long-term academic and career exploration and guidance, visibility and availability as a role model, helping a student envision and weigh future possibilities, and the like, relate more to nurturance than achievement. As Arlie Hochschild wrote, describing darkened hallways with closed office doors in her department at Berkeley, time spent with students was time lost to extending one's vita through research and writing. Consequently, most faculty in the predominantly male department limited their accessibility to students by doing their "work" away from their departmental offices. In the academic world, "productivity" has become evaluated more by grants and publications, rather than by how many students one has encouraged to become "connected knowers" (Belenky et al. 1986). Yet, there is nothing inherently "gender-based" about the range of activities faculty members pursue, and many critics of higher education and its current reward system are male scholars such as Ernest L. Boyer (1990).

Mentoring and the Evolution of American Higher Education

The role of mentoring in academic settings has had surprisingly little recognition (Merriam 1983). Levinson himself observed that

> our system of higher education, although officially committed to fostering the intellectual and personal development of students, provides mentoring that is generally limited in quantity and poor in quality. (1978, 334)

Historically, from the founding of American higher education in the 1600s through the World War II period, the percentage of adolescents, mostly male, who attended college was relatively small and drawn from a selective upper stratum of families. The range of career choices was narrow, and one's career field was often preordained by family traditions or expectations. The percentage of college graduates who went on to doctoral level study was even smaller, and the competition for entry-level academic positions was certainly not what it is today. Those who completed Ph.D.s were overwhelmingly male, and the "old boy network," which was very small in academia prior to World War II, virtually assured appropriate placement for male Ph.D.s. For the limited number of women who completed Ph.D.s, the situation was obviously very different (Hall and Sandler 1983).

The passage of the G.I. Bill, with educational benefits for veterans, opened the doors of higher education to a sizable group of young adults who could not have considered college under other circumstances. It is a little known footnote to history that the leadership of American higher education at the time did not welcome this change in its clientele (Fallows 1989), questioning the motivation and academic ability of returning veterans. Some university administrators and faculty were dismayed that higher education was no longer limited primarily to the "best and brightest," those young people embedded in a network of family money, connections, and career paths.

Particularly since the 1960s, opportunities to go on to higher education have expanded. As the percentage of adolescents interested in higher education increased, as adults began to return to education in increasing numbers, as the range of career possibilities multiplied exponentially, the nature of American higher education has been radically altered. Now institutions of higher education are accepting enormous numbers of people, adolescents and adults, who have potential and are motivated to pursue personal and professional advancement but are uncertain about how to proceed

Meanwhile, the expectations for faculty have also changed significantly. It is no longer enough to be a good teacher and to publish an occasional book or journal article; formerly, the publication of a book might represent twenty years' work or the culmination of an academic career (Erikson was over fifty when his first book was published, and there are many comparable examples). Now, one's name is expected to appear on journal articles as a junior co-author while one is still in graduate school, and on-going research is divided into the sequence of journal articles necessary to extend one's vita, the academic equivalent of media "sound bites." The public's perception of a university faculty member has evolved from the tweedy, absent-minded, pipe-smoking professor to a media figure such as Carl Sagan or to the director of a large research laboratory with a multi-million dollar budget and a large research team, engaged in medical research or research on superconductivity or cold fusion. The president of a major university recently commented that parents want to send their children to prestigious universities but also want tweedy professors with time to spend with students, and that the two objectives were incompatible and parents couldn't have it both ways. This presumed incompatibility captures the pressures that faculty face today and the failure of the reward system in higher education to recognize differences among students, academic disciplines, and faculty strengths.

Students vary considerably in the amount and type of faculty attention they require. A few students enter as freshmen with a declared major and a clearly defined career objective. They maintain this throughout a relatively uneventful undergraduate education, and graduate and go into entry level positions, from social work and nursing to management and engineering, having needed little from faculty beyond actual classroom instruction. But these students are in the minority. As we all know, many arrive uncertain about a major, uncertain about a career objective, including whether or not to continue beyond a bachelor's degree, and uncertain about their identity, values, and so on. Many, particularly minority students, arrive burdened with significant disabilities and obstacles to overcome. Others encounter questions, doubts, and unanticipated alternatives during their undergraduate years. These students need faculty time and attention if they are to persevere and realize their potential. In an increasingly diverse society, we cannot afford to lose the potential contributions of these students through failing to recognize and acknowledge the necessity for investment of faculty time and energy in nurturing and empowering such students.

Mentoring in Higher Education

Mentoring has usually been studied in the context of graduate education, particularly doctoral study, when a student's graduate advisor may play a pivotal role in shaping the student's academic and career direction and often in defining a particular research topic (Hall and Sandler 1983). This is most apparent in the sciences and related applied fields such as medical research and engineering, in which substantive, on-going research programs are directed by senior researchers/principal investigators who supervise a staff of postdoctoral and/or graduate student researchers. When a student is interested in working under a faculty member with such a research program, it may not be enough for a student to be "interested" or to have "potential." Consideration for acceptance may be predicated on perceived compatibility and similarity; demonstrated ability through grades, test scores, and previous writing; and the time and effort involved in integrating the newcomer into the research team. If accepted, the newcomer is often assigned a specific research topic or project that fits into the long-range program. To the extent that mentoring occurs, then, it is largely achievement-oriented, educating the newcomer to the research program and its techniques and equipment; it clearly centers on the mentor's agenda.

Such research teams often become very cohesive working groups (Allport 1987; Kanigel 1986), in which some members stay for a period of years, through lengthy doctoral programs and sometimes continuing as research associates, post-doctoral assistants, or technicians. Such teams frequently produce large numbers of multi-authored publications. These groups often become very competitive in seeking research funding, trying to stay ahead of another team doing similar research, and rushing to publish results before another team (Allport 1987). Rival "empire building" and bitter competition resembling the marketing battles between corporations sometimes occur, as indicated by recent well-publicized incidents that have raised ethical questions (Rosser 1989).

This model of graduate study and research is not readily applied to the humanities and social science disciplines, although there are some exceptions. An eminent historian or philosopher does not build a research team of doctoral students to do the "legwork" to provide data to be synthesized by the principal investigator. A scholar in the humanities is expected to do his or her own fieldwork, synthesis, and writing, and it is considered unethical to rely too heavily on ground work done by one's students. One's students are presumably pursuing their own independent topics, related to but usually distinct from their advisor's interests. Thus, time spent with students may not contribute to one's own list of publications, and in fact probably takes time away from one's own research and writing.

What are graduate students' perceptions of their experiences during graduate school?

An extensive survey of graduate students at 25 institutions shows that the single best predictor of the perceived quality of the graduate department climate is the nature and quality of student-faculty relations, including accessibility and whether the faculty treat the students with respect. A further analysis of the data showed a positive relationship between the number of female faculty and the rating of the environment of learning by women students. (Harnett 1976, cited in Simeone 1987, 102)

The limited data on the differential experiences of male and female graduate students are often not broken down by the gender of the faculty involved, partly because the representation of women as graduate faculty members is so limited. For example, Menges and Exum (1983) summarize data from other studies indicating that women faculty are more likely than men to teach only undergraduate courses and to carry heavier teaching loads.

Berg and Ferber (1983), in a review of the literature on the differential experiences of male and female graduate students, report that female students are viewed as less dedicated and less promising by faculty (predominantly male). In turn, female graduate students are less confident of their academic ability and tend to set lower goals for themselves, leading Berg and Ferber "to speculate whether there is a causal relationship between this perception of faculty and the low self-confidence of women students" (1983, 631). They further report that as graduate students, women are more likely than men to be teaching assistants rather than research assistants. In their analysis of data from a large Midwestern research university, they found a statistically significant difference in faculty-student interaction by gender (1983, 638) and concluded that

> women students are at an inescapable disadvantage in finding mentors
> . . . the inevitable result of rising proportions of women students without
> concomitant changes in the makeup of faculties. (1983, 639)

While the number of women faculty is less than the number of male faculty, evidence suggests that women are more likely to take on what graduate students perceive as mentoring roles. Boyles, in a study of a large research-oriented institution found that "women comprise only 7 percent of the faculty, but act as mentors to 21 percent of men and 37 percent of women graduate students, as indicated by the students themselves" (1988, B3). While the limited evidence available is not conclusive, it is sufficient to suggest that women, because of their socialization to take responsibility for the nurturance and development of others, are more likely to invest time in sustained relationships with students outside of the classroom and beyond their direct responsibilities. There is also evidence that both women and minorities are more likely to invest time in committee work and community service (Hall and Sandler 1983; Menges and Exum 1983), activities that are related to an acceptance of responsibility to others. In fact, these activities represent a continuum of responsibility for the sustenance and maintenance of a network of relationships and a sense of community, from one-to-one relationships to the university as a community to the community within which the university is located.

Patterns of Same-Gender and Cross-Gender Mentoring in Higher Education

This section is based both on the available literature and my own observations. My observations, while not systematic or easily quantifiable, are based on over twenty years' employment in higher education, including opportunities to observe undergraduate and graduate education in a wide variety of institutions in various parts of the country, and on ten years' experience teaching and advising in our graduate program in psychology, which attracts primarily mid-career adult students of both genders and from a variety of ethnic backgrounds.

Same-gender faculty-student advising/mentoring relationships seem most comfortable for both faculty and students and are, therefore, most likely to occur. Because cross-gender relationships are less likely, systematic data on such relationships are limited. Let me discuss briefly the following types of mentoring relationships: male-to-male, female-to-female, male-to-female, and female-to-male.

Male-to-male mentoring relationships tend to center on academic and research-related activities and responsibilities, the preparation of grant proposals and publications, and advice on career advancement—all achievement-related functions. The appropriateness of a man's being in graduate school, his ability to do graduate level work, his role and responsibilities as a graduate student in relation to other life roles—these are rarely issues. Often when an advisor-student relationship lasts over a period of several years, as in a doctoral program, the relationship does develop a personal component—familiarity with each other's personal life and family situation, social activities away from the office or lab, and so on—but this aspect tends to be peripheral, tangential to the primary purpose of the relationship. When such relationships continue after the completion of the protégé's degree, it is rarely as a social relationship or a friendship, but is instead continued for professional reasons.

When a female-to-female advising/mentoring relationship begins, it typically includes both achievement-related and nurturant aspects from the beginning. A woman graduate student is often doubtful of her academic ability in graduate school, unsure of whether she should be in graduate school and concerned about possible conflicts with her other roles and responsibilities. With a male advisor, a woman may feel hesitant to express such doubts, but with a female advisor, she may feel able to acknowledge them. For most of us who are faculty women, there is a immediate sense of empathy, of connectedness with the woman struggling with such issues. Because women students turn to faculty women as role models, and either observe us or ask directly how we juggle multiple roles and balance personal and professional responsibilities, the relationship between a student and a female faculty mentor tends to include both achievement-oriented and nurturant aspects. As a female graduate student progresses, the best of such female-to-female relationships become collaborative, on-going relationships that continue after the degree is completed.

The risk in female-to-female relationships is that the relationship may move from some midpoint on the continuum toward the nurturant direction. A student's lack of self-confidence or her concern over personal issues may become so predominant that the faculty member may become more involved in providing psychosocial support than in keeping academic progress on track. There is some evidence that female faculty may not provide to women clear, specific feedback about inadequate performance and the steps necessary to improve their work to acceptable levels (Hall and Sandler 1983).

Turning to male-to-female relationships, these have been common over the years, since until fairly recently, most women who completed doctoral degrees or other graduate degrees were mentored and/or advised by male faculty (Hall and Sandler 1983). Yet, the limited data that exist are based on fairly small samples or anecdotal accounts (e.g., Clark and Corcoran 1986), and often emphasize difficulties or negative aspects of male-to-female relationships, such as sexual harassment. Given the increasing numbers of female students entering and completing graduate programs, it is reasonable to assume that much effective mentoring of women students by male faculty has occurred across disciplines and throughout the years. Yet, even the best of these relationships seem to have a different quality. There is an effort to maintain a professional distance or reserve, which is certainly understandable in view of the questions that may be triggered by too close or too personal a relationship.

As graduate study is completed, male faculty may consciously "track" male and female graduate students differently, steering female graduates away from the best teaching and research opportunities into more teaching-oriented institutions, including junior colleges (Clark and Corcoran 1986). Colleagues who have served on search committees comment that the letters written for female candidates often include subtle phrases that indicate reservations about a woman's commitment or potential.

I know of no published literature that discusses female-to-male relationships. First of all, such relationships are less likely to exist, given the underrepresentation of women at the upper ranks in graduate and research institutions in most disciplines. For me, there always seems to be a sense of distance in my interactions with male graduate students, as though they feel more concerned about maintaining the hierarchical nature of our relationship than I do. In a similar vein, Arlie Hochschild (1975) describes her discomfort with the deference of male graduate students. There are a variety of possible reasons for male students' response styles to female faculty that go beyond the scope of this paper. However, the effect is that I feel I rarely get to know a male student as a person, to have a sense of who he really is and what he really cares about or values. Thus, I feel limited or constrained in my efforts to guide his professional development. Other female colleagues have reported similar feelings in advising both male students and minority students.

While the evidence for cross-gender patterns is limited, it seems that, for several reasons, this would be an appropriate area for further research in higher education. As higher education becomes more diverse, we need to understand the factors that facilitate and impede effective faculty-student relationships.

Current Trends in Higher Education

It is not essential for a student to have a faculty member as a mentor—obviously many undergraduate and graduate students complete their degrees without ever "connecting" with any faculty member who takes a personal interest in them. However, the affirmation that comes from having even *one* faculty member who cares about a student's progress may be critical to that student's formation of realistic educational and career objectives and in the student's persistence toward the achievement of those objectives (cf. Arnold 1993). We know from attrition rates that many students are dropping out of undergraduate and graduate programs, for reasons that are not necessarily related to their academic ability. There is clearly a loss of potential talent when students are expected to "sink or swim" on their own. But, is there any recognition within higher education today of the significance of faculty time invested in effective mentoring and advising of students?

Clearly, the answer is negative. While some thoughtful observers of American higher education call for a reconsideration of "scholarship" (Boyer 1990), powerful economic and demographic trends have exacerbated the pressures on universities and their faculties. Faculty members are constantly being asked to do more with less—to teach larger and larger classes, to carry larger numbers of advisees, to bring in more grants, to produce more publications, while resources are being reduced, especially in public institutions. As faculty are increasingly stressed, they have less and less time to spend with students and to be involved in the campus as a community. To what extent has this contributed to the increase in campus controversies and tensions, around such varied topics as sexual harassment, date and acquaintance rape, gay rights, ethnic and cultural diversity, and political correctness?

In responding to these various trends and problems, higher education seems to be altering its structure and organization in ways that further remove faculty from contact with students. Specifically, there is a trend toward the creation of "support services," separated from the academic life of the university, that provide specialized services to distinct groups of students. These are termed "student development," "student support services," or "academic support services"—the counseling center, the career development center, the freshman center, the adult learner center, programs and services for minority or non-English-speaking students, and remedial programs euphemistically called "developmental education." Some of these services are clearly necessary and appropriate. To some extent, however, the proliferation and diversification of such specialized services reflects a tendency to categorize and divide students into groups, each different in some way from the "mainstream." Some academic literature today emphasizes the necessity of integrating into the curriculum in all disciplines the intersection of gender, race, ethnicity, and class (cf. Bronstein and Quina 1990). But how do we effectively explore these issues in the classroom, when groups of students are led to believe that their concerns, needs, and differences should be addressed through specialized support services?

This proliferation of support services allows faculty legitimately to excuse themselves from responsibility for everything except actual classroom interaction and grades. Furthermore, if data could be pooled for all such programs (some of which are under student affairs and some under academic affairs), I think we would find that they are predominantly staffed, although not necessarily directed, by women. If verified, this would provide another example of the primary delegation to women of those activities that depend on nurturance and an acceptance of responsibility for others.

What are the implications of this trend? As a developmental

psychologist, reflecting Erikson's concept of generativity, I am concerned that we in higher education are not doing a very good job of guiding and nurturing the next generation. Particularly in four-year colleges and in graduate and professional education, rates of minority attendance and graduation do not reflect the representation of minorities in the population. It is still primarily the privileged, "the best and brightest," who are being encouraged and mentored, while others are relegated to special support programs within the university or to the community colleges. As a female faculty member, I see in this trend another message from the administration: faculty investment of time with students is not recognized as an important and valued function. Indeed, in terms of evaluation, promotion, and tenure, only achievement-oriented functions that produce measurable outcomes will be rewarded.

Conclusions

Mentor was concerned not with his own advancement, but with the nurturance and development of his protégé. Similarly, Aisenberg and Harrington (1988) have suggested that women faculty view their teaching as a process of empowering others.

If American higher education is to meet effectively the needs of an increasingly multicultural, highly technological, and rapidly changing society in the twenty-first century, we need to recognize that the primary mission of education is empowerment. Margaret Mead (1970), writing twenty years ago on the increasing rapidity of social change, observed that adults need to prepare the next generation for a future that cannot even be envisioned. It is our students who will shape the world of the twenty-first century.

It is beyond the scope of this paper to explore how and why the gender patterns of men as achievers and women as nurturers continue to be reproduced. It is clear, however, than many women in higher education value their ability to nurture students and to encourage their students to achieve their potential, and do not want to suppress or sacrifice this to achieve in academe "like men" (Aisenberg and Harrington 1988; Chrisler 1989; and Tidball 1976). Thus, our challenge is to continue to try to change the institutional patterns that do not recognize and reward the values, strengths, and perspectives that women bring to their faculty roles and that limit the voices and visions that women bring to academe.

Works Cited

Aisenberg, Nadya, and Mona Harrington. *Women of Academe: Outsiders in the Sacred Grove.* Amherst: University of Massachusetts Press, 1988.

Allport, Susan. *Explorers of the Black Box: The Search for the Cellular Basis of Memory.* New York: W.W. Norton, 1987.

Arnold, Karen. "Academically Talented Women in the 1980's: The Illinois Valedictorian Project." In *Women's Lives through Time: Educated American Women of the Twentieth Century,* eds. Kathleen Day Hulbert and Diane Tickton Schuster. San Francisco: Jossey-Bass, 1993.

Belenky, Mary F., Blythe M. Clinchy, Nancy R. Goldberger, and Jill M. Tarule. *Women's Ways of Knowing: Development of Self, Voice, and Mind.* New York: Basic Books, 1986.

Berg, Helen M., and Mariane A. Ferber. "Men and Women Graduate Students: Who Succeeds and Why?" *Journal of Higher Education* 54 (1983): 629-648.

Boyer, Ernest L. *Scholarship Reconsidered: The Priorities of the Professoriate.* Princeton, N.J.: Carnegie Foundation for the Advancement of Teaching, 1990.

Boyles, Marcia V. "Letter." *Chronicle of Higher Education* 35:13 (November 1988): B3.

Bronstein, Phyllis, and Katherine Quina. *Teaching a Psychology of People: Resources for Gender and Sociocultural Awareness.* Washington, D.C.: American Psychological Association, 1990.

Chodorow, Nancy. *The Reproduction of Mothering.* Berkeley: University of California Press, 1978.

Chrisler, Joan. "Teacher vs. Scholar: Role Conflict for Women." Paper presented at a conference on Gender in Academe at the University of South Florida, Tampa, November 1989.

Clark, Shirley M., and Mary Corcoran. "Perspectives on the Professional Socialization of Women Faculty." *Journal of Higher Education* 57 (1986): 20-43.

Erikson, Erik. *The Life Cycle Completed.* New York: Norton, 1985.

Fallows, James. *More Like Us.* Boston: Houghton Mifflin, 1989.

Gilligan, Carol. *In a Different Voice: Psychological Theory and Women's Development.* Cambridge, Mass.: Harvard University Press, 1982.

Hall, Roberta M., and Bernice Sandler. "Academic Mentoring for Women Faculty and Students" Project on the Status and Education of Women, Association of American Colleges, Washington, D.C., 1983. ERIC Document ED 240 891.

Hochschild, Arlie. "Inside the Clockwork of Male Careers." In *Women and the Power to Change*, ed. Florence Howe. New York: McGraw-Hill, 1975.

Hulbert, Kathleen D. "Faculty as Mentors in the Career Development of Professional Women." Paper presented at the annual meeting of the American Psychological Association, Atlanta, Georgia, 1988.

Kanigel, Robert. *Apprentice to Genius: The Making of a Scientific Dynasty*. New York: MacMillan, 1986.

Keele, Reba. "Mentoring or Networking: Strong and Weak Ties in Career Development." In *Not as Far as You Think: The Realities of Working Women*, ed. Lynda L. Moore. Lexington, Mass.: Lexington Books, 1986.

Levinson, Daniel H. *The Seasons of a Man's Life*. New York: Knopf, 1978.

Mead, Margaret. *Culture and Commitment: A Study of the Generation Gap*. New York: Doubleday and Company, 1970.

Merriam, Sharan. "Mentors and Protégés: A Critical Review of the Literature" *Adult Education Quarterly* 33 (1983): 161-173.

Menges, Robert J., and William H. Exum. "Barriers to the Progress of Women and Minority Faculty." *Journal of Higher Education* 54 (1983): 123-144.

Moore, Lynda L., ed. *Not as Far As You Think: The Realities of Working Women*. Lexington, Mass.: Lexington, 1986.

Rosser, Sue V. "Saving the Gender at Risk: Women's Studies Methods and Pedagogy for Women and Science." Paper presented at a conference on Gender in Academe at the University of South Florida, Tampa, November 1989.

Simeone, Angela. *Academic Women: Working towards Equality*. South Hadley, Mass.: Bergin and Garvey, 1987.

Speizer, Jeanne J. "Role Models, Mentors, and Sponsors: The Elusive ✓ Concepts." *Signs* 6 (1981): 692-712.

Tidball, M. Elizabeth. "Of Men and Research: The Dominant Themes in American Higher Education Include Neither Teaching nor Women." *Journal of Higher Education* 47 (1976): 373-389.

Vaillant, George. *Adaptation to Life*. Boston: Little Brown, 1977.

Chapter 19

If R2D2 is a Male Robot, Then 10^6 is a Female Nothing

Fran Schattenberg

Look around you, and what do you see? You see people. Look at academic printed matter, and what do you see?

In a 1991 Student Handbook:

> The Provost is the chief academic officer of the University. *He* is responsible for overall development . . . *He* is also responsible for . . . given by the President or *his* designee . . . A student who believes *he* has been denied rights due to *his* religious beliefs . . . No student shall be denied access to *his/her* room . . . (Emphasis added)

In a Faculty/Staff Handbook in use in 1991:

> The Vice President for Employee Relations has as *his* responsibility . . . . The President and *his* executive staff . . . The study of *man* helps the student to understand the world of which *he or she is* a part . . . The Presiding officer of the Faculty Senate *he* then reads . . . *He* shall continue . . . *He* says . . . *He* inquires . . . *He* calls . . . as *he or she* deems necessary . . . each Senator has *his* committee assignment . . . (Emphasis added)

In a 1991 text currently in use:

A scholar is more than a researcher, for while *he* may be gifted . . . *He* is, besides a *man* of broad and luminous learning . . . *He* is never engulfed by mere data, *his* mind is able to see them in the long perspective of *man's* ambitions. (Altick 1981, 19. Emphasis added)

This masculine litany, only a few of the thousands I could cite, should impress upon us that, linguistically, academe is still a man's world, and a woman's only entry into that world is the occasional addition as a secondary, hence subordinate, component in the *he/she* pronoun combination. At worst, she is absent; at best, an afterthought.

There are bitter ironies here, turning in on each other. They are bitter because the possibilities for change were so encouraging when academe first emerged as the primary area for research and for amassing the data to support arguments for change. But today, one still searches in vain for language changes directed toward equality. The civil rights movement and the legislation of the late 1960s spurred interest in discrimination of all types, including discrimination arising out of language. This movement toward equality generated extensive academic research that provided hard data proving that male preferential language socially and psychologically discriminates against women. Academe again seemed to have the potential for utilizing its expertise and power to effect language change. And what are the results of all of this? Twenty-five years later, as you can see from the cited quotations from current academic texts, the promised change has never come to fruition. Nothing is really any different in academic printed matter. Universities continue to present a male-dominated world to their millions of students. Not only is traditional sexist language still ubiquitous, but objections are met by lethargy, boredom, and even derision.

We can indeed ask, and we *should* ask: Who cares that linguistically, academe is populated by male administrators, male faculty and staff, male students, male scholars, male writers, and male researchers? Who cares that there seems to be no groundswell of opinion to eliminate this engrained, conscious, and unconscious language discrimination? Can we get others to care to address the problem of language discrimination against women not only in academe, but everywhere?

My answer to these questions is that I care, and the intention of this essay is to make my readers care as well. This is not just an idle sentence, for *we must all care*. There is too much at stake, particularly since more and more women are participating in all areas of society. They need all the help they can get, because the language that surrounds us every waking moment shapes our lives every hour of every day.

Language has to be changed to describe and create an environment that empowers everyone, not just one sex, to have an equal chance to succeed. Throwing in a few token *he/she-s,* as we saw in the earlier quotations, does not create a gender neutral environment for women. However, the enabling source for change can come from academe with its existent expertise and power, if it decides to mobilize for that effort.

One of the most powerful academic tools for language change is the theory of social constructionism. Pre-dating research into sexist language by some two decades, social constructionism was moving toward "adulthood" at the same time that language research in the mid-1970s to mid-1980s was confirming the original theses of linguistic discrimination. Initially, there was no symbiotic relationship between these two approaches, but social constructionist theory offers a welcome alternative to a rigid set of mandates that explain existence and the formation of human consciousness in absolute terms as an abstract object of contemplation. Feminists such as Luce Irigaray *(Speculum of the Other Woman* 1985) and Dale Spender *(Man Made Language* 1980) have argued that this entrenched patriarchal view is especially antagonistic to women because, among other things, male-dominated language creates an artificial reality that silences, excludes, and oppresses women. In the social constructionist perspective, as the name suggests, reality is a subjective product or construct of continual social interaction as it takes place in our own relative time. Our concepts of the world, our theories of who we are and what we can do are not static and predetermined, but living, organic constructs, reflecting the needs of our own time and place. It is here, in our continual dialogical critique of economic, political, and social arrangements as we act and interact with each other, that language change should occur.

Unfortunately, the potential of social constructionism as a tool for sexist language change has not been fulfilled even though incontrovertible evidence of research data provides the argument for change. The consensus among researchers such as Sally Hacker, Chris Kramarae, Dale Spender, Sandra Bem, Mykol Hamilton, and Johanna DeStafano, to name only a few, is that the constant reiteration of the pronoun "he" as the sole agent causes readers to identify *he* to mean only males (Miller and Swift 1988, 168–71). Donald Mackay translated this discrimination into an astounding statistic. Based on an analysis of over 100 texts in use at his university, he concluded that, in the course of a lifetime, an educated American's exposure to *he* as the sole actor and contributor to society exceeds one million times, or 10^6 (1980, 355). Our language, then, keeps telling us that it is men who do things. As for women, women are nothing. Women cannot "construct" themselves linguistically because they are not even part of the dialogue. They are not envisioned as participants in power politics or as capable of handling positions of power and leadership. This does not mean that some women have not handled power and become leaders, but it is *in spite of language,* not because of it.

Deconstruction is another academic theory that helps us to understand how sexist language can never result in linguistic equality. In deconstruction, *he* (as well as every other word) is not composed of isolated, absolute, inert marks on a page with predetermined values, but is in a constant state of tension, struggle, and discovery. This underlying tumult invites examination as we erase or examine a word to discover the cause of the tension and struggle—its Other. When this is applied to traditional sexist pronoun usage, when we erase *man* or *he* as a general referent for participator and contributor, *she* does not suddenly emerge. There is no "other" in our consciousness. For instance, humanity in general is never called *woman,* and neither *woman* nor *man* is an accurate word to describe the earth's population. Moreover, adding *she* as a presence is not gender neutral, for the male hierarchy is still in place, with *she* only a secondary, subordinate/inferior addition. Even if the common "solution" of using both sexist pronouns is employed, either separately or in the *he/she* combination, in the erasure and undoing of the word, a sex-designated hierarchy remains as a trace, the antithesis of the aim of deconstruction.

Sexist language will always be discriminatory and a perpetuator of inequality because gender is *never* neutral. If sex designator words are eliminated (erased) in the play of presence and absence, it might seem that both sexes "aren't" (don't exist). But what is actually erased is the privileging of one person over another. When we erase the exclusivity of sexist language, this, of necessity, requires a gender-free writing style, a style that concentrates on the general issue at hand, not on the sex of the person referred to. This enables language to focus on how *individuals* function in a society and on what they are doing, not simply on how one sex is functioning and doing. This gender-free editing of the male-dominated description of a scholar cited above shows how academe is a community of equals:

A scholar is more than a researcher who may be gifted in the discovery and assessment of facts, and, at the same time, possesses broad and luminous learning. Never engulfed by mere data, the scholar's mind is able to see them in the long perspective of human ambitions.

The actual technique involves a number of stratagems, starting with the dropping of all sexist words, something that is quite easy to do since English sentence structure is littered with unnecessary pronoun use. For example, "Every practicing scholar, if *he* is candid, has a fund of instructive stories drawn from *his* own experience" (Altick 1981, 126; emphasis added) becomes, "Every practicing scholar, if candid, has a fund of instructive stories drawn from personal experience." Common guideline solutions offer some excellent suggestions for recasting sentences, such as the use of the second person and the use of plurals. But guidelines fail to eliminate sexist language by not prohibiting it entirely; they still include the loophole that it should be avoided whenever possible (Frank and Treichler 1989). We do not need loopholes, because we do not ever have to use sexist language. Below are examples illustrating the total elimination of sexist language.

If an author derived a dominant idea from another, just how did *he* modify it and impress it with the stamp of *his* own intellect? (Altick 1981, 107; emphasis added)

If an author derived a dominant idea from another, just how did the process of modification occur and the imprint of the author's own intellect take place?

But a writer never exists in a vacuum. Whatever private influences are involved, *he* is also the product of *his* age . . . however rebellious *his* attitude toward *his* world may be, *his* mental set is fatefully determined by *his* social and cultural environment. (Altick 1981, 5; emphasis added)

Whatever private influences are involved, the particular age and place influence the writer . . . however rebellious an attitude toward that world may be, one's mind set is fatefully determined by the social and cultural environment.

"Gender free" is what language in academe, and everywhere for that matter, should be all about; not adding *she* as an afterthought, but describing and valuing what *people* can do and what *people* actually do. This is how our books should be transmitting societal values to the millions of students who will engage in their own discourses of creating the world in which they live. They would then create a world where language is not a barrier to an equal chance to learn, contribute, and form a rational self-image based on societal encouragement and approval of both sexes.

This will not occur until you, as part of academe, do care and do something about it. Object to sexist language when and where you see it. Use gender-free language style in all of your conversations and discourse. Nothing will change until *you* do.

Works Cited

Altick, Richard D. *The Art of Literary Research.* 3d ed. New York: W. W. Norton, 1981.

Bruffee, Kenneth. "Social Construction, Language, and the Authority of Knowledge: A Bibliographical Essay." *College English* 48:8 (1986): 773–90.

Faculty/Staff Handbook University of South Florida. Tampa: University of South Florida, N.D. (but internal data indicates it is after 1978).

Frank, Francine, and Paula Treichler. *Language, Gender, and Professional Writing: Theoretical Approaches and Guidelines for Nonsexist Usage.* New York: MLA, 1989.

Irigaray, Luce. *Speculum of the Other Woman.* Ithaca: Cornell University Press, 1985.

Mackay, Donald. "On the Goals, Principles, and Procedures for Prescriptive Grammar: Singular *They.*" *Language in Society* 9 (1980): 349–56.

Miller, Casey, and Kate Swift. *The Handbook of Nonsexist Writing.* 2d ed. New York: Harper, 1988.

Spender, Dale. *Man Made Language.* London: Routledge and Kegan Paul, 1980.

Student Handbook University of South Florida 1991–1992. Tampa: University of South Florida, 1991.

Chapter 20

The Hidden "A-Gender" in Intellectual Discourse: A Dialogical Examination

John Clifford and Janet Mason Ellerby

Clifford:

In the *Republic*, Plato's philosopher king, a prototype for the traditional male intellectual, knew what was best for the society he would rule through informed reason. The privileged status of Plato's intellectual leader was legitimized by default since within the patriarchal context of Athenian culture, no one but such a guardian of guardians would seem logical. And guardian is an apt term since much was protected and forbidden in Plato's ideology, including significant contributions from those who disagreed with him. The carefully proscribed rhetorical education of the elite in Plato's world insured a fairly homogeneous mindset among those with power. Difference was tolerated only within fairly limited parameters among those upper-class males with power. Plato's suspicion of the Sophists, for example, stems from his fear that the hegemony of his intellectual world might be threatened by opposing views about the absoluteness of truth, and so he created for succeeding centuries a caricature of the Sophists as distorters of the truth, as mere rhetorical opportunists. Instead of fairly portraying their commitment to a provisional, contextual truth, Plato discredits them through the seductive brilliance of his Socratic dialogues. Plato seems defensive and rigid about guarding the discourse that would insure the influence of his class and gender.

Although Plato does speak of equality of the sexes in the *Republic*, there is no indication that if this were to come about that women would be able to influence the intellectual discursive structure in any way. Plato's conversation of mankind, for example, would remain intact; women would be expected to adhere to the norms of the dominant discourse already validated. In this paradigm, difference, in the simple sense of variation, is rendered invisible, but more insidiously, difference becomes an epistemological tool to understand and shape reality. Clear oppositions between the absolute and the relative, between the objective and subjective are constructed in order to privilege one against the other. Like the Sophists, women become caricatures, likely to be emotional, subjective, partial, fragmentary, irrational, and circular. More importantly for Plato and his culture, intellectual men could thereby position themselves as reasonable, objective, complete, unified, rational, and linear. Eventually both of these extreme and essentially arbitrary positions became reified in an intellectual discourse that would dominate Western thought for two millennia.

Difference, then, becomes an epistemological weapon. Above Plato's academy door, for example, was the credo, "Let no one enter here who is not a geometer," which might reasonably be read as a representative anecdote for the subject position males have constructed for themselves as dominant intellectuals. In fact, it comes close to being a transhistorical and transcultural motto for a certain type of intellectual whose lineage stretches from Plato to Rousseau, Immanuel Kant, and contemporary conservative intellectuals such as Allan Bloom. "Let no one enter," is self-evidently an exclusionary gesture, already demanding that the site of education and consequently access to power be contingent on specific conditions that are difficult to come by except through the privilege of class and gender. Already we can see that affirmative action is hardly the point. Plato does not automatically encourage entry for the eager, the curious, or the bright, nor does he consider the innovative, the alternative, or the oppositional. His one condition, being a geometer, conjures up the conventional educational wisdom from a generation ago that females do not do well in geometry because it is too abstract, acontextual, and rational; and females are too grounded in the specifics of their emotional context and, of course, neither overly linear nor rational. Plato is probably not consciously using code words for "No girls allowed," especially since his exclusionary gesture is more encompassing. He is, instead, explicitly announcing his commitment to educating in a certain way an already highly constructed audience, namely aristocratic males.

From Plato to Allan Bloom we can look at the intellectual as a defender of the faith. Unlike the bohemian romantic or the oppositional critic, the traditional male intellectual believes it is his duty and responsibility to police, replicate, even purify a discourse that he imagines to be as unproblematically objective and true. In this way, the traditional intellectual becomes an important force in a patriarchal culture that has constructed an epistemology of difference as a strategy to maintain power.

This epistemology invariably positions otherness as inferior. And women, ever since Plato, have been construed within intellectual discourse as the Other. Dissenting men such as the Sophists who have attempted to promote alternative intellectual discourses have also been marginalized, but women have most conveniently served as a rhetorical trope for the inferior Other in order to reinforce a profile of the intellectual that would reinforce the values of those in power. For the Platonic astronomer, for example, objectivity, reason, and an appeal to invariant rules were ideal attributes seemingly made more credible when the Other could stand in for such opposing values as subjectivity, emotion, and the irrational. Gender, therefore, becomes by design an important but unacknowledged dimension of intellectual discourse.

Nevertheless, the traditional intellectual claims to transcend the ephemeral traditions of his time. Plato, Kant, and Bloom believed that they were independent voices upholding objective standards. There is some irony here since the subject positions that male intellectuals have been allowed to assume have always been saturated with cultural values that are thoroughly interested, arbitrary, and, finally, fictional. Objectivity, reason, and the timeless are criteria that intellectuals cloak themselves in, but these concepts are thoroughly problematic.

When we look back at canonical intellectuals from our present perspective, it is hard to avoid the disconcerting feeling that they had little self-consciousness about the ground their discourse was built on. The common postmodern gesture—that it is our obligation as university intellectuals to interrogate the foundations on which our values and scholarly methods rest—was not something that traditional intellectuals took seriously. Consequently, the place that gender played in the intellectual tradition was casually repressed or dismissed as irrelevant. Plato and Aristotle were so convinced that their versions of reason and logic could dominate the production of knowledge that they spent little time wondering if their ideological foundations were actually made of rock or shifting sand. The Sophistic and postmodern spirit of skeptical interrogation appears superficially in Plato's dialogues, but only for a specific end. The enemy of Plato's world view was emotion, uncertainty, fiction, poetry, disorder, and dissent. The constructedness of this remarkable bipolar outlook went without serious challenge for centuries. And for centuries it allowed intellectual men to assume that they could comfortably occupy the position of the one who knows. Perhaps this myopia can be explained as the simple unwillingness of those with privilege to question the appropriateness of the foundations that make their status possible. Perhaps the ideology of the historical moment was so compelling that even the brilliant were compelled to take it as commonsensical.

How else to explain Immanuel Kant's gesture toward equality in which men were naturally constituted to be moral and women to be beautiful. Kant notes that

Deep meditation and long-sustained reflection are noble but difficult, and do not well befit a person in whom unconstrained charms should show nothing but a beautiful nature; women will learn no geometry . . . her philosophy is not to reason but to serve. (quoted in Davis and Finbe 1989, 395–6)

Rousseau's ideas on the education of women in *Emile* are equally exasperating. He notes that "everything that characterizes the fair sex ought to be respected as established by nature" (qtd. in Davis and Finbe 1989, 437). Can Rousseau be so oblivious to social context, to the influence of one's own culture that he can ascribe all behavior to nature? He writes that the "whole education of women ought to relate to men. To please men, to be useful to men, to make herself honored by them . . . to make their lives agreeable and sweet" (qtd. in Davis and Finbe 1989, 439). And later he notes "let us regulate her views according to those of nature and woman will have the education that suits her" (qtd. in Davis and Finbe 1989, 439). It is easy enough to find this sort of bias throughout the Western tradition, but my point is not so much to make explicit the blindness of the great as to suggest that being an intellectual was never simply a matter of intelligence. Ironically, for a group that thought of themselves as autonomous, as far from the madding crowd, the complex rules for intellectual discourse have always been grounded in a cultural tradition that proscribed attitudes quite rigidly. Kant once wrote that the tears a man sheds in pain or over circumstance makes him contemptible since men must shed only magnanimous tears (qtd. in Davis and Finbe 1989, 397). This is the other side of masculine intellectual discourse. Although men appear to be empowered and strong, they are also constrained and weak, disempowered from being fully human. The tradition has allowed them to believe that they were fortunately avoiding the emotional pitfalls and logical flaws that had cast women into such submissive roles. As part of the package, however, they were depriving themselves of alternative modes of knowing.

In support of the dominant, and therefore in support of power and privilege, they diminished their capacity to extend the range and intensity of their own intellectual inquiry. Kant, for example, has something like the right idea in mind in proposing that men and women should complement each other, but relegates the science of astronomy to men and the appreciation of beauty of the stars to women. Step one, of course, would be to suggest that women could also be astronomers, but what was really needed was an interrogation of science itself, an interrogation of tradition itself. It is certainly more equitable for intellectual discourse to be open to men and women but not much is gained if the subject positions available to either men or women are determined a priori. If women can only fulfill certain functions within normal intellectual discourse, little will change. Women must be able not only to inhabit discourse but to alter its ethos, its logos, its structures, its raison d'etre. I also want to extend this notion by suggesting that many male intellectuals in the academy also want to avoid many of the attitudes and conventions associated with the discourse of the traditional intellectual.

Intellectuals in the academy are not accustomed to thinking of their work as intimately connected to social and political forces in the dominant culture. Intellectual work, in literary scholarship or composition teaching, for example, has typically been considered apolitical. Today that posture is increasingly difficult to assume. Theorists such as Kenneth Burke, Michel Foucault, Hélène Cixous, and Raymond Williams have argued convincingly that the neutrality of any discourse is highly suspect, that traditional university intellectuals are neither autonomous nor unrelated to the ideological struggles of our culture. Literary criticism, for example, has until recently been dominated by a critical discourse that tried to be objective by denying the authority of experience, and that tried to eliminate discussions of the sociopolitical world by asserting that the poem was an artifact, autonomous from our own messy lives. Both strategies, of course, simply allowed the status quo. When I was in graduate school, men

and women were socialized into this formalist approach to reading
without noticing the implicit gender bias. Women were simply taught
to read like men while men were taught to read only as this critical
discourse constructed masculinity. The subject position of the
traditional literary critic for centuries has stressed objectivity and
mastery over texts. It was an approach to reading, however, with a
limited range of cognitive and emotional responses. Experience was
suspect and the personal was anathema.

Today this attitude is becoming less prevalent. The traditional
intellectual paradigm is still operative, but there are alternatives. In
literary criticism, for example, reader-oriented approaches allow the
emotional and intellectual concerns of readers to engage in a productive
dialogue with the ideology of the text. Since our culture still constructs
men and women in different ways, students will still respond to texts in
part out of the dynamics of these roles. However, as institutional
intellectuals we can encourage undergraduate and especially graduate
students to explore alternative ways of knowing while we continue to
struggle against the received influence of all dominant discourses. We
can help our students and colleagues become intellectuals who will
encourage multiplicity, diversity, tentativeness, and a rigorous
exploratory critique of their own professional discourse. In this way,
we will be less likely to repeat the pervasive authoritarian patterns that
denied both men and women their full range and vitality as intellectuals.
Our committed intervention can help redirect those constraining
traditions.

Ellerby:

How might I be as an intellectual in academe today? Will I engage
my intellectuality differently if I adopt this subject position? Will my
actions change noticeably? Will I pose different questions to myself
and to others? Will my language become more abstract and
impenetrable? What drawbacks could this subject position include and
what benefits could it provide? What follows is my attempt to answer
these questions. At the heart of the paper lies my effort to find a way
for two subject positions—the intellectual and the political
feminist—which could be construed as oppositional, to be adopted in a
complementary, generative way.

I believe that Professor Clifford has thought of himself as an
intellectual for a long time. Growing up in New York, he discovered
Soho and Greenwich Village; maybe he even heard a group of

bohemian New York intellectuals in a Village coffee house discussing existentialism and said to himself, "That's what I want to be." He seems to feel comfortable with the label and I think it fits him. Growing up in Pasadena, California did not provide me with many intellectual models. The bohemians in my town were long-haired surfers who were explicitly anti-intellectual. There were certainly intellectuals nearby at UCLA and 400 miles north at Berkeley, but their intellectualism became political activism, comingled with everything involved in being counter-cultural. Even so, it was from this political activism of the sixties that the women's movement grew. Unlike the bohemian Soho intellectuals who, according to my stereotype, conversed in galleries and coffee houses about the metaphysics of existentialism and the "cogito," the models that emerged for me involved confrontational women—Angela Davis, Jane Fonda, Joan Baez, Gloria Steinem, Bella Abzug—women whose words mattered to my daily life. It was from their examples and my own life experience that I came to define myself as a political feminist. I never considered being an intellectual, especially since my early academic experience had left me with a sense of exclusion and inferiority that I now know is not atypical and comes with the territory of female. I did not know I wanted to be or could be a college professor until I was thirty and had three children. It did not occur to me until even more recently to consider "intellectual" as a subject position I might adopt.

However, the consequences of taking on that signifier are significant. If I constitute myself as an intellectual, I risk being co-opted by a mode of thought and discourse that in the past I have resisted. When I think of myself as an intellectual, I do feel an accompanying sense of authority, but, given my commitment to equity, authority is a trait I try to relinquish rather than impose. By saying, "Yes, I am an intellectual," I might be expected to change my texts and my tactics. I could find it necessary to fall back on Pierce, Descartes, or Plato to establish the necessary proof of my credibility, rather than to follow Jane Tompkins' example, carry on autobiographically, and take the risk of sounding solipsistic, inconsequential, or trite. Can I be an intellectual and a feminist?

As a woman, a feminist, and an academic, I have come to know things in contradictory ways. I am aligned with, or to use Burke's term "enrolled" in, an interested feminist politics. As an intellectual, Frank Lentricchia maintains, it will by my function "as critical rhetor to uncover, bring into the light, and probe all such alignments" (1983, 149). Certainly I want to continually reevaluate my alignment with the

politics of feminism and the ideologies of feminist criticism and
theory—such self-consciousness is practically a requirement for
postmodernists today—but I choose not to adopt Lentricchia's
description of the academic intellectual who Lentricchia represents
noticeably by the masculine pronoun only. Such an intellectual tends
"to regard *himself* as a cosmopolitan, universal figure, dispassionately
attached *as intellectual* to the society in which *he* lives" (1983, 150;
emphasis added). Such a pose is antithetical to feminist theory which
has, according to Barbara Johnson, reintroduced the personal and the
positional "as a way of disseminating authority and decomposing the
false universality of patriarchally institutionalized meanings" (1988, 69)
that have been given to us throughout cultural history by male
intellectuals. It is in opposition to this figure of the cosmopolitan,
universal, dispassionate intellectual that I assume my first-person
autobiographical stance, insisting on my situatedness by reiterating,
"This is how it looks to me." There is no way that I can be Gramsci's
"traditional intellectual" (1971)—the keeper of culture—since as a
feminist critic I am compelled constantly to interrogate and revise
"culture," nor do I want to be dispassionate about this project; however,
the constraints of my position may become the access route that allows
me to rethink the intellectual enterprise.

Maunuela Fraire maintains that "the practice of self consciousness
is the way in which women reflect politically on their own condition"
(qtd. in Lauretis 1984, 185). In order to be an intellectual and a
feminist, it is important that I continue the practice of "consciousness
raising." Teresa de Lauretis notes that this term has become dated and
more than slightly unpleasant because it "has been appropriated, diluted,
digested and spewed out by the media" (1984, 185). But this
appropriation should not stop me from using this critical instrument that
allows us to analyze social reality and imagine its critical revision. If
I am to be an intellectual and a feminist, I can adopt C. S. Pierce's
"self-analyzing" habit (qtd. in Lauretis 1984, 185). It is through self-
consciousness, or what Lentricchia calls "the widening of consciousness
"(1983, 151), that I can best lay bare the hegemony that keeps me in
the dark. A certain blindness is ineradicable; a partiality of perspective
will contaminate my enterprise. However, because of the whole matrix
of relations that form me—my family, academic institution, class,
nation, and countless other agencies—I have a plurality of spoken and
written voices that can help me to express most authentically and
honestly a self-awareness that is emancipating and empowering. As
Bakhtin reminds me, it is when I take the stance of the monologist in

servitude to one language that I become the very type and example of inauthenticity.

My practice then, if I am to adopt the position of feminist intellectual, is to create a place within my institution where voices can constantly impinge and permeate one another, where language

> enters a dialogically agitated . . . environment of alien words, value judgments and accents, weaves in and out of complex interrelationships, merges with some, recoils from others, intersects with yet a third group. (Bakhtin 1981, 276)

In such an environment language becomes entangled, "shot through with shared thoughts, points of view" (Bakhtin 1981, 276). As an intellectual feminist, it is my responsibility to resist the temptation to fashion a system in my classes whereby my polemics hierarchically order and dominate discussion. I have learned from Hans-Georg Gadamer's *Philosophical Hermeneutics* (1976) and Paul Ricoeur's *The Conflict of Interpretations* (1974) that the process of understanding involves dialogue that will by necessity involve interrogation and dispute. As the facilitator of such dialogues, my goals are to achieve discussions in which the participants accord one another the status of equality—an equality between that which is different rather than that which is similar.

Another difficulty I see infringing on the possibilities offered a feminist intellectual involves the feminist issues that I confront daily, the social issues grounded in the day-to-day experience of women. Perhaps postmodern intellectualism can assist me in clarifying the claims of feminism, yet it also can deter me from one of my most important responsibilities—confronting the oppression of women that derives from race and class. As a feminist, I feel compelled to support and promote social and economic changes that can ensure decent lives for all women. However, as an intellectual, the gap between myself and women further down the socioeconomic scale widens; yet as a feminist, I remain committed to a kind of progress that will end the privilege obtained through the exploitation of women.

Thus, if I am to be an intellectual, it cannot be at the expense of practice. I must not let the lure of the metaphysical draw me away from my efforts to change the reality of poor women's lives and the particular conditions they are facing. By taking on the subject position of intellectual, I risk separating myself from a vision of community that underscores the claims of women as a whole. As a feminist I can begin to expose and, thus, subvert persisting sexual and gender asymmetry; I can foster internal equality within my own institution by making sure my women students receive equal status as discussants within my classroom and that my women peers receive equal status as contributing members to the institution. As a feminist, I am able to link theory and practice. And as a feminist I resist identifying exclusively with my male peers, but consciously work to maintain my primary identification with other women. By remaining in contact with the particular, everyday lives of women in and outside the academy and the real problems they face, I remain committed to social and economic change that will alleviate the oppression of women.

As an intellectual, can I speak from the level of concrete experience, ascribing to the values of care and mutuality, and at the same time, can I move to a level of abstraction, ascribing to the values of neutrality and uncertainty? Presuming that I do take on the subject position of the intellectual, will I also take on the disconcerting mannerisms of an honorary man? The model of the intellectual as male appears to have left women with the unpalatable and unrealistic choice between becoming "male" or not becoming an intellectual. The weight of the history of the intellectual as male makes it extremely difficult for women to fit into that role and even more difficult for them to repudiate it and reconstitute another.

Of course, there are many women who are engaged in the construction of understanding and knowledge and they are intellectuals of our time. They should claim that label and its concomitant authority because they can and do act and write according to the prevailing "xstandards" of "the intellectual." However, women intellectuals must also retain the right to act or write out of a personal experience. What seems to be required, then, is a new conception of "the intellectual" that can take account of sexual asymmetry without subjugating women to men and without subjugating specificity and concretion to abstraction.

Western culture now offers women exceptional possibilities. Opportunity has changed radically for scholarly women who focus their energy on the construction of knowledge. However, although many women are scholars and are respected as such, this does not mean that their energy is not continually interrupted by domestic responsibility. The dissemination of women's energy and focus continues, but, at the same time, women continue to work ambitiously beyond the domestic sphere. While women like me are drawn to the role of the intellectual, the sharp opposition of male and female roles in society continues to make women's experience different from that of their male colleagues.

To be an intellectual in the traditional sense, it seems that one must be able to achieve an amount of detachment that is not available to most women. We are, of necessity, involved in the realm of "doing," whether it be laundry, dinner, and support groups, or teaching, reading, and writing. Is there time enough in a woman's daily life to fit in the subject position of "the intellectual" with the implied requisite time for rumination that the model implies? Can such ruminating be accomplished in the car between school and the grocery store?

There is no doubt that women are intellectual, and we endow our lives with meaning that is no longer limited to service to men and motherhood. We can now make the same claim as men on the role of the academic; the possibility of competing for traditionally male jobs has become a real option, if not yet a general practice. And significantly, from their status as intellectuals, men can no longer claim to speak in the name of humanity at large. But if women are to claim the role of the intellectual, we still face the binary opposition of male/female that continues to constitute a dominate theme of Western culture. This opposition grounds intellectual and discursive patterns in that fundamental difference. Working within discourses largely fashioned by and for men, women still have to struggle for a language of women's representation.

In the fourteenth century, Christine de Pizan overcame her sense of alienation from male theory by elevating "personal experience into a form of wisdom higher than anything literacy and authority can offer" (qtd. in Fox-Genovese 1991, 135). She articulates a tension that still exists between experience and consciousness. Women have made vast gains in the possibility for independent thought, but hostility to that independence has persisted. My question still remains: Will the intellectual liberation of women give them the freedom to think like men or the freedom to think like women—however those categories are constituted? Can women claim the full status of "xintellectual" without losing their identity as women-as-other?

W. E. B. Du Bois, speaking not of women but of black male intellectuals in a white-dominated world, writes the following:

> The Negro is . . . born with a veil, and gifted with second-sight in this American world—a world which yields him no true self-consciousness, but only lets him see himself through the revelation of the other world . . . One ever feels his twoness—an American, a Negro; two souls, two thoughts, two unreconciled strivings; two warring ideals in one dark body. (Du Bois, 1982, 45)

Du Bois refused to forgo either side of his "twoness." It is, says Elizabeth Fox-Genovese, in this "sundered identity, that [Du Bois] wishes to live: distinct, but equal; of, but not wholly assimilated to" (1991, 139). Du Bois provides a framework for how a woman might adopt the subject position of the intellectual, claiming her place within the academy and her equality with her male peers, yet remaining distinct from them and continually resisting assimilation. If I am to take on the subject position of the intellectual, I do not intend to relinquish my focus of gender difference and the corresponding inequalities; instead it becomes vital that I focus attention on difference, not just between men and women, but among women and, for that matter, among men. I must engage with the intellectual tradition while simultaneously engaging that tradition with the experiences of women on new terms.

Women have, up to this point, had little effect on the dominant intellectual tradition and have left disproportionately few intellectual treatises. But their silence has been imposed by the needs of others: their multiple responsibilities of caring for children and for a house while, for many, also earning a living. Men have dominated the intellectual tradition, not on the basis of intrinsic sexual merit, but on the basis of their privileged access to literacy and time. By critiquing the tradition seriously and by deconstructing the ideal of man and the ideal of woman that shape our consciousness, the feminist intellectual can begin to transform this tradition. As a feminist, with my own experiences of socialization and exclusion to draw on, I do not want to turn away from the social opportunity that belongs to the role of the intellectual as I rethink it. It is because of my awareness of sexual asymmetry and difference that I must not turn away from the conversation of intellectuals, even though I know full well that my status will often not be recognized as equal and that my feelings of exclusion and inferiority will resurface time and time again.

Recently, I walked away from a lunch table where my male colleagues were unwilling to give credence to my argument concerning the inequitable financial losses faced by women who divorce. One dismissed me with patronizing humor; the other simply spoke loudly and with few pauses—much like William Bennett—overwhelming me by his stentorian, long-winded retort. My initial reaction was, "Never again will I allow myself to be bullied like that. From now on," I thought, "I'll choose more carefully those with whom I will converse about such topics." Of course, I know that such exclusionary tactics are incompatible with my goal as a feminist and an intellectual, pledged to create dialogue throughout my university community. Ricoeur writes, "To show how the different discourses may interrelate or intersect . . . one must resist the temptation to make them identical" (qtd. in Kearney 1984, 27). I do not plan to walk away again from a discussion—intimidated, angry, and silenced—and miss the opportunity to confront such ploys as dismissive humor or to interrogate a demeaning conception of the place of women in this world. By reconstructing the tradition of the intellectual to complement my beliefs as a political feminist, I can better explore the dialogical possibility of conversation and commit myself to responsible and spirited engagement with those who share my various and diverse communities.

Works Cited

Bakhtin, M. M. *The Dialogic Imagination*. Trans. Caryl Emerson and Michael Holquist; ed. Michael Holquist. Austin: University Press of Texas, 1981.

Bloom, Allan. *The Closing of the American Mind*. New York: Simon and Schuster, 1987.

Davis, Con Robert, and Laurie Finbe, eds. *Literary Criticism and Theory*. New York: Longman, 1989.

Du Bois, W. E. B. *The Souls of Black Folk*. New York: Signet, 1982.

Fox-Genovese, Elizabeth. *Feminism Without Illusions*. Chapel Hill: University Press of North Carolina, 1991.

Gadamer, Hans-Georg. *Philosophical Hermeneutics*. Trans. David E. Linge. Berkeley: University of California Press, 1976.

Gramsci, Antonio. "The Prison Notebooks." In *Selections from Prison Notebooks*, eds. Quinton Hoare and Geoff Nowell-Smith. New York: International Publishers, 1971.

Johnson, Barbara. "Deconstruction, Feminism, and Pedagogy." In *Teaching Literature*, eds. James Engell and David Perkins. Cambridge: Harvard University Press, 1988.

Kearney, Richard. *Dialogues with Contemporary Continental Thinkers*. Manchester: Manchester University Press, 1984.

Lauretis, Teresa de. *Alice Doesn't*. Bloomington: Indiana University Press, 1984.

Lentricchia, Frank. *Criticism and Social Change*. Chicago: University Press of Chicago, 1983.

Plato. *The Collected Dialogues*, eds. Edith Hamilton and Huntington Cairns. Princeton: Princeton University Press, 1961.

Ricoeur, Paul. *The Conflict of Interpretations*. Evanston: Northwestern University Press, 1974.

Afterword

Lagretta Tallent Lenker

> *Comprehensive Examination Question: Compare and contrast the educational theories and opportunities for women in 1540 and 1993. State specific points of comparison and give examples.*

This hypothetical exam, androcentric though it may be, is not as outrageous as it first might appear. In 1540, the three treatises on women's education written by Juan Luis Vives were translated from Latin to English and published in England. By 1600, Vives' works had survived five editions in English and thirty-five editions in other languages (Henderson and McManus 1985, 82), a testament to the popularity and influence of Vives' educational philosophies. Correspondingly in 1993, the American Association of University Women and Wellesley College published *How Schools Shortchange Girls*, a 116–page report on the current state of women's education. This report purports to "present the truth behind . . . [a] myth—that girls and boys receive equal education" (AAUW 1992, v). The report has already had a major impact, being reviewed and cited by major educational publications and in the popular press. Although Vives writes a philosophical treatise—a proscription for the education of women—and the AAUW report offers a critique of existing conditions and some recommendations for change, the two works, written some

450 years apart, reveal five amazingly similar attitudes and circumstances about the education of women in both eras.

First, both Vives and the AAUW writers affirm that the purpose of educating women is to prepare them for life in society. In the Renaissance, "preparation for life in society" meant that the woman would operate strictly in the private and domestic realms. The only justification for a liberal education for a woman would be to make her a "more virtuous Christian." Thus, a woman was effectively eliminated from the academic and political marketplaces of ideas. In the 1990s, access to education, of course, is much more open with U.S. federal laws such as the much-beleaguered Title IX demanding, at least on paper, equal educational opportunities for women. Yet the "private sphere" stereotypes partially originating in Vives' day still affect women in inordinate numbers:

> Thirty-seven percent of female dropouts as compared to only five percent of male dropouts cited family related problems as the reason they left high school. . . . Traditional gender roles place greater family responsibility and stress on adolescent girls rather than their brothers. (AAUW 1992, 48)

In higher education, women are often discouraged or simply not encouraged to enter the traditional masculine fields of math and science. Math is still seen as "something men do" despite reports that the gender gap is closing in that area. Gender differences in science achievement, however, "are not decreasing and may be increasing" (AAUW 1992, 24–25, v). Therefore, women still gravitate to fields that are "uniquely suited to them," ones requiring the social and collaborative skills prized in the private sector rather than the analytical and rational attributes valued in the scientific and professional communities.

Second, in the Renaissance, 90 percent of women were illiterate (Henderson 1985, 91). In the 1990s, overall literacy rates are higher, but not in all fields and disciplines. Women constitute 45 percent of the U.S. work force, but are concentrated in traditionally subordinate or nurturing occupations. As our economy changes, evolving into a "lean and mean" workforce, the role of women in the workforce reflects an equally menacing form of illiteracy:

> Women and children are swelling the ranks of the poor at great cost to society . . . Girls are being steered away from the very courses required for their productive participation in the future of America . . . [which] will require strength in science, math, and technology—subjects girls are still being told are not suitable for them. (AAUW 1992, v)

This more subtle form of illiteracy may yet reverse the advances made in women's education and professional lives and signal a return to the 90 percent illiteracy rate—this time in the very areas that drive our economy.

Third, in Renaissance times, many women were taught to read but not to write, another method of insuring their relegation to the private sphere (Henderson 1985, 88). These women, therefore, had the necessary tools to grasp issues but not to participate in the debates of the times. This muted condition is unfortunately replicated in today's schoolrooms or classrooms: a 1989 survey of book-length works taught in U.S. high school English classes reveals that "the ten books assigned most frequently included only one written by a woman" (AAUW 1992, 62). The choices of writers revealed by this survey underscore most compellingly the elimination of women's voices yet again in the preparation of students to join in society's major debates. The dominant voices that our students hear in our schools are still masculine ones.

Fourth, in keeping with their separatist philosophies, Vives and many of his contemporaries advocated teaching one curriculum for boys and another for girls—since women will neither govern nor teach, they have no need of history, grammar, or logic—subjects which are important for men" (Henderson 1985, 19). Four hundred and fifty years later, educational inequalities are not so blatant. Nevertheless, the National Council of Teachers of Foreign Languages in a 1984 survey record six common forms of bias in curricular and instructional materials:

> exclusion of girls; stereotyping of members of both sexes; subordination or degradation of girls; isolation of materials on women; superficiality of attention to contemporary issues or social problems; and cultural inaccuracy. (AAUW 1992, 63)

Thus, the gender-biased division of the curriculum continues, but in a much more invidious manner.

Finally, Renaissance educators saw women as potential provocateurs of men—even in educational settings (Henderson 1985, 83). This most blatant attempt at "keeping women in their place" has evolved into a situation that *Newsweek* magazine in 1991 labelled "Girls Who Go Too Far." The AAUW writers posit that women, especially young girls, are still inculcated to see themselves as incomplete "without a man"—a compelling transmutation of Renaissance ideology—and therefore often behave aggressively to attract male attention. Women must be taught self-esteem and encouraged to believe in their own worth as individuals. Support and encouragement in the classroom are integral components of this empowering process (*AAUW* 1992, 81), and, in many cases, school serves as the only place where a young woman may find the assistance she needs to become a fulfilled, productive human being.

Thus, vestigial remnants of Vives' educational philosophy are present in our classrooms today. Certainly, evolutionary transformations have occurred even as often well-intended educators attempt to prepare young women for careers for which they are "best suited," that is, for academic disciplines that guarantee a continuation of the educational, societal, and political status quo. Yet, we as educators can and must break the cycle of a system that subtly denies young women the opportunity to choose their own destinies according to their interests and abilities, not according to gender politics.

The contributors to this volume offer suggestions to counter effectively each of the five points of comparison that answer our hypothetical but insightful examination question. For example, educators who wish to amend the traditional segregation and devaluation of the personal/private aspect of life from "the active" realms of commerce and science should consult Carol Mattingly's chapter, "Valuing the Personal," which suggests strategies for validating women's experiences—especially those in the private   real—and adapting strengths gained from traditional women's roles for effective use in the larger society. Those concerned with "levelling the playing field for girls" in disciplines not traditionally perceived as "appropriate" for women would consult Sharyl Bender Peterson's "The Nature and Effects of a Gender-Biased Psychology Curriculum," which models how women's scientific literacy and cognitive skills can be developed. The articles by Linda Woodbridge and Charlotte Templin offer strategies for extracting active participation from women in the classroom, thus preparing females for equal partnership and participation in the societal debates of our times. Those seeking to eliminate gender bias in curriculum development should read Sara Munson Deats' article on developing and teaching courses from a feminist perspective. Equally enlightening is Lisa S. Starks' "Hyper-feminisms" which suggests methods for integrating "feminisms" into the curriculum without conforming to stereotypic "feminist" methodologies. Finally, educators seeking to empower women as whole subjects, not merely as reflections of male-dominated society should study "Woman to Women: Understanding the Needs of our Female Students" by Mary Ann Gawalek, Maggie Mulqueen, and Jill Mattuck Tarule, a chapter that discusses how women can understand their own femininity and can develop the full potential of their own lives.

This brief summary only highlights the excellent recommendations offered by the contributors to this volume. Of course, this collective work alone cannot break the cycle of gender politics that has impeded the development of human kind for centuries. Yet, if we can offer potent strategies for change, present positive role models for educators, and offer hope and encouragement to our students, we will have accomplished our goal. We hope through this book to join in one of the major debates of our times. These essays demonstrate that the role that gender issues play in the academy impacts how society as a whole will script the roles that women are called upon to play. The future of our past depends on how we as educators define these roles.

Works Cited

Henderson, Katherine U, and Barbara F. McManus. *Half Humankind: Contexts and Texts of the Controversy about Women in England, 1540–1640.* Urbana: University of Illinois Press, 1985.

How Schools Shortchange Girls: The AAUW Report: A Study of Major Findings on Girls and Education. Washington, D.C.: AAUW Educational Foundation: National Education Association, 1992.

Suggested Reading

Beth Dalton Williams

Abbott, Sidney, and Barbara Love. *Sappho Was a Right-on Woman: A Liberated View of Lesbianism*. New York: Stein and Day, 1972.

Abel, Elizabeth. *Writing and Sexual Difference*. Chicago: University of Chicago Press, 1980.

Agel, Jerome, ed. *The Radical Therapist*. New York: Ballantine Books, 1971.

Agonito, Rosemary, ed. *History of Ideas on Women: A Sourcebook*. New York: G. P. Putnam's Sons, 1977.

Aisenberg, Nadya, and Mona Harrington. *Women of Academe: Outsiders in the Sacred Grove*. Amherst: University of Massachusetts Press, 1988.

Alcoff, Linda. "Cultural Feminism Versus Post-Structuralism: The Identity Crisis in Feminist Theory." *Signs* 13 (Spring 1988): 405–36.

Alderfer, Hannah, Meryl Altman, Kate Ellis, Beth Jaker, Marybeth Nelson, Esther Newton, Ann Snitow, and Carole S. Vance, eds."Diary of a Conference on Sexuality." In *The Scholar and the Feminist IX: Toward a Politics on Sexuality*. New York: Barnard College Women's Center, 1982.

Allen, Pamela. *Free Space: A Perspective on the Small Group in Women's Liberation*. New York: Times Change Press, 1970.

Alpert, Jane. *Growing Up Underground*. New York: William Morrow, 1981.

Allport, Susan. *Explorers of the Black Box: The Search for the Cellular Basis of Memory.* New York: W. W. Norton, 1987.

Altbach, Edith, ed. *From Feminism to Liberation.* Cambridge, Mass.: Schenkman, 1971.

Althusser, Louis. "Ideology and Ideological State Apparatuses." In *Lenin and Philosophy and Other Essays.* Trans. Ben Brewster. London: New Left Books, 1971.

Altick, Richard D. *The Art of Literary Research.* 3d ed. New York: W. W. Norton, 1981.

Altman, Dennis. *The Homosexualization of America, The Americanization of the Homosexual.* New York: St. Martin's Press, 1982.

American Association of University Professors. "The Annual Report on the Economic Status of the Profession, 1988-1989." *Academe* 75 (March-April 1989): 11, 15, 16, 19.

Anderson, Bonnie S., and Judith Zinsser. *A History of Their Own: From Prehistory to the Present.* New York: Harper and Row, 1988.

Annas, Pamela J. "Style as Politics: A Feminist Approach to the Teaching of Writing." *College English* 47 (April 1985): 360–71.

APA Task Force on Issues of Sexual Bias in Graduate Education. "Guidelines for Nonsexist Use of Language." *American Psychologist* 30 (1975): 682–84.

Ardener, Edwin. "Belief and the Problem of Women." In *Perceiving Women,* ed. Shirley Ardener. London: Malaby Press, 1975.

Ardener, Shirley, ed. *Defining Females: The Nature of Women in Society.* New York: John Wiley, 1978.

Ardill, Susan, and Nora Neumark. "Putting Sex Back into Lesbianism: Is the Way to a Woman's Heart through Her Sadomasochism?" *Gay Information* 11 (Spring 1982): 4–11.

Armstrong, Carol M. "Edgar Degas and the Female Body." In *The Female Body in Western Culture,* ed. Susan R. Suleiman. Cambridge, Mass.: Harvard University Press, 1986.

Arnold, Karen. "Academically Talented Women in the 1980s: The Illinois Valedictorian Project." In *Women's Lives through Time: Educated American Women of the Twentieth Century,* eds. Kathleen Day Hulbert and Diane Tickton Schuster. San Francisco: Jossey-Bass, 1993.

Ashton-Jones, Evelyn, and Dene Kay Thomas. "Composition, Collaboration, and Women's Ways of Knowing: A Conversation with Mary Belenky." *Journal of Advanced Composition* 10.2 (Fall 1990): 275-92.

Ashton-Jones, Evelyn, and Gary Olson, eds. *The Gender Reader*. London: Alleyn and Bacon, 1991.

Association of African Women for Research and Development. "Genital Mutilation: A Statement by the Association of African Women for Research and Development (AAWORD)." *Resources for Feminist Research* 9, no. 1 (March 1980): 7-9.

Association of Salvadoran Women, The. "Participation of Latin American Women in Social and Political Organizations: Reflections of Salvadoran Women." *Monthly Review* 34, no. 2 (June 1982): 11-23.

Atcherson, Esther, and Joanna Jenny. *What About Mentors and Women in Academe?* Educational Resource Information Center (ERIC), 1983. ED 242 642.

Atkinson, Ti-Grace. *Amazon Odyssey*. New York: Links Books, 1974.

Babcock, Barbara. *The Reversible World: Symbolic Inversion in Art and Society*. Ithaca: Cornell University Press, 1978.

Baroja, Julio Caro. *The World of Witches*. Trans. O. N. V. Glendinning. Chicago: University of Chicago Press, 1973.

Barrett, Michèle. *Women's Oppression Today: Problems in Marxist Feminist Analysis*. London: Verso Editions and NLB, 1980.

Barry, Kathleen. *Female Sexual Slavery*. Englewood Cliffs, N.J.: Prentice-Hall, 1979.

—. "Beyond Pornography: From Defensive Politics to Creating a Vision." In *Take Back the Night*, ed. Laura Lederer, 307-12. New York: Bantam Books, 1982.

Barstow, Anne Llewellyn. "Joan of Arc and Female Mysticism." *Journal of Feminist Studies in Religion* I (Fall 1985): 29-42.

—. "On Studying Witchcraft as Women's History: A Historiography of the European Witch Persecutions." *Journal of Feminist Studies in Religion* IV (Fall 1988): 7-19.

Barthes, Roland. *S/Z*. Trans. Richard Miller. New York: Hill and Wang, 1974.

—. *Roland Barthes by Roland Barthes*. Trans. Richard Howard. New York: Hill and Wang, 1977.

—. "The Pleasure of the Text." In *Barthes: Selected Writings*, ed. S. Sontag. London: Fontana, 1982.

—. "The Death of the Author." In *The Rustle of Language*. Oxford: Blackwell: 1986

Basow, Susan A. *Sex-Role Stereotypes: Traditions and Alternatives*. Belmont, Calif.: Brooks-Cole, 1980.

Bass, Ellen, and Laura Davis. *The Courage to Heal-A Guide for Women Survivors of Child Sexual Abuse.* New York: Harper and Row, 1988.

Batsleer, Janet, et al. *Rewriting English: Cultural Politics of Gender and Class.* London: Methuen, 1985.

Baudrillard, Jean. *Selected Writings*, ed. Mark Poster. Stanford: Stanford University Press, 1988.

Bauer, Dale M. "The Other 'F' Word: The Feminist in the Classroom." *College English* 52 (April 1990): 385-96.

Baym, Nina. *Women's Fiction: A Guide to Novels by and about Women in America 1820-1970.* Ithaca: Cornell University Press, 1978.

Baym, Nina, et al., eds. *The Norton Anthology of American Literature.* 3d ed. 2 vols. New York: Norton, 1989.

Beachy, Lucille, and Tom Mathews. "The Lives of Women." *Newsweek* (November 1989): 77.

Beauvoir, Simone de. *The Second Sex.* Trans. H. M. Parshley. New York: Vintage Books, 1952.

Beechy, Veronica. "Women and Production: A Critical Analysis of Some Sociological Theories of Women's Work." In *Feminism and Materialism*, eds. Annette Kuhn and AnnMarie Wolpe, 155-97. Boston: Routledge and Kegan Paul, 1978.

—. "On Patriarchy." *Feminist Review* 3 (1979): 66-82.

Beer, Patricia. *Reader I Married Him: A Study of the Women Characters of Jane Austen, Charlotte Brontë, Elizabeth Gaskell and George Eliot.* London: Macmillan, 1974.

Belenky, Mary Field, Blythe McVicker Clinchy, Nancy Rule Goldberger, and Jill Mattuck Tarule. *Women's Ways of Knowing: The Development of Self, Voice, and Mind.* New York: Basic Books, 1986.

Bell, Currer. "Biographical Notice of Acton and Ellis Bell." In *Wuthering Heights.* Harmondsworth: Penguin, 1982.

Bell, Susan Groag, ed. *Women: From the Greeks to the French Revolution.* Belmont, Calif.: Wadsworth Publishing Co., 1973.

Belsey, Catherine. *Critical Practice.* London: Methuen, New Accents, 1980.

—. *The Subject of Tragedy: Identity and Difference in Renaissance Drama.* London and New York: Methuen, 1985.

Belsey, Catherine, and Jane Moore. *The Feminist Reader.* New York: Blackwell Press, 1989.

Bem, Sandra L. "Probing the Promise of Androgyny." In *Beyond Sex-Role Stereotypes*, eds. Alexandra G. Kaplan and Joan P. Bean, 48-62. Boston: Little, Brown, 1976.

—. "Gender Schema Theory: A Cognitive Account of Sex Typing." *Psychological Review* 83 (1981): 354-64.

Beneria, Lourdes, and Gita Sen. "Accumulation, Reproduction, and Women's Role in Economic Development: Boserup Revisited." *Signs* 7, no. 2 (1981): 279-98.

Benjamin, Jessica. "The Bonds of Love: Rational Violence and Erotic Domination." In *Future of Difference*, eds. Hester Eisenstein and Alice Jardine, 40-70. Boston: G. K. Hall, 1980.

Berg, Helen M., and Mariane A. Ferber. "Men and Women Graduate Students: Who Succeeds and Why?" *Journal of Higher Education* 54 (1983): 629-648.

Bernikow, Louise. *Among Women*. New York: Harmony Books, 1980.

Bernstein, Basil. *Class, Codes and Control: Towards a Theory of Educational Transmissions*. 2d ed. 3 vols. Boston: Routledge and Kegan Paul, 1977.

Berger, Arthur Asa. *Media Analysis Techniques*. The Sage COMMTEXT Series, vol. 10. Beverly Hills: Sage Publications, 1982.

Berger, John. *Ways of Seeing*. London: British Broadcasting Corp., 1972.

—., (producer). *Ways of Seeing, Part I*. British Broadcasting Corp., 1972.

Berkenkotter, Carol, et al. "Conventions, Conversations, and the Writer: Case Study of a Student in a Rhetoric Ph.D. Program." *Research in the Teaching of English* 22 (1988): 9-44.

Betterton, Rosemary. *Looking On: Images of Femininity in the Arts and Media*. London: Pandora, 1987.

—. "How Do Women Look: The Female Nude in the Work of Suzanne Valadon." In *Visibly Female: Feminism and Art: An Anthology*, ed. Hilary Robinson. New York: Universe Books, 1988.

Bick, Barbara, and Nancy C. M. Hartsock. "Parenting and the Human Malaise." *Monthly Review* 31, no. 8 (1980): 47.

Biddle, Arthur W., and Daniel J. Bean with Toby Fulwiler. *Writer's Guide: Life Sciences*. Lexington, Mass.: D.C. Heath and Co., 1987.

Bizzell, Patricia. Review of "What Can We Know, What Must We Do, What May We Hope: Writing Assessment." *College English* 49, no. 5 (September 1987): 575-84.

Blaxall, Martha, and Barbara Reagan. *Women and the Workplace: The Implications of Occupational Segregation*. Chicago: University of Chicago Press, 1976.

Bloom, Allan. *The Anxiety of Influence*. New York: OUP, 1973.

—. *The Closing of the American Mind*. New York: Simon and Schuster, 1987.

Boumelha, Penny. *Thomas Hardy and Women: Sexual Ideology and Narrative Form*. Brighton: Harvester, 1982.

Bowie, Malcolm. "Jacques Lacan." In *Structuralism and Since*, ed. John Sturrock, 116-53. Oxford: Oxford University Press, 1979.

Bowlby, Rachel. *Just Looking: Consumer Culture in Dreiser, Gissing and Zola*. New York and London: Methuen, 1985.

Boxer, Marilyn J., and Jean H. Quatert. *Connecting Spheres: Women in the Western World, 1500 to the Present*. New York: Oxford University Press, 1987.

Boyd, Blanche McCrary. "Growing Up Racist." *Village Voice* 5-11 (August 1982): 1.

Boyer, Ernest L. *Scholarship Reconsidered: The Priorities of the Professoriate*. Princeton, N.J.: Carnegie Foundation for the Advancement of Teaching, 1990.

Boyles, Marcia V. "Letter." *Chronicle of Higher Education* 35:13 (November 1988): B3.

Bridenthal, Renate. "The Dialectics of Production and Reproduction in History." *Radical America* 10, no. 2 (March-April 1976): 3-11.

Bridenthal, Renate, and Claudia Koonz, eds. *Becoming Visible: Women in European History*. Boston: Houghton Mifflin, 1977.

Britton, James. "The Composing Processes and the Functions of Writing." In *Research on Composing*, eds. Charles Cooper and Lee Odell, 13–28. Urbana, Il.: NCTE, 1978.

Britton, James, et al. "The Development of Writing Abilities." In *Schools Council Research Studies Report*. London: Macmillan Education, 1975.

Britton, James N., Nancy C. Martin, and Harold Rosen. *Multiple Marking of Compositions*. London: Her Majesty's Stationery Office, 1966.

Brodky, Linda. "On the Subjects of Class and Gender in 'The Literacy Letters.'" *College English* (February 1989): 125–41.

Bronstein, Phyllis A., and Kathryn Quina. *Teaching a Psychology of People*. Washington, D.C.: American Psychological Association, 1988.

Bronstein, Phyllis A., and Michele Paludi. "The Introductory Psychology Course From a Broader Human Perspective." In *Teaching a Psychology of People*, eds. Phyllis A Bronstein and Kathryn Quina. Washington, D.C.: American Psychological Association, 1988.

Brooten, Bernadette. "Women Leaders in the Ancient Synagogue: Inscriptional Evidence and Background Issues." *Brown Judaic Studies* 36 (1982).

Broude, Norma, and Mary D. Garrard. *Feminism and Art History: Questioning the Litany*. New York: Harper and Row, 1982.

Broverman, Inge, Susan Yogel, Donald Broverman, Frank Clarkson, and Paul Rosenkrantz. "Sex-role Stereotypes: A Current Appraisal." *Journal of Social Issues* 28 (1975): 59–78.

Brown, Elsa Barkley . "African-American Women's Quilting: A Framework for Conceptualizing and Teaching African-American Women's History." *Signs* 14 (1989): 921–29.

Brownmiller, Susan. *Against Our Will: Men, Women and Rape*. New York: Simon and Schuster, 1975.

—. *Femininity*. New York: Linden Press, 1984.

Brownstein, Rachel. *Becoming a Heroine Reading about Women in Novels*. Harmondsworth: Penguin, 1982.

Bruffee, Kenneth. "Social Construction, Language, and the Authority of Knowledge: A Bibliographical Essay." *College English* 48:8 (1986): 773–90.

Bulkin, Elly. "Racism and Writing: Some Implications for White Lesbian Critics." *Sinister Wisdom* 13 (Spring 1980): 3–22.

Bunch, Charlotte. "Not for Lesbians Only." In *Building Feminist Theory: Essays from Quest, A Feminist Quarterly*, eds. Charlotte Bunch et al., 67–73. New York: Longman, 1981.

Bunch, Charlotte, Jane Flax, Alexa Freeman, Nancy Hartsock, and Mary-Helen Manther, eds. *Building Feminist Theory: Essays from Quest, A Feminist Quarterly*. New York: Longman, 1981.

Burke, Carolyn G. "Rethinking the Maternal." In *Future of Difference*, eds. Hester Eisenstein and Alice Jardine, 107–14. Boston: G. K. Hall, 1980.

Burton, Clare. "From the Family to Social Reproduction: The Development of Feminist Theory." Ph.D. diss., Macquarie University, Sydney, 1979.

Butler, Judith. *Gender Trouble: Feminism and the Subversion of Identity*. New York: Routledge, 1990.

Butler, Marilyn. "Feminist Criticism, Late 80s Style." *Times Literary Supplement* 11–17 (March 1988): 283–85.

Byars, Jackie. "Gender Representation in American Family Melodramas of the Nineteen-fifties." Ph.D. diss. University of Texas at Austin, 1983.

Cade (Bambara), Toni, ed. *The Black Woman: An Anthology*. New York: New American Library, 1970.

Cain, William E. *F. O. Matthiessen and the Politics of Criticism*. Madison: University of Wisconsin Press, 1988.

Califia, Pat. "Feminism and Sadomasochism." *Heresies*, no.12 (1981): 30–34.

Cameron, Deborah. *Feminism and Linguistic Theory*. Basingstoke: Macmillan, 1985.

Campbell, Patricia B., and Jeana Wirtenberg. "How Books Influence Children." *IRBC Bulletin* 11 (1980): 3–6.

Cantarella, Eva. *Pandora's Daughters: The Role and Status of Women in Greek and Roman Antiquity*. Trans. Maureen B. Fant. Baltimore: Johns Hopkins University Press, 1987. First printed in 1978.

Carden, Maren Lockwood. *The New Feminist Movement*. New York: Russell Sage Foundation, 1974.

Carnegie Commission on Higher Education. *Opportunities for Women in Higher Education*. New York: McGraw, 1973.

Carter, Angela. *The Sadeian Woman and the Ideology of Pornography*. New York: Pantheon Books, 1978.

—. *The Magic Toyshop*. London: Virago, 1982.

—. "Notes from the Front Line." In *On Gender and Writing*, ed. Michelene Wandor, 69. London: Pandora Press, 1983.

Casey, Kathleen. "The Cheshire Cat: Reconstructing the Experience of Medieval Women." In *Liberating Women's History: Theoretical and Critical Essays*, ed. Berenice Carroll, 224–49. Urbana: University of Illinois Press, 1976.

Cassell, Joan. *A Group Called Women: Sisterhood and Symbolism in the Women's Movement*. New York: David McKay, 1977.

Chadwick, Whitney. *Women, Art, and Society*. London: Thames and Hudson, 1990.

Chamberlain, Mariam K., ed. *Women in Academe: Progress and Prospects*. New York: Russell Sage Foundation, 1988.

Chapman, Rowena, and Jonathan Rutherford. *Male Order—Unwrapping Masculinity*. London: Lawrence and Wishart, 1988.

Chesler, Phyllis. *Women and Madness*. Garden City, N.Y.: Doubleday, 1972.

—. *About Men*. New York: Simon and Schuster, 1978.

Chesler, Phyllis, and Emily Jane Goodman. *Women, Money and Power*. New York: William Morrow, 1976.

Chester, Gail, and Sigrid Nielsen. *In Other Words: Writing as a Feminist*. London: Hutchinson, 1987.

Chicago, Judy. *Through the Flower: My Struggle as a Woman Artist*. Garden City, N.Y.: Doubleday, 1975.

—. *The Dinner Party: A Symbol of Our Heritage*. Garden City, N.Y.: Doubleday, 1979.

Chodorow, Nancy. "Family Structure and Feminine Personality." In *Women, Culture, and Society*, eds. Michelle Zimbalist Rosaldo and Louise Lamphere, 43–66. Stanford: Stanford University Press, 1974.

—. "Oedipal Assymetries and Heterosexual Knots" *Social Problems* 23 (April 1976): 454–68.

—. *The Reproduction of Mothering: Psychoanalysis and the Sociology of Gender*. Berkeley: University of California Press, 1978.

—. "Mothering, Male Dominance, and Capitalism" In *Capitalist Patriarchy*, ed. Zillah Eisenstein. New York: Monthly Review Press, 1979.

—."Gender, Relation, and Difference in Psychoanalytic Perspective" In *Future of Difference*, eds. Hester Eisenstein and Alice Jardine, 3–19. Boston: G. K. Hall, 1980.

Christ, Carol P. "Margaret Atwood: The Surfacing of Women's Spiritual Quest and Vision." *Signs* (Winter 1976).

—. *Diving Deep and Surfacing: Women Writers on Spiritual Quest*. Boston: Beacon Press, 1980.

Christian, Barbara. *Black Women Novelists: The Development of a Tradition*. London: Greenwood Press, 1980.

Cixous, Hélène."The Laugh of the Medusa." Trans. Keith Cohen and Paula Cohen. *Signs* 1 (Summer 1976): 875–93.

—. "Sortis." In *The Newly Born Woman*. Trans. Betty Wing. Minneapolis: University of Minnesota Press, 1986.

Clark, Shirley M., and Mary Corcoran."Perspectives on the Professional Socialization of Women Faculty" *Journal of Higher Education* 57 (1986): 20–43.

Clavir, Judith. "Choosing Either/Or: A Critique of Metaphysical Feminism." *Feminist Studies* 5, no. 2 (Summer 1979): 402–10.

Clément, Catherine. *The Weary Sons of Freud*. London: Verso, 1987.

Coles, William E., Jr., and James Vopat. *What Makes Writing Good*. Lexington, Mass.: Heath, 1985.

Collins, Patricia Hill."The Social Construction of Black Feminist Thought." *Signs* 14 (1989): 745–73.

Combahee River Collective. "A Black Feminist Statement." In *Capitalist Patriarchy*, ed. Zillah Eisenstein. New York: Monthly Review Press, 1979.

Connors, Robert J."Personal Writing Assignments." *College Composition and Communication* 38 (May 1987): 166–83.

Cook, Blanche Wiesen, ed. *Crystal Eastman on Women and Evolution*. Oxford: Oxford University Press, 1978.

—. "The Historical Denial of Lesbianism." *Radical History Review* 20 (Spring-Summer 1979): 60–65.

—. "'Women Alone Stir My Imagination': Lesbianism and the Cultural Tradition." *Signs* 4, no. 4 (Summer 1979): 718–39.

Cooke, Joanne, Charlotte Bunch-Weeks, and Robin Morgan, eds. *The New Woman: A MOTIVE Anthology on Women's Liberation.* Greenwich, Conn.: Fawcett Publications, 1970.

Cooper, Charles R., ed. *The Nature and Measurement of Competency in English.* Urbana, Il.: National Council of Teachers of English, 1981.

Cooper, Charles R., et al. "Studying the Writing Abilities of a University Freshman Class: Strategies from a Case Study." In *New Directions in Composition Research*, 19–52, eds. Richard Beach and Lillian S. Bridwell. New York: The Guilford Press, 1984.

Coote, Anna, and Beatrix Campbell. *Sweet Freedom: The Struggle for Women's Liberation.* London: Picador, 1982.

Cornillon, Susan Koppelman, ed. *Images of Women in Fiction: Feminist Perspectives.* Bowling Green, Ohio: Popular Press, 1972.

Cott, Nancy F., and Elizabeth H. Pleck. *A Heritage of Her Own: Toward a New Social History of American Women.* New York: Simon and Schuster, 1979.

Coward, Rosalind. *Female Desire: Women's Sexuality Today.* London: Paladin, 1984.

—. "This Novel Changes Lives." In *Feminist Literary Theory: A Reader*, ed. M. Eagleton, 155–60. Oxford: Blackwell, 1986.

Coward, Rosalind, and John Ellis. *Language and Materialism: Developments in Semiology and the Theory of the Subject.* London: Routledge and Kegan Paul, 1977.

Crawford, Mary, and Jean Marecek. "Psychology Reconstructs the Female: 1968–1988." *Psychology of Women Quarterly* 13 (1989):141–165.

Culler, Jonathan. *Structuralist Poetics.* London: Routledge and Kegan Paul, 1975.

Culler, Jonathan. "Prolegomena to a Theory of Reading." In *The Reader in the Text: Essays on Audience and Interpretation*, eds. Susan R. Suleiman and Inge Crosman. Princeton: Princeton University Press, 1980.

Cully, Margo, and Catherine Portuges, eds. *Gendered Subjects: The Dynamics of Feminist Teaching.* Boston: Routledge and Kegan Paul, 1975.

Daly, Mary. *Beyond God the Father: Toward a Philosophy of Women's Liberation.* Boston: Beacon Press, 1973.

—. *The Church and The Second Sex.* New York: Harper Colophon, 1975. First printed in 1968.

—. Interview by Australian Broadcasting Company, 5 September 1981. "The Coming Out Show."

___. *Pure Lust: Elemental Female Philosophy.* London: Women's Press, 1984.

—. *Gyn/Ecology: The Metaethics of Radical Feminism.* Boston: Beacon Press, 1990.

Davis, Angela Y. *Women, Culture, and Politics.* New York: Random House, 1981.

Davis, Con Robert, and Laurie Finbe, eds. *Literary Criticism and Theory.* New York: Longman, 1989.

Davis, Natalie Zemon. *Society and Culture in Early Modern France.* Stanford University Press, 1975.

Deats, Sara Munson, and Lagretta T. Lenker, eds. *Youth Suicide Prevention: Lessons from Literature.* New York: Plenum Press, 1989.

—. *The Aching Hearth: Family Violence in Life and Literature.* New York: Plenum Press, 1991.

D.C. Area Feminist Alliance. "Open Letter to Feminist Organizations." *Feminist Studies* 6, no. 3 (Fall 1980): 584.

Deckard, Barbara Sinclair. *The Women's Movement: Political Socioeconomic, and Psychological Issues.* 2d ed. New York: Harper and Row, 1979.

Delphy, Christine. "Women's Liberation in France: The Tenth Year." *Feminist Issues* 1, no. 2 (Winter 1981): 103–12.

Denmark, Florence L. "Integrating the Psychology of Women Into Introductory Psychology." In *The G. Stanley Hall Lecture Series,* eds. C. J. Scherere and A. R. Rogers, vol. 3. Washington, D.C.: American Psychological Association, 1982.

Derrida, Jacques, and Christie V. McDonald. "Choreographies." *Diacritic* 12:2 (1982): 66–76.

Diamond, Arlyn, and Lee R. Edwards, eds. *The Authority of Experience: Essays in Feminist Criticism.* Amherst: University of Massachusetts Press, 1977.

Dickstein, Morris. *Gates of Eden: American Culture in the Sixties.* New York: Basic Books, 1977.

Didion, Joan. "The Women's Movement." In *The White Album,* 109–19. New York: Simon and Schuster, 1979.

Dinnerstein, Dorothy. *The Mermaid and the Minotaur: Sexual Arrangements and Human Malaise.* New York: Harper and Row, 1977.

Donovan, Josephine, ed. *Feminist Literary Criticism: Explorations in Theory.* Lexington: University of Kentucky Press, 1975.

Dreifus, Claudia. *Woman's Fate: Raps from a Feminist Consciousness-raising Group*. New York: Bantam Books, 1973.

Dubois, Ellen Carol. *Feminism and Suffrage: The Emergence of an Independent Women's Movement in America, 1848-1869*. Ithaca, N.Y.: Cornell University Press, 1978.

Du Bois, W. E. B. *The Souls of Black Folk*. New York: Signet, 1982.

Du Plessis, Rachel Blau. *Writing Beyond the Ending: Narrative Strategies of Twentieth-Century Women Writers*. Bloomington: Indiana University Press, 1985.

Dworkin, Andrea. *Woman Hating*. New York: E. P. Dutton, 1974.

—. *Our Blood: Prophecies and Discourses on Sexual Politics*. New York: Harper and Row, 1976.

—. *Pornography: Men Possessing Women*. New York: Perigee/G. P. Putnam's, 1981.

Eagleton, Mary. *Feminist Literary Theory: A Reader*. Oxford: Blackwell, 1986.

Eagleton, Terry. *Marxism and Literary Criticism*. London: Methuen, 1976.

—. "Pierre Macherey and Marxist Literary Criticism." In *Marx and Marxisms*, ed. G. H. R. Parkinson. Cambridge: Cambridge University Press, 1982.

—. *Literary Theory: An Introduction*. Minneapolis: University of Minnesota Press, 1983.

Eaton, Walter Pritchard. *At the New Theatre and Others: American Stage, Its Problems and Performances 1908-1910*. Boston: Small Maynard, 1910.

Ebert, Teresa L. "The 'Difference' of Postmodern Feminism." *College English* 53 (December 1991): 886–904.

Eckenstein, Lina. *Woman under Monasticism*. Cambridge: Cambridge University Press, 1896.

Edholm, Felicity, Olivia Harria, and Kate Young. "Conceptualizing Women." *Critique of Anthropology* 3 , nos. 9–10 (1977): 202–30.

Editors of Questions Féministes. "Variations on Some Common Themes." *Feminist Issues* 1, no.1 (Summer 1980): 3–21.

Edwards, Alison. *Rape, Racism, and the White Women's Movement: An Answer to Susan Brownmiller*. Chicago: Sojourner Truth Organization, n.d.

Edwards, Lee R. *Psyche of Hero: Female Heroism and Fictional Form*. Middleton, Conn.: Wesleyan University Press, 1984.

Ehrenreich, Barbara, and Deidre English. *For Her Own Good: 150 Years of the Experts' Advice to Women*. New York: Anchor/Doubleday, 1978.

Ehrensaft, Diane. "When Women and Men Mother." *Socialist Review*, No. 49 (January-February 1980): 37–72.

Ehrlich, Carol. "The Unhappy Marriage of Marxism and Feminism: Can It Be Saved?" In *Women and Revolution*, 109–33, ed. Lydia Sargent. Boston: South End Press, 1981.

Eichler, Margrit. *The Double Standard: A Feminist Critique of Feminist Social Science*. New York: St. Martin's Press, 1980.

Eisenstein, Hester, ed. *The Scholar and The Feminist III: The Search for Origins*. New York: Barnard College Women's Center, 1976.

—. "Is 'Objectivity' a Code-Word for Male Domination?" Paper presented at the conference, The Second Sex—Thirty Years Later. New York Institute for the Humanities, 28 September 1979.

—. *Contemporary Feminist Thought*. Boston: G. K. Hall, 1983.

Eisenstein, Hester and Alice Jardine, eds. *The Future of Difference*. Boston: G. K. Hall, 1980.

Eisenstein, Hester, and Susan Riemer Sacks. "Women in Search of Autonomy: An Action Design." *Social Change* 5, no. 2 (1975): 4–6.

Eisenstein, Zillah R. "Developing a Theory of Capitalist Patriarchy." In *Capitalist Patriarchy and the Case for Socialist Feminism*. New York: Monthly Review Press, 1979.

—. "Some Notes on the Relations of Capitalist Patriarchy." In *Capitalist Patriarchy and the Case for Socialist Feminism*. New York: Monthly Review Press, 1979.

—. *The Radical Future of Liberal Feminism*. New York: Longman, 1981.

Eisler, Riana. *The Chalice and the Blade: Our History, Our Future*. Cambridge, Mass.: Harper and Row, 1987.

Elbow, Peter. *Writing Without Teachers*. New York: Oxford University Press, 1973.

Ellmann, Mary. *Thinking about Women*. New York: Harcourt, 1968.

Engel, Rosaline E. "Is Unequal Treatment of Females Diminishing in Children's Picture Books?" *The Reading Teacher* (March 1981): 647–52.

English, Deirdre, Amber Hollibaugh, and Gayle Rubin. "Talking Sex: A Conversation on Sexuality and Feminism." *Socialist Review*, no. 58 (July-August 1981): 43–62.

Erikson, Erik. *The Life Cycle Completed*. New York: Norton, 1985.

Espin, Oliva, and Mary Ann Gawelek. "Women's Diversity: Ethnicity, Race, Class and Gender in Theories of Feminist Psychology." In *Theories of Personality and Psychopathology: Feminist Reappraisals*, eds. L. Brown and M. Ballou. New York: Guilford Press, 1992.

Evans, Mari, ed. *Black Women Writers*. London: Pluto, 1985.

Evans, Sara. *Personal Politics: the Roots of Women's Liberation in the Civil Rights Movement and the New Left.* New York: Vintage Books, 1979.

Faderman, Lillian. *Surpassing the Love of Men: Romantic Friendship and Love Between Women from the Renaissance to the Present.* New York: Morrow, 1981.

Fallows, James. *More Like Us.* Boston: Houghton Mifflin, 1989.

Feldman, Edmund Burke. "Ideological Aesthetics." *Liberal Education* (March-April 1989): 8–13.

Ferguson, Ann, and Nancy Folbre. "The Unhappy Marriage of Patriarchy and Capitalism." In *Women and Revolution,* ed. Lydia Sargent, 313–38. Boston: South End Press, 1981.

Ferguson, Ann, Jacquelyn N. Zita, and Kathryn Pyne Addelson. "On 'Compulsory Heterosexuality and Lesbian Existence': Defining the Issues." In *Feminist Theory,* eds. Nanerl O. Keohane, et al., 141–88. Chicago: University of Chicago Press, 1982.

Fetterley, Judith. *The Resisting Reader: A Feminist Approach to American Fiction.* Bloomington, Ind.: Indiana University Press, 1978.

Fetterley, Judith, and Joan Schulz. "A MELUS Dialogue: The Status of Women Writers in American Literature Anthologies." *MELUS* 9 (1982): 3–17.

Fiedler, Leslie. *What Was Literature?* New York: Simon and Schuster, 1982.

Figes, Eva. *Patriarchal Attitudes.* New York: Stein and Day, 1970.

Fiorenza, Elisabeth Schussler. *In Memory of Her: A Feminist Theological Reconstruction of Christian Origins.* New York: Crossroad Publishing, 1983.

—. "Remembering the Past in Creating the Future: Historical-Critical Scholarship and Feminist Biblical Interpretation." In *Feminist Perspectives on Biblical Scholarship,* ed. Adela Yarbro Collins. Chico, Calif.: Scholars Press, 1985.

Firestone, Shulamith. *The Dialectic of Sex: The Case for Feminist Revolution.* New York: Bantam Books, 1970.

Fisher, Elizabeth. *Woman's Creation: Sexual Evolution and the Shaping of Society.* Garden City, N.Y.: Anchor Press/Doubleday, 1979.

Fisher, Jerilyn. "Returning Women in the Feminist Classroom." *Women's Studies Quarterly* XV (Fall/Winter 1987): 90–95.

Fitzgerald, Frances. "The Triumphs of the New Right." *New York Review of Books* (November 1981): 19.

Flax, Jane. "The Conflict Between Nurturance and Autonomy in Mother-Daughter Relationships and Within Feminism." *Feminist Studies* 4, no. 2 (June 1978): 171–89.

—. "Mother-Daughter Relationships: Pschodynamics, Politics, and Philosophy." In *The Future of Difference*, eds. Hester Eisenstein and Alice Jardine. Boston: G. K. Hall, 1980.

Flynn, Elizabeth. "Composing as a Woman." *College Composition and Communication* 39 (December 1988): 423–35.

Foucault, Michel. *The Order of Things. An Archaeology of the Human Sciences.* New York: Vintage/Random, 1973.

—. *The History of Sexuality.* Trans. Robert Hurley. Vols. 1–3. New York: Pantheon, 1978–86.

—. *Madness and Civilization: A History of Insanity in the Age of Reason.* London: Tavistock, 1981.

Fox-Genovese, Elizabeth. *Feminism Without Illusions.* Chapel Hill: University Press of North Carolina, 1991.

—. "Women and the Enlightenment." In *Becoming Visible: Women in European History*, eds. Renate Bridenthal, Claudia Koonz, and Susan Stuard. 2d ed. Boston: Houghton Mifflin, 1987.

Frank, Francine, and Paula Treichler. *Language, Gender, and Professional Writing: Theoretical Approaches and Guidelines for Nonsexist Usage.* New York: MLA, 1989.

Freeman, Derek. *Margaret Mead and Samoa: The Making and Unmaking of an Anthropological Myth.* Cambridge, Mass.: Harvard University Press, 1983.

Freeman, Jo. *The Politics of Women's Liberation: A Case Study of an Emerging Social Movement and Its Relation to the Policy Process.* New York: David McKay, 1975.

—., ed. *Women: A Feminist Perspective.* Palo Alto, Calif.: Mayfield Publishing, 1975.

Freire, Paulo. *Pedagogy of the Oppressed.* Trans. Myra Bergman Ramos. New York: Seabury Press, 1970.

—. *Education for Critical Consciousness.* New York: Herter and Herter, 1973.

Friday, Nancy. *My Mother/Myself.* New York: Delacorte Press, 1977.

Friedan, Betty. *The Feminine Mystique.* New York: Dell Publishing, 1963.

—. *It Changed My Life: Writings on the Women's Movement.* New York: Random House, 1976.

—. *The Second Stage.* New York: Summit Books, 1981.

—. *The Fountain of Age.* New York: Simon and Schuster, 1993.

Fritz, Leah. *Dreamers and Dealers: An Intimate Appraisal of the Women's Movement.* Boston: Beacon Press, 1979.

Gadamer, Hans-Georg. *Philosophical Hermeneutics.* Trans. David E. Linge. Berkeley: University of California Press, 1976.

Gaines, Jane. "Introduction: Fabricating the Female Body." In *Fabrications: Costume and the Female Body,* ed. Jane Gaines and Charlotte Herzog. New York: Routledge, 1990.

Gallop, Jane. *Feminism and Psychoanalysis: The Daughter's Seduction.* Basingstoke: Macmillan, 1982.

—. *Reading Lacan.* Ithaca: Cornell University Press, 1985.

Gawelek, Mary Ann, Eileen Nickerson, Oliva Espin, and Louise Christian. "Intimacy and Autonomy in Women: A Stereoscopic Vision." Forthcoming.

Gergen, Mary McCanney, ed. *Feminist Thought and the Structure of Knowledge.* New York: New York University Press, 1988.

Giarrusso, Roseann, et al. (The Sociology Writing Group, University of California, Los Angeles). *A Guide to Writing Sociology Papers.* 2d ed. New York: St. Martin's Press, 1991.

Giddings, Paula. *When and Where I Enter: The Impact of Black Women on Race and Sex in America.* New York: Bantam, 1984.

Gilbert, Lucia A., June M. Gallessich, and Sherri L. Evans. "Sex of Faculty Role Model and Students' Self-Perceptions of Competency." *Sex Roles* 9 (1983): 597–607.

Gilligan, Carol. *In a Different Voice: Psychological Theory and Women's Development.* Cambridge: Harvard University Press, 1982.

—, ed. *Mapping the Moral Domain: A Contribution to Women's Thinking to Psychological Theory and Education.* Cambridge: Harvard University Press, 1988.

Gilman, Charlotte Perkins. *Herland,* ed. Ann J. Lane. New York: Pantheon Books, 1979.

Gimbutas, Marija. *The Language of the Goddess.* San Francisco: Harper and Row, 1989.

Gintis, Herbert. "Communication and Politics: Marxism and the 'Problem' of Liberal Democracy." *Socialist Review,* nos. 50–51 (March-June 1980): 189–232.

Ginzburg, Carlo. *The Night Battles: Witchcraft and Agrarian Cults in the Sixteenth and Seventeenth Centuries.* Trans. John Tedeschi and Anne Tedeschi. Baltimore: Johns Hopkins University Press, 1983.

Giroux, Jeanne Brady. "Feminist Theory as Pedagogical Practice." *Contemporary Education* 61 (Fall 1989): 6–10.

Glennon, Lynda M. *Women and Dualism: A Sociology of Knowledge Analysis.* New York: Longman, 1979.

Goffman, E. *Gender Advertisements*. London: Macmillan, 1979.

Goldstein, Elyse. "Effects of Same-Sex and Cross-Sex Role Models on the Subsequent Academic Productivity of Scholars." *American Psychologist* 34 (1979): 407–10.

Gombrich, E. H. *Art and Illusion: A Study in the Psychology of Pictorial Representation*. New York: Pantheon, 1960.

Gordon, Linda. *Woman's Body; Woman's Right: A Social History of Birth Control in America*. New York: Grossman Publishers, 1976.

—. "The Struggle for Reproductive Freedom: Three Stages of Feminism." In *Capitalist Patriarchy and the Case for Socialist Feminism*, ed. Zillah R. Eisenstein, 107–32. New York: Monthly Review Press, 1979.

Gordon, Linda, and Ellen Dubois. "Seeking Ecstasy on the Battlefield: Danger and Pleasure in Nineteenth Century Feminist Sexual Thought." Paper presented at the Scholar and the Feminist IX, Barnard College Women's Center Conference, New York, April 1982.

Gornick, Vivian. "Consciousness." In *Essays in Feminism*, 47–68. New York: Harper and Row, 1978

Gornick, Vivian, and Barbara K. Moran, eds. *Woman in Sexist Society: Studies in Power and Powerlessness*. New York: Signet Books, 1972. First printed in 1971.

Gottlieb, Lois C. *Rachel Crothers*. Boston: Twayne, 1979.

Gould, Lois. "Creating a Women's World." *New York Times Magazine* (January 1977): 10.

Grady, Kathleen E. "Sex Bias in Research Design." *Psychology of Women Quarterly* 5 (1981): 628–37.

Graff, Gerald, and William E. Cain. "Peace Plan for the Canon Wars." *National Forum* (Summer 1989): 7–9.

Gramsci, Antonio. "The Prison Notebooks." In *Selections from Prison Notebooks*, eds. Quinton Hoare and Geoff Nowell-Smith. New York: International Publishers, 1971.

Grant, Judith. "I Feel Therefore I Am: A Critique of Female Experience as the Basis for a Feminist Epistemology." *Women and Politics* 7(Fall 1987): 99–114.

Gray, Vicky A. "The Image of Women in Psychology Textbooks." *Canadian Psychological Review* 18 (1977): 46–55.

Greene, Gayle, and Coppelia Kahn, eds. *Making a Difference; Feminist Literary Criticism*. New York: Methuen, 1985.

Greer, Germaine. *The Female Eunuch*. New York: Bantam Books, 1972. First printed in 1971.

Griffin, Gail B. *Calling: Essays on Teaching in the Mother Tongue.* Pasadena, Calif.: Trilogy Books,1992.

Griffin, Susan. *Woman and Nature: The Roaring Inside Her.* New York: Harper and Row, 1978.

—. *Rape: The Power of Consciousness.* San Francisco: Harper and Row, 1979.

—. *Pornography and Silence: Culture's Revenge Against Nature.* New York: Harper and Row, 1981.

—. "The Way of All Ideology." *Signs* 7, no. 3 (Spring 1981): 641–60.

Gross, Elizabeth. "On Speaking About Pornography." *Scarlett Woman* 13 (Spring 1981): 16–21.

Gross, Harriet Engel, Jessie Bernard, Alice J. Dan, Nona Glazer, Judith Lorber, Martha McClintock, Niles Newton, and Alice Rossi. "Considering 'A Biosocial Perspective on Parenting.'" *Signs* 4, no. 4 (Summer 1979): 695–717.

Guthrie, Robert V. *Even the Rat Was White: A Historical View of Psychology.* New York: Harper and Row, 1976.

Halcomb, R. "Mentors and the Successful Woman. *"Across the Board* 26 (1980): 13–18.

Hall, Roberta M., and Bernice R. Sandler. *Academic Mentoring for Women Students and Faculty: A New Look at an Old Way to Get Ahead.* Educational Resource Information Center (ERIC), 1983. ED 240 891.

Hamilton, Roberta. *The Liberation of Women: A Study of Patriarchy and Capitalism.* London: George Allen and Unwin, 1978.

Haraway, Donna Jeanne. *Primate Visions: Gender, Race, and Nature in the World of Modern Science.* New York: Routledge, 1989.

—. *Simians, Cyborgs, and Women: The Reinvention of Nature.* New York: Routledge, 1991.

Harding, Sandra. *Rediscovering Reality: Feminist Perspectives on Epistemology, Metaphysics, and Philosophy of Science.* Boston: D. Reidel, 1983.

—. *The Science Question in Feminism.* Ithaca: Cornell University Press, 1986.

—., ed. *Feminism and Methodology: Social Science Issues.* Indiana: Indiana University Press, 1987.

Harkin, Patricia, and John Schlib. *Contending with Words: Composition and Rhetoric in a Postmodern Age.* New York: Modern Language Association, 1991.

Harris, Ann Sutherland, and Linda Nochlin. *Women Artists: 1550-1950.* New York: Los Angeles County Museum of Art, Alfred A. Knopf, 1977.

Hartmann, Heidi. "Capitalism, Patriarchy, and Job Segregation by Sex." In *Women and the Workplace: The Implications of Occupational Segregation,* eds. Martha Blaxall and Barbara Reagan, 137–69. Chicago: University of Chicago Press, 1976.

Hatton, Billie Jo, Susan Jones, Judith Worell, and Patricia Atkins. "The Experience of Feminist Professors of Psychology." Paper presented at the annual meeting of the Eastern Psychological Association, Washington, D.C., April 1993.

Hawkins, Harriett. *Classics and Trash: Traditions and Taboos in High Literature and Popular Modern Genres.* Hemel Hempstead: Harvester, 1990.

Hawkesworth, Mary E. "Knowers, Knowing, Known: Feminist Theory and Claims of Truth." *Signs* 14 (1989): 533–57.

Heilbrun, Carolyn G.. *Toward a Recognition of Androgny.* New York: Alfred A. Knopf, 1973.

—. *Reinventing Womanhood.* New York: W. W. Norton, 1979.

—. *Writing a Woman's Life.* New York: W. W. Norton, 1988.

Herlihy, David. "Land, Family, and Women in Continental Europe 701–1200." *Traditio* 18 (1962): 89–120.

Herschberger, Ruth. *Adam's Rib.* New York: Harper and Row, 1970. First printed in 1948.

Hirsch, E. D., Jr. "English and the Perils of Formalism." *The American Scholar* (Summer 1984): 369–79.

Hochschild, Arlie. "Inside the Clockwork of Male Careers". In *Women and the Power to Change,* ed. Florence Howe. New York: McGraw-Hill, 1975.

Hole, Judith, and Ellen Levine. *Rebirth of Feminism.* New York: Quadrangle, 1971.

Hollander, Anne. *Seeing Through Clothes.* New York: Viking, 1978.

Hollibaugh, Amber, and Cherrie Moraga. "What We're Rollin Around in Bed With—Sexual Silences in Feminism: A Conversation Toward Ending Them." *Heresies,* no. 12 (1981): 58–62.

hooks, bell. *"Ain't I a Woman:" Black Women and Feminism.* Boston: South End Press, 1981.

—. *Talking Back: Thinking Feminist, Thinking Black.* Boston: South End Press, 1989.

—. *Black Looks: Race and Representation.* Boston: South End Press, 1992.

Hosken, Fran P. *The Hosken Report: Genital/Sexual Mutilation of Females*. Lexington, Mass.: WIN News, 1979.

Hubbard, Ruth, Mary Sue Henifin, Barbara Fried, Vicki Druss, and Susan Leigh Starr. *Women Look at Biology Looking at Women: A Collection of Feminist Critiques*. Cambridge, Mass.: Schenkman Publishing Co., 1979.

Hulbert, Kathleen D. "Faculty as Mentors in the Career Development of Professional Women." Paper presented at the annual meeting of the American Psychological Association, Atlanta, Georgia, 1988.

Hull, Debra B., and John H. Hull. "A Note on the Evaluation of Stereotypical Masculine, Feminine and Neutral Behaviors of Children." *Journal of Genetic Psychology* 147 (1986): 135–37.

Huppert, George. *After the Black Death: A Social History of Early Modern Europe*. Bloomington: Indiana University Press, 1986.

International Visual Literacy Association. *Membership Brochure*. Blacksburg, Va.: International Visual Literacy Association, 1990.

Irigaray, Luce. *Speculum of the Other Woman*. Ithaca: Cornell University Press, 1985.

—. *The Sex Which Is Not One*. Trans. Catherine Porter and Carolyn Burke. Ithaca: Cornell University Press, 1985.

Jaggar, Alison. "Feminist Politics." In *Feminist Frameworks: Alternative Theoretical Accounts of the Relations between Women and Men*, eds. Alison Jaggar and Paula Rothenberg. New York: McGraw-Hill, 1978.

—. *Feminist Politics and Human Nature*. New York: Rowman Press, 1983.

Jameson, Frederic. *The Political Unconscious: Narrative as a Socially Symbolic Act*. Ithaca: Cornell University Press, 1981.

Janeway, Elizabeth. *Man's World, Woman's Place: A Study in Social Mythology*. New York: Dell Publishing, 1971.

—. *Between Myth and Morning: Women Awakening*. New York: William Morrow, 1974.

—. "Who is Sylvia? On the Loss of Sexual Paradigms." *Signs* 5, no. 4 (Summer 1980): 573–89.

—. *Powers of the Weak*. New York: Alfred A. Knopf, 1980.

—. *Cross-Sections from a Decade of Change*. New York: William Morrow, 1982.

Jardine, Alice. *Gynesis: Configurations of Woman and Modernity*. Ithaca: Cornell University Press, 1985.

—. "Death Sentences: Writing Couples and Ideology." In *The Female Body in Western Culture*, ed. Susan R. Suleiman. Cambridge, Mass.: Harvard University Press, 1986.

Jarratt, Susan. "Feminism and Composition: The Case for Conflict." In *Contending with Words: Composition in the Post-Modern Era*, eds. Patricia Harkin and John Schilb. New York: Modern Language Association, 1991.

Jay, Nancy. "Gender and Dichotomy." *Feminist Studies* 7, no. 1 (Spring 1981): 38–56.

Jehlen, Myra. "Archimedes and the Paradox of Feminist Criticism." *Signs* 6, no. 4 (Summer 1981) 575–601.

Johnson, Barbara. "Deconstruction, Feminism, and Pedagogy." In *Teaching Literature*, eds. James Engell and David Perkins. Cambridge: Harvard University Press, 1988.

Johnston, Jill. *Lesbian Nation: The Feminist Solution*. New York: Simon and Schuster, 1974.

Jolliffe, David. *The Content of Composition: Subjects and Genres in College Writing Instruction*. Forthcoming.

Jordan, Judith. "Empathy and Self Boundaries." In *Women's Growth and Connection*, eds. Judith Jordan, Alexandra Kaplan, Jean Baker Miller, Irene Stiver, and Janet Surrey. New York: Guilford Press, 1991.

Joseph, Gloria I., and Jill Lewis. *Common Differences: Conflicts in Black and White Perspectives*. Garden City, N.Y.: Anchor Books, 1981.

Journet, Debra. "Forms of Discourse and the Sciences of the Mind: Luria, Sacks, and the Role of Narrative in Neurological Case Histories." *Written Communication* 7 (April 1990): 171–99.

Kanigel, Robert. *Apprentice to Genius: The Making of a Scientific Dynasty*. New York: MacMillan, 1986.

Kanter, Rosabeth Moss. *Men and Women of the Corporation*. New York: Basic, 1977.

Kaplan, Alexandra G., and Joan P. Bean, eds. *Beyond Sex-Role Stereotypes: Readings Toward a Psychology of Androgyny*. Boston: Little Brown, 1976.

Katz, Elihu. "The Return of the Humanities and Sociology." *Journal of Communication*. ("Ferment in the Field: Communications Scholars Address Critical Issues and Research Tasks of the Discipline") 33, no. 3 (Summer 1983): 51–52.

Kaufer, David S., and Cheryl Geisler. "Novelty in Academic Writing." *Written Communication* 8 (1989): 236–311.

Kazickas, Jurate, and Lynn Sherr. *The Woman's Calendar for 1980*. New York: Universe Books, 1979.

Kearney, Richard. *Dialogues with Contemporary Continental Thinkers*. Manchester: Manchester University Press, 1984.

Keele, Reba. "Mentoring or Networking: Strong and Weak Ties in Career Development." In *Not as Far as You Think: The Realities of Working Women*, ed. Lynda L. Moore. Lexington, Mass.: Lexington Books, 1986.

Keller, Evelyn F. "Gender and Science." *Psychoanalysis and Contemporary Thought* 1 (1978): 409–33.

—. "Feminism and Science." *Signs* 7, no. 3 (Spring 1982): 589–602.

—. *Reflection on Gender and Science*. New Haven, Conn.: Yale University Press, 1985.

Kelly, Joan. "The Social Relations of the Sexes: Methodological Implications of Women's History." *Signs* 1, no. 4 (Summer 1976): 809–24.

—. "The Doubled Vision of Feminist Theory." *Feminist Studies* 5, no. 1 (Spring 1979): 216–27.

—. "Early Feminist Theory and the *Querelle des Femmes, 1400-1789*." *Signs* 8, no. 1 (Autumn 1982): 4–28.

Keohane, Nannerl O., Michelle Z. Rosaldo, and Barbara C. Gelpi, eds. *Feminist Theory: A Critique of Ideology*. Chicago: University of Chicago Press, 1982.

Kessler, Suzanne J., and Wendy McKenna. *Gender: An Ethnomethodological Approach*. New York: John Wiley, 1978.

Kessler-Harris, Alice. *Out to Work: A History of Wage-Earning Women in the United States*. New York: Oxford University Press, 1982.

Kimmel, Ellen, Judith Worell, Judith Daniluk, Mary Ann Gawalek, Cathy Lerner, and Geraldine Stahley. "Process and Outcome in Feminist Pedagogy." Paper presented at the First National Conference on Education and Training in Feminist Practice, Boston, Mass., July 1993.

King, Margaret Leah. "The Religious Retreat of Isotta Nogarola (1418-1466): Sexism and its Consequences in the Fifteenth Century." *Signs* (Summer 1978): 807–31.

—. "Book-lined cells: Women and Humanism in the Early Italian Renaissance." In *Beyond their Sphere: Learned Women of the European Past*, ed. Patricia Labalme, 66–90. New York: New York University Press, 1984.

Klaits, Joseph. *Servants of Satan: The Age of the Witch Hunts*. Bloomington: Indiana University Press, 1985.

Kleinbaum, Abby. "Women in the Age of Light." In *Becoming Visible: Women in European History*, eds. Renate Bridenthal and Claudia Koonz, 217–35. Boston: Houghton Mifflin, 1977.

Koedt, Anne, Ellen Levine, and Anita Rapone, eds. *Radical Feminism*. New York: Quadrangle, 1973.

Komarovsky, Mirra. "Cultural Contradictions and Sex Roles." *American Journal of Sociology* 52 (1946): 184–89.

—. "Functional Analysis of Sex Roles." *American Sociological Review* 15, no. 4 (August 1950): 508–16.

—. *Women in the Modern World: Their Education and Their Dilemmas*. Boston: Little Brown, 1953.

Kors, Alan C., and Edward Peters. *Witchcraft in Europe 1100-1700: A Documentary History*. Philadelphia: University of Pennsylvania Press, 1984.

Kramarae, Cheris, and Paula A. Treichler. *A Feminist Dictionary*. Boston: Pandora, 1985.

Kreiling, Albert. "Toward a Cultural Studies Approach for the Sociology of Popular Culture." *Communication Research* 5 (July 1978): 240–63.

Kristeva, Julia. "Women's Time." *Signs* 7 (1981): 13–35. Trans. Alice Jardin and Harry Blake. Reprinted in *The Feminist Reader*, 197–98, 214–17.

—. "Revolution in Poetic Language." In *The Kristeva Reader*, ed. Toril Moi. Oxford: Blackwell, 1986.

Kroker, Arthur, and Marilouise Kroker. *Body Invaders: Panic Sex in America*. New York: St. Martin's Press, 1987.

Kronik, John W. "On Men Mentoring Women: Then and Now." *Profession 90* (1990): 52–57.

Krupnick, Catherine. "Women and Men in the Classroom: Inequality and Its Remedies." *On Teaching and Learning* (1985): 19-25.

Kuhn, Annette, and Ann Marie Wolpe, eds. *Feminism and Materialism: Women and Modes of Production*. London: Routledge and Kegan Paul, 1978.

Kuhn, T. *The Structure of Scientific Revolutions*. Chicago: University of Chicago Press, 1962.

Labalme, Patricia H. *Beyond their Sex: Learned Women of the European Past*. New York: New York University Press, 1984.

Landa, A. "Setting the Context for Theory." *Lesley College Collaborative Project Newsletter* I (1989): 1–2.

Lanham, Richard A. "The Extraordinary Convergence: Democracy Technology, Theory, and the University Curriculum." *South Atlantic Quarterly* 89 (1990): 27–50.

Larner, Christina. *Enemies of God: The Witch-Hunt in Scotland*. Baltimore: Johns Hopkins University Press, 1981.

Lasch, Christopher. *Haven in a Heartless World: The Family Besieged.* New York: Basic Books, 1979.

Lauter, Paul. "Race and Gender in the American Literature Canon." *Feminist Studies* 9 (1983): 435–63.

Lavine, Ann. "Subject Matter and Gender." In *Teaching Writing: Pedagogy, Gender, and Equity*, eds. Cynthia L. Caywood and Gillian R. Overing. Albany: SUNY Press, 1987.

Laws, Judith Long. "The Psychology of Tokenism: An Analysis." *Sex Roles* 1 (1975): 51–67.

—. *The Second X: Sex Role and Social Role.* New York: Elsevier, 1979.

Lauretis, Teresa de. *Alice Doesn't.* Bloomington: Indiana University Press, 1984.

Lawson, Bruce, Susan Sterr Ryan, and W. Ross Winterowd. *Encountering Student Text: Interpretive Issues in Reading Student Writing.* Urbana, Il.: National Council of Teachers of English, 1989.

Lazarre, Jane. *On Loving Men.* New York: Dial Press, 1980.

—. *The Mother Knot.* New York: McGraw-Hill, 1976.

Leacock, Eleanor. "History, Development, and the Division of Labor by Sex: Implications for Organization." *Signs* 7, no. 2 (1981): 474–91.

Lear, Martha Weinman. "The Second Feminist Wave." *New York Times Magazine* (March 1968): 24.

Lederer, Laura, ed. *Take Back the Night: Women on Pornography.* New York: William Morrow, 1980.

Lentricchia, Frank. *Criticism and Social Change.* Chicago: University Press of Chicago, 1983.

Lerner, Gerda. "The Lady and the Mill Girl: Changes in the Status of Women in the Age of Jackson." *Midcontinent American Studies Journal* 10 (Spring 1969): 5–14.

—. *The Female Experience: An American Documentary.* Indianapolis, Ind.: Bobbs-Merrill, 1977.

—. *The Majority Finds Its Past.* New York: Oxford University Press, 1979.

—. *The Creation of Patriarchy.* New York: Oxford University Press, 1986.

Levine, Suzanne, Harriet Lyons, Joanne Edgar, Ellen Sweet, and Mary Thom. *The Decade of Women: A Ms. History of the Seventies in Words and Pictures.* New York: Paragon Books, 1980.

Levinson, Daniel J., et al. *The Seasons of a Man's Life.* New York: Knopf, 1987.

Lewis, Diane. "A Response to Inequality: Black Women, Racism, and Sexism." *Signs* 3, no 2 (Winter 1977): 339–61.

Lips, Hilary M., and Nina Lee Colwill. *The Psychology of Sex Differences*. Englewood Cliffs, N.J.: Prentice-Hall, 1978.

Lloyd-Jones, Richard. "Primary Trait Scoring." In *Evaluating Writing: Describing Measuring, Judging*, 33–66, eds. Charles R. Cooper and Lee Odell. Urbana, Il.: National Council of Teachers of English, 1977.

Loos, Anita. *Kiss Hollywood Goodbye*. New York: Random House, 1975.

Lorber, Judith, Rose Laub Coser, Alice S. Rossi, and Nancy Chodorow. "On *The Reproduction of Mothering*: A Methodological Debate." *Signs* 6, no. 3 (Spring 1981): 481–514.

Lorde, Audre. "The Master's Tool Will Never Dismantle the Master's House." In *This Bridge Called My Back: Writings by Radical Women of Color*, eds. Cherrie Morago and Gloria Anzaldua. Watertown, Mass.: Persephone Press, 1981.

Lott, Bernice. "The Potential Enrichment of Social/Personality Psychology through Feminist Research and Visa Versa." *American Psychologist* 40 (1985): 155–164.

Lugones, Maria C. "On the Logic of Pluralist Feminism." In *Feminist Ethics*, ed. Claudia Card. Lawrence: University of Kansas Press, 1991.

Lugones, Maria C., and Elizabeth Spelman. "Have We Got a Theory For You! Feminist Theory, Cultural Imperialism and the Demand for 'The Woman's Voice.'" *Woman's Studies International Forum* 6 (1983): 573–581.

Lykes, M. Brinton, and Abigail J. Stewart. "Evaluating the Feminist Challenge to Research in Personality and Social Psychology: 1963-1968." *Psychology of Women Quarterly* 10 (1986): 393–412.

Lyons, Nona. "Two Perspectives: On Self, Relationships and Morality." *Harvard Educational Review* 52(2) (May 1983): 125–145.

Lyons, William, Don Scroggins, and Patra Bonham Rule. "The Mentor in Graduate Education." *Studies in Higher Education* 15 (1990): 277–85.

Mackay, Donald. "On the Goals, Principles, and Procedures for Prescriptive Grammar: Singular *They*." *Language in Society* 9 (1980): 349–56.

MacKinnon, Catharine. "Feminism, Marxism, Method, and the State: An Agenda for Theory." *Signs* 7, no. 3 (Spring 1982): 515–44.

Madison, D. Soyini. *The Woman That I Am: The Literature and Culture of Contemporary Women of Color*. New York: St. Martin's Press. 1994.

Maeroff, Gene. "Female President Settles in Comfortably at University of Chicago." *New York Times* (March 1980).

Mahoney, Deirdre. "A Woman's Solitude, Silence, Interruptions and Work: Negotiating a Self." Paper presented at the Wyoming Conference on Rhetoric. Laramie, June 1991.

Manderson, Lenore. "Self, Couple, and Community: Recent Writings on Lesbian Women." *Hecate* 6, no. 1 (1980): 67–79.

Marable, Manning. "Black Nationalism in the 1970s: Through the Prism of Race and Class." *Socialist Review*, nos. 50–51 (March-June 1980): 57–108.

Marcuse, Herbert. *One-dimensional Man*. London: Sphere, 1968.

Marks, Elaine, and Isabelle de Courtrivon, eds. *New French Feminisms: An Anthology*. Amherst, Mass.: University of Massachusetts Press, 1980.

McConnell-Ginet, Sally. "Linguistics and Feminist Challenge." In *Women and Language in Literature and Society*, eds. Sally McConnell-Ginet, et al. New York: Praeger, 1980.

McGann, Jerome J. "The Religious Poetry of Christina Rossetti." *Critical Inquiry* 10 (September 1983): 127–44.

McGlen, Nancy E., and Karen O'Connor. *The Struggle for Equality in the Nineteenth and Twentieth Centuries*. New York: Praeger, 1983.

McNally, Colleen, and Arnold S. Wolfe. "Deconstructing Images: Understanding the Role of Images in the Social Production of Meaning." In *Investigating Visual Literacy*, eds. Darrell Beauchamp, Judy Clark Baca, and Roberts Braden. Conway, Ark.: International Visual Literacy Association, 1991.

McNamara, Joann, and Suzanne F. Wemple. "Sanctity and Power: The Dual Pursuit of Medieval Women." In *Becoming Visible*, eds. Renate Bridenthal and Claudia Koonz, 90–118. Boston: Houghton Mifflin, 1977.

Mead, Margaret. *Culture and Commitment: A Study of the Generation Gap*. New York: Doubleday, 1970.

Medea, Andra, and Kathleen Thompson. *Against Rape*. New York: Farrar, Straus, and Giroux, 1974.

Mellon, John C. *National Assessment and the Teaching of English*. Urbana, Il.: National Council of Teachers of English, 1975.

Members of Samois, eds. *Coming to Power: Writings and Graphics on Lesbian S/M*. San Francisco: Samois, 1981.

Menges, Robert J., and William H. Exum. "Barriers to the Progress of Women and Minority Faculty." *Journal of Higher Education* 54 (1983): 123-144.

Merriam, Sharan. "Mentors and Protégés: A Critical Review of the Literature." *Adult Education Quarterly* 33 (1983): 161–73.

Milkman, Ruth. "Organizing the Sexual Division of Labor: Historical Perspectives on 'Women's Work' and the American Labor Movement." *Socialist Review*, no. 49 (January-February 1980): 95–150.

Miller, Casey, and Kate Swift. *The Handbook of Nonsexist Writing*. 2d ed. New York: Harper, 1988.

Miller, Jean Baker. *Toward a New Psychology of Women*. New York: Basic Books, 1976.

—. "The Development of Women's Sense of Self." In *Women's Growth and Connection*, eds. Judith Jordan, Alexandra Kaplan, Jean Baker Miller, Irene Stiver, and Janet Surrey. New York: Guilford Press, 1986.

Millet, Kate. *Sexual Politics*. New York: Avon Books, 1971. First printed in 1970.

—. *Flying*. New York: Alfred A. Knopf, 1974.

—. *Sita*. New York: Farrar Straus and Giroux, 1977.

—. *The Prostitution Papers*. New York: Ballantine Books, 1976.

—. *The Basement: Meditations on a Human Sacrifice*. New York: Simon and Schuster, 1979.

Millum, Trevor. *Images of Women: Advertising in Women's Magazines*. London: Chatto and Windus, 1987.

Mitchell, Juliet. *Woman's Estate*. New York: Vintage Books, 1973. First printed in 1971.

—. *Psychoanalysis and Feminism*. New York: Pantheon Books, 1974.

Moi, Toril. "Feminist, Female, Feminism." In *Modern Literary Theory*, eds. Ann Jefferson and Donald Robey. London: 1986. Reprinted in *The Feminist Reader*, 115–24.

Molyneux, Maxine. "Socialist Societies Old and New: Progress Toward Women's Emancipation?" *Monthly Review* 34, no. 3 (July-August 1982): 56–100.

Monter, E. William. "Inflation and Witchcraft: The Case of Jean Bodin." In *Action and Conviction in Early Modern Europe: Essays in Honor of E. H. Harbison*, eds. Theodore K. Rabb and Jerrold E. Siegel, 371–89. Princeton: Princeton University Press, 1969.

—. "The Historiography of European Witchcraft: Progress and Prospects." *The Journal of Interdisciplinary History* II (1972): 435–51.

—. "The Pedestal and the Stake: Courtly Love and Witchcraft." In *Becoming Visible*, eds. Renate Bridenthal and Claudia Koonz, 119–36. Boston: Houghton Mifflin, 1977.

—. "Protestant Wives, Catholic Saints, and the Devil's Handmaid: Women in the Age of Reformations." In *Becoming Visible*, eds. Renate Bridenthal and Claudia Koonz, 203–11. Boston: Houghton Mifflin, 1977.

Moore, Lynda L., ed. *Not as Far As You Think: The Realities of Working Women*. Lexington, Mass.: Lexington, 1986.

Moraga, Cherrie, and Gloria Anzaldúa, eds. *This Bridge Called My Back: Writings by Radical Women of Color*. Watertown, Mass.: Persephone Press, 1981.

Morgan, Elaine. *The Descent of Woman*. New York: Bantham Books, 1972.

Morgan, Robin. *Sisterhood is Powerful: An Anthology of Writings from the Women's Liberation Movement*. New York: Vintage Books, 1970.

—. *Going Too Far: The Personal Chronicle of a Feminist*. New York: Random House, 1977.

—. "A Quantum Leap in Feminist Theory." *Ms.* (December 1982): 101.

—. *The Anatomy of Freedom: Feminism, Physics, and Global Politics*. New York: Doubleday/Anchor, 1982.

Mulqueen, Margaret. *On Our Own Terms: Redefining Competence and Feminity*. Albany: SUNY Press, 1992.

Myron, Nancy, and Charlotte Bunch, eds. *Lesbianism and the Women's Movement*. Baltimore: Diana Press, 1975.

Nathan, George Jean. "The Status of the Female Playwright." In *The Entertainment of a Nation*. New York: Knopf, 1941.

National Assessment of Educational Progress. *Writing Achievement, 1969-79. Results from the Third National Writing Assessment*. Denver, Colo.: Education Commission of the States, 1980.

Newkirk, Thomas. "Anatomy of a Breakthrough: Case Study of a College Freshman Writer." In *New Directions in the Composing Process*, eds. Richard Beach and Lillian Bridwell. New York: Guilford, 1983.

Nin, Anais. "Lectures, Seminars, and Interviews." In *A Woman Speaks: The Lectures, Seminars, and Interviews of Anais Nin*, ed. EvelynHinz. Chicago: Swallow Press, 1975.

Oakley, Ann. *Women's Work: The Housewife, Past and Present*. New York: Vintage, 1974.

—. *Subject Woman*. New York: Pantheon Books, 1981.

O'Connell, Agnes N., and Nancy Felipe Russo. *Models of Achievement: Reflections of Eminent Women in Psychology*. Vols. I and II. New York: Columbia University Press, 1983, 1988.

O'Faolain, Julia, and Lauro Martines, eds. *Not in God's Image: Women in History from the Greeks to the Victorians*. New York: Harper Torchbooks, 1973.

Oglesby, Carl, ed. *The New Left Reader*. New York: Grove Press, 1969.

Ohmann, Richard. "The Shaping of a Canon: U.S. Fiction, 1960-1975." *Critical Inquiry* 10 (1983): 199–223. Reprinted in *Politics of Letters*. Middletown: Wesleyan UP, 1987: 68–91.

Olin, Margaret. "Forms of Respect: Alois Reigel's Concept of Attentiveness." *The Art Bulletin* 71 (June 1989): 284–99.

Olson, Gary A., and Lester Faigley. "Language, Politics, and Composition: A Conversation with Noam Chomsky." *Journal of Advanced Composition* 11 (1991): 1–35.

Ott, J.S. *The Organizational Culture Perspective*. Pacific Grove, Calif.: Brooks/Cole Publishing, 1989.

Pagels, Elaine H. "What Became of God the Mother? Conflicting Images of God in Early Christianity." *Signs* 2, no. 2 (Winter 1976): 293–303.

—. *Adam, Eve, and the Serpent*. New York: Random House, 1988.

Parker, Rozsika, and Griselda Pollock. *Old Mistresses: Women, Art, and Ideology*. New York: Pantheon, 1981.

Parlee, Mary Brown. "Appropriate Control Groups in Feminist Research." *Psychology of Women Quarterly* 5 (1981): 637–644.

Peplau, Ann, and E. Conrad. "Beyond Non-Sexist Research: The Perils of Feminist Methods in Psychology." *Psychology of Women Quarterly* 13 (1989): 379–400.

Percival, Elizabeth. "Sex Bias in Introductory Psychology Textbooks: Five Years Later." *Canadian Psychology* 25 (1984): 35–42.

Perry, Donna M. "Making Journal Writing Matter." In *Teaching Writing: Pedagogy, Gender, and Equity*, eds. Cynthia L. Caywood and Gillian R. Overing. Albany: SUNY Press, 1987.

Perry, Mary Elizabeth. *Gender and Disorder in Early Modern Seville*. Princeton: Princeton University Press, 1990.

Petchesky, Rosalind Pollack. "Reproductive Freedom: Beyond 'A Woman's Right to Choose.'" *Signs* 5, no. 4 (Summer 1980): 661–85.

—. "Antiabortion, Antifeminism, and the Rise of the New Right." *Feminist Studies* 7, no. 2 (Summer 1981): 206–46.

—. *Reproductive Freedom: The Social and Political Dimensions of Birth Control.* New York: Longman. Forthcoming.

Peterson, Sharyl Bender. "Survey of Publishers: Report and Implications for Publishers' Roles Regarding Mainstreaming Gender and Diversity into Psychology Textbooks." Paper presented at the 100th Annual Meeting of the American Psychological Association, Washington, D.C., 1992.

Peterson, Sharyl Bender, and Mary Alyce Lach. "Gender Stereotypes in Children's Books: Their Prevalence and Influence on Cognitive and Affective Development." *Gender and Education* 2 (1990): 185–197.

Peterson, Sharyl Bender, and Traci Kroner. "Gender Biases in Textbooks for Introductory Psychology and Human Development." *Psychology of Women Quarterly* 16 (1992): 17–36.

Phillips, William. "Comment: Further Notes Toward a Definition of the Canon and the Curriculum." *Partisan Review* 2 (1989): 175–78.

Piercy, Marge. *Vida.* New York: Summit Books, 1979.

Plaskow, Judith. *Standing Again at Sinai: Judaism from a Feminist Perspective.* San Francisco: Harpercollins, 1990.

Plato. *The Collected Dialogues*, eds. Edith Hamilton and Huntington Cairns. Princeton: Princeton University Press, 1961.

Plotke, David. "Facing the 1980s." *Socialist Review*, no. 49 (January-February 1980): 7–35.

Pollock, Griselda. *Vision and Difference: Femininity, Feminism, and Histories of Art.* London and New York: Routledge, 1988.

—. "Women, Art, and Ideology: Questions for Feminist Art Historians." In *Visibly Female: Feminism and Art: An Anthology*, ed. Hilary Robinson. New York: Universe Books, 1988.

Pomeroy, Sarah. *Goddesses, Whores, Wives, and Slaves: Women in Classical Antiquity.* New York: Schocken Books, 1975.

Poster, Mark. "Introduction." In *Baudrillard: Selected Writings*, ed. Mark Poster. Stanford: Stanford University Press, 1988.

Pringle, Rosemary. "The Dialectics of Porn." *Scarlet Woman* 12 (March 1981): 3–10.

Progoff, Ira. *At a Journal Workshop: The Basic Text and Guide for Using the Intensive Journal.* New York: Dialogue House Library,1975.

Raymond, Janice. *The Transsexual Empire: The Making of the She-Male.* Boston: Beacon Press, 1979.

Réage, Pauline. *Story of O.* Trans. S. D'estree. New York: Grove Press, 1965.

Reimer, James D. "Becoming Gender Conscious: Writing about Sex Roles in a Composition Class." In *Teaching Writing: Pedagogy, Gender, and Equity*, eds. Cynthia L. Caywood and Gillian R. Overing. Albany: SUNY Press, 1987.

Reiter, Rayna R., ed. *Toward an Anthropology of Women*. New York: Monthly Review Press, 1975.

Rich, Adrienne. *Of Woman Born: Motherhood as Experience and Institution*. New York: W. W. Norton, 1976.

——. *The Dream of a Common Language: Poems 1974-1977*. New York: W. W. Norton, 1978

——. *On Lies, Secrets, and Silence: Selected Prose, 1966-1978*. New York: W. W. Norton, 1979.

——. "Compulsory Heterosexuality and Lesbian Existence." *Signs* 5, no. 4 (Summer 1980): 631–60.

Ricoeur, Paul. *The Conflict of Interpretations*. Evanston: Northwestern University Press, 1974.

Robinson, Lillian S. "What Culture Should Mean." *Nation* 25 (September 1989): 319–21.

Rogers, Katherine. *The Troublesome Helpmate*. Seattle: University of Washington Press, 1966.

Rosaldo, Michelle Zimbalist, and Louise Lamphere, eds. *Woman, Culture, and Society*. Stanford: Stanford University Press, 1974.

——. "The Use and Abuse of Anthropology: Reflections on Feminism and Cross-Cultural Understanding." *Signs* 5, no. 3 (Spring 1980): 389–417.

Rose, Phyllis. *Writing on Women: Essays in a Renaissance*. Middletown, Conn.: Wesleyan University Press, 1985.

Rose, Willie Lee. "Reforming Women." *New York Review of Books*. (October 1982): 47.

Rosenberg, Rosalind. *Beyond Separate Spheres: Intellectual Roots of Modern Feminism*. New Haven: Yale University Press, 1982.

Rosser, Sue V. "Saving the Gender at Risk: Women's Studies Methods and Pedagogy for Women and Science." Paper presented at a conference on Gender in Academe, University of South Florida, Tampa, Fl., November 1989.

Rossi, Alice S., ed. "A Biosocial Perspective on Parenting." *Daedalus: Journal of the American Academy of Fine Arts and Sciences* 106, no. 2 (Spring 1977): 1–31.

——. *The Feminist Papers: From Adams to de Beauvoir*. New York: Columbia University Press, 1982.

Rossman, Michael. *On Learning and Social Change: Transcending The Totalitarian Classroom*. New York: Vintage Books, 1972.

Roszak, Theodore. *The Making of a Counter Culture.* New York: Doubleday, 1969.

Rothman, Sheila M. *Woman's Proper Place: A History of Changing Ideals and Practices, 1870 to the Present.* New York: Basic Books, 1978.

Rowbotham, Sheila. *Woman's Consciousness, Man's World.* London: Penguin Books, 1973.

—. *Women, Resistance, and Revolution: A History of Women and Revolution in the Modern World.* New York: Vintage Books, 1974. First printed in 1972.

Rowbotham, Sheila, Lynne Segal, and Hilary Wainwright. *Beyond the Fragments: Feminism and the Making of Socialism.* London: Merlin Press, 1979.

Ruddick, Sara. "Maternal Thinking." *Feminist Studies* 6, no. 2 (Summer 1980): 342–67.

Ruddick, Sara, and Pamela Daniels, eds. *Working It Out: 23 Women Writers, Scientists, and Scholars Talk About Their Lives and Work.* New York: Pantheon Books, 1977.

Russell, Diane E. H., and Nicole van de Ven, eds. *Proceedings of the International Tribunal on Crimes Against Women.* Millbare, Calif.: Les Femmes, 1976.

Russell, Jeffrey Burton. *Witchcraft in the Middle Ages.* Ithaca: Cornell University Press, 1972.

Ruth, Sheila, ed. *Issues in Feminism: A First Course in Women's Studies.* Boston: Houghton Mifflin, 1980.

Sacks, Susan Riemer, and Hester Eisenstein. "Feminism and Psychological Autonomy: A Study in Decision-Making." *Personnel and Guidance Journal* 57 (April 1979): 419–23.

Sanford, Linda, and Mary Ellen Donovan. *Women and Self-Esteem: Understanding and Improving the Way We Think and Feel About Ourselves.* New York: Penguin, 1984.

Sargent, Lydia, ed. *Women and Revolution: A Discussion of the Unhappy Marriage of Marxism and Feminism.* Boston: South End Press, 1981.

Sarris, Greg. "Storytelling in the Classroom: Crossing Vexed Chasms." *College English* 52 (February 1990): 169–85.

Sawchuck, Kim. "A Tale of Inscription/Fashion Statements." In *Body Invaders: Panic Sex in America.* New York: St. Martin's Press, 1987.

Scarborough, Elizabeth, and Laurel Furomoto. *Untold Lives: The First Generation of American Women Psychologists.* New York: Columbia University Press, 1987.

Schafran, Lynn Hecht. "Sandra O'Connor and the Supremes: Will the First Woman Make a Difference?" *Ms.* (October 1981): 71.

Schilb, John. "Ideology and Composition Scholarship." *Journal of Advanced Composition* 8 (1988): 22–29.

Schneir, Miriam, ed. *Feminism: The Essential Historical Writings.* New York: Random House, 1972.

Schniedewind, Nancy, and Ellen Davidson. *Open Minds to Equality: Learning Activities to Promote Race, Sex, Class, and Age Equality.* Englewood Cliffs, N.J.: Prentice-Hall, 1983.

Schneede, Uwe M. *Surrealism.* Trans. Maria Pelikan. New York: Harry N. Abrams, 1973.

Scholes, Robert. *Semiotics and Interpretation.* New Haven: Yale University Press, 1982.

Schur, Edwin M. *Labeling Women Deviant: Gender, Stigma, and Social Control.* New York: Random House, 1984.

Schweickart, Patrocinio. "The Challenge of Diversity." *ADE Bulletin* 88 (Winter 1988): 21–26.

See, Katherine O'Sullivan. "Feminism and Political Philosophy." *Feminist Studies* 8, no. 1 (Spring 1982): 179–94.

Shavlik, Donna, and Judith Touchton. "Women as Leaders." In *Leaders for a New Era*, ed. M. Green. New York: Macmillan, 1988.

Shavlik, D., Judith Touchton, and Carol Pearson. *New Agenda of Women for Higher Education.* Washington, D.C.: American Council on Education, 1988.

Sherif, Carolyn W. "Bias in Psychology." In *Feminism and Methodology*, ed. S. Harding. Bloomington: Indiana University Press, 1987.

Sherman, Julia A., and Evelyn Torton Beck. *The Prism of Sex: Essays in the Sociology of Knowledge.* Madison: University of Wisconsin Press, 1979.

Showalter, Elaine. "Feminism Criticism in the Wilderness." In *The New Feminist Criticism; Essays on Women, Literature, and Theory*, ed. Elaine Showalter. New York: Pantheon Books, 1985.

—. "Piecing and Writing." In *The Poetics of Gender*, ed. Nancy K. Miller. New York: Columbia University Press, 1986.

Shulman, Alix Kates. "Sex and Power: Sexual Bases of Radical Feminism." *Signs* 5, no. 4 (Summer 1980): 590–604.

—. "Dancing in the Revolution: Emma Goldman's Feminism." *Socialist Review*, no. 62 (March-April 1982): 31–44.

Simeone, Angela. *Academic Women: Working Towards Equality.* South Hadley, Mass.: Bergin and Garvey, 1987.

Simons, Margaret. "Racism and Feminism: A Schism of Sisterhood." *Feminist Studies* 5 (1979): 384–401.

Sinfield, Alan. "Give an Account of Shakespeare and Education . . ." In *Political Shakespeare: New Essays in Cultural Materialism*, eds. Jonathan Dollimore and Alan Sinfield. Ithaca: Cornell University Press, 1985.

Shapiro, Eileen, Florence Haseltine, and Mary Rowe. "Moving Up: Role Models, Mentors and the Patron System." *Sloan Management Review* 19 (1978): 51–58.

Sheehy, G. "The Mentor Connection: The Secret Link in the Successful Women's Life." *New York* (April 1976): 33–39.

Simeone, Angela. *Academic Women: Working Towards Equality.* South Hadley, Mass.: Bergin, 1987.

Smith, Barbara Herrnstein. *Contingencies of Value: Alternative Perspectives for Critical Theory.* Cambridge: Harvard University Press, 1988.

Smith, Dorothy. "A Women's Perspective as a Radical Critique of Sociology." In *Feminism and Methodology*, ed. Sandra Harding. Indiana: Indiana University Press, 1987.

Snitow, Ann Barr. "Thinking About the Mermaid and the Minotaur." *Feminist Studies* 4, no. 2 (June 1978): 190–98.

—. "Mass Market Romance: Pornography for Women is Different." *Radical History Review* 20 (Spring-Summer 1979): 141–61.

—. "The Front Line: Notes on Sex in Novels by Women, 1969-79." *Signs* 5, no. 4 (Summer 1980): 702–18.

Sokoloff, Natalie J. *Between Love and Money: The Dialectics of Women's Home and Market Work.* New York: Praeger, 1980.

Solsten, Judith W. *Literacy, Gender and Work: In Families and in School.* Norword, N.J.: Albex Publishing Company, 1993.

Spacks, Patricia. "Selves in Hiding." In *Women's Autobiography*, ed. Estelle C. Jelinek. Bloomington: Indiana University Press, 1980.

Speizer, Jeanne J. "Role Models, Mentors, and Sponsors: The Elusive Concepts," *Signs* 6 (1981): 692-712.

Spelman, Elizabeth V. *Inessential Woman: Problems of Exclusion in Feminist Thought.* Boston: Beacon Press, 1988.

Spender, Dale. *Man Made Language.* London: Routledge and Kegan Paul, 1980.

Stage, Sarah. "Women's History and 'Woman's Sphere' Major Works of the 1970s." *Socialist Review*, nos. 50–51 (March-June 1980): 245–53.

Stanley, Liz, and Sue Wise. *Breaking Out: Feminist Consciousness and Feminist Research.* London: Routledge and Kegan Paul, 1983.

Starhawk. *The Spiral Dance: A Rebirth of the Ancient Religion of the Great Goddess.* San Francisco: Harper and Row, 1979.

—. *Dreaming the Dark: Magic, Sex, and Politics.* Boston: Beacon Press, 1982.

—. *Truth or Dare: Encounters with Power, Authority, and Mystery.* San Francisco: Harper and Row, 1987.

Steeves, H. Leslie. "Feminist Theories and Media Studies." *Critical Studies in Mass Communication* 4 (June 1987): 95–135.

Steffens, Henry J., and Mary Jane Dickerson with Toby Fulwiler. *Writer's Guide: History.* Lexington, Mass.: D. C. Heath and Co., 1987.

Sternburg, Janet, ed. *The Writer and Her Work.* New York: W. W. Norton, 1991.

Sternglass, Marilyn S. "Applications of the Wilkinson Model of Writing Maturity to College Writing." *College Composition and Communication* 33 (1982): 167–75.

Stevens, Gwendolyn, and Sheldon Gardner. *The Women of Psychology: Vol. I: Pioneers and Innovators.* Cambridge, Mass.: Schenkmen Publishing Company, 1982.

—. *The Women of Psychology: Vol. II: Expansion and Refinement.* Cambridge, Mass.: Schenkman Publishing Company, 1982.

Stimpson, Catharine R., and Ethel Spector Person, eds. *Women: Sex and Sexuality.* Chicago: University of Chicago Press, 1980.

Stone, Lawrence. "The Rise of the Nuclear Family in Early Modern England: The Patriarchal Stage." In *The Family in History*, ed. Charles Rosenberg, 13–57. Philadelphia: The University of Pennsylvania Press, 1975.

—. *The Family, Sex, and Marriage in England, 1500-1800.* New York: Harper Torchbooks, 1979.

Stone, Merlin. *When God Was A Woman.* New York: Harcourt Brace Jovanovich, 1978.

Stuard, Susan. "The Dominion of Gender: Women's Fortunes in the High Middle Ages." In *Becoming Visible*, eds. Renate Bridenthal, Claudia Koonz, and Susan Stuard, 153–72. 2d ed. 1987.

Surrey, J. "The 'Self-in-Relation': A Theory of Women's Development." In *The Stone Center Work In Progress Papers* 13 (1983): 1–9.

Takalan, Sauli, Alan Purves, and Annette Buckmaster. "On the Interrelationships between Language, Perception, Thought anCulture and Their Relevance to the Assessment of Written Composition." *Evaluation in Education: An International Review Series* 5, no. 3 (1982): 317–42.

Taylor, Letta. "Abortion Battle Continues Nationwide." *Guardian* (July 1980): 4.

Tidball, M. Elizabeth. "Perspectives on Academic Women and Affirmative Action." *Educational Record* 54 (1973): 130–35.

—. "Of Men and Research: The Dominant Themes in American Higher Education Include Neither Teaching nor Women." *Journal of Higher Education* 47 (1976): 373-389.

Tinsley, A., C. Secor, and S. Kaplan, eds. *Women in Higher Education Administration.* San Francisco: Jossey-Bass, 1983.

Tompkins, Jane. *Sensational Designs: The Cultural Work of American Fiction 1790-1860.* New York: Oxford University Press, 1985.

Thompson, Martha. "Comment on Rich's 'Compulsory Heterosexuality and Lesbian Existence.'" *Signs* 6, no. 4 (Summer 1981): 790–94.

Tiger, Lionel, and Robin Fox. *The Imperial Animal.* New York: Delta, 1971.

Tong, Rosemarie. *Feminist Thought: A Comprehensive Introduction.* Boulder, Colo.: Westview Press, 1989.

—. *Feminist Philosophies: Problems, Theories, and Applications.* Englewood Cliffs, N.J.: Prentice-Hall, 1992.

—. *Feminine and Feminist Ethics.* Belmont, Calif.: Wadsworth Publishing Co., 1993.

Unger, Rhoda Kessler. "Sex as a Social Reality: Field and Laboratory Research." *Psychology of Women Quarterly* 5 (1983): 645–53.

Vaillant, George. *Adaptation to Life.* Boston: Little Brown, 1977.

Vicinus, Martha. "Sexuality and Power: A Review of Current Work in the History of Sexuality." *Feminist Studies* 8, no.1 (Spring 1982): 134–56.

Vida, Ginny, ed. *Our Right to Love: A Lesbian Resource Book.* Englewood Cliffs, N.J.: Prentice-Hall, 1978.

Wallace, Michele. *Black Macho and the Myth of the Super-Woman.* New York: Dial Press, 1979.

Wallston, Barbara Strudler. "What are the Questions in the Psychology of Women? A Feminist Approach to Research." *Psychology of Women Quarterly* 5 (1981): 597–617.

Walsh, Mary Roth. "The Psychology of Women Course: A Continuing Catalyst for Change." *Teaching of Psychology* 12 (1986): 198–203.

Weber, C.E. "Mentoring." *Directors and Boards* (1980): 17–24.

Weber, Max. "Spinning Out Capital: Women's Work in the Early Modern Economy." In *Becoming Visible,* eds. Renate Bridenthal,Claudia Koonz, and Susan Stuard, 220–49. 2d ed. 1987.

Webster, Paula. "Pornography and Pleasure." *Heresies,* no. 12 (1981): 48–51.

Weiler, Kathleen. *Women Teaching for Change: Gender, Class, and Power*. South Hadley, Mass.: Bergin and Garvey, 1988.

Weinbaum, Batya. *The Curious Courtship of Women's Liberation and Socialism*. Boston: South End Press, 1978.

Weitzman, Lenore J., Deborah Eifler, Elizabeth Hokada, and Catherine Ross. "Sex-Role Socialization in Picture Books for Preschool Children." *American Journal of Sociology* 77 (1972): 1125–50.

Whipple, B. "Collaborative Learning: Recognizing It When We See It." *AAHE Bulletin* (October 1987): 3–7.

White, R.W. *Lives in Progress: A Study of the Natural Growth of Personality*. New York: Holt, Rinehart and Winston, 1975.

Wiesner, Merry E. "Women's Work in the Changing City Economy, 1500-1650." In *Connecting Spheres*, Marilyn J. Boxer and Jean H. Quatert, 64–74. New York: Oxford University Press, 1987.

Williamson, Judith. *Decoding Advertisements*. London: Marion Boyars, 1978.

Willis, Ellen. *Beginning to See the Light: Pieces of a Decade*. New York: Wideview Books, 1981.

—. "Peace in Our Time? Betty Friedan's No-Win Feminism." *Village Voice Literary Supplement* 2 (November 1981): 1.

—. "Sisters Under the Skin? Confronting Race and Sex." *Village Voice Literary Supplement* 8 (June 1982): 1.

Wilson, Elizabeth. *Adorned in Dreams: Fashion and Modernity*. Berkeley: University of California Press, 1985.

—. "All the Rage." In *Fabrications: Costume and the Female Body*, ed. Jane Gaines and Charlotte Herzog. New York: Routledge, 1990.

Wittig, Monique. *Les Guérillières*. Trans, David LeVan. New York: Viking, 1971.

—. "One is Not Born a Woman." *Feminist Issues* 1, no. 2 (Winter 1981): 47–54.

Woolf, Virginia. *A Room of One's Own*. New York: Harcourt, Brace, and World, Inc., 1929.

—. *Three Guineas*. New York: Harcourt/Brace, 1938.

Woolsey, Lorette. "Psychology and the Reconciliation of Women's Double Bind: To be Feminine or to be Fully Human." *Canadian Psychological Review* 18 (1977): 66–78.

Worell, Judith, "Feminist Frameworks: Retrospect and Prospect." *Psychology of Women Quarterly* 14 (1990): 1–7.

—. "Gender in Close Relationships; Public Policy vs. Personal Prerogative." *Journal of Social Issues*, 49(3) (1993): 203–18.

Worell, Judith, and Faye J. Crosby. "The Feminist Teaching Project: Interim Report." Preliminary report submitted to the Women's College Coalition, Washington, D.C., November 1992.

Wright, William. *Lillian Hellman: The Image, The Woman.* New York: Simon and Schuster, 1986.

Yates, Gayle Graham. *What Woman Want: The Ideas of the Movement.* Cambridge: Harvard University Press, 1975.

Zinn, Maxine Baca, Lynn Webber Cannon, Elizabeth Higginbotham, and Bonnie Thorton Dill. "The Costs of Exclusionary Practices in Women's Studies." *Signs* 11 (1986): 290–303.

Index

About the Editors

Sara Munson Deats is director of the English Graduate Program and co-director of the Center for Applied Humanities at the University of South Florida. She received her B.A. from UCLA in 1967 and continued her academic study, first at Stanford University, then at UCLA, receiving her Ph.D. in 1970. Dr. Deats, a specialist in renaissance drama, has been an English professor at the University of South Florida since 1970. She is author of numerous journal articles and co-editor of *Youth Suicide Prevention: Lessons from Literature* (Plenum Press 1989) and *The Aching Hearth: Family Violence in Life and Literature* (Plenum Press 1991).

Lagretta Tallent Lenker is co-director of the Center for Applied Humanities and director of the Division of Lifelong Learning at the University of South Florida. She received her B.A. from the University of Tennessee, her M.S. from Florida State University, and her Ph.D. in English literature from the University of South Florida. Dr. Lenker is also the co-editor of *Youth Suicide Prevention: Lessons from Literature* and *The Aching Hearth: Family Violence in Life and Literature*.

About the Contributors

Evelyn Ashton-Jones teaches rhetoric and composition at the University of Southern Mississippi, where she also directs the writing center and serves as senior editor of the *Journal of Advanced Composition.*

Meredith Butler serves as Dean and Director of University Libraries at the University at Albany, SUNY. Prior to her appointment as Dean, Ms. Butler served as Assistant Vice President for Academic Planning and Development at the University at Albany. She received degrees from the Ohio State University and Syracuse University. She represents the University Libraries in the Association of Research Libraries, the American Library Association, and the Research Libraries Group and has a joint faculty appointment in Albany's School of Information Science and Policy. She is the author of numerous articles on a variety of topics related to academic libraries, and the status of women in higher education.

John Clifford is Professor of English at the University of North Carolina at Wilmington where he teaches courses in theory, rhetoric, and literature. He taught high school for ten years in Brooklyn, New York, and teaches in the summer at Northeastern, Harvard, and the University of Pennsylvania. He has published dozens of articles and a number of textbooks, including *Modern American Prose* and *Constellations. Writing Theory and Critical Theory*, forthcoming.

Blanche Radford Curry received her Ph.D. in philosophy from Brown University and is Visiting Assistant Professor of Philosophy at Eckerd College. Her research interests and publications are in multicultural, feminist theory, moral and social value inquiry, and cultural diversity theory. She is an assistant editor of the "American Philosophical Association's Newsletter on the Black Experience," a member of the editorial board of *Hypatia: Journal of Feminist Philosophy*, a Fulbright-Hayes Japan Fellow, and the recipient of two teaching awards.

Gloria DeSole serves as Senior Advisor to the President for Affirmative Action and Employment Planning and Director of the Affirmative Action Office at the University of Albany, SUNY. She is an adjunct associate professor in the Department of Women's Studies. Dr. DeSole has edited two books and written a number of articles on women and academic issues. She writes, consults, and lectures widely on contemporary concerns in higher education, most particularly on violence against women, social change, affirmative action, and sexual harassment.

Janet Mason Ellerby is Assistant Professor of English at the University of North Carolina at Wilmington. She is interested in narrative, psychoanalytic and feminist theories. She has published in *Reader* and *Signs* and has forthcoming essays in *Teaching Wallace Stevens* (Knoxville, University of Tennessee Press) and *The Text and Beyond* (Tuscaloosa, University of Alabama Press). Her current projects include locating transgressions of the conventional romance and reconfiguations of the nuclear family in contemporary fiction.

Mary Ann Gawelek is Dean and Associate Professor in the Counseling Psychology and Expressive Therapies Division of the Graduate School, Lesley College. Teaching and scholarly interests are focused on psychology of women, issues of diversity, clinical training, and professional ethics.

Judith M. Green received her Ph.D. from the University of Minnesota and is currently Associate Professor of Philosophy at Eckerd College, where she teaches feminist theory, social and political philosophy, ethics, and philosophy of political transformation. She is the author of two forthcoming books, *Women's Place in Aristotle's World: A Feminist Critique and Retrieval* and *Community, Dignity, and Equality: From Democratic Ideal to Democratic Reality.* She is be co-editor of *Philosophy and Cultural Diversity: Motives, Methods, and Models for Curricular Transformation.*

Brenda Gross is co-editor of the forthcoming anthology, *Writing and Gender* (Harlow, England, Longman) and is currently completing a book on the New York Artists Theatre for Gordon and Breach/London. Her essays appear in *New Perspectives on Women and Comedy* (London, Gordon and Breach 1992) and in *Notable Women in American Theatre* (Lanham, Maryland, University Press of America 1989). She earned her Ph.D. from the Graduate Center of the City University of New York and, for the past four years, has been an Assistant Professor of English at Barnard College.

Suzan Harrison, Assistant Professor of Rehtoric at Eckerd College, teaches courses in composition, literature, and women's and gender studies. Her research interests include feminist literary theory and criticism, African-American literature, and Southern literature. She is currently working on a book-length study of Eudora Welty's novels.

Kathleen Day Hulbert is Associate Professor of Psychology at the University of Massachusetts, Lowell. She holds a B.A. in political science with a minor in history, from Northwestern University, and a doctorate in human development from Boston University. Her interests include career development from adolescence through adulthood, adult work and family roles for women and men, adult learning and career change, and sociohistorical and cross-cultural perspectives on life-span development. Dr. Hulbert is co-editor of *Women's Lives Through Time: Educated American Women of the Twentieth Century* (San Francisco, Jossey-Bass 1993, with Diane Tickton Schuster).

Carolyn Johnston, Professor of American Studies and History, is the author of *Sexual Power: Feminism and the Family in America* (Tuscalosa, Alabama, University of Alabama Press 1992) which was nominated for a Pulitzer Prize. She received her Ph.D. in history from the University of California at Berkeley, and currently serves as the coordinator of the Women's and Gender Studies Program at Eckerd College.

Linda E. Lucas, Associate Professor of Economics at Eckerd College, has research interests in feminist economic theory and marine resource policy. She received her Ph.D. in economics from the University of Hawaii. She has been a Fulbright Professor of economics in Mexico City, a Research Fellow at the East-West Center, Director of Latin American Studies at the Helen Kellogg Institute for International Studies, and currently holds a federal advisory appointment with the Gulf of Mexico Fishery Management Council.

Carol Mattingly received her M.A. and Ph.D. from the University of Louisville. She is Assistant Professor of English at Louisiana State University.

Colleen McNally is a professional artist and art educator currently on the faculty of Lake Forest College. She teaches, does research, and gives public lectures on the topics of women artists and images of women in art. She exhibits her sculpture nationally and regionally and has received state and local art grants. She also serves on the Board of Directors of the Chicago Chapter of the Women's Caucus for Art.

Maggie Mulqueen is an adjunct faculty member of the Counseling and Psychology Program at Lesley College and on the faculty at the Center for Addiction Studies, Cambridge City Hospital, Harvard Medical School. She is author of *On Our Own Terms: Redefining Competence and Femininity* (Albany, SUNY Press 1992). Her clinical and research interests involve understanding the relationship between competence development for women and self-esteem.

Virginia Nees-Hatlen is Associate Professor of English at the University of Maine, where she also teaches in the Women's Studies Program.

Judith Ochshorn, Professor of Women's Studies at the University of South Florida, co-founded that department twenty-one years ago. Author of *The Female Experience and the Nature of the Divine* (Bloomington, Indiana University Press, 1981) and related essays, her primary areas of interest are women's history, feminist spirituality, and feminist theory-building.

Gary A. Olson teaches in the graduate program for rhetoric and composition at the University of South Florida, where he edits the *Journal of Advanced Composition.*

Sharyl Bender Peterson holds a joint administrative-academic position at The Colorado College. She serves as a counselor and as the research coordinator in the Career Center. She also teaches in the Psychology Department, and most recently, has been appointed research associate to head a major institutional project. Her recent research is in gender representations in college-level textbooks, and she has developed a coding system that is being widely used to evaluate gender, family, and cultural representations in many types of college textbooks.

Eleanor Roffman is a feminist educator and therapist who is on the faculty at Lesley College in Cambridge, Massachusetts. Her practice specialty is working with survivors of abuse and addictions. Dr. Roffman is committed to providing quality education to counselors-in-training from a multicultural perspective. She is dedicated to facilitating expression that challenges the racist, sexist, heterosexist, and class biased forums of the status quo. She feels privileged and nourished by the opportunities her work provides for her to integrate ideology and action.

Fran Schattenberg is completing her Ph.D. in English at the University of South Florida. She has done editorial consulting on removing sexist language from documents in the private and public sector, including insuring the St. Petersburg (Florida) City Charter was gender-free. She has written articles and given papers and talks on sexist language in academe and in the public sector. She was a language witness before the Florida Supreme Court Commission on Gender Bias.

Lisa S. Starks, who recently received her Ph.D. from the University of South Florida, has published on both Renaissance and gender studies, including an essay on Jean Rhys' *Wide Sargasso Sea* in *The Aching Hearth* and an article (with Sara Munson Deats) on antitheatricality in Marlowe's *Jew of Malta* in *Theatre Journal.* In her dissertation, entitled *Identity as Performance: Shakespeare's English History Plays and the Construction of the Gendered Subject,* she employs contemporary perspectives on gender and identity.

Jill Mattuck Tarule is Dean and Professor in Organizational Counseling and Foundational Studies in the College of Education and Social Services, University of Vermont. A co-author of *Women's Ways of Knowing: The Development of Self, Voice and Mind*, her teaching and research focuses on human development, emphasizing epistemological development and institutional and pedagogical design.

Charlotte Templin received her Ph.D. from Indiana University and is Professor of English and Chair of the English Department at the University of Indianapolis. She has published articles on women writers, e.g., Erica Jong, Margaret Atwood, Marietta Holley; and interviews with Jong, Molly Peacock, and others. She is completing *Feminism and the Politics of Literary Reputation: The Example of Erica Jong*, and co-editing (with Carole Taylor of Bates College) *Literary Reputation and the Woman Writer*, a collection of interviews and essays.

Beth Dalton Williams is an art history student and technical assistant at the University of South Florida. She is also an exhibiting artist at the university.

Arnold S. Wolfe is Assistant Professor of Communication at Illinois State University where he does research and teaches courses in mass media theory and criticism. He has published work in *Critical Studies in Mass Communication* and is pursuing further investigation into issues of visual literacy.

Linda Woodbridge is Professor of English at Pennsylvania State University, where she teaches Renaissance literature. She has published *Women and the English Renaissance: Literature and the Nature of Womankind, 1540-1620* (Urbana, Il., University of Illinois Press 1984), *Shakespeare: A Selective Bibliography of Modern Criticism* (West Cornwall, Conn., Locust Hill Press 1988), the co-edited *True Rites and Maimed Rites: Ritual and Anti-Ritual in Shakespeare and His Age* (Urbana, Il., University of Illinois Press 1992), and articles on Shakespeare, Marlowe, Webster, and other authors, in such journals as *Shakespeare Quarterly, Renaissance Quarterly, English Literary Renaissance*, and *Texas Studies in Literature and Language*. Her new book *The Scythe of Saturn: Shakespeare and Magical Thinking* is forthcoming, as is her edition of *A Chaste Maid in Cheapside* for the Oxford *Complete Works of Middleton*.

Judith Worell is Professor and Chair in the Department of Educational and Counseling Psychology at the University of Kentucky. She was a recent recipient of the Distinguished Leader for Women in Psychology Award from the American Psychological Association and was the Distinquished Psychologist of the year for the Kentucky Psychological Association. She is editor of *Psychology of Women Quarterly*, and author of five books. Her most recent book, co-authored with Pam Remer, is *Feminist Perspectives in Therapy: An Empowerment Model for Women* (Chichester, New York, Wiley 1992). Her research focuses on feminist pedagogy, feminist identity development, and gender in close relationships.